VOLUME SIXTY TWO

INTERNATIONAL REVIEW OF RESEARCH IN DEVELOPMENTAL DISABILITIES

Contemporary Issues in Evaluating Treatment in Neurodevelopmental Disorders

VOLUME SIXTY TWO

INTERNATIONAL REVIEW OF RESEARCH IN DEVELOPMENTAL DISABILITIES

Contemporary Issues in Evaluating Treatment in Neurodevelopmental Disorders

Edited by

ANNA J. ESBENSEN

Division of Developmental and Behavioral Pediatrics, Cincinnati Children's Hospital Medical Center; Department of Pediatrics, University of Cincinnati College of Medicine, Cincinnati, OH, United States

EMILY K. SCHWORER

Division of Developmental and Behavioral Pediatrics, Cincinnati Children's Hospital Medical Center, Cincinnati, OH, United States

ELSEVIER

ACADEMIC PRESS

An imprint of Elsevier

Academic Press is an imprint of Elsevier
50 Hampshire Street, 5th Floor, Cambridge, MA 02139, United States
525 B Street, Suite 1650, San Diego, CA 92101, United States
The Boulevard, Langford Lane, Kidlington, Oxford OX5 1GB, United Kingdom
125 London Wall, London EC2Y 5AS, United Kingdom

First edition 2022

ISBN: 978-0-323-98883-4
ISSN: 2211-6095

For information on all Academic Press publications
visit our website at https://www.elsevier.com/books-and-journals

Publisher: Zoe Kruze
Acquisitions Editor: Mariana Kuhl
Developmental Editor: Naiza Ermin Mendoza
Production Project Manager: Abdulla Sait
Cover Designer: Matthew Limbert

Typeset by STRAIVE, India

Contents

Contributors

Dawn Adams
Autism Centre of Excellence, Griffith University, Queensland, Australia

Georgie Agar
School of Psychology, University of Birmingham, Birmingham, United Kingdom

Debbie Allen
School of Psychology, University of Wolverhampton, Wolverhampton, United Kingdom

Elizabeth Berry-Kravis
Department of Pediatrics, Neurological Sciences, Anatomy and Cell Biology, Rush University Medical Center, Chicago, IL, United States

Stacey Bissell
School of Psychology, University of Birmingham, Birmingham, United Kingdom

Justin Cheuk Yin Chung
School of Psychology, University of Birmingham, Birmingham, United Kingdom

Isabel C.H. Clare
Department of Psychiatry, University of Cambridge, Cambridge, United Kingdom

Hayley Crawford
Mental Health and Wellbeing Unit, Division of Health Sciences, Warwick Medical School, University of Warwick, Coventry, United Kingdom

Louise Daniel
Specialist Assessment Service, University Hospitals Birmingham NHS Foundation Trust, Birmingham, United Kingdom

Jennifer Davila Valdes
Texas State University, San Marcos, TX, United States

Lucy Deeprose
School of Psychology, University of Surrey, Guildford, United Kingdom

Andrea DeMaria
Purdue University, West Lafayette, IN, United States

Georgina Edwards
School of Psychology, College of Health and Life Sciences, Aston University, Birmingham, United Kingdom

Katherine Ellis
Clinical, Educational and Health Psychology, University College London, London, United Kingdom

Anna J. Esbensen
Division of Developmental and Behavioral Pediatrics, Cincinnati Children's Hospital Medical Center; Department of Pediatrics, University of Cincinnati College of Medicine, Cincinnati, OH, United States

Cristan Farmer
Neurodevelopmental and Behavioral Phenotyping Service, National Institute of Mental Health, Bethesda, MD, United States

Deborah J. Fidler
Human Development and Family Studies, Colorado State University, Fort Collins, CO, United States

Victoria Fleming
Waisman Center; School of Human Ecology, University of Wisconsin-Madison, Madison, WI, United States

Laura Groves
School of Psychology, University of Birmingham, Birmingham; Department of Neuroscience, Psychology and Behaviour, University of Leicester, Leicester, United Kingdom

Amanda C. Gulsrud
Department of Psychiatry and Biobehavioral Sciences, Semel Institute for Neuroscience and Human Behavior, University of California, Los Angeles, Los Angeles, CA, United States

Lisa Hamrick
Purdue University, West Lafayette, IN, United States

Benjamin Handen
Department of Psychiatry, University of Pittsburgh, Pittsburgh, PA, United States

Sigan L. Hartley
Waisman Center; School of Human Ecology, University of Wisconsin-Madison, Madison, WI, United States

Mary Heald
Learning Disability Service, Lancashire and South Cumbria NHS Foundation Trust, Preston, United Kingdom

Christy L. Hom
Department of Psychiatry and Human Behavior, University of California, Irvine School of Medicine, Orange, CA, United States

Laura Hopp
Texas State University, San Marcos, TX, United States

Shemaya L. Hurd-Thomas
Department of Psychiatry, University of Cambridge, Cambridge, United Kingdom

Lauren Jenner
School of Psychology, University of Surrey, Guildford, United Kingdom

Aaron J. Kaat
Feinberg School of Medicine, Northwestern University, Chicago, IL, United States

Breanne Kearney
Institute of Cognitive Neuroscience, University College London, London, United Kingdom

Bridgette L. Kelleher
Purdue University, West Lafayette, IN, United States

Sharon Krinsky-McHale
New York State Institute for Basic Research in Developmental Disabilities, Staten Island, NY, United States

Elizabeth A. Laugeson
Department of Psychiatry and Biobehavioral Sciences, Semel Institute for Neuroscience and Human Behavior, University of California, Los Angeles, Los Angeles, CA, United States

Sandy Magaña
University of Texas at Austin, Austin, TX, United States

Carolyn McCormick
Purdue University, West Lafayette, IN, United States

Christine T. Moody
Department of Psychiatry and Biobehavioral Sciences, Semel Institute for Neuroscience and Human Behavior, University of California, Los Angeles, Los Angeles, CA, United States

Jo Moss
School of Psychology, University of Surrey, Guildford, United Kingdom

Chris Oliver
School of Psychology, University of Birmingham, Birmingham, United Kingdom

Effie Pearson
School of Psychology, College of Health and Life Sciences, Aston University, Birmingham, United Kingdom

Tyra Protho
Purdue University, West Lafayette, IN, United States

Allison B. Ratto
Children's National Hospital, Washington, DC, United States

Caroline Richards
School of Psychology, University of Birmingham, Birmingham, United Kingdom

Mandy Rispoli
Purdue University, West Lafayette, IN, United States

Rachel Royston
Division of Psychiatry, University College London, London, United Kingdom

Hillary K. Schiltz
Department of Psychiatry and Biobehavioral Sciences, Semel Institute for Neuroscience and Human Behavior, University of California, Los Angeles, Los Angeles, CA, United States

Emily K. Schworer
Division of Developmental and Behavioral Pediatrics, Cincinnati Children's Hospital Medical Center, Cincinnati, OH, United States

Amanda Seidl
Purdue University, West Lafayette, IN, United States

Lauren Shelley
School of Psychology, College of Health and Life Sciences, Aston University, Birmingham, United Kingdom

Delta Smith
Purdue University, West Lafayette, IN, United States

Kayla Smith
Mental Health and Wellbeing Unit, Division of Health Sciences, Warwick Medical School, University of Warwick, Coventry, United Kingdom

Joanne Tarver
School of Psychology, College of Health and Life Sciences, Aston University, Birmingham, United Kingdom

Audrey Thurm
Neurodevelopmental and Behavioral Phenotyping Service, National Institute of Mental Health, Bethesda, MD, United States

Angela John Thurman
University of California Davis Health, MIND Institute and Department of Psychiatry and Behavioral Sciences, Sacramento, CA, United States

Hayley Trower
Mental Health and Wellbeing Unit, Division of Health Sciences, Warwick Medical School, University of Warwick, Coventry, United Kingdom

Sandra B. Vanegas
Texas State University, San Marcos; University of Texas at Austin, Austin, TX, United States

Kelly Wade
School of Psychology, University of Birmingham, Birmingham, United Kingdom

Jane Waite
School of Psychology, College of Health and Life Sciences, Aston University, Birmingham, United Kingdom

Alice Welham
School of Psychology, University of Leicester, Leicester, United Kingdom

Lucy Wilde
School of Psychology and Counselling, Open University, Milton Keynes, United Kingdom

Kate Woodcock
Centre for Applied Psychology and the Institute for Mental Health, School of Psychology, University of Birmingham, Birmingham, United Kingdom

Preface

This special volume of the *International Review of Research in Developmental Disabilities* includes seven chapters centered around contemporary issues in evaluating treatment in neurodevelopmental disorders. We sought chapters that focused on current methodology and highlighted key challenges in currently available methods for measuring outcomes in clinical trials involving individuals with intellectual and developmental disabilities. Advances in basic research and intervention science continue to inform clinical trials. Yet, as these advances are applied to individuals with intellectual and developmental disabilities, challenges continue to arise, which initiated this deeper look into assessment techniques and methodology. The chapters in this volume share the goal of disseminating best practice for outcome measurement in neurodevelopmental disabilities, including progress to date and identification of areas where additional work is needed.

The first three chapters cover central issues or methodological advances in outcome measures for individuals with intellectual and developmental disabilities. In Chapter 1, Cristan Farmer, Aaron Kaat, Elizabeth Berry-Kravis, and Audrey Thurm present a rigorous analysis of endpoint selection and narrow in on the challenges faced by studies that target developmental outcomes. Study design and psychometrics of developmental measures are reviewed, providing insight into nuances of scoring options and interpretation, which are essential to the success of measuring developmental concepts in clinical trials.

In Chapter 2, Bridgette Kelleher and colleagues cover the innovative use of remote assessment in the context of monitoring treatment outcomes. This chapter shares historically relevant examples and practical cost–benefit information on remote monitoring of outcomes. Both the benefits and challenges of this methodology are included, along with contextual discussion relating to the COVID-19 pandemic that has brought this methodology to the forefront of data collection methods for many researchers, including those studying intellectual and developmental disabilities.

Chapter 3 by Sandra Vanegas, Laura Hopp, Jennifer Davila Valdes, and Sandy Magaña provides an important overview of issues that researchers and professionals must consider while identifying and measuring outcomes for individuals with developmental disabilities from diverse backgrounds. Their scoping review highlights gaps that must be addressed to ensure measures are available that are appropriate for diverse groups and culturally responsive.

The next four chapters concentrate on the assessment of outcomes for specific subgroups of individuals with neurodevelopmental disorders. First, in Chapter 4, Chris Oliver and colleagues review distress and challenging behavior present among people with profound or severe intellectual disability and complex needs. In addition to summarizing nine domains that influence well-being and challenging behavior, strategies for assessment and suggestions for measurement of these domains among individuals with profound or several intellectual disability are provided for researchers and clinicians.

Chapters 5 and 6 address outcome measurement topics in Down syndrome relating to the preparation for future clinical trials. In Chapter 5, by Anna Esbensen, Emily Schworer (the coeditors of this *IRRDD* series), Deborah Fidler, and Angela Thurman, considerations for measurement in children and adolescents are reviewed, with a focus on cognition, language, and behavioral/psychopathology outcomes. Specific aspects of the behavioral and medical phenotype associated with Down syndrome are discussed.

Chapter 6, by Victoria Fleming, Christy Hom, Isabel Clare, Shemaya Hurd-Thomas, Sharon Krinsky-McHale, Benjamin Handen, and Sigan Hartley, focuses on cognitive outcome measures used to track symptoms of Alzheimer's disease dementia in adults with Down syndrome. The chapter reviews Alzheimer's disease-related pathology and dementia symptomology in Down syndrome. Specific attention is paid to measures sensitive to tracking cognitive decline appropriate for large-scale clinical trials for Alzheimer's disease dementia prevention in adults with Down syndrome.

Chapter 7, the final chapter of the volume by Christine Moody, Hillary Schiltz, Allison Ratto, Amanda Gulsrud, and Elizabeth Laugeson, addresses the measurement of social skill for individuals with autism spectrum disorder. The chapter includes a detailed evaluation of available questionnaires, observational measures, and qualitative interviews. Neurobiological indices and diversity are noted as next steps for advancing measurement of social skills in autism treatment work.

We thank the authors for their insightful contributions and Naiza Mendoza at Elsevier for her excellent guidance as Developmental Editor. This collection of articles adds to the ongoing progress in outcome measurement in neurodevelopmental disorders and, we hope, will spur others to advance evidence-based clinical interventions for this population.

Anna J. Esbensen
Emily K. Schworer
May 10, 2022

CHAPTER ONE

Psychometric perspectives on developmental outcome and endpoint selection in treatment trials for genetic conditions associated with neurodevelopmental disorder

Cristan Farmer[a], Aaron J. Kaat[b], Elizabeth Berry-Kravis[c], and Audrey Thurm[a]

[a]Neurodevelopmental and Behavioral Phenotyping Service, National Institute of Mental Health, Bethesda, MD, United States
[b]Feinberg School of Medicine, Northwestern University, Chicago, IL, United States
[c]Department of Pediatrics, Neurological Sciences, Anatomy and Cell Biology, Rush University Medical Center, Chicago, IL, United States

Contents

Abstract

Development in domains like motor ability, thinking and learning, social abilities, and communication are important areas of concern for individuals affected by genetic conditions associated with neurodevelopmental disorder (GCAND). Challenges associated with clinical trials in rare conditions, such as limited information about natural history,

International Review of Research in Developmental Disabilities, Volume 62
ISSN 2211-6095
https://doi.org/10.1016/bs.irrdd.2022.05.001

small sample size, and heterogeneous presentation, have been well-described. However, little attention has been paid to the additional complications conferred by use of developmental outcomes in these studies. Change is inherent to developmental concepts, which complicates the establishment of psychometric profiles that is already challenged by heterogeneous populations. Further, change in developmental concepts during a clinical trial may be difficult to interpret. This is especially true for disorders which are associated with significant delay or even decline, where decreases in age-based normative scores may be caused by active degeneration or slower-than-expected growth. Choices in the selection of the concept of interest, the clinical outcome assessment, and the endpoint may mitigate these issues. In this chapter, we review essential background information about those choices and discuss additional considerations and unresolved challenges that investigators in GCAND may face when the concept is developmental in nature, in order to prompt future efforts.

Abbreviations

CGI clinical global impression
ClinRO clinician-rated outcome
COA clinical outcome assessment
FDA Food and Drug Administration
GCAND genetic conditions associated with neurodevelopmental disorder
ID intellectual disability
ObsRO observer-reported outcome
PerfO performance-based outcome
PRO patient-reported outcome

1. Introduction

The Food and Drug Administration (FDA), guided by the Orphan Drug Act, defines a rare disease as one that affects fewer than 200,000 people in the United States. More than half of rare genetic conditions affect children (Wright, FitzPatrick, & Firth, 2018), and neurodevelopmental disorders such as intellectual disability (ID) are predominant aspects of many (Sanders et al., 2019). In fact, with well over 1000 conditions described (Maia, Nabais Sá, Melo-Pires, de Brouwer, & Jorge, 2021), a genetic diagnosis is now likely for the majority of individuals with severe or profound ID. For these rare genetic conditions associated with neurodevelopmental disorder (GCAND), development in domains like motor ability, thinking and learning, social abilities, and communication are potential targets for intervention. There has been a great deal of momentum in pharmaceutical clinical trials (e.g., Fragile X syndrome; Aishworiya, Valica, Hagerman, &

Restrepo, 2022) and gene or genomic therapy (e.g., Angelman syndrome and Rett syndrome; Copping, McTighe, Fink, & Silverman, 2021; Jensen, Gøtzsche, & Woldbye, 2021) for GCAND. This is true also of several conditions which might be more generally considered metabolic or neurodegenerative, but which have clearly demonstrated relationships to neurodevelopmental disorders (e.g., Poletti & Biffi, 2019).

One major aspect of clinical trial design is selection of the outcome, or how efficacy of the intervention will be defined. This starts with the concept, or the aspect of the individual that is hoped to change with treatment. The concept must be of significant clinical meaning to patients, caregivers, and clinicians, and the clinical outcome assessment (COA) used to assess it must have good psychometric properties (i.e., be valid, reliable, and responsive to change). The endpoint defines exactly how a COA will be used to assess efficacy (e.g., how the COA will be scored, at which timepoint comparison will be made). For clinical trials of GCAND, there are many obstacles to this process of concept, COA and endpoint selection, including limited information about the natural history of the disorder, small sample sizes, and heterogeneous presentations (see Fig. 1; Benjamin et al., 2017). However, less attention has been paid to the additional challenges that arise when the outcome of interest is developmental in nature, as it often is in GCAND. In order to develop and provide evidentiary support for the use of developmental outcomes in GCAND trials, investigators may need to employ qualitative and quantitative psychometric approaches not necessary for common diseases or even rare diseases with non-developmental outcomes. In this chapter, we offer general background information on the selection of concepts, outcome assessments, and endpoints, in service of discussing the particular challenges in assessment and endpoint selection for clinical trials targeting developmental outcomes in GCAND. Although we focus specifically on GCAND, the challenges and potentially mitigating actions should apply to all clinical trials in populations with severe neurodevelopmental disability, regardless of the etiology.

2. Developmental concept selection for GCAND clinical trials

In any clinical trial, a concept is "the aspect of an individual's clinical, biological, physical, or functional state or experience that the assessment is intended to capture (or reflect)" (p. 12; FDA, 2009). The investigator must synthesize a variety of quantitative and qualitative information, such as

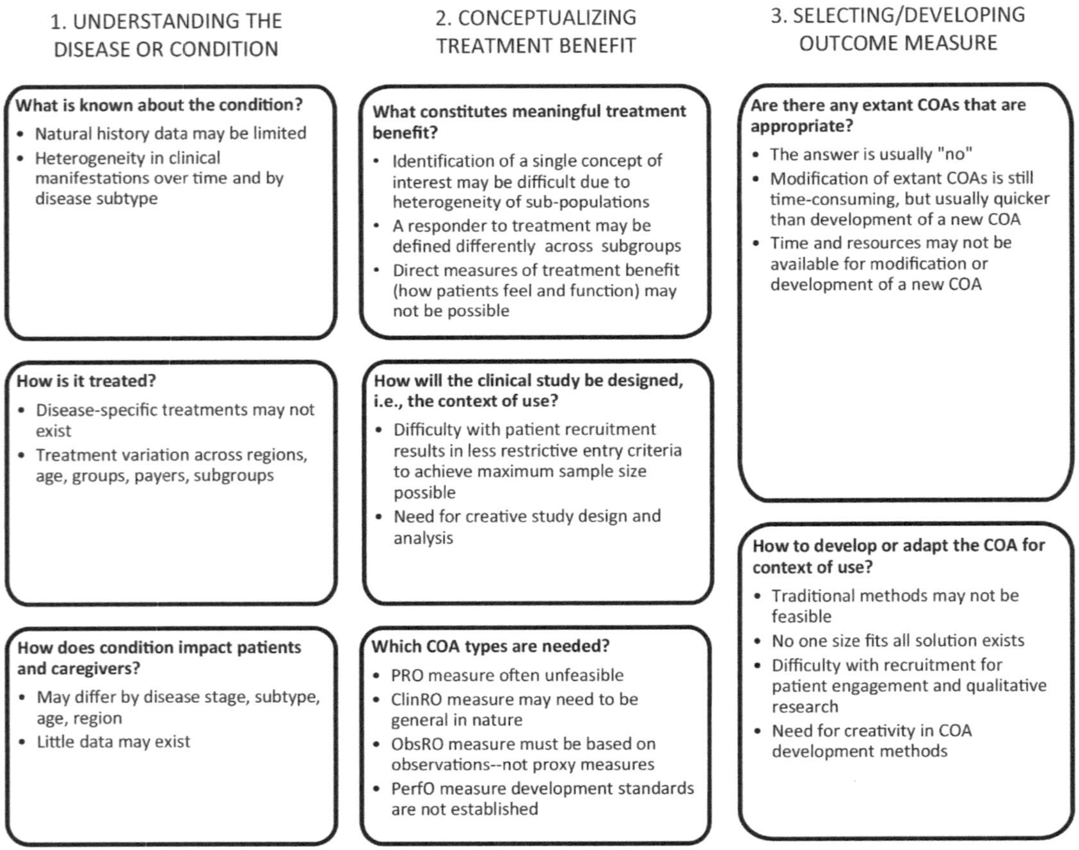

Fig. 1 Challenges for implementing COA endpoints in rare disease clinical trials. This schematic, based on the FDA's roadmap (https://www.fda.gov/media/87004/download), lists the challenges to COA selection faced by stakeholders in the intervention development process for rare conditions. ClinRO = clinician-reported outcome; COA = clinical outcome assessment; COI: concept of interest; COU = context of use; ObsRO = observer-reported outcome; PerfO = performance outcome; PRO = patient-reported outcome; RD = rare disease. *Reprinted with permission, Benjamin, K., Vernon, M. K., Patrick, D. L., Perfetto, E., Nestler-Parr, S., & Burke, L. (2017). Patient-reported outcome and observer-reported outcome assessment in rare disease clinical trials: An ISPOR COA emerging good practices task force report. Value in Health, 20(7), 838–855.*

natural history data, patient and stakeholder input, and basic science about the intervention, in order to determine which concepts are relevant to a study. The natural history of a disease, or the course it takes in the absence of intervention, outlines the universe of relevant concepts. For example, developmental concepts might be motor abilities, social skills, language and communication abilities, and cognitive abilities, depending on the profile of the condition.

However, not all clinically relevant concepts are appropriate candidates for a clinical trial; the investigator must decide which ones *could* be changed by the intervention. This decision is partially informed by the intervention's mechanism of action, which is informed by basic science. Importantly, however, this is also determined in part by the concept itself. Can the concept *be* changed, especially on the timescale of the study? When the concept of interest is developmental, there are at least two unique features to consider. First, developmental concepts may have a window—or point in development—at which change in the concept becomes much less possible. For example, language development is considered to have a critical period of development, making acquisition of speech after the age of 5 years less likely (Pickett, Pullara, O'Grady, & Gordon, 2009). Second, change in some developmental outcomes may require learning, which takes time—perhaps longer than classical clinical trial designs typically allow. Interventions are unlikely to "reveal" latent abilities of which a child is capable but not exhibiting. More likely, intervention creates the conditions under which abilities are learned; in this case, the behavioral manifestation of treatment effects on broad developmental concepts like cognitive ability, language, or socialization require that the child has sufficient time to learn these skills. This is true even if a trial includes recommended adjunctive therapies (e.g., speech therapy for a minimally verbal child), a strategy which may maximize the manifestation of improvements in developmental outcomes. In general, it is important to remember that not all clinically meaningful concepts are appropriate for use as trial outcomes, and developmental concepts may require extra scrutiny.

Even after the universe of concepts relevant to a disorder has been narrowed to those which might be appropriate for a clinical trial, the remaining concepts do not necessarily possess clinical meaning or importance to those living with GCAND. Although it may seem axiomatic, the idea that patient input is necessary to this process has only recently been formalized in the regulatory guidelines under the general umbrella of "patient-focused drug development" (FDA, 2018; Hudson & Collins, 2017; Perfetto, Burke,

Oehrlein, & Epstein, 2015). In other words, the clinical meaning of a concept can only be determined by asking patients and/or their families/caregivers.

Though incomplete understanding of natural history, heterogeneity of presentation, diversity of patient experience, and small population size affect the process of developing patient-centered outcomes in rare conditions (Benjamin et al., 2017), researchers in GCAND have had some success. For example, mixed (qualitative and quantitative) methods were used to integrate input from patients, caregivers, and clinicians regarding the clinical meaning of concepts and scores on the Niemann-Pick Type C Severity Scale (Patterson et al., 2021). The effect of qualitative caregiver input on this process is illustrated by the reduction of the original 12 domains into 5, including 1 case where 2 domains considered separable by experts (cognition and memory) were judged by caregivers as highly interrelated if not the same thing.

Similar methods have been used to establish the clinical meaningfulness of the Aberrant Behavior Checklist—Community Edition, which has been modified for use in Fragile X syndrome (Merikle et al., 2021) and to develop a utility index[1] for this scale (Kerr et al., 2015). As illustrated by the methods used in these examples, caregivers are of particular importance in establishing clinical meaning within GCAND. Because an individual with GCAND may have limited insight (or ability to convey insight) into their condition, caregivers are often a rich source of information regarding the clinical meaning of concepts and outcome measures. The process of concept elicitation and selection (as well as outcome evaluation) must include family and/or caregivers as essential stakeholders.

3. Clinical outcome assessments (COA) in GCAND

Clinical outcome assessment (COA) is an umbrella term used by the FDA for an outcome that may be influenced by human motivation or judgment (Walton et al., 2015). The COA is the method for measuring a concept of interest in a given study. Like concept selection, COA selection involves the synthesis of a great deal of information from a variety of sources. The end goal is to identify a measure for each concept that is "fit for purpose," a

[1] A utility index is a scoring model frequently used in economics and population health research; scores are represented as quality of life adjusted years (QoLAY) where a score of 0 is "as good as dead" and 1 represents perfect or full health.

summary term for the regulatory conclusion that a measure is adequate for the proposed use (FDA-NIH Biomarker Working Group, 2016). Whether a measure is fit for purpose depends on several related factors, including the intended use (context, study design, study population), its psychometric profile (validity, reliability, and responsiveness), and its clinical meaningfulness in the population, including its ability to be administered and communicated in a clear and understandable way (FDA, 2018). Importantly, a mismatch between study design, analytic plan, and COA can have a major impact on the statistical power of the trial to detect an effect, and on the ability to interpret the effect as clinically meaningful. In this section, we introduce the types of COAs that might be encountered in GCAND clinical trials, and mention some strengths and weaknesses when used for developmental concepts. We then discuss the types of psychometric evidence that must be provided for a selected COA, and how the derivation and interpretation of this information is impacted by GCAND and developmental concepts.

3.1 Categories of COA

General statements about limitations or areas of caution when COAs measure developmental concepts can be made based on who completes the COA (Fig. 2). Performance outcomes (PerfOs) are direct assessments of an individual. Their use in GCAND trials is limited in at least two ways. First, the cognitive and language demands of the PerfO may exceed the capacity of an individual with neurodevelopmental disability, such as lack of understanding of the instructions or differences in motivation that are not related to the construct of interest. As a result, a PerfO that may be well-established in the general population may not be appropriate for all members of a GCAND group. This is not insurmountable (DiStefano, Sadhwani, & Wheeler, 2020; Thurm et al., 2021), but it does require special attention, including additional work to establish the psychometric profile of the modified PerfO. This could take the form of modifying and standardizing administration instructions, as has been done for the Bayley Infant and Toddler Development scales in Angelman's syndrome (Sadhwani et al., 2021). Ideally, this will be accompanied by empirical demonstration of the psychometric properties, as in the NIH Toolbox for the Assessment of Neurological and Behavioral Function batteries (Gershon et al., 2013; Weintraub et al., 2013). For that adaptation, a multidisciplinary neurodevelopmental disorder research group developed and validated a

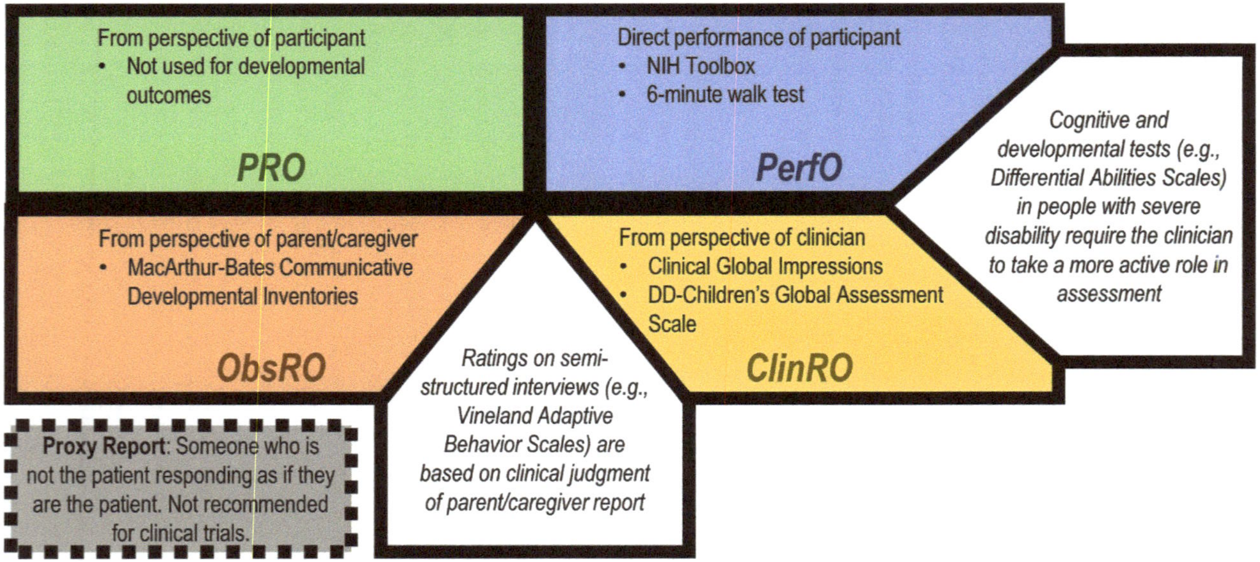

Fig. 2 Categories of clinical outcome assessment. Schematic illustrates how COAs may be categorized based on the responder, and that COAs for developmental concepts often combine aspects of more than one category. For each category, examples of COAs sometimes used in CGAND or neurodevelopmental disability studies are provided. *Adapted from FDA. (2018). Methods to identify what is important to patients & select, develop or modify fit-for-purpose clinical outcomes assessments. Patient-focused drug development guidance public workshop. FDA Maryland, USA. Retrieved from https://www.fda.gov/media/116277/download.*

specialized manual for administration in individuals with mild-to-moderate ID (but not severe-to-profound, which may describe a large proportion of those with GCAND), complete with strategies intended to improve feasibility such as a visual schedule and the use of a token board (Shields et al., 2020).

The second issue surrounding PerfOs relates more generally to the types of developmental concepts that they might measure. As mentioned before, interventions are rarely expected to reveal some behavior or skill that was simply obscured by symptoms of GCAND; improvement in developmental concepts often requires sufficient time to allow for some degree of learning. As a result, PerfOs targeting very specific developmental concepts (e.g., change in vocabulary, ability to attend) may be more likely to change over the relatively short duration of a clinical trial than PerfOs of more general concepts like cognitive ability (e.g., IQ tests).

The emphasis on patient-focused drug development has made patient-reported outcomes (PRO), which obtain measurements directly from the patient without interpretation from others, popular. While PROs are extremely common in clinical trials for adolescents and adults without neurodevelopmental disorder, they are less common in other populations where the degree of an individual's insight into their own state may affect their ratings (Benjamin et al., 2017). There are reasons to believe that some individuals with neurodevelopmental disorder can report on some symptom domains; for example, one observational study of adults with mild-to-moderate ID described feasible self-report of stigma, depressive symptoms, and anxious symptoms (Ali, King, Strydom, & Hassiotis, 2015). However, developmental concepts may be uniquely resistant to self-assessment because they tend to require insight which exceeds the individual's current level of ability. As with PerfOs, the cognitive and language demands of a PRO may exceed the capabilities of many members of a GCAND sample, and any use of a PRO in these studies must be accompanied by meaningful qualitative and quantitative data supporting the validity of the instrument. While people with GCAND must be involved in all aspects of research, including the design and evaluation of COAs, researchers should treat with caution PROs of developmental concepts.

Global clinician-reported outcomes (ClinROs) like the Clinical Global Impressions Severity and Improvement scales, which have been frequently used in GCAND trials (e.g., Berry-Kravis et al., 2020; Glaze et al., 2019; Kolevzon et al., 2021), are overall judgments made by a clinician. Global ClinROs may be particularly attractive in trials for GCAND, because the vague definition of the variables can account for heterogeneous presentation (e.g., the original version of the Clinical Global Impressions improvement (CGI-I) scale asks, "Compared to the patient's condition at admission...this patient's condition is: [rated on 7-point scale]") (Busner & Targum, 2007). Even in general population research, it is challenging to evaluate the psychometric properties of global ClinROs and to interpret the result as meaningful benefit (Marquis, Cano, Hobart, Isaac, & RN10, 2017). Great care must be taken to establish how the information used to make a rating is ascertained, which facilitates interrater reliability by ensuring that raters are making judgments based on the same information. Validity of ClinROs is facilitated by ensuring that the anchors for each rating are defined so that an equal degree of clinical meaning is reflected in 1-unit changes across the scale. Several examples of well-anchored CGIs for GCANDs exist (e.g., Berry-Kravis et al., 2020; Glaze et al., 2019; Kolevzon et al., 2021; Neul et al., 2022); the development processes for these scales involves the creation of disorder-specific systematic interviews and training materials, as well as qualitative evaluations of clinical meaning. It is worth noting that for developmental outcomes, adequate anchoring may be likely to require systematic interviews resembling (but perhaps less detailed than) the semi-structured developmental evaluations described below.

Because caregivers often possess the broadest and deepest understanding of the study participant, observer report outcomes (ObsROs) are a commonly used method in clinical trials for individuals with neurodevelopmental disabilities. It should be noted that ObsROs are *not* proxy reported outcomes. Proxy report refers to someone who is not the patient responding as if that person *were* the patient, such as rating internal emotions (e.g., sadness) rather than behaviors which are thought to reflect an internal emotion (e.g., crying). Proxy reports are not generally recommended for usage in clinical trials (FDA, 2009). This means that ObsROs are not used for the assessment of the information that is internal to the patient, only that which can be observed. ObsROs are often surveys, which are advantageous due to their simplicity and ease of use; they are usually inexpensive and do not usually require the involvement of a clinician or even an in-person visit. The Aberrant Behavior Checklist—Community Edition modified for Fragile X syndrome (Merikle et al., 2021), introduced above, is an example of an ObsRO.

Symptom-based concepts that may be relevant to GCAND, like disruptive behaviors, are readily quantified via ObsRO. However, the complexity of many developmental concepts (e.g., language, social-emotional) would require a large number of items to represent the concept when the developmental range is not very narrow. For example, to capture expressive language ability across development, a scale would need items ranging from non-word utterances to single words to phrase speech to complex speech, and each level would require a number of detailed questions. As a result, traditional pencil-and-paper ObsROs for developmental concepts may require that parents and caregivers respond to many items with little relevance to their child/dependent; this can be a major source of frustration (Kelleher et al., 2020).

With proper quantitative methodology (e.g., item response theory) during scale creation, a broad ObsRO can be narrowed using basal/ceiling and skip rules, or item sets. Because the items on a developmental COA can be arranged from easiest to hardest, it is possible to identify a threshold in the number of failed items after which an individual is no longer likely to attain a passing score (ceiling rule; the inverse is the basal rule). Skip rules may be identified through dependencies in the items (e.g., if an individual does not use single words, items which require phrase speech may be skipped) or through quantitative procedures (e.g., a given response on one item may be associated with a near-perfect probability of a given response on another item). Item sets, or groups of items that yield equivalent estimates of the individual's ability, may be derived such that only a subset of test items need be administered at any given time. These methods can be generally referred to as computerized adaptive testing, which maximize assessment efficiency by selectively administering the items most relevant to a person's level of functioning. Computerized adaptive testing methods, which are implemented both during scale development and COA administration, promise to improve this experience, and new ObsROs of developmental concepts are beginning to take advantage (Bishop et al., 2019; Dumas et al., 2012).

Up to this point, we have discussed ObsROs in the survey format, wherein the observer rates a series of individual items. Recently, researchers have created global ratings based on caregiver report, called CaGIC or CaGI-I (Caregiver Global Impression of Change or Caregiver Global Impression of Improvement) (e.g., Berry-Kravis, Porter, Mak, & VanMeter, 2021; Merikle et al., 2021), which possess similar advantages, and require the same level of care in constructing, as ClinRO CGIs. Another ObsRO approach that may prove useful in GCAND clinical trials are personalized endpoints, versions of which have been called "target problem ratings" (Sheridan et al., 2021). An example of this was piloted in a phase 2 clinical trial wherein caregivers of individuals with Fragile X selected and rated on a visual analog scale the problems most important to them (Berry-Kravis et al., 2012). The advantage of this approach is that the COA inherently possesses clinical meaning for the individual in the study, and this endpoint was more responsive to treatment than the others in this particular trial. However, this degree of specificity to the participant makes generalizability difficult. It is difficult to interpret change in a target symptom measure at the group level (i.e., what effect can be expected as a result of the intervention), because the specific construct of interest is idiosyncratic to the participant. Further, it is important that the clinician anchors the target symptoms to a domain which is a target concept for the study and likely to be affected by the intervention. This may be mitigated by requiring the clinician to map the target problem onto predefined domains (e.g., Berry-Kravis et al., 2020), or allowing respondents to select a specific problem from a given domain (e.g., Berry-Kravis et al., 2021). This personalized approach may also be combined with electronic administration to yield real-time, individualized observer ratings of behavior, as in the Janssen Autism Knowledge Engine system (Ness et al., 2019).

Specifically for developmental concepts, the most robust ObsROs are actually a blend of ClinRO and ObsRO. An important example is the semi-structured interview, a format often used in developmental and psychiatric evaluation. For the evaluation of concepts relating to neurodevelopmental disability, measures like the Vineland Adaptive Behavior Scales Comprehensive Interview (Sparrow, Cicchetti, & Saulnier, 2016) are administered to parents or caregivers by a skilled clinician, who makes ratings informed by, but not identical to, the observer's report. Semi-structured interviews like the Vineland Comprehensive Interview possess a blend of advantages of both methods, namely, the clinician's knowledge of the concept and the observer's knowledge of the subject. When administered appropriately, the semi-structured interview can avoid the frustrating experience of low-relevance items described above.

Direct assessments of developmental concepts, too, usually require a degree of clinical observation and judgment in administration and scoring, distinguishing them from IQ tests. Among individuals with GCAND (and those with ID more generally), limitations that are unrelated to the concept of interest may require test modifications and accommodations (Soorya, Leon, Trelles, & Thurm, 2018; Thompson et al., 2018). For example, limitations in motoric abilities might interfere with finger pointing as a response modality on a cognitive test; if this is not considered during administration, the motoric impairment might be mistaken for a cognitive impairment.

Owing to the degree of clinical judgment needed to administer and score these tests, direct assessments of developmental concepts in GCAND have qualities of both PerfOs and ClinROs.

While these "hybrid" assessments allow for the integration of clinician expertise with observer report and participant performance, and therefore make possible the valid and reliable assessment of clinically meaningful concepts, they are often more costly to administer than their ObsRO or PerfO counterparts. These modalities often require longer administration time and significant training and expertise (e.g., to establish interrater reliability). This must be accounted for in the design of the study. However, some of these measures (especially the semi-structured interviews) can be administered remotely, meaning that the use of central raters trained to very high fidelity can be a way of reducing site burden from administration time and increasing consistency and reliability of the measures.

Another useful categorization of COAs differentiates domain-general and condition-specific measures. Many concepts of interest in clinical trials are domain-general, or common across multiple diagnoses (e.g., fatigue, physical function, pain). Developmental concepts, like cognitive ability or language ability, tend to be domain-general concepts and have domain-general COAs. There have been recent federally supported large-scale efforts to develop domain-general measures such as the Patient-Reported Outcomes Measurement Information System (PROMIS) (Cella et al., 2010, 2007), the Quality of Life in Neurological Disorders (Neuro-QoL) system (Cella et al., 2012; Gershon et al., 2012; Lai et al., 2012), and the NIH Toolbox (Gershon et al., 2013; Weintraub et al., 2013). The use of domain-general measures has many advantages, including reducing the burden on the investigator to develop a COA for each condition, and increasing comparability across trials.

Other times, however, the manifestation of a concept in a particular population may be different enough to warrant a condition-specific COA, like the CGI scales described above. This is the motivation for multicomponent endpoints, described below. However, it has been pointed out that if every rare condition requires its own COA, the process of developing the COA will be overly burdensome, the research utility of characterizing participants across diagnoses is reduced, and the entire process becomes self-defeating (Aman, 2012). To the extent that rare conditions share common characteristics, the use of domain-general COAs as much as possible will reduce the time and cost associated with identifying and developing appropriate outcomes (Critical Path Institute, 2021). For example, widespread use of items or scales from sources such as PROMIS, Neuro-QoL, and NIH Toolbox will result in a wealth of psychometric data, some of which could serve as the foundation for the disease-specific information. Thus, investigators must weigh the benefits of a disease-specific COA with the costs; a domain-general measure with satisfactory qualitative and quantitative evidence to support its intended use may be preferable. No matter whether the COA is condition-specific or domain-general, there must exist sufficient reason to believe that it has psychometric qualities sufficient for use in clinical trials. Next, we turn our attention to the definition and evaluation of the psychometric properties of a COA.

3.2 Psychometric properties

Current psychometric thinking follows an argument-based approach (Cronbach, 1988), which is to say that the relevant type of psychometric evidence for a given COA depends on the intended use. Psychometric properties are not inherent to the instrument; they exist relative to how a score from a test is to be used and interpreted (American Educational Research Association, American Psychological Association, & National Council on Measurement in Education, 2014). Further, psychometric properties exist in degrees (vs categorically "valid" or "not valid"). The investigator must compile sufficient evidence to demonstrate that a particular COA is fit-for-purpose—that is, the COA is a valid and reliable measure of a particular concept, and that it is responsive to clinically meaningful change, within a particular population, given the design of the study. A vast amount of psychometric information may exist for a given COA, especially if it is domain-general. But a determination must still be made: How relevant are those data to the population one wishes to study, and to the way in which the scale is intended to be used?

Often, the answer is that data from the general population are not reflective of the psychometric properties of a special population. For example, a panel of expert judges determined that the majority of COAs validated for the measurement of anxiety in typically developing children are not appropriate clinical trial COAs for children with ASD (Lecavalier et al., 2014). However, investigators in GCAND hoping to evaluate the psychometric profile of a COA face an inconvenient synergy between small population size and heterogeneity in the population, especially in key characteristics such as age, cognitive ability, and language level (Benjamin et al., 2017), creating smaller and smaller subpopulations within which COAs might be validated. Further, many of the concepts of interest are developmental in nature and therefore evolve over time even within a person. As a result, a COA with a good psychometric profile may nevertheless become inappropriate over time within the same person; for example, while a developmental language test may have good psychometric properties for a given sample at younger ages, as their language develops its psychometric properties will suffer (requiring replacement with more complex methods like language sampling).

The psychometric properties of a COA are specific to the context of use, or the purpose of the assessment. It is common for developmental COAs to have been developed for a diagnostic context. Thus, while these measures may have adequate psychometric properties when used to diagnose a condition, they are ill-suited to a clinical response context (FDA-NIH Biomarker Working Group, 2016). An example relevant to GCAND trials is the Autism Diagnostic Observation Schedule (ADOS; Lord et al., 2012), a measure that is appropriate for most diagnostic contexts but not originally developed for, and therefore poorly suited to, the monitoring or response context (Anagnostou et al., 2015). The characteristics of a measure which make scores useful for diagnostic differentiation (e.g., reflecting behaviors which are most different between groups with and without ASD) result in lack of sensitivity to change in behaviors which are clinically meaningful to ASD severity but that are not "high value" diagnostic indicators (Kanne et al., 2014). Similarly, it is not reasonable to assume that a COA that is fit-for-purpose in one trial will be appropriate for another trial, especially if the population differs. This is of particular relevance to GCAND trials where developmental concepts are of interest, as much of the psychometric data on relevant COAs is derived from the general population.

Especially for investigators in GCAND, establishing that a COA is fit-for-purpose is not a matter of citing off-the-shelf psychometric data from a manual. Rather, it is the construction of an argument that requires thoughtful and often creative use of available information. For example, psychometric data from populations that share key characteristics may be useful. Groups like the Developmental Synaptopathies Consortium of the Rare Diseases Clinical Research Network could prove to be a rich source for such data (e.g., Rare Diseases Clinical Research Network, 2021). The use of domain-general COAs will likely be essential to this process (Critical Path Institute, 2021). Finally, both researchers and regulatory bodies must allow for an evolving understanding of what type of evidence is necessary and feasible for demonstrating fitness of purpose in rare disease clinical trials

(Benjamin et al., 2017)—the rote application of standards and guidelines used for large sample research will result in too few appropriate COAs. In the remainder of this section, we discuss specific types of psychometric information and special considerations for developmental COAs.

3.2.1 Validity

Because the results of clinical trials—the effect of an intervention on the COA—are the basis of the language eventually used in labeling and promotion of intervention, the FDA is charged with ensuring that clinicians and patients can understand the documented benefit of the intervention (Edwards, Slagle, Rubright, & Wirth, 2018). Perhaps as a result, FDA guidance tends to emphasize content validity, which it considers paramount; no amount of evidence for other types of measurement properties can overcome a lack of content validity (FDA, 2009). Validity evidence relates to the interpretation of the effect of the intervention but does not necessarily affect the statistical power of the study. Thus, validity data address whether the assessment contains the right questions, whether the participants understand those questions and are responding in the way that is intended, or whether the "score [is] composed of the appropriate and sufficiently comprehensive elements to be the basis for labeling language that is not overly promotional or potentially false or misleading" (Edwards et al., 2018). Evidence for content validity often comes from qualitative research, including focus group testing, cognitive interviews, and proof that relevant experts contributed to the item derivation (p. 31, FDA, 2009). Importantly, researchers need to integrate into their studies the qualitative methodology that is required to generate evidence of content validity (FDA, 2020). Several recent studies offer examples of such designs, including work in Fragile X (Merikle et al., 2021) and Angelman syndromes (Willgoss et al., 2021).

3.2.2 Reliability

Reliability is the extent to which a COA yields a consistent and reproducible estimate of the treatment effect (FDA, 2009). The most relevant types of evidence for clinical trials are test-retest and interrater reliability because these are understood to define the amount of variability in a score that can be attributed to real change as opposed to measurement error. These are often assessed using intraclass correlation coefficients or other statistics appropriate for evaluating not just the consistency of ratings but their absolute agreement (Hayes & Krippendorff, 2007; Koo & Li, 2016). Minimizing this value by maximizing test-retest and interrater reliability will increase the power of a study to detect an effect.

Because psychometric properties depend on the intended use, the most relevant test-retest data will utilize a period of time that is comparable to that which will be used in the study. Meaning, test-retest reliability with a follow-up period of 1 day may not accurately reflect test-retest reliability with a follow-up period of 6 weeks. However, the establishment of test-retest reliability over a relevant time period is difficult for developmental measures, as the nature of developmental constructs is to change over time. Thus, it is challenging (if not impossible, in some cases) to disentangle measurement error from true developmental changes in the underlying construct. For this reason, the period over which test publishers typically evaluate test-retest reliability of developmental measures is usually about 2 weeks. For the Mullen Scales of Early Learning (Mullen, 1995), for example, the test-retest data in the normative sample were based on a mean time to follow-up of 11 days. It is difficult to say whether this test-retest value is a good estimate of the test-retest reliability for follow-up of 3–6 months, as might be found in a clinical trial (e.g., Gengoux et al., 2015). Given that assessment of test-retest reliability requires stability of the target concept, precise estimates corresponding to longer follow-up periods may simply be infeasible, and shorter periods may have to suffice. For example, many validation studies in GCANDs have used 1–3 month periods: the NIH Toolbox Cognitive battery (Shields et al., 2020) and the KiTAP executive function measure (Knox et al., 2012) in Fragile X syndrome, and expressive language sampling for both Fragile X syndrome and Down syndrome (Abbeduto et al., 2020; Thurman et al., 2021).

Interrater reliability is the extent to which independent evaluators produce similar ratings of the same target (American Psychological Association, 2020). Thus, it is a crucial aspect of the psychometric profile, especially for trials that involve multiple sites or comparison to external controls (i.e., data that were not collected during the current study). Interrater reliability may have more to do with the training procedures than the content of the COA. Intra-rater reliability, or the consistency of ratings from a single individual, is also relevant to clinical trials in GCAND. Across long trials, or between separate trials, raters may experience drift over time. As described above in the section on ClinROs, the development and implementation of training procedures required to achieve and maintain inter- and intrarater reliability can be extensive and come at a high cost, but the improvement in statistical power is usually worth the expenditure (Perkins, Wyatt, & Bartko, 2000).

3.2.3 Responsiveness

Responsiveness is the degree to which the COA detects meaningful change in a concept. While a scale that is responsive must have some degree of reliability and validity, responsiveness also integrates the concept of clinical meaning. If the concept of interest has changed in a way that is meaningful to the patient, has the COA also changed? Statistical evidence for the responsiveness of a COA is often indirect. A COA can be evaluated for responsiveness by correlating change in it to change on a separate measure for which responsiveness has been demonstrated (i.e., convergent change). A second method is to evaluate the effect size of change in a group known to have changed (e.g., if there is a method of defining a "responder" that does not involve the COA under investigation, the between-group difference [responders vs non-responders] on the COA under investigation, or the pre-post effect size within responders is evidence for the responsiveness of the COA).

Ignoring issues of measurement error, which relate more directly to reliability, the question of responsiveness usually has to do with the granularity of the scale. A scale can only detect change at intervals determined by the items which compose it, and increased granularity is achieved through additional items. For example, a scale with items for "walks with assistance" and "walks 20 steps independently" will fail to detect change in a child who becomes able to walk 10 steps independently. For COAs of developmental concepts, increased granularity comes at a cost; investigators must carefully weigh improved responsiveness against the burden of a longer scale on participants and clinicians. For example, the Vineland Adaptive Behavior Scales (Sparrow et al., 2016) has increased the number of items on its Receptive Communication domain from 13 items in the first edition, 20 items in the second edition, and 39 items on the third edition. As a result, the most recent edition of the Vineland appears to do a better job at discriminating among individuals with ID (Farmer, Adedipe, Bal, Chlebowski, & Thurm, 2020). In the ClinRO section above, we mentioned that increasingly complex systematic interviews to facilitate CGI ratings would approach the semi-structured interviews used for developmental assessment. Whether the time cost of a more granular measure (like the Vineland) outweighs its benefit relative to a less granular measure (like a ClinRO CGI for functioning) depends on the amount of granularity necessary to detect clinically meaningful change. There is a point of diminishing return, but it is unique to the condition under study.

Not all increases in granularity yield improvements in responsiveness. In the clinical trial setting, COAs tend to have more granularity at particular levels of the construct being measured. This is common in tests of developmental concepts. For example, the Weschler Intelligence Scale for Children (Wechsler, 2014) was developed to measure the cognitive ability of children aged 6–16 years, and the content of the test is therefore calibrated to provide the most precise estimates for children with abilities in that range. There are relatively few items on the test that provide information about cognitive ability commensurate with ages younger than 6, because the granularity has been focused elsewhere. While the scale is likely to be responsive to change in the 10–11 year age equivalent range, it is less likely to detect change in the 3–4 year age equivalent range. Thus, whether a COA possesses adequate responsiveness depends on how it reflects the nature of the concept in the population of interest, and the amount of change which would be considered clinically meaningful. Because it is primarily driven by test content, there is not much that the statistical design or analysis of a study can do to rectify a lack of responsiveness in a COA.

4. Endpoint selection for developmental COAs

"Endpoint" and "COA" are not interchangeable terms; the endpoint includes information about how the information from a COA will be used to quantify the effect of treatment, such as the scoring method, the density and timing of assessment points, and the statistical analysis. While concept and COA selection is focused on clinical significance, statistical significance plays a more prominent role in endpoint selection. In this section, we discuss aspects of endpoint selection that affect both clinical and statistical significance, with a focus on issues that uniquely affect developmental concepts.

4.1 Timing of endpoints

The endpoint contains information about the timing of its assessment, both the duration of follow-up and the number of repetitions. For various reasons, including practice/learning effects and respondent fatigue, the manuals of many measures of developmental concepts suggest that assessments are repeated at intervals no shorter than 6 months to 1 year. If the endpoint must occur at a briefer interval, an alternative COA may be required. However, as described in the section on psychometric data, it is possible that the concerns in the general population (e.g., practice/learning effects) may be less relevant to the GCAND population. More densely repeated measures may be allowable in some samples, which would be advantageous to study power, which is increased with additional timepoints. This is becoming increasingly important as N-of-1 studies, where densely repeated measurements are used to establish trajectory, emerge as a common approach to evaluate gene therapy and other agents directed at genetic correction. As described above, computerized adaptive testing methods (e.g., portions of the NIH Toolbox Cognitive Battery) and alternate forms (e.g., Peabody Picture Vocabulary Test), can relieve the need for administration of all or the same items every time. This may be particularly useful in limiting practice effects, which are less likely to occur when an examinee does not complete all of the items on each assessment occasion.

4.2 Types of endpoints

4.2.1 Dichotomous endpoints

A clinical response endpoint is created by determining the minimum amount of change thought to be clinically meaningful and applying this threshold to each study participant to yield a dichotomous responder variable. The interpretation of the resulting endpoint is intended to reflect the individual response to treatment and to directly inform the real-life treatment decisions that clinicians, patients, and families must make. Responder analysis is common in clinical trials, and is accepted and even promoted by regulatory bodies (p. 24, FDA, 2009). However, the known limitations of this approach (Snapinn & Jiang, 2007) are exacerbated in rare disease research. First, there is unlikely to be a one-size-fits-all threshold for clinically significant change in a developmental concept, because the amount of change that is meaningful is likely to depend on what abilities the participant already has. Second, although the response threshold must be supported with empirical data, derived through anchor-based or distributional methods (Crosby, Kolotkin, & Williams, 2003), the specific value is still arbitrary. For example, in a study of risperidone for the treatment of irritability associated with DSM-IV autistic disorder, the primary endpoint was clinical response at 8 weeks, defined by a 25% reduction in Aberrant Behavior Checklist Irritability subscale score and a CGI Improvement score of 1 or 2 (McDougle et al., 2005). Thus on this response scale, a child with 85% improvement is indistinguishable from a child with 25% improvement, despite experiencing what is very likely to be a clinically significant difference in treatment effect. By the same token, a child with 24% improvement is considered qualitatively distinct from the child with 25% improvement, despite experiencing functionally equivalent effects. Although evaluated on an ordinal scale, ClinROs like the CGI also represent a categorization of a continuous construct and are subject to the same statistical and interpretive limitations as binary response variables.

The loss of information that results from response classification affects the interpretability of the results, but perhaps more seriously for GCAND trials, it usually causes a major reduction in statistical power (Senn, 2005; Snapinn & Jiang, 2007). The exact difference in power between a continuous endpoint and its dichotomized (or categorized) form depends on the distribution of the continuous response and the extremity of the threshold, but a reduction of up to 50% is well within the realm of possibility (Deyi, Kosinski, & Snapinn, 1998). From a statistical and design perspective, this reduction in power must be redressed with additional sample size, a luxury not available to GCAND investigators. Therefore, if an appropriate continuous endpoint (or COA) exists, it is usually preferable to a categorized endpoint like responder status or CGI.

4.2.2 Multidomain responder index

Given a single concept of interest, the statistical implications of dichotomizing a continuous response into categorical are clearly negative: reduced power. However, in GCAND, it is often the case that there is no one single concept of interest. For this reason, the multidomain responder index (MDRI) has been offered up as an attractive endpoint formulation (Tandon & Kakkis, 2021). An MDRI is a type of composite endpoint based on applying responder criteria to multiple COAs (or domains of a single COA), which potentially allows for the detection of treatment effects across participants with heterogeneous presentation. To our knowledge, an MDRI endpoint has been described in only one published report of a GCAND clinical trial (Berry-Kravis et al., 2020). In that phase 2 Fragile X study, a "subject-specific efficacy score" was calculated by summing ratings of clinically meaningful improvement across several domains. Improvements of at least 20% on the study Obs/ClinROs were coded as +1, worsening of at least 20% was coded as −1. The use of MDRI allows the investigator to select multiple endpoints, ideally of similar clinical value, without increasing the risk of Type I error. The MDRI still amounts to a categorization of continuous information sources, which always confers a loss of power for the individual domain, but in the event that treatment effects are scattered across multiple domains, the use an MDRI may increase the ability of a study to detect a clinically meaningful effect. While this is being used in trials of non-GCAND conditions which span multiple domains (e.g., motor function, milestone attainment, sleep, vision) (Tandon & Kakkis, 2021), there remains much work to be done to demonstrate that it is a viable approach (FDA, 2019). A unique issue is that in addition to the difficulty in establishing responder thresholds described above, the MDRI approach also requires that the deterioration/worsening thresholds be symmetric (i.e., a score of −1 is equivalent in clinical meaning to a score of +1).

4.2.3 Multicomponent endpoints

Another approach common to rare disease research is the multicomponent endpoint, which is also a composite of several COAs (or domains of a single COA). Unlike the MDRI, the comprising variables are *not* binarized based on response criteria. Because multicomponent endpoints combine ratings of clinically relevant concepts, they may be better suited for use in a diagnostic context rather than response monitoring. For example, the Niemann-Pick Type C Severity Scale (NPC-SS; Patterson et al., 2021) is a multicomponent endpoint; the 5-domain version contains severity ratings for ambulation, fine motor, swallowing, cognition, and speech. Each domain is scored on its own metric, and the resulting scores are summed to total. The statistical efficiency of a multicomponent endpoint is strongly reliant on the relationships among the domains that comprise it, and is maximized when the domains are not strongly correlated (Sankoh, Li, & D'Agostino Sr, 2014). This is attractive when the disorder under study is multifaceted and has no widely accepted endpoints, or when the treatment effect may manifest in different areas across participants, as is often the case in GCAND. However, one must address many considerations in the selection of components (Tandon & Kakkis, 2021): Are all of the components equally clinically meaningful? If not, how should they be weighted? Will all components respond in favor of the drug, even if not at the same rate? Given that it may reflect a large change in any one component or mild changes in some number of components, what is the clinical meaning of a treatment effect on a multicomponent endpoint? A significant amount of qualitative data, from parents/caregivers and clinicians, will be necessary to evaluate these queries. For example, the NPC-SS study mentioned above elicited feedback from parents/caregivers to establish that a 1-point change on any component was judged as clinically relevant (Patterson et al., 2021). This is also a risk from a statistical perspective, as incomparability in scale and variance of the constituent components will yield the multicomponent outcome uninterpretable. Statistical power is also a consideration; if the intervention only affects a portion of the multicomponent endpoint for a given participant, the effect size (i.e., ratio of change to overall variability in the multicomponent outcome) will be small and will therefore require larger sample sizes to achieve adequate power. One variation on the multicomponent endpoint is a Monte Carlo approach, wherein significant change on some combination of outcomes (e.g., any two of four COAs) will be taken as evidence of clinical benefit (Berry-Kravis et al., 2020).

4.3 Scoring of developmental COAs

The remainder of this chapter is focused on considerations that are not specific to standardized developmental tests, but are made most explicit when using them: how should the COA be scored? Developmental concepts are expected to change over time in some predictable way, and so measures of these concepts are often norm-referenced. Norm-referencing makes it possible to contextualize the performance of a child against that of their age-based peers. Most norm-referenced tests offer a suite of scoring options: raw scores, scaled or standard scores, age equivalents, and ability scores (Fig. 3). As described below, raw scores and age equivalents generally do not possess adequate measurement properties to serve as endpoints in clinical trials and scaled or standard scores have significant limitations when used in GCAND. Thus, which score is used as an endpoint is a major decision that affects both the interpretability and statistical power of a clinical trial.

4.3.1 Raw scores

Two aspects of the raw score are important to consider when evaluating an endpoint. First, because raw scores are typically unweighted, each item has equal influence over the raw score. This type of score is often used for surveys (ObsRO), especially when the concept does *not* have a strong developmental arc. For example, the Repetitive Behavior Scale—Revised (Bodfish, Symons, Parker, & Lewis, 1999) Stereotyped Behavior subscale score is the sum of six items (Lam & Aman, 2007). Thus, a rating of 3 on "whole body" is treated as equally reflective of stereotyped behavior as a rating of 3 on either of "head," "hand/finger" or "locomotion," or as a rating of 1 on all three of those items. Whether items have the same degree of relationship to the measured concept can be framed as an empirical question that is readily answered using a factor analytic or item response theory framework, but even when the factorial validity of a scale has been evaluated, this assumption of equal weighting is usually not addressed (DiStefano, Zhu, & Mindrila, 2009). Qualitative information relating to content validity can also guide evaluation of this assumption, especially in the context of treatment trials. Are the items comprising the scale equally likely to respond to

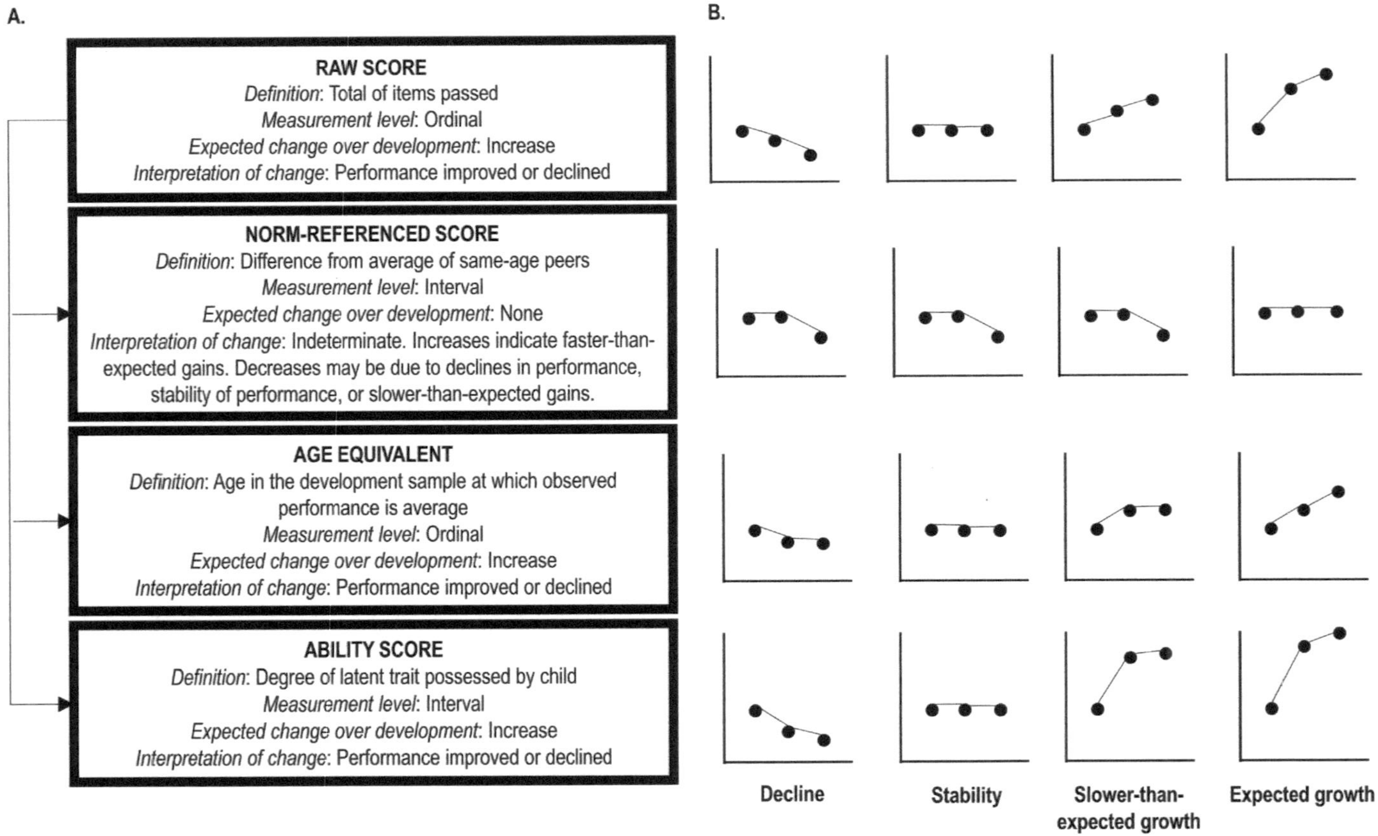

Fig. 3 Summary of score types common to standardized developmental measures. (A) Many standardized tests provide norm-referenced scores to facilitate the comparison of children across ages. Within the same test, performance may be expressed by several types of scores, described here. Aspects of the scores, such as their measurement level, how they are expected to change over time, and how change over time is interpreted affect their viability as endpoints in clinical trials for GCAND. *Expected change over development* refers to the general population over the entire developmental period. (B) The illustrative patterns (not real data) show the score (Y axis) over time (X axis) within a hypothetical child. Note that the pattern of norm-referenced scores is identical (and decreasing) for decline, stability, and slower-than-expected growth.

treatment? Will equally weighting the items dilute the treatment effect, thereby reducing the power of the study? The considerations noted above for multicomponent outcomes apply to raw scores, as well.

The second salient aspect of the raw score is its measurement level. While the items comprising the raw score are often clearly measured at the ordinal level, it may be less obvious that the raw score itself is therefore also measured at the ordinal level. It is common to sum ordinal variables and treat them as continuous. This requires the assumption that there is a continuous variable underlying the ordinal variable, like age (e.g., 16 months, 18 months, 20 months) underlying age category (e.g., 12–18 months, 19–24 months). In the case of raw scores, however, the ordinal categories are not evenly spaced, unless a test has been very carefully constructed. As a result, the raw score can change faster wherever there are more items (sometimes referred to as the item gradient, Bracken, 1988), which means that changes or differences are not comparable across the range of the scale. To make these assumptions clear, let us consider a hypothetical example.

Imagine a gross motor questionnaire with three items that can easily be arranged by increasing difficulty: sitting, walking, running. Each item is scored as a pass (+1) or fail (+0) and summed. More capable children have higher scores than those who are less capable, consistent with an ordinal interpretation of the total score. To interpret this score at the interval level, however, one must assume that the difference in motor ability required to move from sitting to walking is the same as moving from walking to running. Notice that raw scores have the undesirable property of being entirely dependent upon the composition of the scale; if "standing" were added, the intervals would be between sitting and standing, standing and walking, etc. Generating items that measure the construct with constant granularity across the full range is particularly difficult, perhaps especially for developmental concepts which by definition manifest differently with age. As a result, the meaning of change in raw score is often not easily interpretable, lacking content validity. For these reasons, raw scores are not likely to be suitable endpoints for a COA of any concept of interest (Grimby, Tennant, & Tesio, 2012), but especially for developmental COAs.

4.3.2 Norm-referenced scores

Often, a raw score is compared to the distribution of scores in some relevant comparison group, which for developmental COAs is usually based on chronological age. This is a norm-referenced score, and on developmental tests usually takes the form of a scaled score (typically with a population mean and standard deviation of 10 ± 3) or a standard score (population mean and standard deviation of 100 ± 15), and occasionally as a T-score (population mean and standard deviation of 50 ± 10). Unlike raw scores, norm-referenced scores have an interval measurement level, in that changes/differences are in standard deviation units. In other words, a 1-point difference in the scaled score has the same meaning (which is, "1/3 of the population standard deviation"), whether it is moving from a score of 4–5 or 14–15. In general samples, an increase in norm-referenced scores can be interpreted as improvement above and beyond what might be expected purely as a result of development, though it is worth noting that development samples are cross-sectional (i.e., each normative age group is composed of different individuals). Improvement in abilities that is commensurate with age-related expectations will result in static scores.

Given the nature of developmental constructs, meaningful within-subject decreases in norm-referenced scores rarely occur in the general population. For those working with GCAND, however, the presence of severe disability and even degeneration makes decreasing standard scores likely (Bishop, Farmer, & Thurm, 2015). Consider a hypothetical child with a degenerative GCAND. Treatment is initiated, and over time, the child's standard scores in language and cognition measures decrease. If this reflects active ongoing degeneration, the conclusion may be that the intervention was ineffective. If the decrease in standard scores instead reflects slower-than-expected improvements in abilities or stability, the conclusion may instead be that the intervention was successful. Although these two causes have dramatically different clinical meaning, it is not possible to distinguish them based on the standard score alone. An inconvenient feature of norm-referenced scores is that especially when the starting value is low, a decrease can be caused by deterioration, stability, or slower-than-expected improvement in the target concept (Fig. 3B). This significantly limits the validity of norm referenced scores when the natural history of a GCAND is characterized by severe disability and/or degeneration.

Norm-referenced scores are also known to exhibit poor reliability at extreme values (e.g., Oosterhuis, van der Ark, & Sijtsma, 2015), where "extreme" refers to scores more than 2 SD away from the average of the individual's normative age group (approximately the 2nd percentile). For many concepts of interest, individuals with neurodevelopmental disability are likely to fall far below this threshold. Test developers are well-aware of this decrease in reliability at the extremes of scaled or standard scores, and as a result, most standardized tests do not offer scaled or standard scores

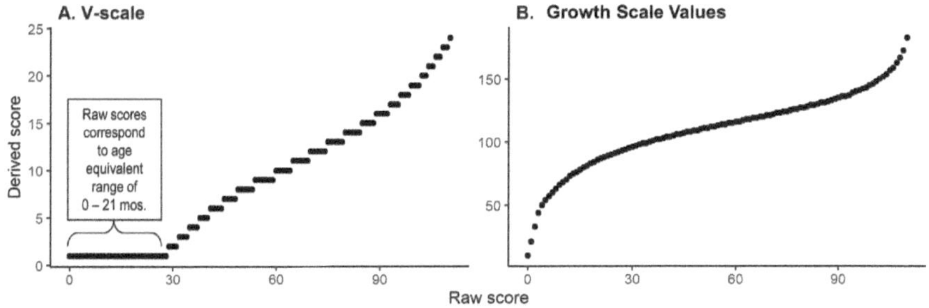

Fig. 4 Floor effect in Vineland-3 Personal subdomain V-scale scores. (A) The relationship between raw scores and V-scale score (population mean = 15, SD = 3) for a child aged 60 months is plotted. All raw scores less than 28 receive V-scale scores of 1, despite reflecting a wide range of skills (age equivalents between birth and 21 months); this is known as a floor effect. (B) The relationship between ability scores (called Growth Scale Values on the Vineland-3) and raw scores is plotted. Unlike for V-scale scores, there is no floor effect on ability scores for this subdomain. As a result, within-person change below a raw score of 28 can be detected. *Figure derived from: https://support.pearson.com/usclinical/s/article/Vineland-3-Scoring-Tables*

at levels more than 4 SD below average. This induces what is referred to as a "floor effect," wherein all participants below some threshold are given the same score (Hessl et al., 2009) (Fig. 4A), which dramatically reduces responsiveness. Floor effects obscure important variability. The figure illustrates that for a 60-month-old, Vineland Personal subdomain age equivalents between 0 and 21 months all receive the same V-scale score of 1. In practice, floor effects prevent the detection of change for individuals who are too-low functioning. For example, progression of dementia among adults with Down syndrome is challenging to quantify, because they may have been at the floor of cognitive tests prior to onset (Snyder et al., 2020). Some investigators working in ID, where floor effects on a COA can cause a work stoppage, have used publisher's data to calculate deviation scores below the publisher's threshold (Sansone et al., 2014), but these scores may not be suitable trial endpoints due to the aforementioned limitations in reliability. In summary, norm-referenced scores are poor candidates for endpoints in GCAND clinical trials because they have compromised validity, reliability, and responsiveness.

4.3.3 Age equivalents

Age equivalent scores are criterion-referenced scores, where the criterion is the age at which that score would be considered average. Returning to the vignette described above, when faced with decreasing standard scores, a clinician may turn to age equivalents to determine whether the standard scores are a result of decline (decreasing age equivalent) or slower-than-expected growth (stable or increasing age equivalent). Age equivalents possess great clinical value, but their statistical limitations have been well-documented (Bracken, 1988). Regarding their use as endpoints in clinical trials, the main limitation is that, like raw scores, age equivalents are ordinal. Because of the non-linear nature of development, a 1-month change in age equivalent means something very different depending on whether the starting point was 12 months or 12 years. Thus, the limitations described for raw scores apply to age equivalents, making them poorly suited to use as endpoints in GCAND clinical trials.

4.3.4 Person ability scores

A third type of score, the person ability score, can shed light on whether decreasing norm-referenced scores are due to actual decline or slower-than-expected growth. They are available on many developmental tests, and though they may have a test-specific name (e.g., Growth Scale Value, Growth Score, Change Sensitive Scale), all person ability scores result from the Rasch or item response theory calibration of a measure. Put simply, these psychometric models assume that an individual's score on a particular item depends on both the person's ability and the difficulty of the item. Through latent variable methods, person ability and item difficulty are estimated on the same scale. When a person's ability exceeds the difficulty of the item, they are more likely to pass an item than to fail it. Using data from a large sample, test developers can identify a difficulty level for each item (a process called "calibration"). Thus, based on the number or pattern of items passed by an individual, their ability level can be estimated (for detailed description: Edwards, 2009; Kean, Brodke, Biber, & Gross, 2018; Van der Linden, 2018).

In contrast with norm-referenced scores, for which a decrease may result from decline, stability, or even increase in raw score, ability scores have a monotonic relationship with raw scores. As raw scores increase, so do ability scores (Fig. 4B). However, while raw scores are influenced by the distribution of difficulty in the items, ability scores adjust for this variability. As a result, a 1-point change in ability corresponds to a consistent difference in the underlying trait, no matter the level. Thus, like norm-referenced scores, ability scores are measured at the interval level. Unlike norm-referenced scores, however, change is attributable to a change in the underlying trait. The reliability and responsiveness is also less affected by floor effects for ability scores than for norm-referenced scores (Farmer et al., 2020; Farmer, Thurm, Troy, & Kaat, 2022). Ability scores have a conditional standard error of measurement, meaning that the reliability of a score can be precisely determined. Both measurement at the interval level and the availability of precise reliability estimates are especially attractive for trials which rely on the patient as their own control, where no comparison group exists. In these studies, the endpoint of interest may be the difference in slope (rate of change) of pre-intervention/natural history measurements and post-intervention measurements. The interval measurement level means that the rate of change in ability scores is comparable across time and level of the underlying trait, and the standard error of measurement can be used to better understand the statistical significance of the within-person change.

The intended use of ability scores is to track change over time within an individual; to harmonize this with the terms used in this chapter, ability scores are used to establish the statistical significance of change, but not the clinical significance of change. The scale of ability scores does not have any meaning; in fact, test developers impose a variety of transformations to make them more familiar-feeling to users. One way to increase the interpretability of change in ability score might be to use the corresponding age equivalents as a guide, such that the ability score is the endpoint for analysis, but it is transformed into age equivalent for interpretation. In educational settings, the definition of meaningful change is typically determined by content-matter experts (e.g., what score is indicative of proficiency, or what amount of change is expected between the start and end of fifth grade?). To establish interpretive levels for GCAND trials, something similar, using panels composed of experienced clinicians, parents, caregivers, and other stakeholders will likely be necessary. One promising avenue for assigning clinical significance to change in ability scores in GCAND trials is through criterion-referencing. A given change in ability score can be expressed as a specific change in the probability of passing a particular item (Benson, Beaujean, Donohue, & Ward, 2016; Tillmann, 2021). For example, a minimal clinically important difference in ability score might be defined based on the magnitude of increase required to improve by 25% the probability of passing an item such as, "Walks independently." While the clinical meaning of the increase in ability scores is yoked to some individual item, the information used to calculate the ability score comes from the entire test, likely allowing for a more precise and responsive endpoint (vs pass/fail of the individual item).

Finally, we note that although this section was focused on standardized developmental tests, where the decision between score types is most obvious, the preceding discussion could apply to most types of COAs. The distinction lies in that standardized developmental tests have usually been developed using the methods necessary to produce the various score derivations (norm-referenced scores, age equivalents, ability scores). Strictly speaking, there is no reason that these methods (i.e., item response theory) could not be applied to ObsRO surveys, for example. This is perhaps most feasible for domain-general measures, where sufficient sample sizes might be obtained across GCANDs rather than within. In summary, when a standardized developmental test is used as a COA in GCAND clinical trials, the investigators usually have the ability to select one of several score types as the endpoint. Raw scores and age equivalents are unsuitable for this purpose and should be avoided; norm-referenced scores (like IQ) may have poor validity, reliability, and responsiveness when used in individuals with significant impairment. Although a significant amount of qualitative work will be necessary to establish the content validity of ability scores, for researchers in GCAND they likely represent the most powerful endpoint for standardized developmental COAs.

5. Discussion

The challenges associated with COA and endpoint selection in clinical trials for GCAND are well-known though not necessarily resolved (Benjamin et al., 2017). That GCAND often onset during early childhood is mentioned as contributing to these challenges, but there has been little discussion of the effects of targeting developmental concepts. Developmental concepts, like motor ability, thinking and learning, social abilities, and communication, are challenging to measure even in the typical population, because they by definition manifest differently over time in very complex ways. In populations affected by neurodevelopmental disability, such as those with autism spectrum disorder, the unresolved challenges of identifying appropriate COAs have been discussed extensively (Grzadzinski, Janvier, & Kim, 2020). These challenges are enhanced by the small population, increased incidence of severe ID, and phenotypic heterogeneity observed in GCAND. Even after a COA has been selected, the particular endpoint used may greatly affect the power of a study and the validity of its interpretation. While members of various fields have coalesced to address the challenges inherent to the study of rare conditions, the effectiveness of these efforts will be enhanced by acknowledging and explicitly addressing the difficulty of evaluating developmental concepts. In this chapter, we discussed a variety of hurdles to the process of identifying adequate COAs and endpoints of developmental concepts in clinical trials for GCAND, each of which is intertwined with the others.

The first hurdle is the identification of specific concepts that hold meaning for patients, families, and clinicians and that may reasonably be expected to change during the surveillance period of a study. Improvement in developmental domains is dissimilar to improvement in psychiatric conditions, where symptoms like depressed mood or inattention are being removed. Improvement in developmental domains requires the acquisition of new behaviors, which necessarily takes time. Although a change in trajectory may result in large differences much later in development, during the timeframe of a study these improvements may appear minor. For trials where a developmental concept is targeted, the length of the study should be tailored accordingly. Still, this emphasizes the importance of identifying a COA that measures the concept of interest with a high degree of reliability and responsiveness, so that earlier, smaller effects might be detected. These psychometric properties, along with content validity, are not properties of the COA itself but rather exist relative to the context in which the scale will be used and how scores will be interpreted.

For investigators in GCAND, the relativity of psychometric data presents a second hurdle: psychometric data on developmental COAs that are relevant to the population under study may be difficult or impossible to obtain, due to small population size and phenotypic heterogeneity. Natural history studies, which may be used as external controls for trials where randomization is not possible or ethical, can also be an invaluable source for psychometric data. To obtain psychometric data from a natural history study requires that it be planned with psychometric evaluation in mind, employing standard batteries alongside unproven scales, and evaluating their content validity through qualitative methods. Investigators in GCAND should consider building in such qualitative and quantitative work into all studies, recognizing the interrelationship among these first two hurdles. Because many developmental concepts are domain-general, the use of standard assessment batteries (and data sharing) will allow for investigators interested in one GCAND to support a COA using data from phenotypically similar conditions. Finally, after a COA is selected, the investigator must decide upon the endpoint, or the operationalization of how the COA will be used to evaluate the intervention. Especially for developmental outcomes, there are several options within a test (i.e., score types), and across all types of outcomes the investigator has several options for analyzing the test output (e.g., untransformed score, response, multicomponent index, composite index).

Endpoint selection comprises the final hurdle discussed in this chapter. Multicomponent endpoints, which attempt to account for heterogeneity through the unweighted combination of relevant COA scores, are common in GCAND but they suffer from a lack of responsiveness and difficulty with interpretation and therefore require a significant amount of qualitative and quantitative development. Given the small sample sizes in GCAND trials, the decrease in power associated with binary endpoints (responder/non-responder) is untenable. Composite endpoints, where multiple COAs are converted into response binaries and combined, hold promise for use in GCAND, but their validation depends on agreement about what constitutes similar levels of clinically meaningful change across developmental concepts. The difficulty of defining meaningful change cannot be overestimated, but the inclusion of qualitative studies as mentioned above will help to make it possible. While the hyper-specificity of multicomponent and composite endpoints to the GCAND population under study may be useful from a statistical power perspective, the creation of these types of endpoints requires a significant amount of work that may not be feasible for a measure that can only be used in a single condition.

Even if the endpoint is a single domain-general COA score, many developmental measures have multiple score options. Norm-referenced scores were intended for the diagnostic context and have poor reliability and validity in a context of use as an outcome measure, which is exacerbated when they are low, as is often the case in GCAND. Importantly, it can be impossible to distinguish between deterioration and slower-than-expected improvement, or to detect improvement beneath the floor, based solely on norm-referenced scores. Ability scores, which index absolute performance on an interval scale, have better reliability and limited floor effects, and may afford investigators more power to detect treatment effects. While the advantages of ability scores are most notable for the type of standardized tests used for developmental outcomes, the statistical methodology that produces ability scores (item response theory) could be applied to any type of COA that meets the technical requirements.

The challenges discussed in this chapter must be contextualized within the tide of genetic reversal and pathway-targeted treatments emerging from basic science, which may be outpacing our ability to identify the highest quality outcomes. There exists great urgency to apply these treatments as early as possible within an individual with GCAND, given the higher likelihood of benefit if treatment targeting a developmental concept is enacted early in development, and the large clinical and economic burden of these conditions. With respect to developmental outcomes in GCAND clinical trials, perfect may be the enemy of good. This chapter highlights areas that require attention when developing new measures and modifying/validating existing measures for use in the GCAND clinical trial context. There is urgent work to be done on validation of potential endpoints through natural history or endpoint-enabling studies as new treatments for GCANDs are going through the pre-clinical development process. In the meantime, however, considerations discussed above can help guide the selection of optimal COAs and endpoints from what is currently available, so that clinical trials can proceed when treatments are ready for human trials.

Acknowledgment

This research was supported in part by the Intramural Research Program of the NIMH (ZIC-MH002961).

Disclosures

Cristan Farmer, Aaron Kaat, and Audrey Thurm make no disclosures. Elizabeth Berry-Kravis has received funding from Acadia, Alcobra, AMO, Asuragen, Avexis, Biogen, BioMarin, Cydan, Erydel, Fulcrum, GeneTx, GW, Ionis, Jaguar, Lumos, Marinus, Neuren, Neurogene, Neurotrope, Novartis, Orphazyme, Ovid, Retrophin, Roche, Seaside Therapeutics, Taysha, Tetra, Ultragenyx, Yamo, Zynerba, and Vtesse/Sucampo/Mallinckrodt Pharmaceuticals, to consult on trial design or run clinical or lab validation trials in genetic neurodevelopmental or neurodegenerative disorders, all of which is directed to RUMC in support of rare disease programs; Dr. Berry-Kravis receives no personal funds and RUMC has no relevant financial interest in any of the commercial entities listed.

References

Abbeduto, L., Berry-Kravis, E., Sterling, A., Sherman, S., Edgin, J. O., McDuffie, A., et al. (2020). Expressive language sampling as a source of outcome measures for treatment studies in fragile X syndrome: Feasibility, practice effects, test-retest reliability, and construct validity. *Journal of Neurodevelopmental Disorders*, *12*(1), 1–23.

Aishworiya, R., Valica, T., Hagerman, R., & Restrepo, B. (2022). An update on psychopharmacological treatment of autism Spectrum disorder. *Neurotherapeutics*. https://doi.org/10.1007/s13311-022-01183-1.

Ali, A., King, M., Strydom, A., & Hassiotis, A. (2015). Self-reported stigma and symptoms of anxiety and depression in people with intellectual disabilities: Findings from a cross sectional study in England. *Journal of Affective Disorders*, *187*, 224–231. https://doi.org/10.1016/j.jad.2015.07.046.

Aman, M. G. (2012). Aberrant behavior checklist: Current identity and future developments. *Clinical and Experimental Pharmacology*, *2*(3). https://doi.org/10.4172/2161-1459.1000e114.

American Educational Research Association, American Psychological Association, & National Council on Measurement in Education. (2014). *Standards for educational and psychological testing*. Washington, DC: American Educational Research Association.
American Psychological Association. (2020). *APA dictionary of psychology*. Retrieved from dictionary.apa.org.
Anagnostou, E., Jones, N., Huerta, M., Halladay, A. K., Wang, P., Scahill, L., et al. (2015). Measuring social communication behaviors as a treatment endpoint in individuals with autism spectrum disorder. *Autism*, *19*(5), 622–636.
Benjamin, K., Vernon, M. K., Patrick, D. L., Perfetto, E., Nestler-Parr, S., & Burke, L. (2017). Patient-reported outcome and observer-reported outcome assessment in rare disease clinical trials: An ISPOR COA emerging good practices task force report. *Value in Health*, *20*(7), 838–855.
Benson, N. F., Beaujean, A. A., Donohue, A., & Ward, E. (2016). W scores: Background and derivation. *Journal of Psychoeducational Assessment*, *36*(3), 273–277. https://doi.org/10.1177/0734282916677433.
Berry-Kravis, E., Harnett, M. D., Reines, S. A., Reese, M. A., Ethridge, L. E., Outterson, A. H., et al. (2021). Inhibition of phosphodiesterase-4D in adults with fragile X syndrome: A randomized, placebo-controlled, phase 2 clinical trial. *Nature Medicine*, *27*(5), 862–870.
Berry-Kravis, E., Hessl, D., Rathmell, B., Zarevics, P., Cherubini, M., Walton-Bowen, K., et al. (2012). Effects of STX209 (arbaclofen) on neurobehavioral function in children and adults with fragile X syndrome: A randomized, controlled, phase 2 trial. *Science Translational Medicine*, *4*(152), 152ra127-152ra127.
Berry-Kravis, E., Horrigan, J. P., Tartaglia, N., Hagerman, R., Kolevzon, A., Erickson, C. A., et al. (2020). A double-blind, randomized, placebo-controlled clinical study of trofinetide in the treatment of fragile X syndrome. *Pediatric Neurology*, *110*, 30–41.
Berry-Kravis, E., Porter, F. D., Mak, C., & VanMeter, S. (2021). *Adrabetadex for the treatment of Niemann-pick disease type C1*. Orlando, FL, USA: Paper presented at the WORLD Symposium.
Bishop, S., Farmer, C., Kaat, A., Georgiades, S., Kanne, S., & Thurm, A. (2019). The need for a developmentally based measure of social-communication skills. *Journal of the American Academy of Child and Adolescent Psychiatry*, *58*(6), 555.
Bishop, S., Farmer, C., & Thurm, A. (2015). Measurement of nonverbal IQ in autism spectrum disorder: Scores in young adulthood compared to early childhood. *Journal of Autism and Developmental Disorders*, *45*(4), 966–974. https://doi.org/10.1007/s10803-014-2250-3.
Bodfish, J. W., Symons, F. J., Parker, D. E., & Lewis, M. H. (1999). Repetitive behavior scale–revised. *Journal of Autism and Developmental Disorders*.
Bracken, B. A. (1988). Ten psychometric reasons why similar tests produce dissimilar results. *Journal of School Psychology*, *26*(2), 155–166.
Busner, J., & Targum, S. D. (2007). The clinical global impressions scale: Applying a research tool in clinical practice. *Psychiatry (Edgmont (Pa.: Township))*, *4*(7), 28–37.
Cella, D., Lai, J. S., Nowinski, C., Victorson, D., Peterman, A., Miller, D., et al. (2012). Neuro-QOL: Brief measures of health-related quality of life for clinical research in neurology. *Neurology*, *78*, 1860–1867. https://doi.org/10.1212/WNL.0b013e318258f744.
Cella, D., Riley, W., Stone, A., Rothrock, N., Reeve, B., Yount, S., et al. (2010). The patient-reported outcomes measurement information system (PROMIS) developed and tested its first wave of adult self-reported health outcome item banks: 2005–2008. *Journal of Clinical Epidemiology*, *63*(11), 1179–1194. https://doi.org/10.1016/j.jclinepi.2010.04.011.
Cella, D., Yount, S., Rothrock, N., Gershon, R., Cook, K., Reeve, B., et al. (2007). The patient-reported outcomes measurement information system (PROMIS): Progress of an

NIH roadmap cooperative group during its first two years. *Medical Care, 45*(5), S3–S11. https://doi.org/10.1097/01.mlr.0000258615.42478.55.
Copping, N. A., McTighe, S. M., Fink, K. D., & Silverman, J. L. (2021). Emerging gene and Small molecule therapies for the neurodevelopmental disorder Angelman syndrome. *Neurotherapeutics, 18*(3), 1535–1547. https://doi.org/10.1007/s13311-021-01082-x.
Critical Path Institute. (2021). *Rare disease clinical outcome assessment consortium*. Retrieved from https://c-path.org/programs/rd-coac/.
Cronbach, L. J. (1988). Five perspectives on validity argument. *Test Validity*, 3–17.
Crosby, R. D., Kolotkin, R. L., & Williams, G. R. (2003). Defining clinically meaningful change in health-related quality of life. *Journal of Clinical Epidemiology, 56*(5), 395–407.
Deyi, B. A., Kosinski, A. S., & Snapinn, S. M. (1998). Power considerations when a continuous outcome variable is dichotomized. *Journal of Biopharmaceutical Statistics, 8*(2), 337–352.
DiStefano, C., Sadhwani, A., & Wheeler, A. C. (2020). Comprehensive assessment of individuals with significant levels of intellectual disability: Challenges, strategies, and future directions. *American Journal on Intellectual and Developmental Disabilities, 125*(6), 434–448.
DiStefano, C., Zhu, M., & Mindrila, D. (2009). Understanding and using factor scores: Considerations for the applied researcher. *Practical Assessment, Research and Evaluation, 14*(1), 20.
Dumas, H. M., Fragala-Pinkham, M. A., Haley, S. M., Ni, P., Coster, W., Kramer, J. M., et al. (2012). Computer adaptive test performance in children with and without disabilities: Prospective field study of the PEDI-CAT. *Disability and Rehabilitation, 34*(5), 393–401. https://doi.org/10.3109/09638288.2011.607217.
Edwards, M. C. (2009). An introduction to item response theory using the need for cognition scale. *Social and Personality Psychology Compass, 3*(4), 507–529.
Edwards, M. C., Slagle, A., Rubright, J. D., & Wirth, R. J. (2018). Fit for purpose and modern validity theory in clinical outcomes assessment. *Quality of Life Research, 27*(7), 1711–1720. https://doi.org/10.1007/s11136-017-1644-z.
Farmer, C., Adedipe, D., Bal, V., Chlebowski, C., & Thurm, A. (2020). Concordance of the Vineland adaptive behavior scales, second and third editions. *Journal of Intellectual Disability Research, 64*(1), 18–26.
Farmer, C., Kaat, A. J., Thurm, A., Anselm, I., Akshoomoff, N., Bennett, A., et al. (2020). Person ability scores as an alternative to norm-referenced scores as outcome measures in studies of neurodevelopmental disorders. *American Journal on Intellectual and Developmental Disabilities, 125*(6), 475–480.
Farmer, C., Thurm, A., Troy, J., & Kaat, A. J. (2022). Comparing ability and norm-referenced scores as clinical trial outcomes for neurodevelopmental disabilities: A simulation study. *PsyArXiv*. https://doi.org/10.31234/osf.io/p4vjx.
FDA. (2009). *Patient-reported outcome measures: Use in medical product development to support labeling claims*. Marylanf, USA: FDA (Retrieved from: https://www.fda.gov/regulatory-information/search-fda-guidance-documents/patient-reported-outcome-measures-use-medical-product-development-support-labeling-claims).
FDA. (2018). Methods to identify what is important to patients & select, develop or modify fit-for-purpose clinical outcomes assessments. In *Patient-focused drug development guidance public workshop*. Maryland, USA: FDA. Retrieved from https://www.fda.gov/media/116277/download.
FDA. (2019). *Incorporating clinical outcome assessments into endpoints for regulatory decision-making*. Maryland, USA: FDA (Retrieved from: https://www.fda.gov/media/132505/download).
FDA. (2020). *Patient-focused drug development: Collecting comprehensive and representative input*. Maryland: Silver Spring (Retrieved from: https://www.fda.gov/media/139088/download).

FDA-NIH Biomarker Working Group. (2016). *BEST (biomarkers, endpoints, and other tools) resource [internet].*
Gengoux, G. W., Berquist, K. L., Salzman, E., Schapp, S., Phillips, J. M., Frazier, T. W., et al. (2015). Pivotal response treatment parent training for autism: Findings from a 3-month follow-up evaluation. *Journal of Autism and Developmental Disorders, 45*(9), 2889–2898. https://doi.org/10.1007/s10803-015-2452-3.
Gershon, R., Lai, J., Bode, R., Choi, S., Moy, C., Bleck, T., et al. (2012). Neuro-QOL: Quality of life item banks for adults with neurological disorders: Item development and calibrations based upon clinical and general population testing. *Quality of Life Research, 21*(3), 475–486. https://doi.org/10.1007/s11136-011-9958-8.
Gershon, R., Wagster, M. V., Hendrie, H. C., Fox, N., Cook, K. F., & Nowinski, C. J. (2013). NIH toolbox for assessment of neurological and behavioral function. *Neurology, 80*(11 Supplement 3), S2–S6. https://doi.org/10.1212/WNL.0b013e3182872e5f.
Glaze, D. G., Neul, J. L., Kaufmann, W. E., Berry-Kravis, E., Condon, S., Stoms, G., et al. (2019). Double-blind, randomized, placebo-controlled study of trofinetide in pediatric Rett syndrome. *Neurology, 92*(16), e1912–e1925.
Grimby, G., Tennant, A., & Tesio, L. (2012). The use of raw scores from ordinal scales: Time to end malpractice? *Journal of Rehabilitation Medicine, 44*(2), 97–98.
Grzadzinski, R., Janvier, D., & Kim, S. H. (2020). Recent developments in treatment outcome measures for young children with autism Spectrum disorder (ASD). *Seminars in Pediatric Neurology, 34*, 100806. https://doi.org/10.1016/j.spen.2020.100806.
Hayes, A. F., & Krippendorff, K. (2007). Answering the call for a standard reliability measure for coding data. *Communication Methods and Measures, 1*(1), 77–89. https://doi.org/10.1080/19312450709336664.
Hessl, D., Nguyen, D. V., Green, C., Chavez, A., Tassone, F., Hagerman, R. J., et al. (2009). A solution to limitations of cognitive testing in children with intellectual disabilities: The case of fragile X syndrome. *Journal of Neurodevelopmental Disorders, 1*(1), 33–45.
Hudson, K. L., & Collins, F. S. (2017). The 21st century cures act—A view from the NIH. *New England Journal of Medicine, 376*(2), 111–113.
Jensen, T. L., Gøtzsche, C. R., & Woldbye, D. P. D. (2021). Current and future prospects for gene therapy for rare genetic diseases affecting the brain and spinal cord. *Frontiers in Molecular Neuroscience, 14*, 695937. https://doi.org/10.3389/fnmol.2021.695937.
Kanne, S. M., Mazurek, M. O., Sikora, D., Bellando, J., Branum-Martin, L., Handen, B., et al. (2014). The autism impact measure (AIM): Initial development of a new tool for treatment outcome measurement. *Journal of Autism and Developmental Disorders, 44*(1), 168–179.
Kean, J., Brodke, D. S., Biber, J., & Gross, P. (2018). An introduction to item response theory and Rasch analysis of the eating assessment tool (EAT-10). *Brain impairment: a multidisciplinary journal of the Australian Society for the Study of Brain Impairment, 19*(Spec Iss 1), 91–102. https://doi.org/10.1017/BrImp.2017.31.
Kelleher, B., Halligan, T., Garwood, T., Howell, S., Martin-O'Dell, B., Swint, A., et al. (2020). Brief report: Assessment experiences of children with neurogenetic syndromes: caregivers' perceptions and suggestions for improvement. *Journal of Autism and Developmental Disorders*, 1–8.
Kerr, C., Breheny, K., Lloyd, A., Brazier, J., Bailey, D. B., Berry-Kravis, E., et al. (2015). Developing a utility index for the aberrant behavior checklist (ABC-C) for fragile X syndrome. *Quality of Life Research, 24*(2), 305–314. https://doi.org/10.1007/s11136-014-0759-8.
Knox, A., Schneider, A., Abucayan, F., Hervey, C., Tran, C., Hessl, D., et al. (2012). Feasibility, reliability, and clinical validity of the test of attentional performance for children (KiTAP) in fragile X syndrome (FXS). *Journal of Neurodevelopmental Disorders, 4*(1), 1–12.

Kolevzon, A., Ventola, P., Keary, C. J., Heimer, G., Neul, J. L., Adera, M., et al. (2021). Development of an adapted clinical global impression scale for use in Angelman syndrome. *Journal of Neurodevelopmental Disorders, 13*(1), 1–13.

Koo, T. K., & Li, M. Y. (2016). A guideline of selecting and reporting intraclass correlation coefficients for reliability research. *Journal of Chiropractic Medicine, 15*(2), 155–163. https://doi.org/10.1016/j.jcm.2016.02.012.

Lai, J. S., Nowinski, C., Victorson, D., Bode, R., Podrabsky, T., McKinney, N., et al. (2012). Quality-of-life measures in children with neurological conditions: Pediatric neuro-QOL. *Neurorehabilitation and Neural Repair, 26*(1), 36–47. https://doi.org/10.1177/1545968311412054.

Lam, K. S., & Aman, M. G. (2007). The repetitive behavior scale-revised: Independent validation in individuals with autism spectrum disorders. *Journal of Autism and Developmental Disorders, 37*(5), 855–866.

Lecavalier, L., Wood, J. J., Halladay, A. K., Jones, N. E., Aman, M. G., Cook, E. H., et al. (2014). Measuring anxiety as a treatment endpoint in youth with autism spectrum disorder. *Journal of Autism and Developmental Disorders, 44*(5), 1128–1143.

Lord, C., Rutter, M., DiLavore, P., Risi, S., Gotham, K., & Bishop, S. (2012). *Autism diagnostic observation schedule, second edition (ADOS-2).* Los Angeles, CA: Western Psychological Services Torrance.

Maia, N., Nabais Sá, M. J., Melo-Pires, M., de Brouwer, A. P. M., & Jorge, P. (2021). Intellectual disability genomics: Current state, pitfalls and future challenges. *BMC Genomics, 22*(1), 909. https://doi.org/10.1186/s12864-021-08227-4.

Marquis, P., Cano, S., Hobart, J., Isaac, M., & RN10, L. B. B. (2017). Clinician-reported outcome (ClinRO) assessments of treatment benefit: Report of the ISPOR clinical outcome assessment emerging good practices task force. *Value in Health, 20*, 140–152.

McDougle, C. J., Scahill, L., Aman, M. G., McCracken, J. T., Tierney, E., Davies, M., et al. (2005). Risperidone for the core symptom domains of autism: Results from the study by the autism network of the research units on pediatric psychopharmacology. *American Journal of Psychiatry, 162*(6), 1142–1148.

Merikle, E., Patel, V., Dobbins, T., Griesser, J., Tich, N., Sebree, T., et al. (2021). Meaningful change thresholds for the aberrant behavior checklist-community fragile X syndrome (ABC-CFXS) in children and adolescents with FXS. In *Paper presented at the ISPOR (Professional Society for Health Economics and Outcomes Research), Virtual.*

Mullen, E. M. (Ed.). (1995). *Mullen scales of early learning.* Circle Pines, MN: American Guidance Service.

Ness, S. L., Bangerter, A., Manyakov, N. V., Lewin, D., Boice, M., Skalkin, A., et al. (2019). An observational study with the Janssen autism knowledge engine (JAKE(®)) in individuals with autism Spectrum disorder. *Frontiers in Neuroscience, 13*, 111. https://doi.org/10.3389/fnins.2019.00111.

Neul, J. L., Percy, A. K., Benke, T. A., Berry-Kravis, E., Glaze, D. G., Peters, S. U., et al. (2022). Design and outcome measures of LAVENDER, a phase 3 study of trofinetide for Rett syndrome. *Contemporary Clinical Trials, 106704.*

Oosterhuis, H. E. M., van der Ark, L. A., & Sijtsma, K. (2015). Sample size requirements for traditional and regression-based norms. *Assessment, 23*(2), 191–202. https://doi.org/10.1177/1073191115580638.

Patterson, M. C., Lloyd-Price, L., Guldberg, C., Doll, H., Burbridge, C., Chladek, M., et al. (2021). Validation of the 5-domain Niemann-pick type C clinical severity scale. *Orphanet Journal of Rare Diseases, 16*(1), 79. https://doi.org/10.1186/s13023-021-01719-2.

Perfetto, E. M., Burke, L., Oehrlein, E. M., & Epstein, R. S. (2015). Patient-focused drug development: A new direction for collaboration. *Medical Care, 53*(1), 9–17.

Perkins, D. O., Wyatt, R. J., & Bartko, J. J. (2000). Penny-wise and pound-foolish: The impact of measurement error on sample size requirements in clinical trials. *Biological Psychiatry*, *47*(8), 762–766. https://doi.org/10.1016/S0006-3223(00)00837-4.

Pickett, E., Pullara, O., O'Grady, J., & Gordon, B. (2009). Speech acquisition in older nonverbal individuals with autism: A review of features, methods, and prognosis. *Cognitive and Behavioral Neurology*, *22*(1), 1–21. https://doi.org/10.1097/WNN.0b013e318190d185.

Poletti, V., & Biffi, A. (2019). Gene-based approaches to inherited neurometabolic diseases. *Human Gene Therapy*, *30*(10), 1222–1235. https://doi.org/10.1089/hum.2019.190.

Rare Diseases Clinical Research Network. (2021). *Developmental Synaptopathies consortium*. Retrieved from https://www1.rarediseasesnetwork.org/cms/DSC.

Sadhwani, A., Rietman, A., Hiruma, L., Ten Hooven-Raadstaake, M., Navis, C., ... Wheeler, A. (2021). Bayley Scales of Infant and Toddler Development, third and fourth editions (Bayley-III/Bayley-4): Standardizing administration for individuals with Angelman syndrome.

Sanders, S. J., Sahin, M., Hostyk, J., Thurm, A., Jacquemont, S., Avillach, P., et al. (2019). A framework for the investigation of rare genetic disorders in neuropsychiatry. *Nature Medicine*, *25*(10), 1477–1487.

Sankoh, A. J., Li, H., & D'Agostino, R. B., Sr. (2014). Use of composite endpoints in clinical trials. *Statistics in Medicine*, *33*(27), 4709–4714.

Sansone, S. M., Schneider, A., Bickel, E., Berry-Kravis, E., Prescott, C., & Hessl, D. (2014). Improving IQ measurement in intellectual disabilities using true deviation from population norms. *Journal of Neurodevelopmental Disorders*, *6*(1), 16. https://doi.org/10.1186/1866-1955-6-16.

Senn, S. (2005). Dichotomania: An obsessive compulsive disorder that is badly affecting the quality of analysis of pharmaceutical trials. In *Proceedings of the International Statistical Institute, 55th Session, Sydney*.

Sheridan, E., Gillespie, S., Johnson, C. R., Lecavalier, L., Smith, T., Swiezy, N., et al. (2021). Using parent target problem narratives to evaluate outcomes in children with autism Spectrum disorder. *Research on Child and Adolescent Psychopathology*, *49*(11), 1527–1535. https://doi.org/10.1007/s10802-021-00843-8.

Shields, R. H., Kaat, A. J., McKenzie, F. J., Drayton, A., Sansone, S. M., Coleman, J., et al. (2020). Validation of the NIH toolbox cognitive battery in intellectual disability. *Neurology*, *94*(12), e1229–e1240. https://doi.org/10.1212/wnl.0000000000009131.

Snapinn, S. M., & Jiang, Q. (2007). Responder analyses and the assessment of a clinically relevant treatment effect. *Trials*, *8*(1), 31. https://doi.org/10.1186/1745-6215-8-31.

Snyder, H. M., Bain, L. J., Brickman, A. M., Carrillo, M. C., Esbensen, A. J., Espinosa, J. M., et al. (2020). Further understanding the connection between Alzheimer's disease and down syndrome. *Alzheimer's & Dementia*, *16*(7), 1065–1077.

Soorya, L., Leon, J., Trelles, M. P., & Thurm, A. (2018). Framework for assessing individuals with rare genetic disorders associated with profound intellectual and multiple disabilities (PIMD): The example of Phelan McDermid syndrome. *The Clinical Neuropsychologist*, *32*(7), 1226–1255. https://doi.org/10.1080/13854046.2017.1413211.

Sparrow, S. S., Çicchetti, D. V., & Saulnier, C. A. (2016). *Vineland-3: Vineland adaptive behavior scales*. PsychCorp.

Tandon, P. K., & Kakkis, E. D. (2021). The multi-domain responder index: A novel analysis tool to capture a broader assessment of clinical benefit in heterogeneous complex rare diseases. *Orphanet Journal of Rare Diseases*, *16*(1), 183. https://doi.org/10.1186/s13023-021-01805-5.

Thompson, T., Coleman, J. M., Riley, K., Snider, L. A., Howard, L. J., Sansone, S. M., et al. (2018). Standardized assessment accommodations for individuals with intellectual disability. *Contemporary School Psychology*, *22*(4), 443–457. https://doi.org/10.1007/s40688-018-0171-4.

Thurm, A., Halladay, A., Mandell, D., Maye, M., Ethridge, S., & Farmer, C. (2021). Making research possible: Barriers and solutions for those with ASD and ID. *Journal of Autism and Developmental Disorders*. https://doi.org/10.1007/s10803-021-05320-1.

Thurman, A. J., Edgin, J. O., Sherman, S. L., Sterling, A., McDuffie, A., Berry-Kravis, E., et al. (2021). Spoken language outcome measures for treatment studies in down syndrome: Feasibility, practice effects, test-retest reliability, and construct validity of variables generated from expressive language sampling. *Journal of Neurodevelopmental Disorders*, *13*(1), 1–17.

Tillmann, J. (2021). Endpoints in clinical trials. In *Paper presented at the Roche Innovation Center, Basel, Switzerland.*

Van der Linden, W. J. (2018). *Handbook of item response theory: Three volume set*. CRC Press.

Walton, M. K., Powers, J. H., III, Hobart, J., Patrick, D., Marquis, P., Vamvakas, S., et al. (2015). Clinical outcome assessments: Conceptual foundation—Report of the ISPOR clinical outcomes assessment–emerging good practices for outcomes research task force. *Value in Health*, *18*(6), 741–752.

Wechsler, D. (2014). *WISC-V: Technical and interpretive manual*. Bloomington, MN: Pearson.

Weintraub, S., Dikmen, S. S., Heaton, R. K., Tulsky, D. S., Zelazo, P. D., Bauer, P. J., et al. (2013). Cognition assessment using the NIH toolbox. *Neurology*, *80*(11 Supplement 3), S54–S64. https://doi.org/10.1212/WNL.0b013e3182872ded.

Willgoss, T., Cassater, D., Connor, S., Krishnan, M. L., Miller, M. T., Dias-Barbosa, C., et al. (2021). Measuring what matters to individuals with Angelman syndrome and their families: Development of a patient-centered disease concept model. *Child Psychiatry and Human Development*, *52*(4), 654–668. https://doi.org/10.1007/s10578-020-01051-z.

Wright, C. F., FitzPatrick, D. R., & Firth, H. V. (2018). Paediatric genomics: Diagnosing rare disease in children. *Nature Reviews Genetics*, *19*(5), 253–268.

CHAPTER TWO

Remotely monitoring treatment outcomes in patients with neurogenetic syndromes: A family-centered perspective

Bridgette L. Kelleher, Tyra Protho, Lisa Hamrick, Delta Smith, Carolyn McCormick, Andrea DeMaria, Mandy Rispoli, and Amanda Seidl
Purdue University, West Lafayette, IN, United States

Contents

Abstract

Remote assessment has been ongoing for years, however, the integration of remote protocols while considering the unique needs of patients with neurogenetic syndromes (NGS) is lacking. The need for remotely monitoring treatment outcomes has intensified with the ongoing COVID-19 pandemic due to closures, travel mandates, and COVID-19 related health concerns in individuals with NGS. Beyond the COVID-19 pandemic, remote assessment may become the "status quo" and potential benefits and caveats that should be considered. In this review, we first define remote assessment, reasons for conducting remote assessment including enhancing access to research, reducing participant burden, and reducing financial costs and conserving staff. Next, we address reasons to not conduct remote assessment including the digital divide, digital inequities in technology literacy, impact on rapport, trust-building, and community-centered work, particularly for marginalized populations, and task and method constraints.

International Review of Research in Developmental Disabilities, Volume 62
ISSN 2211-6095
https://doi.org/10.1016/bs.irrdd.2022.05.002

We then describe our remote assessment efforts centered around the caregiver, and future directions and next steps with an emphasis on user experiences (UX), ongoing need to address issues of access and equity and the importance of a whole-family approach given the heterogeneity of experiences in families with NGS.

In the context of the COVID-19 pandemic, the question of *why* we should develop remote assessment tools is perhaps too obvious. In some ways, the pandemic has made familiar an experience to many that was previously thought of as only affecting few: not being able to physically access the connections typical of day-to-day life. Now, issues of access have touched everyone, bringing a sudden interest and investment in leveraging digital tools to rebuild scientific research programs and clinical care. This rapid shift and interest have come with a flurry of data collection methods and tools pivoting into the virtual stratosphere. With this shift came great successes and ingenuity, with teams rallying together to alter their protocols to be administered remotely (see Dikkala et al., 2021, for review). Many of these changes will likely outlive the COVID-19 pandemic itself and become "status quo." However, as COVID-19 restrictions begin to change and the scientific community approaches a new normal, it is time to pause and ask ourselves the critical questions we may not have had time to ask as we rapidly navigated the unknown. For example, "*What should be the standards of remote assessment?*", *"How do we create inclusive remote assessment spaces?"* and—quite importantly—*"When should remote methods be avoided?"*

These questions are particularly important in the context of research on individuals with neurogenetic syndromes (NGS) associated with intellectual and developmental disabilities (IDD). Even prior to COVID-19, families of people with NGS often lacked local access to providers with expertise in their child's medical needs (DeMaria et al., 2022; Kelleher, Halligan, Garwood, et al., 2020). To access experts with knowledge of their child's disability, some families would and continue to travel great distances; however, families who are able to do so successfully often have greater financial resources, employment flexibility, and child behavioral compliance, substantially biasing participation cohorts (DeMaria et al.). Remote assessment offers an appealing solution to these challenges, and several remote assessment methods were underway prior to COVID-19. For example, remote technology was being used for parent-facilitated interventions (Nelson et al., 2018; Vismara, McCormick, Young, Nadhan, & Monlux, 2013) and autism screening (Parmanto, Pulantara, Schutte, Saptono, & Mccue, 2013; Talbott et al., 2019). In our work, we had begun developing a remote "laboratory" for collecting assessment data from NGS families (Kelleher, Halligan, Witthuhn, et al., 2020). These early efforts highlight the promise for remote assessment in NGS and related populations predated COVID-19 and will remain long after the field has settled into a "new normal."

Numerous recent developments that have accelerated the need for remote assessment tools in NGS. First, there is an acute need for clinical measures that can be deployed in natural history studies and treatment trials for NGS patients (Abbeduto et al., 2020; Berry-Kravis et al., 2013; Budimirovic et al., 2017; Erickson et al., 2017; Schwartz et al., 2016; Soorya, Leon, Trelles, & Thurm, 2018; Thurm, Kelleher, & Wheeler, 2020). Given trials are often enrolling geographically-distributed cohorts, remote assessment tools—if properly developed and validated—could ease burden for families and facilitate more representative patient cohorts. The COVID-19 pandemic itself has also accelerated the need for remote assessment tools for NGS. Indeed, the COVID-19 pandemic has disproportionately affected therapeutic, medical, and educational services in NGS and similar groups (Jeste et al., 2020; Murphy, Pinkerton, Bruckner, & Risser, 2021; Neece, McIntyre, & Fenning, 2020; Turk, Landes, Formica, & Goss, 2020). Travel also comes with higher risk for NGS patients due to increased complications of COVID-19 in people with IDD (Bauer, 2018). In other words, the pandemic has accelerated demand for remote assessment options in a population that was already primed for this need prior to the pandemic.

Importantly, although substantial progress in remote assessment has been made during the COVID-19 pandemic, the nature by which these most recent tools were developed is fundamentally different than from the typical "status quo" of scientific progress, with some notable exceptions (Izmailova, Ellis, & Benko, 2020). Rather than thoroughly planning novel assessment tools with the support of guided by patient input, feasibility studies, rigorous piloting, and validation, many tools and techniques were rapidly tested and deployed, analogous to "building the plane while flying it." This abbreviated process—although arguably necessary in many cases—has come with risks. For example, it is possible that methods will not be acceptable to patient communities (feasibility) or produce reliable and valid data. Missing data rates may be higher due to technology "glitches" that were previously solvable with on-site technology experts in clinical research centers. Importantly, although remote assessment is often thought to *improve* access, it is possible that the added burden on patients' technology access and literacy will intensify demographic health disparities. Particularly given the biased demographic composition of most trials, it is likely the methods and tools developed to rapidly "go virtual" in current samples may still not meet the needs of underserved communities—and could perhaps even intensify disparities that were previously present.

The purpose of this review is to pause and reflect on the status quo for remote assessment research in NGS. Our goal is to characterize key considerations when deploying remote assessments for NGS populations, with a focus on practical considerations and "lessons learned" from our team's development of phenotyping tools both prior to and during and prior to the pandemic. Together, our goal is to help scientists who are using remote tools pause, critically self-evaluate their methods, and methodically approach their next line of work. We conclude by sharing our own hopes for the future of remote assessment work and the impact these approaches will have on the field.

1. What is remote assessment?

Remote data collection methods have been around for decades yet have advanced in scope in response to the COVID-19 pandemic. Here, we refer to *remote assessments* as data collection tools that can be completed by patients and their caregivers from a location distinct from their provider. Within this broad definition, it could be argued that many common assessment tools—particularly informant report measures—are already remote-assessment compatible. However, as the practical constraints and complexity of the assessment tool increase, remote deployment becomes less common and, in many cases, implausible. As such, considering "*What is remote assessment?*" is a first step to understanding the status quo—and limits—of these methods.

To decide whether measures can be deployed remotely, it is helpful to consider existing frameworks for categorizing clinical assessments. One useful metric is the Food and Drug Administration (FDA)'s categorization of clinical outcome assessments (COAs). Per FDA, a COA is "a measurement of a patient's symptoms, overall mental state, or the effects of a disease or condition on how the patient functions" (FDA-NIH Biomarker Working Group, 2016). The FDA defines several types of outcome measures, including patient-reported outcome (PRO), observer-reported outcome (ObsRO), clinician-reported outcome (ClinRO), and performance outcome (PerfO). Of note, not all assessment tools have been classified as COAs; to be declared a COA, an assessment measure must pass a series of regulatory approvals, including rigorous validation in the intended patient population. However, given COA development is a major focus for NGS clinical trials, the FDA framework provides a useful taxonomy for considering remote compatibility of commonly used assessment measures. The following definitions are adapted from the FDA glossary (FDA-NIH Biomarker Working Group, 2016).

- *Patient-reported outcomes (PRO)* are derived from the direct report of the patient without any interpretation by a caregiver or clinician, including via rating scales or self-reported frequency of symptoms. Given challenges many people with NGS experience self-reporting symptoms, these measures are not a primary focus of outcome measure development in NGS.
- *Observer-reported outcomes (ObsRO)* are based on observed symptoms, events, and/or behaviors based on a caregiver or other informant who observes the patient in day-to-day life. ObsRO tools are commonly used in NGS populations and include rating scales and reports of frequencies of events.
- *Clinician-reported outcomes (ClinRO)* are based on reports from a trained healthcare provider or professional; these measures typically require a provider to make clinical judgments based on observable behaviors or features of the patient. ClinRO measures may include rating scales and clinical findings that must be interpreted by a trained professional, such as to quantify clinical events that require clinical observation and/or use of biomarker data (e.g., neuroimaging).
- *Performance outcomes (PerfO)* are based on standardized tasks completed by the patient using pre-set instructions. Measures may be completed by the patient independently or administered by a professional with appropriate expertise. Examples include standardized measures of symptoms (e.g., vocal maturity during a standardized observation) and neuropsychological or "IQ" batteries.

The FDA's categories of COAs do not determine whether an assessment tool is compatible with remote administration. However, a few key elements of these definitions do "track" with remote capacity. These factors have been considered across a number of commentaries published in response to COVID-19 (Izmailova et al., 2020). First, it is important to consider *who is administering the assessment*. Measures administered by a caregiver, rather than by a clinician, have been more commonly used in remote contexts for NGS. Another consideration is *what materials are required for the assessment*; COAs that only require access to web-based surveys or pen-and-paper forms are much simpler to deploy virtually than those that require standardized materials and manipulatives. A related concern is *whether a trained examiner is required to deploy the COA in real-time*; many PerfO measures deployed in NGS require a professional administrator, and ClinRO and PerfO tools both often require professional interpretation of the data. Finally, the *portability of the method* is paramount; particularly for neuroimaging and other ClinRO tools, it may not be possible or feasible to move the devices outside of standardized clinical and laboratory spaces.

In many cases, factors related to portability and examiner training constrain COAs to in-person administration; deploying a magnetic resonance imaging scan, for example, is completely infeasible outside of a laboratory setting due to both the equipment itself and the expertise needed to safely operate it (Izmailova et al., 2020). However, there are some spaces in which creativity can overcome initial constraints, particularly through technology. For example, trained examiners can use teleconferencing software to observe and engage with participants in real-time, facilitating ClinROs without in-person assessment (Kelleher, Halligan, Witthuhn, et al., 2020; Parmanto et al., 2013). Similarly, materials can be shipped to families—either to allow them to access remote assessment platforms (e.g., through a laptop and "hotspot") or to administer simple PerfO tasks at home (e.g., sending a set of toys so that an experimental task can be implemented similarly across households) (Kelleher, Halligan, Witthuhn, et al., 2020). In some cases, wearable biosensors and other portable technologies can be used to collect PerfO assays without any live examiner interaction (Nelson et al., 2018; Rapela, Lin, Westerfield, Jung, & Townsend, 2012; Xu, Yapanel, Gray, & Gilkerson, 2008). Central to our work, the caregiver can also be trained to administer PerfO assessments to a level of fidelity comparable to an examiner, blending both the standardization of clinic-based administration with the comfort and ease of home-based assessments (Kelleher, Halligan, Witthuhn, et al., 2020). In the context of these and other advances in remote assessments, it has been proposed that virtual clinical trials could become a "new normal" for some populations (Alemayehu, Hemmings, Natarajan, & Roychoudhury, 2022).

A central first question to address prior to remotely deploying any assessment tool, however, is *why?* Changing the status quo in the ways we describe comes at a sometimes-considerable cost, practically and perhaps financially. In -person administration is historically the status quo for a reason; from the perspective of the researcher, it is likely simpler and easier to achieve a highly standardized testing session if the participant simply comes to a clinic. So, particularly as COVID-19 restrictions subside, why pursue remote assessment for NGS populations? When is it worth it … and when is it not?

2. Why remote assessment?

There are many advantages and considerations when using remote assessment, including capacity to enhance access, reduce participant burden, and conserve costs. Here, we briefly summarize each of these potential benefits.

Enhancing access. From its onset, the very inception and expansion of the modern-day internet has centered around themes of community and access (Pease, 2013), and deploying assessments remotely holds great promise for enhancing accessibility, particularly for geographically restricted NGS families who often do not live near specialty clinics or clinical trial sites (DeMaria et al., 2022). Timely, high-quality assessments are a particular challenge for children with NGS and other forms of neurodevelopmental disorders, particularly given the disruptions to in-person services associated with COVID-19 (Jeste et al., 2020). Access to effective assessments is important at multiple stages of the "diagnostic odyssey" for NGS patients (Carmichael, Tsipis, Windmueller, Mandel, & Estrella, 2015), including initial diagnosis, early treatments, school/individualized education plan processes, and medication management. However, families of NGS patients often report substantial challenges accessing informed providers who are able to provide appropriate assessments in community contexts.

Many caregivers have reported feeling uninformed, unsupported, and distraught after initial genetic diagnoses, even if the diagnosis itself is perceived as helpful (Carmichael, Pembrey, Turner, & Barnicoat, 1999; Goodwin et al., 2015). Some of this dissatisfaction appears to carry forward as NGS caregivers continue to pursue assessments for their child's continued care. For example, in our mixed-methods study of assessment experiences among NGS caregivers (Kelleher, Halligan, Garwood, et al., 2020), most respondents did not "agree" that assessments were positive experiences, and individuals often reported challenges around communication with providers. Indeed, there have been numerous efforts across rare disease communities to increase patient access to highly skilled, specialized providers through establishment of developmental disability clinics, such as the Down Syndrome Clinic at Boston Children's Hospital, the Fragile X Research and Treatment Center at the University of California Davis

MIND Institute, or the Angelman Syndrome Foundation Clinic at the University of North Carolina. However, for most patients, travel to even a developmental disability regional clinic can be a burden. As such, remote connection methods offer a powerful tool for enabling patients to engage with providers with the expertise most critical to their care.

Reducing participant burden. Remote assessments may also ease participation burden for NGS families. For most NGS families, participating in trials requires substantial time commitment, including to prepare for the session, arrange childcare or transportation for other children, complete screening questions, communicate with the staff, and travel to the session location. Although many NGS caregivers report that a trials' potential to directly benefit the patient is their primary motivator for participation (D'Amanda, Peay, Wheeler, Turbitt, & Biesecker, 2019; Turbitt et al., 2021), convenience of logistics and demands of the study are commonly considered, as well (D'Amanda et al., 2019; WhiteWhite, Chevette, Hillerstrom, & Esbensen, 2022). Examples of logistical inconveniences noted by caregivers have included substantial travel to the trial site, high numbers of appointments, and challenges taking time off work (D'Amanda et al., 2019; White et al., 2022), while study demand concerns expressed by caregivers have included potential risks of participation, time commitment, and study compensation (White et al., 2022). These findings add to a broader literature on individual differences that may affect trial engagement.

The type of activities involved in a trial are also closely related to perceived burden. Recently, Getz et al. (2020) collected data on the perceived burden of a variety of aspects of clinical trial participation, to establish an objective metric of burden that could be applied to existing, registered protocols. Respondents rated a variety of procedural, convenience, lifestyle, and caregiver involvement factors that would influence their perceived burden of trial participation, yielding an average "burden score" for each aspect (scale 1–100). Across assessment types, respondents rated invasive procedures (e.g., biopsies, lumbar punctures) as most burdensome (average score = 75.2) relative to questionnaires (41.8), routine examinations (41.5), lab tests and blood work (46.4), and noninvasive procedures such as physiological monitoring (44.3). Interestingly, over 80% of patients reported not being willing to travel more than 1 h to their appointments or stay for more than 3 h at their appointments, and 76% described having to travel via plane to participate as "somewhat" or "very" burdensome. White et al. (2022) reported similar findings in a recent survey of parents of children with Down syndrome. Here, non-invasive procedures (e.g., surveys, journals, wearable devices) were again rated more favorably than more invasive procedures such as neuroimaging techniques, ingesting medication, or receiving injections. Although results may vary in other NGS populations, these findings can provide a baseline understanding of the relative burden cost of various trial components and underscore the importance of travel and time in patients' perceived willingness to complete trial activities.

Reducing financial costs and conserving staff. The majority of costs incurred for human subjects clinical trials relate to clinical procedures (Sertkaya, Wong, Jessup, & Beleche, 2016). Indeed, participants who attend in-person sessions often require transportation costs, may have to take off work, or pay for childcare for other children. Remote research studies, if administered flexibly, may reduce some of these costs. From the researcher perspective, telehealth studies also have the potential to increase staffing efficiency, allowing providers to see a greater number of patients in a shorter amount of time. Remote studies may also reduce burden on physical infrastructure, such as assessment and office space. Indeed, cost-savings have been reported in a variety of telehealth-based studies. For example, deploying autism interventions virtually has been estimated to reduce costs by as much as 64% (Lindgren et al., 2016), aligning with a variety of study designs that have similarly reported cost savings in a variety of populations (Dinesen et al., 2016; Shore, Brooks, Savin, Manson, & Libby, 2007). In our own projects, deploying a research assessment protocol remotely also yielded cost savings, however, with some important caveats relevant to NGS populations. The rate of savings was lower in our protocol (6–30%) than reported by traditional in person protocols for neurodevelopmental conditions but only emerged once a critical mass of 7 monthly assessments occurred (Kelleher, Halligan, Witthuhn, et al., 2020). Here, we review a few factors that may be influencing whether a given protocol does, indeed, save costs, particularly for NGS groups:

First, telehealth has greater savings capacity *when the materials needed to complete the activity are readily available to the patient.* If materials must be sent to participants, the added costs of duplicate kits and shipping must be considered and can add considerable costs. In our published cost analysis of our remote assessment protocol (Kelleher, Halligan, Witthuhn, et al., 2020), for example, we budgeted 11 days of "use" for each testing kit, including time spent packing, shipping, using, shipping, and unpacking the kit. As such, we estimated administering 24 remote assessments per month would require 9 kits for remote assessment relative to 3 kits for in-person assessments. At low costs, the higher number of kits required for remote assessment may be negligible, however for more expensive equipment, the added cost of duplicate kits may overshadow other cost savings.

Second, telehealth may be more cost-effective *when the patient sample is geographically distributed.* The cost savings of remote research exponentially improves when a patient would otherwise need to travel a great distance to engage in the project. Again pulling from our published cost-analysis, we estimated each remote assessment (in 2020) would save an estimated \$1238 in travel and \$570 in lost wages, based on an average trip of 2.5 days and 1.5 nights for a national sample of NGS families. Compared to the "travel cost" of shipping an assessment kit round-trip (\$90), the financial implications of removing patient travel were extensive.

Third, telehealth may be particularly beneficial *when the alternative is research staff traveling to individual patients.* Although not the most common format for NGS research, a number of studies have recognized the burden of patient travel and have elected to build research protocols around traveling staff. This method may solve many barriers to remote assessment—particularly the need for an on-site examiner to deploy ObsrO or PerfO assays. However, requiring staff to travel substantially reduces the thruput of participants within a given study *and* inflates the labor costs of conducting an assessment. As an example, we can use the current NIH rate for postdoctoral scholar salary (\$53,760) and an estimated fringe rate of 25% to estimate the cost for each administered assessment across a 12-month period months (assuming 48 weeks of assessment per year). Based on a weekly staffing cost of \$1400 per assessor, and an average of 2.5 days of travel per traveling assessment, a staff person could administer 2 in-person assessments per week at a rate of \$700/assessment, or 5 remote assessments per week at a rate of \$280/assessment. These costs are, of course, added to the travel costs that are incurred by staff. In other words, remote assessment cuts staffing costs by over half relative to traveling assessment formats. Of note, these costs savings are less substantial when staff travel to collect data at a patient "hub," such as collecting data at conferences focused on patient communities.

3. Why *not* remote assessment?

Although remote assessments can facilitate access, reduce burden, and reduce costs, it is equally important to consider limitations of these approaches. Here, we review a few key challenges to consider in the context of remote assessment.

The digital divide. A primary barrier to remote assessment is the *availability of technology and internet access.* In the wake of the COVID-19 pandemic, access to broadband internet has been proposed as a "social determinant of health" (Benda, Veinot, Sieck, & Ancker, 2020). However as of 2021, what is commonly referred to as a "digital divide" persists: according to recent reports, approximately 32% of US households lack a home computer with high-speed internet access, 22% lack a smartphone with a data plan necessary for digital access, and 14% lack any digital access to the internet (Curtis et al., 2022; Sheet, 2019). These disparities are most pronounced at lower income levels; among Americans who report <$30,000 annual household income, only 86% report using the internet and 57% report home broadband access, compared to 99% usage and 92% home access for Americans with incomes >$75,000 (Sheet, 2019). The "divide" is also stratified across race and ethnicity, with white families reporting greater access to home broadband (80%) than Black (71%) and Hispanic (65%) families. The reasons for the digital divide varies, but likely include geographical constraints, poverty, and technical capacities in a given location or household. These barriers underscore that remote assessments—if reliant on a patient's technology—will likely exclude a substantial portion of the population, including low-income and marginalized demographic groups. The added barriers of this digital divide are particularly concerning given the well-established health disparities and under-representation of many minoritized groups in research studies (Di Pietro & Illes, 2014; Ratto et al., 2017; Sullivan, 2013).

Digital inequities in technology literacy. A related but distinct challenge of remote assessment is *digital inequality.* Digital inequality refers to the variability in abilities and resulting experiences of internet users for whom access itself is not a barrier. Here, the goal is to understand technology's "differentiated use" among active users, rather than solely focusing on who is accessing technology at all (DiMaggio, Hargittai, Celeste, & Shafer, 2004). In response to the rapid shift to digital health innovation observed during COVID-19, Crawford and Serhal (2020) updated a popularized model of health equity (Dover & Belon, 2019) to include digital health. In this updated framework, the authors stipulate core "digital determinants of health", including access, uptake, and literacy of digital health; a person's beliefs, values, and cultural norms surrounding digital health; and the integration of digital health resources into societal infrastructures (Crawford & Serhal, 2020). In their model, these digital determinants interact with other intermediate factors—such as a person's biology, environment, coping skills, and health—to impact health outcomes. As an example of how this framework manifests in current research, one study of digital technology uptake after COVID-19 found that in contrast to users with high self-reported technology skills, those who self-reported poorer skills generally *decreased* digital communication at the start of the pandemic, perhaps because they could no longer access social supports necessary to use technology effectively (Nguyen et al., 2020).

Crawford and Serhal (2020) also prescribe four helpful guideposts for digital health equity: (1) equal access *and* outcomes related to digital health across sociodemographic characteristics, (2) healthcare providers capable of providing equitable digital health services, (3) attention to issues of measurement and quality for digital health access and outcomes, and (4) integration of stakeholders from marginalized groups in the digital health movement. Although Crawford and Serhal's framework helps conceptualize an individual's orientation toward digital health, large-scale solutions are needed to make digital equity a reality. The World Health Organization (WHO) has proposed a strategy and action plan within their *Global Strategy on Digital Health 2020–25* plan (World Health Organization, 2021) that highlights global, structural infrastructure must be addressed, including global collaboration, digital health governance, and person-centered healthcare systems.

Impact on rapport, trust-building, and community-centered work. Remote connectedness undoubtedly expands the *quantity* of connections a single person can make, however, there is controversy around the impact of digitization on *quality* of such connections. Although early reports suggest generally comparable satisfaction in telehealth vs in-person services across a variety of treatment formats (Eannucci, Hazel, Grundstein, Nguyen, & Gallegro, 2020; Yuen et al., 2015), findings have been mixed among studies of children with neurodevelopmental disorders. For example, a large caregiver-report survey revealed lower satisfaction with behavioral, speech/language, and occupational services for children with autism when deployed via telehealth (Ferguson, Jimenez-Muñoz, Feerst, & Vernon, 2021), and record reviews during COVID-19 suggest that a substantial minority (40%) of patients within a hospital network initially declined telehealth-based services when clinics shut down, particularly if their child was not currently exhibiting severe problem behaviors (Aranki, Wright, Pompa-Craven, & Lotfizadeh, 2022). In contrast, however, some studies have reported strong satisfaction among families and clinicians engaged in virtual autism assessments (Alfuraydan, Croxall, Hurt, Kerr, & Brophy, 2020). The variability in satisfaction and uptake of remote-format clinical care highlights the complex impact of virtual delivery on patient engagement.

Telehealth-based research also requires an added layer of trust. Within early intervention, home visits by providers are typical and recommended practice (Ciupe & Salisbury, 2020), and families who receive in-person intervention services in a familiar setting (i.e., their home) have typically shown an increased level of comfort and trust, relative to in-person services delivered elsewhere (Tomlin & Hadadian, 2007). Although some studies have reported similar caregiver satisfaction when intervention studies are deployed in-person or via telehealth (Corona et al., 2021), building trust between the provider and family in telehealth settings may require added effort, creativity, and recognition of risks (Bernhardt & King, 2022; Goldstein & Glueck, 2016). One challenge in rapport building is the possibility of poor bandwidth or connection limiting video quality, preventing a provider from delivering or interpreting nonverbal cues (Goldstein & Glueck, 2016). However another important concern is the added vulnerability and fear of judgment that participants may experience when their homes are on virtual display to providers; much like an in-person home visit, families who participate in telehealth research cannot always control what a clinician might see or hear. These challenges may be particularly difficult for participants who are not technologically fluent in how to enhance privacy in their home, such as by "blurring" their teleconferencing background or using the "mute" function.

These challenges contribute to a concerning possibility that digital care will compromise already damaged trust between providers and marginalized patient communities. Indeed, a large nationally representative study that oversampled racial/ethnic minority patients observed lower post-COVID-19 telehealth uptake among non-white patients (Zhang et al., 2021). A related cross-sectional analysis of family medicine health records revealed lower uptake of telehealth visits for rural and Black patients, with lower uptake of full audio/visual recordings among patients who were Black, older age, living in urban areas, and who did not use private insurance. These findings parallel well-established disparities in which individuals from ethnic and racially diverse backgrounds are underrepresented in research. For example, relative to non-Black peers, Black children with autism are more likely to receive delayed diagnoses or are "missed" altogether (Corbie-Smith, Thomas, & St George, 2002; Le Cook, Trinh, Li, Hou, & Progovac, 2017; Mandell et al., 2009; Webb Hooper, Nápoles, & Pérez-Stable, 2020), receive fewer and lower-quality services from early childhood throughout their lifetimes

(Eilenberg, Paff, Harrison, & Long, 2019), and may receive genetic testing or counseling at lower rates (Shea, Newschaffer, Xie, Myers, & Mandell, 2014). Furthermore, given the recently intensified racial tensions in the United States, many Black families are experiencing amplified race-related stress in what has been called a "pandemic on a pandemic" as racial trauma and medical health disparities collide (Laurencin & Walker, 2020). In this context, reducing disparities in minoritized populations requires building rapport and trust, which can be challenging to do in an entirely virtual space. It is possible that given these challenges, some remote assessment protocols are not the most appropriate option and may indeed amplify pre-existing disparities, rather than reduce them.

Task and method constraints. A final additional caveat to remote assessment is the need to select tools that can be rigorously deployed in a remote space. Like any other COA, remote assessment tools must meet rigorous standards for feasibility, reliability, robustness to practice effects, and validity. It is important to consider whether the desired methods to assess a construct translate appropriately to a remote setting. For example, event-related paradigms requiring millisecond precision—such as studies of event-related potentials (ERP)—may be more difficult to implement remotely due to potential lags and interruptions in internet connectivity that may occur in real-time. Some standardized assessment tools may be impossible to administer remotely due to the need for examiners to have a specific level of training, or constraints outlined by publishers in terms of acceptable formats for use. Tasks may also require more from caregivers than would be feasible or reasonable. For example, experimental tasks requiring a confederate would not be feasible to implement in a home setting without examiners present. Finally, there are situations in which in-person evaluation is simply necessary for safety, such as over the course of pharmaceutical trials. It is important to note that in these cases, remote assessment could still be used to supplement ongoing evaluations, potentially increasing the density or overall quantity of assessments. However, in these cases, remote assessment may present one of many "tools" to implement patient-centered trials, in conjunction with in-person visits.

4. Our approach to remote assessment: Centering the caregiver

Since 2016 (pre-pandemic), our research group has maintained a primary focus on leveraging remote assessment as a primary tool for conducting both observational and experimental data from NGS families. Across a variety of study designs and patient groups, we have developed a general framework for conceptualizing, designing, and implementing remote data collection studies. Throughout this work, we assume a family systems perspective whereby the caregiver is an active member of our research team. Here, we describe this approach, including examples and lessons learned.

A historic time for caregiver involvement. The arc of caregiver involvement as active agents in the research process has fluctuated across history. At one extreme, some of the field's foundational studies were implemented by research scientists on their children, prior to the era of modern research ethics. For example, Piaget (1971) developed his infamous stages of cognitive development on mostly uncontrolled observations generated from his children. Piaget's theories have since been criticized for narrowly focusing on his experiences and culture (DePalma, Matusov, & Hayes, 2000), and the field subsequently moved toward more objective, experimental designs, with the vast majority of subsequent developmental research occurring in structured, standardized laboratory settings. In contrast to the early days of Piaget, it is currently standard practice for caregivers to be completely removed from the testing location while their child is engaging in standardized assessments, particularly when the child is old enough to engage with the examiner independently. This status quo reflects a heavy emphasis on maintaining standardization of protocols, with the hopes that standardized circumstances will facilitate consistent comparisons of scores and results across patients. Indeed, standardization is at the heart of COA development and is a critical aspect of rigorous trial design.

However, at the same time, there are signs our current methods are not working as well as we would like. Some NGS clinical trials are failing, potentially due, in part, to flaws in the design and stability of findings in COAs (Berry-Kravis et al., 2013; Budimirovic et al., 2017; Jacquemont et al., 2014; Jeste, Frohlich, & Loo, 2015). For example, early, highly anticipated trials of mavoglurant in fragile X syndrome (FXS) failed when primarily behavior-rating COAs did not detect unique improvements in the FXS group (Berry-Kravis et al., 2016), despite follow-up studies suggesting effects of the drug on alternate PerfO eye tracking assays (Hessl et al., 2019). Now, mavoglurant is being re-probed in active clinical trials in FXS that integrate more innovative PerfO assays *and* parent-meditated intervention, including telehealth-based parent feedback and coaching, demonstrating a break from traditional paradigms and measures used in past trials. Of note, concerns about the integrity, generalizability and stability of developmental research findings are not unique to NGS trials and are being widely discussed in the broader developmental literature (Davis-Kean & Ellis, 2019), spurned in part by the suggestion that the science is facing a "replication crisis" (Open Science Collaboration, 2015). As these historic events converge, our field is again examining our methods, assumptions, and biases to produce data that are reliable and reproducible, and that can be used to monitor the success of clinical trials.

Now, the COVID-19 pandemic has further flipped many standardized protocols upside down, requiring examiners to "break protocol" to safely collect data, often with the blessing of test publishers who are quickly releasing digital deployment guidelines (Pearson, 2021). Caregivers are uniquely able to safely participate in sessions when examiners cannot. Against this scientific backdrop, our team has begun to re-conceptualize the role of the caregiver in the assessment process. Specifically, we have integrated caregivers at each step of the design and deployment of our remote assessment studies, including by ultimately placing them in the "driver's seat" as the official facilitators of our standardized protocols. Here, we offer three facets to this caregiver-centered approach:

Seeking caregiver input at multiple stages of the research process. A first step to engaging caregivers in research is to seek and value their input. Caregivers can be integrated into the research process using a variety of formal research methods, including surveys, focus groups, and "think tanks." For example, in designing our primary remote assessment protocol, we conducted early mixed-methods surveys to characterize NGS caregivers' experiences surrounding assessment, intending to document their suggestions for improvement (Kelleher, Halligan, Garwood, et al., 2020). Through this work, we identified specific ways caregivers desired to be more involved in the assessment process, such as by helping present materials in a way the child would understand, or by defining the types of feedback information they would receive. More recently, we have begun to integrate patient communities, clinical scientists, and engineers to collectively tackle challenges facing the uptake of wearable biosensors in clinical trials. To do so, we have implemented a series of systematic literature reviews, focus groups, and collaborative design meetings to both identify gaps in existing biosensor technologies *and* partner with engineers to design and pilot solution prototypes.[1] Through this work, caregivers

[1] This study is funded by a grant from the Purdue Institute for Integrative Neuroscience "Grand Challenges" Competition (MPI Carolyn McCormick and Bridgette Kelleher).

have identified several patient barriers that interfere with wearable device uptake, including interpreting instructions that contain substantial jargon, using devices without live support from a trained examiner, relying on support staff who are unfamiliar with the NGS phenotype, and using devices with different platforms or hardware. This project highlights the utility of engaging directly with patient communities at each stage of the study design process, including in the selection and development of materials.

Importantly, there are also a variety of less formal ways researchers can seek and integrate caregiver input. Many NGS patient groups host regular scientific and family-focused meetings, which can be a time for researchers to engage socially with the patient community, share scientific findings, and receive feedback on current projects. Social media is also a highly active virtual space for patient communities; many communities host open social groups where researchers can learn about the experiences of families and needs of communities. Consistent with community-engaged work, researchers can also engage with patient communities by participating in walks, meet-ups, and other fundraising events, where appropriate and welcome by the patient groups. Of course, in each of these formats, researchers must take care to respect the privacy and boundaries of patient groups; for example, it would be inappropriate to join a virtual forum designated exclusively for caregivers. However, patient communities are often eager to engage with the research community in the context of mutual appreciation, boundaries, and respect.

Customizing the assessment experience to the needs of families. A second step to engaging caregivers and families in remote research has been to customize the assessment experiences to their needs, particularly as related to *access* and *child compliance.* In terms of access, each of our studies includes a pre-assessment interview (online or via phone) in which we probe the family's needs surrounding access. As part of this process, we probe numerous topics relevant to access (Fig. 1) and offer potential solutions. For example, if technology access is a challenge, we offer any necessary technology to engage in the study (e.g., tablets, "hot spots"), including prepaid shipping. If children are home during the session, we can offer "busy bags" of activities or a spare tablet pre-loaded with a preferred video to keep them entertained. As part of the consent process, caregivers are assured that they are not responsible for lost or damaged equipment, minimizing the potential that caregivers might be nervous about borrowing laboratory devices for research purposes.

1. Access to computer
2. Access to Wifi in home
3. Quiet space
4. Childcare
5. Child compliance
6. Pet care
7. Privacy from family members
8. Anticipated disruptions
9. Safety planning
10. Plan if disconnected

Fig. 1 Sample topics to probe before remote assessment.

It is also important to consider whether families may benefit from support for child compliance. One particularly helpful aspect of attending research sessions at clinics is the on-site availability of highly skilled clinicians, including those with behavioral training to help a patient adjust to and complete their assessment tasks. Although home-based assessments may lead to fewer problem behaviors in general, it is still possible—and often likely—that challenges will emerge during the session. Here, it can be helpful for examiners to ask in advance about the child's potential challenges and interests, to provide coaching in real-time for the family during the assessment. The examiner may also send physical supports, such as practice materials, reward charts, and desensitization protocols to help the families prepare for the assessment. Ideas for desensitization and preparation protocols have been published previously, including as related to collecting neuroimaging data from children with autism spectrum disorder (Webb et al., 2015). Within our current work, prior to implementing our remote electroencephalogram protocol in Angelman syndrome,[2] we send families practice caps fitted with 3-D printed electrodes and child-friendly stickers that simulate the feel of the real cap and electrodes (Foti et al., 2021). We also include a habituation plan to help the child practice wearing the cap and stickers, developed in consultation with behavior analysts (Harold, Galvez-Ortega, Kelleher, & Foti, 2020), and pre-load a tablet with a favorite movie to entertain the child during setup. This protocol has resulted in 100%

[2] This study is funded by a grant from the Indiana Clinical and Translational Research Institute (PI Dan Foti).

successful EEG data collection across all six patients currently enrolled in our feasibility trial (Foti et al.) a notable success given the commonly reported challenges of completing EEGs in Angelman patients (Kelleher, 2021).

Actively involving caregivers in the assessment process. Building from these efforts, we have now designed and deployed a host of remote assessment protocols for children ages 3 months to 18 years that center the caregiver as an active facilitator. Perhaps our most widely used protocol is PANDABox (Parent Assisted NeuroDevelopmental Assessment), an open science, telehealth-based assessment protocol for collecting high quality, integrated clinical, behavioral, and spectral assays (e.g., heart activity, acoustics) from children ages 3–60 months of age, with and without rare disorders. In contrast to standard neuropsychological assessments, PANDABox includes a series of classic "laboratory tasks" that are appropriate for a wide spectrum of abilities and are administered by caregivers in the family home. To minimize burden, caregivers receive live teleconferencing support from a trained assessor who adjusts the pace of the assessment and manages all technology remotely. In this way, PANDABox combines the *standardized control* of a laboratory-based performance assessment with the *convenience, naturalistic comfort, and access* afforded by home-based assessment. Our published findings (Kelleher, Halligan, Witthuhn, et al., 2020) indicate that PANDABox is highly feasible and acceptable to caregivers and generates high quality, integrated, "laboratory-grade" data at low cost. Specifically, results indicated that PANDABox required low resources to administer and was well received by families, with high caregiver fidelity (94%) and infant engagement (91%), as well as high caregiver-reported satisfaction (97% positive), including among caregivers with limited technology literacy. Missing data were low for video frames (3%) and vocalization recordings (6%) and moderate for heart rate (25% fully missing, 13% partially missing), in part due to wearable device programming issues that have since resolved. These data suggest PANDABox is a feasible, low-cost method for collecting laboratory-grade data remotely. More recently, we received additional NIH funding to develop an open science platform to standardize administration for additional user sites, ensuring rigor and reproducibility and furthering scalability.

Importantly, several family-centered procedures are critical to PANDABox' success. First, we ship all materials (Fig. 2) to families using a small, prepaid crate, which they leave on their doorstep for pickup after the assessment. Second, we provide highly scaffolded coaching for families throughout the assessment; using remote access technology, we display all prompts and instructions for them on the provided computer, monitor

Fig. 2 PANDABox materials.

the fidelity of their administration, offer real-time feedback if necessary, and manage all technical demands (e.g., opening and closing files, adjusting volume). Where possible and necessary, we remain on the phone with families during teleconferencing to ensure they feel supported, even as they open and close the other technology tools. We also allow families to pause and restart the assessment as needed to facilitate the child's best effort. These procedures ensure that families with limited technological literacy can successfully engage in sessions and have contributed to the project's success.

Thinking forward to analysis. As with any assessment tool, remote data collection methods can produce large volumes of data. Indeed, big data approaches are becoming more and more common and offer tremendous advantages for advancing the ecological validity of the data we collect, particularly in early development. Often a single snapshot of early developmental behaviors is not representative of a child's typical behavior—factors such as setting, interaction partners, sleep, hunger, or sickness can lead to behavior significantly varying hour by hour and day by day. Using big data allows researchers to collect behavior samples over wider time frames, which are potentially more robust to fluctuations in typical behavior. Thus, big data approaches can present a solution to questions of the validity of information collected in early development from populations with IDD.

As the name implies, big data approaches result in immense quantities of data, which can be difficult to manage, clean, and analyze. These issues commonly arise in remote assessment settings, particularly when researchers can collect large volumes of data from wearable devices or other home-based monitoring systems. One solution is to automate these processes to minimize the time and person-hours required to move from data collection to analysis. Some programs already exist to assist in this process. For example, the Language Environment Analysis (LENA) system takes daylong recordings of children's vocalizations and automatically tags speakers within the recording and counts utterances produced by the child as well as words heard in their immediate environment (Gilkerson & Richards, 2009). In clinical settings, LENA can be a powerful tool for rapidly summarizing a child's skills relative to peers (Weil & Middleton, 2010); however, LENA's utility as a COA is questionable because (1) the device has not been developed or normed for NGS, (2) the automated algorithms produce some error (e.g., mistaking infant-directed speech for children's speech (Bulgarelli & Bergelson, 2019; VanDam & Silbert, 2016), and (3) LENA focuses primarily on quantity variables (e.g., count of utterances) that we have shown are less sensitive to NGS-related risks than "quality" metrics such as vocalization pitch and duration (Hamrick, Seidl, & Tonnsen, 2019). As such, we worked with computer scientists to develop a post-processing pipeline to efficiently clean, code, and analyze vocalization data collected during and after PANDABox sessions. This pipeline (Semenzin, Hamrick, Seidl, Kelleher, & Cristia, 2021) uses LENA's tagging capacity to isolate and segment sounds LENA says are produced by the child, input these .wav segments into a user-friendly software program, and present these sounds to minimally trained coders who verify the sound is indeed produced by a child (e.g., clean the data) *and* rate the maturity of the vocalization. Scripts are then applied to these cleaned, coded data to generate estimates of the child's canonical babbling ratio, pitch range, and average vocalization duration. Using this semi-automated approach, we can pair LENA's *efficiency* in tagging longform recordings—which would otherwise take hundreds of hours of coding time per recording—with *rigor* of human-verified "checks" and supplemental coding, providing rich estimates of vocal development. Given the volume of data produced by home assessments—developing these types of semi-automated approaches will be critical to efficiently analyzing and outputting variables.

Consistent with our goal to integrate caregivers in the research process, it is also possible that caregivers could actively participate in the coding and processing of "big data" generated through NGS trials. For example, we recently tested whether citizen scientists—lay community members interested in contributing to science by engaging in simple tasks online—could accurately clean and classify vocalizations as part of our post-processing pipeline. Our results (Semenzin et al., 2021) suggested that despite some variability in annotation at the level of the vocalization segment, citizen scientists produced overall estimates of summary codes (e.g., linguistic and canonical proportions) that strongly correlated with summary codes generated by gold-standard coders ($0.821 < r < 0.938$), with similar coding quality for files generated from children with and without NGS. These findings suggest that caregivers could actively support not just data collection but also more rapid data coding and dissemination as citizen scientists.

5. Next steps and future directions

We anticipate remote assessment is here to stay, including beyond the current bounds of the COVID-19 pandemic. With this context in mind, we share three considerations for the future.

We are not the first people to center the caregiver experience. As we "re-standardize" our assessment protocols around families and remote contexts, we have found ourselves bumping into a parallel literature base: user experience (UX). UX is broadly defined as the experience a user has when using a certain product or technology and plays an integral role in accessibility of telehealth-based research. The term "user experience," coined by Donald Norman in 1993, has a rich history that precedes the field's formal creation. While there are many different areas where the idea of user experience grew, one area commonly cited in UX research is that of the telephone's design. Almost 75 years ago, psychologist John E. Karlin was hired to work with Bell Telephone Laboratories to redesign early versions of the telephone. In redesigning the original model, one of the goals was to ease its usability and mold its accessibility to that of the average user (Karlin, 1962). From there, the field of human factors and user experience continued to grow in popularity. Today, we see substantial push for technologies to prioritize the user experience and usability as a means to maximize their demand and continued use.

Although the UX framework is typically used to describe commercial product development, many of the core principles can be applied to the development of remote assessment tools. For example, UX is conceptualized as the intersection of three factors: (1) the interactive system of the experience (e.g., brand, function, performance, presentation, capacities),

(2) the prior factors that give rise to the user's internal state, such as their experiences, attitudes, and personality, and (3) the context in which the experience occurs (ISO 9241-210; as described in Rico-Olarte, López, and Kepplinger (2018). Using this frame, we can consider how caregivers and NGS patients may interact with our remote assessment tools by asking questions such as *What are the key components of the system that are compatible and incompatible with the NGS phenotype? How might the child or caregiver's prior assessment experiences prepare them for the current session—in supportive ways or not? What individual factors might determine whether a user participates successfully in the remote assessment? What internal states (*e.g., *hunger, tiredness) might influence their participation, and how might we address these challenges head-on?* In this way, UX science can provide a complementary framework for optimizing remote assessment methods for our intended user groups.

Telehealth alone will not solve issues of access and equity. It is important to reiterate that simply offering remote monitoring options does not entirely address the issue of diversity and representation in clinical research and services. There may be several factors that impact the acceptability or appeal of remote assessment for families from diverse backgrounds beyond simply reducing travel burden. As previously stated, some families may have limited access to wireless internet, making remote connection challenging to arrange. Having clear protocols to address this need can ensure that this does not become an additional barrier for families to participate in services. One solution may be to include wireless hotspots among the other materials being provided to families. It may also be helpful to develop protocols that can easily be adapted to be completed in community settings that often provide free wireless internet (e.g., libraries, community centers). This may require additional steps to ensure the participating family's privacy, including potentially partnering with the community setting directly to arrange appropriate testing and/or intervention environment without placing the coordination burden on the family.

Technology literacy is another consideration when developing remote assessment protocols. It is easy to fall into the misunderstanding that technology use is universal in these times; however, it is important to consider the range of familiarity families, and caregivers, in particular, may have with using technology. Certain demographic factors, such as a caregiver's age or cultural perspectives on technology use, may impact a caregiver's inclination toward engaging in telehealth services. Some caregivers may be proficient in one type of technology (e.g., smartphones) but less familiar with using laptops or tablets. Others may be tentative to engage with software or apps that are new or unfamiliar. It is possible that mentioning telehealth services would deter some families from even inquiring about services in the first place. As such, ensuring that recruitment materials highlight that proficiency with technology is not a requirement or that there are a variety of supports available to assist with managing the technology can alleviate these road-blocks for families.

Beyond making technology and remote services accessible, it is important to consider the needs of the families that will be participating when designing remote assessment and intervention protocols. How will this research or these services benefit them? How can we ensure that the time they contribute to these remote protocols are justified in terms of what information or services they leave with? Do the benefits truly outweigh the risks, particularly in the context of potential past experiences of discrimination and trauma many minoritized patients report in medical settings? A driving force behind these decisions can be thinking about what supports this community may need to participate in research, both logistically (e.g., childcare support) and/or emotionally (e.g., buy-in from the research team).

One way to garner acceptance of research within a particular community is to invest in those communities themselves. Families may be more likely to engage with organizations that they see references to within their day-to-day lives. This could mean volunteering at local community centers, sponsoring family-friendly events, or providing informational series on topics most relevant to the community. Furthermore, this engagement creates opportunities for your team to understand any community-specific stressors that may impact participation in research (e.g., local policy, neighborhood crime, natural disasters), for which your team may be able to offer support to those participating in research and the community more broadly. Building these partnerships not only increases familiarity with your team and research program but increases the benefits families receive from engaging with your research.

Caregiver needs exist beyond the remote assessment session. It is important to remember that our research and/or clinical work with families does not exist in a vacuum. The competition between research demands and other life experiences is particularly salient in telehealth context. Although the provider or researcher may perceive that "popping in" to a family's home for a short web-based session is a simple process, the participating family may have faced many barriers to make the session possible. Some of these barriers may be straightforward, such as having access to technology, childcare, or even time to participate in the session. Others may seem more peripheral but may nevertheless be impacting the quality of the information gathered during your session. For example, caregivers struggling with their mental health may have difficulty providing ample reports of their child's behavior. Similarly, caregivers whose children have not been sleeping or eating well may have difficulty focusing on other aspects of their child's behavior that may be relevant to the goal of your session.

Taking time to understand the broader context from which a family or participant is joining your session has several benefits, including by contextualizing the data being collected, ensuring the family has access to necessary resources, and providing context to build rapport. While it would be overwhelming to attempt to assess every aspect of a family's functioning in the context of a short research or clinical session, there may be approaches that can streamline this process or ensure its functionality within the primary purpose of the session. Proactively, many screeners exist for common stressors or challenges that may be affecting the family in day-to-day life, including those for mental health, diet and/or feeding challenges, sleep behaviors, and access to resources like meals, transportation, and social support. Of course, it is important to consider the balance between gathering relevant contextual information and the burden placed on families to provide this information before or during your session. In some cases, a series of simple or targeted screening questions may be sufficient to get a sense of the contextual factors impacting the family. For service providers with ongoing contact with families, screening questions can be used to decide whether more detailed information would be helpful or necessary.

6. Final thoughts

The purpose of this review was to consider when and how remote assessment can best serve the need of NGS communities. Building from our line of remote assessment development work, we advocate for a family-centered approach that recognizes and centers the caregiver as a key agent in the assessment process. We also highlight the potential impact of remote assessment on diverse and marginalized groups, including potential opportunities and risks. Together, work from our team and others suggests that in the right circumstances and with proper planning, remote assessment can greatly improve access, reach, and quality of clinical trials in NGS.

Acknowledgments

Funding for this work was provided by K23MH111955 (PI Kelleher) and F31DC018219 (PI Hamrick).

References

Abbeduto, L., Berry-Kravis, E., Sterling, A., Sherman, S., Edgin, J. O., McDuffie, A., et al. (2020). Erratum: Expressive language sampling as a source of outcome measures for treatment studies in fragile X syndrome: Feasibility, practice effects, test-retest reliability, and construct validity. *Journal of Neurodevelopmental Disorders, 12*(1), 1–23. https://doi.org/10.1186/s11689-020-09314-5.

Alemayehu, D., Hemmings, R., Natarajan, K., & Roychoudhury, S. (2022). Perspectives on virtual (remote) clinical trials as the "new Normal" to accelerate drug development. *Clinical Pharmacology and Therapeutics, 111*(2), 373–381. https://doi.org/10.1002/cpt.2248.

Alfuraydan, M., Croxall, J., Hurt, L., Kerr, M., & Brophy, S. (2020). Use of telehealth for facilitating the diagnostic assessment of autism Spectrum disorder (ASD): A scoping review. *PLoS One, 15*(7 July), 1–16. https://doi.org/10.1371/journal.pone.0236415.

Aranki, J., Wright, P., Pompa-Craven, P., & Lotfizadeh, A. D. (2022). Acceptance of telehealth therapy to replace in-person therapy for autism treatment during COVID-19 pandemic: An assessment of patient variables. *Telemedicine and E-Health, 00*(00), 1–8. https://doi.org/10.1089/tmj.2021.0397.

Bauer, I. (2018). When travel is a challenge: Travel medicine and the 'dis-abled' traveller. In *Vol. 22. Travel medicine and infectious disease* (pp. 66–72). USA: Elsevier. https://doi.org/10.1016/j.tmaid.2018.02.001.

Benda, N. C., Veinot, T. C., Sieck, C. J., & Ancker, J. S. (2020). Broadband internet access is a social determinant of health! *American Journal of Public Health, 110*(8), 1123–1125. https://doi.org/10.2105/AJPH.2020.305784.

Bernhardt, C., & King, C. (2022). Telehealth and food insecurity screenings: Challenges and lessons learned. *mHealth, 8*, 10. https://doi.org/10.21037/mhealth-21-31.

Berry-Kravis, E., Des Portes, V., Hagerman, R., Jacquemont, S., Charles, P., Visootsak, J., et al. (2016). Mavoglurant in fragile X syndrome: Results of two randomized, double-blind, placebo-controlled trials. *Science Translational Medicine, 8*(321), 321ra5. https://doi.org/10.1126/scitranslmed.aab4109.

Berry-Kravis, E., Hessl, D., Abbeduto, L., Reiss, A. L., Beckel-Mitchener, A., & Urv, T. K. (2013). Outcome measures for clinical trials in fragile X syndrome. *Journal of Developmental and Behavioral Pediatrics, 34*(7), 508–522. https://doi.org/10.1097/DBP.0b013e31829d1f20.

Budimirovic, D. B., Berry-Kravis, E., Erickson, C. A., Hall, S. S., Hessl, D., Reiss, A. L., et al. (2017). Updated report on tools to measure outcomes of clinical trials in fragile X syndrome. *Journal of Neurodevelopmental Disorders, 9*(1), 1–36. https://doi.org/10.1186/s11689-017-9193-x.

Bulgarelli, F., & Bergelson, E. (2019). Look who's talking: A comparison of automated and human-generated speaker tags in naturalistic day-long recordings. *Behavior Research Methods, 52*(2), 641–653. https://doi.org/10.3758/s13428-019-01265-7.

Carmichael, B., Pembrey, M., Turner, G., & Barnicoat, A. (1999). Diagnosis of fragile-X syndrome: The experiences of parents. *Journal of Intellectual Disability Research: JIDR, 43*(Pt. 1), 47–53. https://doi.org/10.1046/j.1365-2788.1999.43120157.x.

Carmichael, N., Tsipis, J., Windmueller, G., Mandel, L., & Estrella, E. (2015). "Is it going to hurt?": The impact of the diagnostic odyssey on children and their families. *Journal of Genetic Counseling, 24*(2), 325–335. https://doi.org/10.1007/s10897-014-9773-9.

Ciupe, A., & Salisbury, C. (2020). Examining caregivers' independence in early intervention home visit sessions. *Journal of Early Intervention, 42*(4), 338–358. https://doi.org/10.1177/1053815120902727.

Corbie-Smith, G., Thomas, S. B., & St George, D. M. (2002). Distrust, race, and research. *Archives of Internal Medicine, 162*(21), 2458–2463. https://doi.org/10.1001/archinte.162.21.2458.

Corona, L. L., Stainbrook, J. A., Simcoe, K., Wagner, L., Fowler, B., Weitlauf, A. S., et al. (2021). Utilization of telemedicine to support caregivers of young children with ASD and their part C service providers: A comparison of intervention outcomes across three models of service delivery. *Journal of Neurodevelopmental Disorders, 13*(1), 1–13. https://doi.org/10.1186/s11689-021-09387-w.

Crawford, A., & Serhal, E. (2020). Digital health equity and COVID-19: The innovation curve cannot reinforce the social gradient of health. *Journal of Medical Internet Research, 22*(6), e19361. https://doi.org/10.2196/19361.

Curtis, M. E., Clingan, S. E., Guo, H., Zhu, Y., Mooney, L. J., & Hser, Y. I. (2022). Disparities in digital access among American rural and urban households and implications for telemedicine-based services. *The Journal of Rural Health, 38*(3), 512–518. https://doi.org/10.1111/jrh.12614.

D'Amanda, C. S., Peay, H. L., Wheeler, A. C., Turbitt, E., & Biesecker, B. B. (2019). Fragile X syndrome clinical trials: Exploring parental decision-making. *Journal of Intellectual Disability Research, 63*(8), 926–935. https://doi.org/10.1111/jir.12605.

Davis-Kean, P. E., & Ellis, A. (2019). An overview of issues in infant and developmental research for the creation of robust and replicable science. In *Vol. 57. Infant behavior and development* Elsevier Ltd. https://doi.org/10.1016/j.infbeh.2019.101339.

DeMaria, A. L., Dykstra, C., King, H., Felicicchia, R., Kelleher, B. L., & McCormick, C. E. B. (2022). Reproductive healthcare access and genetic testing decision-making among women with increased likelihood of having a child with autism. *Women's Reproductive Health, 3*, 1–20. https://doi.org/10.1080/23293691.2022.2054669. Advanced online publication.

DePalma, R., Matusov, E., & Hayes, R. (2000). Sociocultural critique of Piaget and Vygotsky sociocultural critique of Piaget and Vygotsky. *New Ideas in Psychology, 18*, 215–239.

Di Pietro, N. C., & Illes, J. (2014). Disparities in Canadian indigenous health research on neurodevelopmental disorders. *Journal of Developmental & Behavioral Pediatrics, 35*(1), 74–81.

Dikkala, R., Khanna, R., Matthews, C., Dodge, J., Raja, S., Hu, C., et al. (2021). Doing remote controlled studies with humans: Tales from the COVID trenches. In *2021. Proceedings—2021 IEEE/ACM 13th international workshop on cooperative and human aspects of software engineering, CHASE* (pp. 113–116). https://doi.org/10.1109/CHASE52884.2021.00022.

DiMaggio, P., Hargittai, E., Celeste, C., & Shafer, S. (2004). From unequal access to differentiated use: A literature review and agenda for research on digital inequality. *Social Inequality, 1*, 355–400.

Dinesen, B., Nonnecke, B., Lindeman, D., Toft, E., Kidholm, K., Jethwani, K., et al. (2016). Personalized telehealth in the future: A global research agenda. *Journal of Medical Internet Research, 18*(3), e53. https://doi.org/10.2196/jmir.5257.

Dover, D. C., & Belon, A. P. (2019). The health equity measurement framework: A comprehensive model to measure social inequities in health. *International Journal for Equity in Health, 18*(1), 1–12. https://doi.org/10.1186/s12939-019-0935-0.

Eannucci, E. F., Hazel, K., Grundstein, M. J., Nguyen, J. T., & Gallegro, J. (2020). Patient satisfaction for telehealth physical therapy services was comparable to that of in-person services during the COVID-19 pandemic. *HSS Journal, 16*, 10–16. https://doi.org/10.1007/s11420-020-09800-5.

Eilenberg, J. S., Paff, M., Harrison, A. J., & Long, K. A. (2019). Disparities based on race, ethnicity, and socioeconomic status over the transition to adulthood among adolescents and young adults on the autism spectrum: A systematic review. *Current Psychiatry Reports, 21*(5), 32. https://doi.org/10.1007/s11920-019-1016-1.

Erickson, C. A., Davenport, M. H., Schaefer, T. L., Wink, L. K., Pedapati, E. V., Sweeney, J. A., et al. (2017). Fragile X targeted pharmacotherapy: Lessons learned and future directions. *Journal of Neurodevelopmental Disorders, 9*(1), 1–14. https://doi.org/10.1186/s11689-017-9186-9.

FDA-NIH Biomarker Working Group. (2016). *BEST (Biomarkers, EndpointS, and other Tools) resource*. Silver Spring (MD)/Bethesda: Food and Drug Administration (US) (Glossary)/National Institutes of Health United States.

Ferguson, E. F., Jimenez-Muñoz, M., Feerst, H., & Vernon, T. W. (2021). Predictors of satisfaction with autism treatment services during COVID-19. *Journal of Autism and Developmental Disorders, 19*(0123456789), 1–12. https://doi.org/10.1007/s10803-021-05232-0.

Foti, D., Kelleher, B. L., Galvez-Ortega, K., Harold, R., Gombas, S., & Haarer, A. (2021). Update on the development of a novel telehealth EEG assessment protocol for Angelman syndrome. In *Paper presentation at the 2021 Angelman biomarker and outcome measure Alliance, Austin, TX*.

Getz, K., Sethuraman, V., Rine, J., Peña, Y., Ramanathan, S., & Stergiopoulos, S. (2020). Assessing patient participation burden based on protocol design characteristics. *Therapeutic Innovation & Regulatory Science, 54*(3), 598–604. https://doi.org/10.1007/s43441-019-00092-4.

Gilkerson, J., & Richards, J. A. (2009). Impact of adult talk, conversational turns, and TV during the critical 0-4 years of child development. In *The power of talk* (2nd ed., pp. 1–36). LENA Foundation.

Goldstein, F., & Glueck, D. (2016). Developing rapport and therapeutic alliance during telemental health sessions with children and adolescents. *Journal of Child and Adolescent Psychopharmacology, 26*(3), 204–211.

Goodwin, J., Schoch, K., Shashi, V., Hooper, S. R., Morad, O., Zalevsky, M., et al. (2015). A tale worth telling: The impact of the diagnosis experience on disclosure of genetic disorders. *Journal of Intellectual Disability Research: JIDR, 59*(5), 474–486. https://doi.org/10.1111/jir.12151.

Hamrick, L. R., Seidl, A., & Tonnsen, B. L. (2019). *Acoustic properties of early vocalizations in infants with fragile X syndrome. Vol. 12* (11th ed., pp. 1663–1679). Autism Research.

Harold, R., Galvez-Ortega, K., Kelleher, B., & Foti, D. (December 2020). Development and implementation of a novel remote EEG protocol for studying Angelman syndrome. In *Symposium presentation at the 2020 Foundation for Angelman Syndrome Therapeutics Translational Research Symposium, virtual*.

Hessl, D., Harvey, D., Sansone, S., Crestodina, C., Chin, J., Joshi, R., et al. (2019). Effects of mavoglurant on visual attention and pupil reactivity while viewing photographs of faces in fragile X syndrome. *PLoS One, 14*(1), e0209984.

Izmailova, E. S., Ellis, R., & Benko, C. (2020). Remote monitoring in clinical trials during the COVID-19 pandemic. *Clinical and Translational Science, 13*(5), 838–841. https://doi.org/10.1111/cts.12834.

Jacquemont, S., Berry-Kravis, E., Hagerman, R., von Raison, F., Gasparini, F., Apostol, G., et al. (2014). The challenges of clinical trials in fragile X syndrome. *Psychopharmacology, 231*(6), 1237–1250. https://doi.org/10.1007/s00213-013-3289-0.

Jeste, S. S., Frohlich, J., & Loo, S. K. (2015). Electrophysiological biomarkers of diagnosis and outcome in neurodevelopmental disorders. *Current Opinion in Neurology, 28*(2), 110–116. https://doi.org/10.1097/WCO.0000000000000181.

Jeste, S., Hyde, C., Distefano, C., Halladay, A., Ray, S., Porath, M., et al. (2020). Changes in access to educational and healthcare services for individuals with intellectual and developmental disabilities during COVID-19 restrictions. *Journal of Intellectual Disability Research*, *64*(11), 825–833. https://doi.org/10.1111/jir.12776.

Kelleher, B. L. (December 2021). Bringing together caregivers, clinical scientists, and engineers to improve wearable biosensors for Angelman syndrome trials. Paper presentation at the 2021 Angelman biomarker and outcome measure Alliance, Austin, TX.

Karlin, J. E. (1962). Human factors engineering and research in telephone systems engineering. *IRE Transactions on Education*, *2*, 71–75.

Kelleher, B. L., Halligan, T. A., Garwood, T. E., Howell, S. M., Martin-O'Dell, B., Swint, A., et al. (2020). Brief report: Assessment experiences of children with neurogenetic syndromes: Caregivers' perceptions and suggestions for improvement. *Journal of Autism and Developmental Disorders*, *50*, 1443–1450.

Kelleher, B. L., Halligan, T., Witthuhn, N., Neo, W. S., Hamrick, L., & Abbeduto, L. (2020). Bringing the laboratory home: PANDABox telehealth-based assessment of neurodevelopmental risk in children. *Frontiers in Psychology*, *11*, 1634.

Laurencin, C. T., & Walker, J. M. (2020). A pandemic on a pandemic: Racism and COVID-19 in blacks. *Cell Systems*, *11*(1), 9–10. https://doi.org/10.1016/j.cels.2020.07.002.

Le Cook, B., Trinh, N. H., Li, Z., Hou, S. S. Y., & Progovac, A. M. (2017). Trends in racial-ethnic disparities in access to mental health care, 2004-2012. In *Vol. 68 (1). Psychiatric services* (pp. 9–16). American Psychiatric Association. https://doi.org/10.1176/appi.ps.201500453.

Lindgren, S., Wacker, D., Suess, A., Schieltz, K., Pelzel, K., Kopelman, T., et al. (2016). Telehealth and autism: Treating challenging behavior at lower cost. *Pediatrics*, *137*(Suppl), S167–S175. https://doi.org/10.1542/peds.2015-2851o.

Mandell, D. S., Wiggins, L. D., Carpenter, L. A., Daniels, J., DiGuiseppi, C., Durkin, M. S., et al. (2009). Racial/ethnic disparities in the identification of children with autism spectrum disorders. *American Journal of Public Health*, *99*(3), 493–498. https://doi.org/10.2105/AJPH.2007.131243.

Murphy, A., Pinkerton, L. M., Bruckner, E., & Risser, H. J. (2021). The impact of the novel coronavirus disease 2019 on therapy service delivery for children with disabilities. *Journal of Pediatrics*, *231*, 168–177. https://doi.org/10.1016/j.jpeds.2020.12.060.

Neece, C., McIntyre, L. L., & Fenning, R. (2020). Examining the impact of COVID-19 in ethnically diverse families with young children with intellectual and developmental disabilities. *Journal of Intellectual Disability Research*, *64*(10), 739–749. https://doi.org/10.1111/jir.12769.

Nelson, S., McDuffie, A., Banasik, A., Tempero Feigles, R., Thurman, A. J., & Abbeduto, L. (2018). Inferential language use by school-aged boys with fragile X syndrome: Effects of a parent-implemented spoken language intervention. *Journal of Communication Disorders*, *72*(May 2017), 64–76. https://doi.org/10.1016/j.jcomdis.2018.02.007.

Nguyen, M. H., Gruber, J., Fuchs, J., Marler, W., Hunsaker, A., & Hargittai, E. (2020). Changes in digital communication during the COVID-19 global pandemic: Implications for digital inequality and future research. *Social Media + Society*, *6*(3), 2056305120948255. https://doi.org/10.1177/2056305120948255.

Open Science Collaboration. (2015). Estimating the reproducibility of psychological science. *Science*, *349*(6251), aac4716.

Parmanto, B., Pulantara, I. W., Schutte, J. L., Saptono, A., & Mccue, M. P. (2013). An integrated telehealth system for remote Administration of an Adult Autism Assessment. *Telemedicine and E-Health*, *19*, 2. https://doi.org/10.1089/tmj.2012.0104.

Pearson. (2021). *Telepractice and the WISC-V* (pp. 1–15). NCS Pearson, Inc.

Pease, R. L. (2013). A brief history of the NSREC. *IEEE Transactions on Nuclear Science*, *60*(3), 1668–1673. https://doi.org/10.1109/TNS.2013.2239661.

Piaget, J. (1971). *The child's conception of the world*. Littlefield Adams.

Rapela, J., Lin, T. Y., Westerfield, M., Jung, T. P., & Townsend, J. (2012). Assisting autistic children with wireless EOG technology. In *Proceedings of the annual international conference of the IEEE Engineering in Medicine and Biology Society, EMBS* (pp. 3504–3506). https://doi.org/10.1109/EMBC.2012.6346721.

Ratto, A. B., Anthony, B. J., Pugliese, C., Mendez, R., Safer-Lichtenstein, J., Dudley, K. M., et al. (2017). Lessons learned: Engaging culturally diverse families in neurodevelopmental disorders intervention research. *Autism*, *21*(5), 622–634. https://doi.org/10.1177/1362361316650394.

Rico-Olarte, C., López, D. M., & Kepplinger, S. (2018). Towards a conceptual framework for the objective evaluation of user experience. In A. Marcus, & W. Wang (Eds.), *Design, user experience, and usability: Theory and practice* (pp. 546–559). Springer International Publishing.

Schwartz, L., Holland, A., Dykens, E., Strong, T., Roof, E., & Bohonowych, J. (2016). Prader-Willi syndrome mental health research strategy workshop proceedings: The state of the science and future directions. *Orphanet Journal of Rare Diseases*, *11*(1), 1–7. https://doi.org/10.1186/s13023-016-0504-1.

Semenzin, C., Hamrick, L., Seidl, A., Kelleher, B. L., & Cristia, A. (2021). Describing vocalizations in young children: A big data approach through citizen science annotation. *Journal of Speech, Language, and Hearing Research*, *64*(7), 2401–2416. https://doi.org/10.1044/2021_JSLHR-20-00661.

Sertkaya, A., Wong, H. H., Jessup, A., & Beleche, T. (2016). Key cost drivers of pharmaceutical clinical trials in the United States. *Clinical Trials (London, England)*, *13*(2), 117–126. https://doi.org/10.1177/1740774515625964.

Shea, L., Newschaffer, C. J., Xie, M., Myers, S. M., & Mandell, D. S. (2014). Genetic testing and genetic counseling among medicaid-enrolled children with autism spectrum disorder in 2001 and 2007. *Human Genetics*, *133*(1), 111–116. https://doi.org/10.1007/s00439-013-1362-8.

Sheet, M. F. (2019). *Internet/broadband, mobile, social media*. Pew Research Center.

Shore, J. H., Brooks, E., Savin, D. M., Manson, S. M., & Libby, A. M. (2007). An economic evaluation of telehealth data collection with rural populations. *Psychiatric Services*, *58*(6), 830–835.

Soorya, L., Leon, J., Trelles, M. P., & Thurm, A. (2018). Framework for assessing individuals with rare genetic disorders associated with profound intellectual and multiple disabilities (PIMD): The example of Phelan McDermid syndrome. *The Clinical Neuropsychologist*, *32*(7), 1226–1255. https://doi.org/10.1080/13854046.2017.1413211.

Sullivan, A. L. (2013). School-based autism identification: Prevalence, racial disparities, and systemic correlates. *School Psychology Review*, *42*(3), 298–316.

Talbott, M. R., Dufek, S., Zwaigenbaum, L., Bryson, S. E., Brian, J., Smith, I. M., et al. (2019). Brief report: Preliminary feasibility of the TEDI: A novel parent-administered telehealth assessment for autism Spectrum disorder symptoms in the first year of life. *Journal of Autism and Developmental Disorders*, *50*(9), 3432–3439.

Thurm, A., Kelleher, B., & Wheeler, A. (2020). Outcome measures for core symptoms of intellectual disability: State of the field. *American Journal on Intellectual and Developmental Disabilities*, *125*(6), 418–433.

Tomlin, A. M., & Hadadian, A. (2007). Early intervention providers and high-risk families. *Early Child Development and Care*, *177*(2), 187–194. https://doi.org/10.1080/03004430500379234.

Turbitt, E., D'Amanda, C., Hyman, S., Weber, J. D., Bridges, J. F. P., Peay, H. L., et al. (2021). Parent clinical trial priorities for fragile X syndrome: A best-worst scaling. *European Journal of Human Genetics: EJHG*, *29*(8), 1245–1251. https://doi.org/10.1038/s41431-021-00922-w.

Turk, M. A., Landes, S. D., Formica, M. K., & Goss, K. D. (2020). Intellectual and developmental disability and COVID-19 case-fatality trends: TriNetX analysis. *Disability and Health Journal, 13*(3), 100942. https://doi.org/10.1016/j.dhjo.2020.100942.

VanDam, M., & Silbert, N. H. (2016). Fidelity of automatic speech processing for adult and child talker classifications. *PLoS One, 11*(8), 1–13. https://doi.org/10.1371/journal.pone.0160588.

Vismara, L. A., McCormick, C., Young, G. S., Nadhan, A., & Monlux, K. (2013). Preliminary findings of a telehealth approach to parent training in autism. *Journal of Autism and Developmental Disorders, 43*(12), 2953–2969. https://doi.org/10.1007/s10803-013-1841-8.

Webb, S. J., Bernier, R., Henderson, H. A., Johnson, M. H., Jones, E. J., Lerner, M. D., et al. (2015). Guidelines and best practices for electrophysiological data collection, analysis and reporting in autism. *Journal of Autism and Developmental Disorders, 45*(2), 425–443.

Webb Hooper, M., Nápoles, A. M., & Pérez-Stable, E. J. (2020). COVID-19 and racial/ethnic disparities. *JAMA: The Journal of the American Medical Association, 323*(24), 2466–2467, American Medical Association. https://doi.org/10.1001/jama.2020.8598.

Weil, L. W., & Middleton, L. (2010). Use of the LENA tool to evaluate the effectiveness of a parent intervention program. *Perspectives on Language Learning and Education, 17*(3), 108–111. https://doi.org/10.1044/lle17.3.108.

White, A. N., Chevette, M., Hillerstrom, H., & Esbensen, A. (2022). Parental perspectives on research for down syndrome. *Journal of Applied Research in Intellectual Disabilities, 35*(1), 179–187. https://doi.org/10.1111/jar.12937.

World Health Organization. (2021). *Global strategy on digital health 2020–2025*. World Health Organization. Retrieved from: https://www.who.int/docs/default-source/documents/gs4dhdaa2a9f352b0445bafbc79ca799dce4d.pdf.

Xu, D., Yapanel, U., Gray, S., & Gilkerson, J. (2008). *Signal processing for young child speech language development*. Wocci: First Workshop on Child, Computer and Interaction.

Yuen, E. K., Gros, D. F., Price, M., Zeigler, S., Tuerk, P. W., Foa, E. B., et al. (2015). Randomized controlled trial of home-based telehealth versus in-person prolonged exposure for combat-related PTSD in veterans: Preliminary results. *Journal of Clinical Psychology, 71*(6), 500–512.

Zhang, D., Shi, L., Han, X., Li, Y., Jalajel, N. A., Patel, S., et al. (2021). Disparities in telehealth utilization during the COVID-19 pandemic: Findings from a nationally representative survey in the United States. *Journal of Telemedicine and Telecare*, 1–8. https://doi.org/10.1177/1357633X211051677. January 2022.

Further reading

Atassi, N., Yerramilli-Rao, P., Szymonifka, J., Yu, H., Kearney, M., Grasso, D., et al. (2013). Analysis of start-up, retention, and adherence in ALS clinical trials. *Neurology, 81*(15), 1350–1355. https://doi.org/10.1212/WNL.0b013e3182a823e0.

Borno, H. T., Zhang, L., Siegel, A., Chang, E., & Ryan, C. J. (2018). At what cost to clinical trial enrollment? A retrospective study of patient travel burden in cancer clinical trials. *The Oncologist, 23*(10), 1242–1249. https://doi.org/10.1634/theoncologist.2017-0628.

Luu, S., Province, H., Berry-Kravis, E., Hagerman, R., Hessl, D., Vaidya, D., et al. (2020). Response to placebo in fragile x syndrome clinical trials: An initial analysis. *Brain Sciences, 10*(9), 1–17. https://doi.org/10.3390/brainsci10090629.

Probst, J. C., Laditka, S. B., Wang, J.-Y., & Johnson, A. O. (2007). Effects of residence and race on burden of travel for care: Cross sectional analysis of the 2001 US National Household Travel Survey. *BMC Health Services Research*, 7(1), 40. https://doi.org/10.1186/1472-6963-7-40.

CHAPTER THREE

Evaluating outcomes within culturally diverse contexts for children and youth with developmental disabilities

Sandra B. Vanegas[a,b], **Laura Hopp**[a], **Jennifer Davila Valdes**[a], **and Sandy Magaña**[b]
[a]Texas State University, San Marcos, TX, United States
[b]University of Texas at Austin, Austin, TX, United States

Contents

Abstract

Greater attention and focus are being paid to outcome measures used in evaluating treatment gains and long-term outcomes for children and youth with developmental delays/disabilities (DD). However, much of this research does not include racially/ethnically and linguistically diverse participants, nor does it consider the relevance of chosen outcome measures for these distinct cultural groups. As a result, there exists a substantial gap in knowledge on treatment efficacy and application for diverse communities of children and youth with DD. We begin by describing the key issues researchers and professionals must consider in identifying and measuring outcomes

International Review of Research in Developmental Disabilities, Volume 62
ISSN 2211-6095
https://doi.org/10.1016/bs.irrdd.2022.05.003

for children and youth with DD from diverse backgrounds. These issues include identifying meaningful outcomes, recognizing the language needs, and ensuring the accessibility of the outcome measures. Furthermore, consulting with community stakeholders, especially individuals with DD and their families, is vital. Finally, we present a literature review on the developmental outcomes of diverse populations of children and youth with DD. This review gives insight into how researchers and other professionals can work to ensure outcome measures are culturally responsive and for diverse groups.

Abbreviations

ASD	autism spectrum disorder
BASC-2	Behavior Assessment System for Children, 2nd edition
BOTMP	Bruininks-Oseretsky Test of Motor Proficiency
BRIEF	Behavior Rating Inventory of Executive Function
CBCL	Child Behavior Checklist
CP	cerebral palsy
CSBS-DP	Communication Symbolic Behavior Scales Developmental Profile
DBC	Developmental Behavior Checklist
DCMA	Dyadic Communication Measure for Autism
DD	developmental delay/disability
DS	down syndrome
ECBI	Eyberg Child Behavior Inventory
ESCS	Early Social-Communication Scale
GMFM-88	Gross Motor Function Measure-88
HINE	Hammersmith Infant Neurological Examination
ICHOM	International Consortium for Health Outcomes Measurement
ID	intellectual disability
IERPR	Instrument for the Evaluation of Results in Pediatric Rehabilitation
SON 2 1/2-7	Snijders-Oomen Nonverbal Intelligence Test 2 1/2-7
SSIS	Social Skills Improvement System
VABS	Vineland Adaptive Behavior Scales
WISC-III	Wechsler Intelligence Scale for Children-III
WPPSI-III	Wechsler Preschool and Primary Scale of Intelligence-III

1. Introduction

Discussions about outcomes for children and youth with developmental delays/disabilities (DD) have become more prevalent as researchers reflect on the efficacy and effectiveness of programs and support for children and youth with DD. Although reviews of outcome measures for specific conditions, including autism spectrum disorders (ASD), Down syndrome

(DS), Fragile X syndrome, and intellectual disability (ID), have been published, these reviews have not adequately described the racial/ethnic and linguistic diversity of their samples (Abbeduto et al., 2020; Berry-Kravis et al., 2013; Esbensen et al., 2017; Keeling et al., 2017; Kelleher & Wheeler, 2020; Trembath, Westerveld, & Shellshear, 2016). Furthermore, reviews of interventions services, and treatments for DD also demonstrate that many studies have limited, if any, descriptions on the racial/ethnic and linguistic diversity of their samples (Fannin, 2017; Steinbrenner et al., 2022; West et al., 2016). For the few published studies that report on these diverse characteristics, we continue to see that most intervention, service, and treatment research includes homogenous samples that do not adequately represent the rich racial, ethnic, and linguistic diversity of our communities. Furthermore, research on interventions that reflects diversity across race, ethnicity, and language only emerges when the authors have a focused perspective on diverse populations (Koly et al., 2021; Magaña et al., 2019, 2021; Simpson, 2021). This lack of research is alarming given that published research on interventions, services, and treatments are used to inform evidence-based practices and are often used by health care practitioners and health insurance providers to outline recommended and covered therapeutic services for all communities. Beyond the direct impact on children and youth with DD and their families, implementing ineffective interventions or interventions not validated for diverse populations can yield high costs and financial risk for schools and providers (Scheibel, Zane, & Zimmerman, 2022). Thus, there remains a significant gap between what we know are effective interventions, services, and treatments for DD and what is effective for children and youth with DD from diverse racial/ethnic and linguistic backgrounds. At the core of this issue are the outcomes that are measured to determine the effects of interventions, services, and treatments. If measured outcomes are not responsive to the cultural and linguistic needs of children and youth with DD and their families, then any effects resulting from interventions, services, and treatments will be unknown.

Several recent initiatives on autism have been undertaken to review outcome measures (McConachie et al., 2015, 2018) and develop a standard set of outcomes for consistent implementation worldwide (International Consortium for Health Outcomes Measurement (ICHOM), 2021). Although many outcomes often reflect certain targets for specific interventions or programs, less attention has been dedicated to examining whether the outcomes identified by researchers and practitioners are also meaningful and important to children and youth, and their families. In this paper, we highlight cultural considerations in defining and measuring outcomes for children and youth with DD from diverse racial/ethnic and linguistic backgrounds and present a literature review on the state of research on outcomes across diverse communities.

2. Cultural considerations in defining and measuring outcomes for DD

2.1 Meaningful outcomes for DD

A primary concern when identifying outcome measures for children and youth with DD, especially from racially/ethnically and linguistically diverse backgrounds, is the relevance of said outcome for the child/youth and their family. For example, researchers may pursue outcomes directly linked to skills taught in an intervention or program that have been deemed necessary for a Western idealized life trajectory. However, when we consider the vast diversity of opportunities and environments in which children and youth with DD reside, it becomes much more important to take into account what will be meaningful for this child/youth within their environment, culture, and society. These issues are critical if we truly engage in culturally responsive approaches when working with and for diverse communities. Vanegas, Magaña, Zeng, and Pavon (2021) found that although many transition support programs and services focus on independent living, this outcome was not deemed appropriate nor important for racially/ethnically diverse youth with DD and their families. If we were to designate only independent living as the desired outcome, youth with DD from racially/ethnically diverse backgrounds would not meet these outcomes and thus would be assumed to need additional support (Vanegas et al., 2021).

To identify priorities for meaningful outcomes, engagement of the community is essential. Tomlinson et al. (2014) adopted the Child Health and Nutrition Research Initiative methods to identify research priorities for ID and ASD (Rudan et al., 2008). The authors assembled an expert panel ($n = 63$) representing a range of geographical regions, gender identities, professional backgrounds (i.e., research, non-governmental organization), and focal areas of work (Tomlinson et al., 2014). Research questions were contributed by the expert panel and ranked on answerability, feasibility, applicability and impact, support within the context, and equity. Research questions were then grouped into priority areas and distinct goals.

The highest priority goals included advancing identification, screening, and early intervention, as well as improving awareness, prevention, and promotive interventions. The authors provided sample research questions to help frame these goals into actionable, responsive approaches to research that reflect the communities served. Sample questions include: "What is the effectiveness and efficiency of family-mediated early intervention on the future health and well-being of children with developmental disabilities in low resource settings?," "What is the availability, cost and efficacy of early intervention and rehabilitation programs for children with developmental disabilities in low and low-middle income countries?" and "What are the most effective ways of promoting the rights to health and education of children with developmental disabilities in low and low-middle income countries?" (Tomlinson et al., 2014, p. 1126). These research questions center on ways to improve the general quality of life, health, and well-being for persons with DD and their families.

Other efforts to engage stakeholders have been demonstrated by researchers in England, which may serve as a model for other researchers who desire to engage in similar work to inform outcome measures. McConachie et al. (2015) engaged ASD stakeholders (i.e., autistic persons, parents, and professionals) to explore beneficial outcomes for children with ASD, identify the best ways to assess these skills and determine key information needed for improved evaluations. Engagement took place across several methods including consultations, surveys, and discussions. The authors compiled all shared information to determine which outcomes to measure and whether agreement would be reached across all stakeholder groups. The findings showed a marked difference between parents and professionals on important outcomes. For example, parents focused on measuring happiness, anxiety, fears, and self-esteem; whereas, professionals focused on peer social interaction, play skills, and attention. The discussions revealed that parents were focused more on the "big picture" as they have a comprehensive view of the child across days, times, and environments. Professionals were often limited by what tools they had available, shaping the evaluation to focus on specific outcomes. In final discussions, an autistic person and parents discussed the need to focus on what a child can do vs what the child cannot do (social model of disability); on the other hand, professionals recognized they were focused on identifying challenges (medical model of disability). These perspectives may be limited in scope as all participants resided in the United Kingdom. No other demographic information was reported on participants. Including input from a variety of stakeholders with diverse lived experiences and who know more about the needs of autistic communities and others with DD is important in determining the meaningful outcomes for children and youth with DD.

2.2 Language of outcome measures

The language of outcome measures is another concern, given the diverse language experiences within and across communities. Many outcomes are often evaluated in only one language (e.g., English), neglecting the breadth of the child's linguistic experience and skills (Liao et al., 2021). This limited evaluation may be due to the limited availability of assessments developed and validated for other languages. A review of speech assessments in languages other than English revealed a total of 30 speech assessments covering 19 languages (McLeod & Verdon, 2014). The authors reported that most assessments were designed for monolingual speakers while only seven assessments were norm-referenced, suggesting that there are limited ways to capture consistent, reliable, and valid outcome measures for many linguistically diverse communities for children and youth with DD. One way to address this issue would be to translate or adapt existing tools for use with other languages and cultures. However, many studies that report on translated or adapted tools do not adequately detail the methods to translate, validate and ensure cultural equivalence in the assessment measures (Maldonado, Chandna, & Gladstone, 2019; Soto et al., 2015). Furthermore, translation methods often rely on forward and back translation, which may be insufficient and prone to errors such as literal translations, complex vocabulary, incorrect grammar, and inappropriate use of idioms (Hawkins, Cheng, Elsworth, & Osborne, 2020; van Widenfelt, Treffers, de Beurs, Siebelink, & Koudijs, 2005). Several efforts have been proposed to ensure that translated or adapted tools are culturally relevant and psychometrically sound (DuBay & Watson, 2019; International Test Commission, 2017; van Widenfelt et al., 2005). One method outlines how to achieve equivalence across language, constructs, and operations by engaging a stepwise adaptation process that includes translations, quality review, consensus, pre-testing, and psychometric testing (DuBay & Watson, 2019). These procedures are important to consider when translating or adapting measures for linguistically diverse communities. Without them, the outcome measures used with children and youth with DD may not accurately capture the changes, growth, or results that researchers and professionals intend to measure.

2.3 Accessibility of outcome measures

Additional considerations are needed to ensure that outcome measures, when identified, are accessible to diverse, global communities. For example, the Autism project team, as part of the International Consortium for Health Outcomes Measurement, developed two tracks in identifying outcomes focused on: (1) outcome measures that could be integrated within health insurance reimbursement models, and (2) outcome measures that were free or low cost and could be used within any healthcare system (International Consortium for Health Outcomes Measurement (ICHOM), 2021). This approach was necessary as many outcome measures and questionnaires have significant fees for training, licensing, administration, use, and scoring. These costs can be burdensome for some and impossible for others given the limited resources often reported in low resource areas within high-income countries and across low- and middle-income countries. Other initiatives have also been underway to identify and increase the accessibility of free and open assessment measures for disabilities. For example, the disabilitymeasures.org website is a centralized repository of assessment measures available to researchers and clinicians. The website contains vetted measurements with direct information on how to access and use the measures. The Mapi Research Trust, a non-profit focused on the distribution of clinical outcome measures is another resource for translated measurement tools. This organization connects authors with language adaptation services to create a translated tool that is conceptually equivalent to the original measure.

Overall, to effectively engage with diverse communities of children and youth with DD, researchers and providers must recognize and act upon these cultural considerations to ensure that outcomes are culturally responsive and relevant to the communities they reflect. We conducted a scoping review to ascertain how outcome measures have been captured within the literature, with a focus on culturally diverse, DD communities.

3. Scoping review of outcome measures in intervention studies

This scoping review examines the state of research on outcome measures used for children and youth with DD from diverse racial/ethnic and linguistic backgrounds. We focused this review on intervention studies that evaluated child-level outcomes for infants, children and youth (ages 0–18) with DD, broadly defined as including the following conditions: ASD, cerebral palsy (CP), DD, DS, Fragile X syndrome, and ID. Although we recognize the value and importance of parent and family-level outcomes (see Hu, Wang, & Fei, 2012; Jansen-van Vuuren et al., 2022; Meral, Cavkaytar, Turnbull, & Wang, 2013), we focused on child-level outcomes due to the limited research on this population. We focused on studies that implemented an intervention or program through a quasi-experimental or randomized controlled design. We highlight research studies that include a majority sample ($\geq$50% of sample) of racially/ethnically or linguistically diverse populations or those that have taken place in underrepresented areas. We have organized this literature review by select developmental domains as outcomes: behavior, cognition and development, health and physical development, language and communication, and social and emotional skills. Although many studies on children and youth with DD focus on reducing symptoms as an outcome, we have taken a strengths-based approach, recognizing that symptoms associated with many DD conditions may represent a developmental difference and not a developmental deficit. Therefore, we do not include a discussion of deficit-oriented measures.

Our review is not exhaustive, but rather includes representative examples from the literature. We searched for "outcome measures," "developmental disability," and "racially/ethnically diverse." We further limited our search to studies that included the age range covering infancy through young adulthood, study designs that focused on experimental or quasi-experimental designs and studies that were published between 2000 and 2022. Authors selected representative articles to capture geographical diversity. Overall, we present 17 studies that have examined 30 outcome measures across 12 countries. We structure the literature review on outcome measures by domains (behavior, cognition and development, health and physical development, language and communication, and social and emotional skills) and we describe whether measures were culturally and linguistically adapted for their respective communities. We then draw attention to the psychometric properties of the outcome measures, when available. An overview of the outcome measures described is shown in Table 1.

3.1 Outcomes measures: Behavior

Overall, eight measures were identified that evaluated behavior, including adaptive behavior, for children and youth (0–18 years) with ASD, ASD + ID,

Table 1 Overview of outcome measures described in scoping literature review of intervention research with culturally diverse populations.

Outcome measure by domain	Study	Countries used	Child conditions	Ages of participants	Psychometric properties	Languages used	Cultural adaptations
Behavior							
Avoidant Behaviors Scale	Siller, Swanson, Gerber, Hutman, and Sigman (2014)	United States	ASD	0–6 years	ICC = 0.89	English	None reported
Behavior Assessment System for Children, 2nd edition	Parladé et al. (2020)	United States	ASD	3–7 years	Validity (α = 0.81–0.96) Test-retest reliability (r = 0.77–0.90)[a]	English	None reported
Behavior Rating Inventory of Executive Functioning	Parladé et al. (2020)	United States	ASD	3–7 years	Internal consistency (α = 0.82–0.98)[a] Test-retest reliability (r = 0.72–0.84)[a]	English	None reported
Child Behavior Checklist	Feitosa, Muzzolon, Rodrigues, de S Crippa, and Zonta (2017)	Brazil	CP	6–18 years	Not reported	Not reported	Validated in Brazil
Developmental Behavioral Checklist	Divan et al. (2019)	India	ASD	2–9 years	Not reported	Not reported	None reported
Eyberg Child Behavior Inventory	Brookman-Frazee, Roesch, Chlebowski, Baker-Ericzen, and Ganger (2019)	United States	ASD	5–13 years	Intraclass correlation coefficient = (0.67–0.69)	Not reported	None reported
	Parladé et al. (2020)	United States	ASD	3–7 years	Validity (α = 0.94)[a] Test-retest reliability (r = 0.75)[a]	English	None reported
Proximity and Contact Seeking Behaviors Scale	Siller et al. (2014)	United States	ASD	0–6 years	ICC = 0.86	English	None reported
Vineland Adaptive Behavior Scales	Bordini et al. (2020)	Brazil	ASD + ID	3–6 years	Not reported	Not reported	None reported
	Divan et al. (2019)	India	ASD	2–9 years	Not reported	Marathi and Hindi	None reported

Continued

Table 1 Overview of outcome measures described in scoping literature review of intervention research with culturally diverse populations.—cont'd

Outcome measure by domain	Study	Countries used	Child conditions	Ages of participants	Psychometric properties	Languages used	Cultural adaptations
	Rahman et al. (2016)	Pakistan & India	ASD	2–9 years	Not reported	Translated into Urdu, Konkani, and Marathi	Culturally adapted but not described
Cognition and Development							
Bayley Scales of Infant and Toddler Development	Russell, van Heerden, van Vuuren, Venter, and Joubert (2016)	South Africa	DS	0–3.5 years	Inter-rater reliability (Kappa = 0.97)	Not reported	None reported
Mullen Scales of Early Learning	Siller, Hutman, and Sigman (2013)	United States	ASD	0–6 years	Not reported	English	None reported
Quality of Play Questionnaire-Parent	Ong et al. (2021)	Malaysia	ASD	7–12 years	Reliability (Conflict, $r=0.75$; Engage, $r=0.70$ Disengage, $r=0.74$)	Not reported	None reported
Snijders-Oomen Nonverbal Intelligence Test 2 ½-7	Bordini et al. (2020)	Brazil	ASD + ID	3–6 years	Not reported	Translated into Brazilian Portuguese	Standardized and validated in Brazilian Portuguese
Study developed measure of literacy skills	Felix, Mena, Ostos, and Maestre (2017)	Mexico	DS	6–15 years	Not reported	Spanish	None reported
Health and Physical Development							
Bruininks-Oseretsky Test of Motor Proficiency	Rahman and Rahman (2010)	Saudi Arabia	DS	10–13 years	Not reported	Not reported	None reported
Gross Motor Function Measure-88	Habib-Hasan, Sheikh, Hoodbhoy, Azam, and O'Neil (2020)	Pakistan	DS	0–5 years	Not reported	Translated in multiple languages	None reported

Hammersmith Infant Neurological Examination	Tann et al. (2021)	Uganda	CP	0.5 years	Not reported	Not reported	Not reported
Instrument for the Evaluation of Results in Pediatrics Rehabilitation	Feitosa et al. (2017)	Brazil	CP	6–18 years	Not reported	Translated to Brazilian Portuguese	None reported
Language and Communication							
Communication and Symbolic Behavior Scales Developmental Profile	Rahman et al. (2016)	Pakistan & India	ASD	2–9 years	Not reported	Translated but not described	Culturally adapted but not described
Communication DEALL Developmental Checklist	Karanth, Shaista, and Srikanth (2010)	India	ASD	2–6 years	Not reported	Not reported	None reported
Dyadic Communication Measure for Autism	Divan et al. (2019)	India	ASD	2–9 years	Inter-rater reliability (Parent acts, $r=0.90$; Child communication initiations, $r=0.93$; Mutual shared attention, $r=0.96$)	Not reported	None reported
	Rahman et al. (2016)	Pakistan & India	ASD	2–9 years	Inter-rater reliability: Parental synchrony, (Pakistan, $r=0.92$; India, $r=0.90$); Child initiations (Pakistan, $r=0.84$; India, $r=0.58$–0.98); Mutual shared attention (Pakistan, $r=0.98$; India, $r=0.98$)	Translated but not described	Culturally adapted selection of toys used for naturalistic play
Early Social-Communication Scale	Chiang, Chu, and Lee (2016)	Taiwan	ASD	2–4 years	Inter-rater reliability (Alternate gaze, $r=0.94$; Pointing, $r=0.81$)	Not reported	None reported
MacArthur Communicative Development Inventory	Rahman et al. (2016)	Pakistan & India	ASD	2–9 years	Not reported	Translated but not described	Culturally adapted but not described

Continued

Table 1 Overview of outcome measures described in scoping literature review of intervention research with culturally diverse populations.—cont'd

Outcome measure by domain	Study	Countries used	Child conditions	Ages of participants	Psychometric properties	Languages used	Cultural adaptations
Social and Emotional Skills							
Contextual Assessment of Social Skills	Rabin, Israel-Yaacov, Laugeson, Mor-Snir, and Golan (2018)	Israel	ASD	12–17 years	Internal consistency ($\alpha = 0.84$) Inter-rater agreement ($r = 0.86$)	Not reported	None reported
Empathy Quotient	Rabin et al. (2018)	Israel	ASD	12–17 years	Internal consistency ($\alpha = 0.82$)	Not reported	None reported
Loneliness and Social Dissatisfaction Questionnaire	Rabin et al. (2018)	Israel	ASD	12–17 years	Internal consistency ($\alpha = 0.80$)	Not reported	None reported
Parent-child Interaction	Chiang et al. (2016)	Taiwan	ASD	2–4 years	Inter-rater reliability (Unengaged/Other engagement, $r = 0.98$; Object engagement, $r = 0.94$; Child-initiated supported joint engagement, $r = 0.86$; Parent-initiated joint engagement, $r = 0.88$; child-initiated coordinated joint engagement, $r = 0.85$; Parent-initiated coordinated joint engagement, $r = 0.92$)	Not reported	None reported
Quality of Socialization Questionnaire	Rabin et al. (2018)	Israel	ASD	12–17 years	Internal consistency (Parent $\alpha = 0.79$; Adolescent $\alpha = 0.72$)	Not reported	None reported
Social Responsiveness Scale-2	Rabin et al. (2018)	Israel	ASD	12–17 years	Not reported	Not reported	Not reported
Social Skills Improvement System	Ong et al. (2021)	Malaysia	ASD	7–12 years	Reliability ($r = 0.88$)	Not reported	None reported
	Rabin et al. (2018)	Israel	ASD	12–17 years	Internal consistency (Parents $\alpha = 0.86$, Teachers $\alpha = 0.91$)	Not reported	None reported
Test of Adolescent Social Skills Knowledge	Rabin et al. (2018)	Israel	ASD	12–17 years	Not reported	Not reported	None reported

[a]Psychometric properties reported are for the original measure and not for the study sample.
Notes: The table is organized alphabetically by domain and then alphabetically by outcome measure; ASD = Autism spectrum disorder, CP = Cerebral palsy, DD = Developmental delay/disability, DS = Down syndrome, ID = Intellectual disability.

and CP across seven studies. These studies encompassed four countries (Brazil, India, Pakistan, United States) and evaluated 493 children and youth. The eight measures included the Avoidant Behaviors Scale (Ainsworth, Blehar, Waters, & Wall, 1978), Behavior Assessment System for Children, 2nd edition (BASC-2; Reynolds & Kamphaus, 2004), Behavior Rating Inventory of Executive Function (BRIEF; Gioia, Isquith, Guy, & Kenworthy, 2000; Gioia, Espy, & Isquith, 2002), Child Behavior Checklist (CBCL; Achenbach & Rescorla, 2001), Developmental Behavioral Checklist (DBC; Witwer & Lecavalier, 2007), Eyberg Child Behavior Inventory (ECBI: Eyberg & Pinctus, 1999), Proximity and Contact Seeking Behaviors Scale (Ainsworth, 1977), and the Vineland Adaptive Behavior Scales (VABS; Sparrow, Balla, & Cicchetti, 1984; Sparrow, Cicchetti, & Balla, 2008; Sparrow, Cicchetti, & Saulnier, 2016).

3.1.1 Cultural and linguistic adaptation

The Avoidant Behaviors Scale and the Proximity and Contact Seeking Behaviors Scale (Ainsworth et al., 1978) were used in the United States with racially/ethnically diverse children with ASD between 0 and 6 years of age (Siller et al., 2014) to measure attachment-related outcomes through a brief separation-reunion scenario. Although the sample included a diverse racial/ethnic composition (Latino = 47.2%; White = 22.2%; Asian = 11.1%; Black = 8.3%), the study was only administered in English and excluded non-English speaking participants. Furthermore, no information was provided on cultural or linguistic adaptations for either measure. Despite relying on observational coding, no information was provided on whether the coders were from the same racial/ethnic background as the parent-child dyad, which may impact how specific behaviors were interpreted and coded.

The BASC-2 (Reynolds & Kamphaus, 2004) and the BRIEF (Gioia et al., 2000, 2002) were both used in one study in the United States with children with ASD and children with disruptive behavior who were between 3 and 7 years of age (Parladé et al., 2020). The sample included primarily Latino children (68.75%); however, all study procedures were completed in English. Whether the BASC-2 or the BRIEF were adapted or validated for racially/ethnically diverse populations or whether any cultural or linguistic adaptations were made for this study was not reported (Parladé et al., 2020).

The CBCL was used in Brazil with children and youth with CP who were between 6 and 18 years of age. Feitosa et al. (2017) mentioned that the CBCL had been validated in Brazil but did not describe the validation process of the CBCL and whether it included cultural and linguistic adaptation. The authors referred to the manual indicating that the CBCL had been used in over 80 countries. We assume the CBCL had undergone translation of some kind for use in Brazil, but this information was not available in the study. The DBC was used in India with children with ASD who were between 2 and 9 years of age (Divan et al., 2019). The study delivered the intervention in Marathi or Hindu, based on family preferences; however, no explicit mention was made of the languages used in delivering the DBC or if any items had been culturally or linguistically adapted for the sample.

The ECBI was used across two studies in the United States that targeted children with ASD who were between 3 and 13 years of age (Brookman-Frazee et al., 2019; Parladé et al., 2020). Both studies included a predominantly Latino sample (59.90% and 68.75%, respectively). Brookman-Frazee et al. (2019) reported that children were eligible to participate if they spoke English or Spanish, yet the authors did not report whether the outcome assessments were administered or available in Spanish, whether the measure was validated for Spanish-speaking populations, or if any adaptations were made to the outcome measure for this study. Parladé et al. (2020) only included children whose parents opted for receiving services in English, thus, it is assumed that the ECBI was administered in English. No other information was provided by the study authors on any cultural or linguistic adaptations.

The VABS was used in three separate studies conducted in Brazil, India, and Pakistan and focused on children with ASD between 2 and 9 years of age for two studies (Divan et al., 2019; Rahman et al., 2016) and children with ASD + ID in one study (Bordini et al., 2020). For the study in Brazil, the authors reported using the first edition of the VABS (Sparrow et al., 1984); however, no additional information about the language and cultural adaptations were provided (Bordini et al., 2020). It is assumed that the VABS was administered in Brazilian Portuguese. However, the language was not directly stated by the authors (Bordini et al., 2020). Rahman et al. (2016) did not report which version of the VABS they used with their sample in Pakistan and India. The authors shared that the intervention was delivered in Urdu, English, Konkani, Marathi and that all questionnaires were translated into these preferred languages (Divan et al., 2015) following established methods (Bhui, Mohamud, Warfa, Craig, & Stansfeld, 2003). The Bhui et al. (2003) paper provided a commentary on common issues in the cultural adaptation of measures used with adolescents and adults from South Asian,

African, and Caribbean origins. They highlighted several recommendations, such as the need for conceptual adaptations, considerations for the idioms used to describe conditions and symptoms, and recognition that translations, including forward-back translations and expert committee reviews, take extensive time and effort. We followed up with the Divan et al. (2015) article, to ascertain the adaptation process. This study, however, only reported on the cultural adaptation process for the PASS intervention, which involved qualitative studies, expert-led modifications of the manual, adaptation workshops with local and national experts, and pilot cases led by regional specialists in child development. No details were included about the translation or linguistic adaptation process for the VABS. Finally, Divan et al. (2019) reported that they used the second edition of the VABS (Sparrow, Cicchetti, & Balla, 2005) and that all materials were translated into Marathi, while the intervention was delivered in Marathi or Hindi; however, no information was included on the linguistic translations or adaptations. Overall, behavioral outcome measures were administered to highly diverse samples across the world; however, most studies did not elaborate on the cultural or linguistic adaptation of these measures or on the cultural match between participants and research staff.

3.1.2 Psychometric properties

Siller et al. (2014) reported excellent intraclass correlation coefficients for the Avoidant Behaviors Scale (ICC $=0.89$) and for the Proximity and Contact Seeking Behaviors Scale (ICC $=0.86$) across coders. No information was available about other psychometric properties for these two measures. The BASC-2 was reported to have good validity ($\alpha=0.81$–0.96) and reliability (test-retest, $r=0.77$–0.90) based on a past study (Reynolds & Kamphaus, 2004). This past study reported that the norm samples matched the race/ethnicity population estimates from the 2001 U.S. census. No information was provided on the validity or reliability for the current study (Parladé et al., 2020). Psychometric properties for the BRIEF were reported (Parladé et al., 2020) as reflecting good internal consistency ($\alpha=0.82$–0.98) and test-retest reliability ($r=0.72$–0.84) based on the measure developers (Gioia et al., 2002). No psychometric properties were reported for the CBCL used in Brazil with children with CP (Feitosa et al., 2017). No psychometric properties were reported for the DBC used by Divan et al. (2019) in their study of children with ASD. Brookman-Frazee et al. (2019) reported significant variability for the ECBI (Intraclass correlation coefficient $=0.67$–0.69) at the child/therapist level, but variability was minimal at the program level. Parladé et al. reported that the reliability (test-retest, $r=0.75$) and validity ($\alpha=0.94$) of the ECBI were acceptable for racially/ethnically diverse populations based on a past study (Gross et al., 2007), but did not report for their study (Parladé et al., 2020). Gross et al. (2007) recruited a racially/ethnically diverse sample (African American = 28.7%; Latino = 46.8%; and non-Latino White = 24.5%) of parents of young children (2- to 4-year-olds) to establish the reliability and validity of the ECBI. Gross et al. included a Spanish translation of the ECBI, which was developed using translation and back-translation by the publisher and approved by the instrument author. Overall, Gross et al. reported good internal consistency ($\alpha=0.86$–0.95) for the entire sample, with no differences found between language of the questionnaire. However, further examination revealed differences across racial/ethnic groups and socioeconomic groups. African American children were rated lower on the Intensity Scale compared to Latino and White children. Furthermore, Latino children and children in the low-income group were more likely to have clinical level scores on the Problem Scale, a finding that was more pronounced among children whose parents completed the Spanish-language questionnaire (Gross et al., 2007). Information about the psychometric properties of the VABS were not reported in the studies included in our scoping literature review (Bordini et al., 2020; Divan et al., 2019; Rahman et al., 2016). Overall, psychometric properties were reported for most behavioral outcome measures, with some discussion by the study authors on the use of their outcome measure with diverse samples. However, most psychometric properties reported were from the original validation study and did not reflect the populations in which the measure was being used.

3.2 Outcomes measures: Cognition and development

For cognition and development, five measures were included as outcomes for infants, children and youth (0–15 years) with ASD, DS, and ASD + ID. These measures included the Bayley Scales of Infant and Toddler Development (Bayley, 2006), Mullen Scales of Early Learning (Mullen, 1995), Quality of Play Questionnaire—Parent (Frankel & Mintz, 2008), Snijders-Oomen Nonverbal Intelligence Test 2 ½-7 (SON 2 ½-7; Laros, Reis, & Tellegen, 2010), and a study developed measure of literacy skills (Felix et al., 2017). These studies were conducted across five countries: Brazil, Malaysia, Mexico, South Africa, and the United States. A total of 195 children and youth were evaluated on these measures.

3.2.1 Cultural and linguistic adaptation

The Bayley Scales of Infant and Toddler Development was used in South Africa with infants and children with DS between 0 and 3.5 years of age (Russell et al., 2016). The authors reported that the overall study included a range of languages (English, Afrikaans, Sesotho, Xhosa and isiZulu); however, no information was provided on how the Bayley Scales were linguistically adapted or translated for use with these languages. No other information was provided on cultural adaptations. The Mullen Scales of Early Learning Expressive Language subscale was used in one study in the United States with children with ASD who were between 0 and 6 years of age. The sample included a diverse sample of children from Latino (47.2%), White (22.2%), Asian (11.1%), Black (8.3%), and mixed racial/ethnic (11.1%) backgrounds. Although the study only included English-speaking families, no details were included whether any linguistic or cultural adaptations were made to the outcome measure. The Quality of Play Questionnaire – Parent was used in Malaysia with children with ASD who were between 7 and 12 years of age (Ong et al., 2021). The sample included children whose parents reflected a range of racial/ethnic groups (Malay, Chinese, Indian). However, no information was included in the study on any cultural or linguistic adaptations or even which language was used for the administration of the questionnaire or intervention. The SON 2 ½-7 was used in Brazil with children with ASD + ID who were between 3 and 6 years of age (Bordini et al., 2020). The authors cited two studies that standardized and validated the SON 2 ½-7 in Brazilian Portuguese (Karino, Laros, & De Jesus, 2011; Laros et al., 2010). Laros et al. (2010) reported on Brazilian test standards that were stratified by sex, age, educational status, and demographic variables. The author reported that because the SON 2 ½-7 was a nonverbal IQ measure, no translations were needed. No cultural or linguistic adaptations for the SON 2 ½-7 were reported by Karino et al. (2011). The measure of literacy skills was specifically created for Mexican children with DS who were between 6 and 15 years of age (Felix et al., 2017). The measure was administered in Spanish. As this measure was not imported from another geographical region or linguistic community, no cultural or linguistic adaptations were implemented. These studies demonstrate that outcome measures for cognition and development need to be adapted to reflect the cultural norms, include available and culturally relevant toys, and establish culturally relevant testing norms.

3.2.2 Psychometric properties

Inter-rater reliability (Kappa = 0.97) was reported for the Bayley Scales of Infant and Toddler Development based on the scores derived by the test administrator and the test observer (Russell et al., 2016). No other psychometric properties were reported for the Bayley Scales. No psychometric properties were reported the Mullen Scales of Early Learning by the study authors (Siller et al., 2013). Ong et al. (2021) reported reliability coefficients for the Quality of Play Questionnaire – Parent for the three subscales: Conflict, $r = 0.75$; Engage, $r = 0.70$, and Disengage, $r = 0.74$. No other psychometric properties were reported for the outcome measure. The SON 2 ½-7 did not have any psychometric properties reported by the study authors (Bordini et al., 2020). However, the authors cited other studies which presented psychometric properties on the Brazilian adaptation. Laros et al. (2010) reported that the SON 2 ½-7 had positive convergent validity with the Raven's Colored Progressive Matrices ($r = 0.77$) and the Columbia Mental Maturity Scale ($r = 0.62$). Reliability coefficients for the SON 2 ½-7 were also high, $r = 0.91$ for the full scale. The authors did report that they obtained a limited range of nonverbal IQ scores, as their sample did not reflect the entire spectrum of cognitive abilities. Karino et al. (2011) conducted another validation study with Brazilian children between the SON 2 ½-7 and the Wechsler Preschool and Primary Scale of Intelligence-III (WPPSI-III) and the Wechsler Intelligence Scale for Children-III (WISC-III). Moderate correlations between the SON 2 ½-7 total scores and the WPPSI-III total score ($r = 0.75$) and the WISC-III ($r = 0.69$; Karino et al., 2011). The authors of both studies reported that the SON 2 ½-7 had adequate psychometric properties for use in Brazil as no other standardized measure existed. For the study developed measure of literacy skills, the authors did not describe its development, reliability, or validity (Felix et al., 2017). Handwriting quality was evaluated through subjective judgment made by a therapist. Yet, no information was shared whether the therapist was blinded to the child's condition (intervention, control), or if multiple therapists were involved, and whether there was interrater reliability between therapists. Limited psychometric properties were reported for outcome measures used to capture cognition and development, even though authors included well-established standardized assessment tools. More validation studies, as those described for the SON 2 ½-7, are needed to ensure that these outcome measures are valid and reliable for use with populations that were not reflected in the original validation studies.

3.3 Outcomes measures: Health and physical development

Overall, four outcome measures were identified to measure health and physical development among infants, children, and youth (0–18 years) with CP and DS. These studies were conducted across four countries (Brazil, Pakistan, Saudi Arabia, and Uganda). The outcome measures included the Bruininks-Oseretsky Test of Motor Proficiency (BOTMP; Bruininks & Bruininks, 2005), Gross Motor Function Measure-88 (GMFM-88; Russell et al., 1998), Hammersmith Infant Neurological Examination (HINE; Haataja et al., 1999), and the Instrument for the Evaluation of Results in Pediatrics Rehabilitation (IERPR; de Assis, Forlin, Bruck, Antoniuk, & dos Santos, 2008). These outcome measures captured outcomes for 130 infants, children, and youth between 0 and 18 years of age.

3.3.1 Cultural and linguistic adaptation

The BOTMP was used in Saudi Arabia to evaluate infants and children with DS who were between 0 and 5 years of age (Rahman & Rahman, 2010). No other information was provided on cultural or linguistic adaptations that were made for the study. The GMFM-88 was used to measure outcomes for Pakistani children with DS who were between 0 and 5 years of age (Habib-Hasan et al., 2020). The authors remarked that the GMFM-88 allowed for parent input when children were unable to demonstrate specific tasks. The authors further described that the GMFM-88 had been translated into multiple languages and that it was considered an international gold standard. However, no other information was provided on whether any cultural or linguistic adaptations were made to this measure, or whether the instructions had been translated for use with Pakistani children. The HINE was used with infants who were 6 months old with CP in Uganda (Tann et al., 2021). The HINE was reported as a supported assessment tool for infants with CP based on a review (Novak et al., 2017); however, no other information was shared on the cultural or linguistic adaptation of the HINE and its validity with Ugandan infants. The IERPR was used in Brazil with children with CP between 6 and 18 years of age (Feitosa et al., 2017). The authors reported that the measure was initially adapted from the Pediatric Outcomes Data Collection Instrument, a measure developed by the Pediatric Orthopaedic Society of North America. The IERPR was translated into Portuguese following a forward-back translation process completed by a native speaker. The translated version of the measure was then evaluated by an expert judge (de Assis et al., 2008) and standard scores followed the original version (Haynes & Sullivan, 2001). No other information was reported on cultural adaptations to the measure or to the standard norms used for scores. Overall, outcome measures that evaluated health and physical development were all reported to be used in regions outside of the original validation or development of the measures; yet no information was described by the authors on how they adapted the outcome measure for the culture and language of their sample. More information outlining the translation and modification of items is needed to ensure the cultural relevance of outcomes measured.

3.3.2 Psychometric properties

The BOTMP had acceptable construct validity based on a past study (Miles, Nierengarten, & Nearing, 1988; Rahman & Rahman, 2010). However, Miles et al. (1988) only reported on the existing psychometric data available in the manuals of common measures of physical ability. These authors did report that the BOTMP had satisfactory test-retest reliability ($r = 0.60$–0.89) and was validated with 800 children without any conditions stratified against the 1970 census data. No other information was reported on the psychometric properties or whether more recent validation samples were available. No psychometric properties were reported for the GMFM-88 were reported by the study authors (Habib-Hasan et al., 2020). Although the authors of the reviewed study (Tann et al., 2021) did not include psychometric properties of the HINE in their report, the authors referenced a review that provided this information (Novak et al., 2017). This review showed that the HINE had high sensitivity for detecting CP before (90% sensitivity) and after (90% sensitivity) 5 months of age. The authors further recommended the HINE for use in low- and middle-income countries, especially when MRIs were not readily available. No other psychometric data was available. No psychometric properties were reported for the IERPR by the reviewed study (Feitosa et al., 2017); however, the authors referenced a validation study (de Assis et al., 2008), however, this study did not report on any psychometric properties of the adapted IERPR, but rather reported on changes in scores after children and youth (1–17 years) received botulinum toxin injections (de Assis et al., 2008). Overall, the psychometric properties reported for health and physical development did not reflect adequate, recent validations for the populations they were used. Although the authors provided justification for using the outcome measure, the referenced articles did not provide the needed information (e.g., validity with other measures, inter-rater reliability, test-retest reliability).

3.4 Outcomes measures: Language and communication

Language and communication outcomes were measured using five measures in children (2–9 years) with ASD across three countries (India, Pakistan, and Taiwan), and included a total of 169 children published in four studies. The outcomes were measured with the following tools: Communication and Symbolic Behavior Scales Developmental Profile (CSBS-DP; Wetherby & Prizant, 2003), Communication DEALL Developmental Checklist (Karanth, 2007), Dyadic Communication Measure for Autism (DCMA; Aldred, Green, Emsley, & McConachie, 2012), Early Social-Communication Scale (ESCS; Mundy et al., 2003), and MacArthur Communicative Development Inventory (Fenson, Marchman, Thal, Reznick, & Bates, 2007).

3.4.1 Cultural and linguistic adaptation

The CSBS-DP and the MacArthur Communicative Development Inventory were used in a study that took place across Pakistan and India with children with ASD who were between 2 and 9 years of age (Rahman et al., 2016). The authors shared that the intervention was delivered in Urdu, English, Konkani, Marathi and that all questionnaires were translated into these preferred languages (Divan et al., 2015) following established methods (Bhui et al., 2003). Following up with Bhui et al. (2003), we observed a discussion on common issues with the cultural adaptation processes and recommendations for conceptual adaptations, translations that incorporated forward and back translations, and expert committee review. The Divan et al. (2015) study did not include any relevant details regarding the linguistic or cultural adaptation of the measures. The Communication DEALL Developmental Checklist was used in India with children with ASD who were between 2 and 6 years of age (Karanth et al., 2010). This measure was specifically created for children who were participating in the intervention program, Communication DEALL. The measure was developed from data of 360 children who ranged from 0 to 6 years of age. As the measure was created locally, the authors did not report any cultural or linguistic adaptations made to the measure. The DCMA was implemented in India and Pakistan by two separate studies that evaluated children with ASD who were between 2 and 9 years of age

(Divan et al., 2019; Rahman et al., 2016). Rahman et al. (2016) reported that a set of age-appropriate toys used for the DCMA were culturally adapted (e.g., stainless steel kitchen utensils in place of stacking toys). Divan et al. (2019) reported in their study that the DCMA had strong feasibility for use in Asian communities based on prior studies (Green et al., 2010; Rahman et al., 2016). Rahman et al. (2016) provided limited information on the cultural adaptations (see above) but did not report on linguistic adaptations. Green et al. (2010) evaluated the DCMA with primarily White children (57.24%) with ASD in the UK who resided in households where English was spoken. The ESCS was administered in Taiwan to children with ASD who were between 2 and 4 years of age (Chiang et al., 2016). The authors did not report any cultural or linguistic adaptations made to the measure for their sample in Taiwan. Overall, some adaptations were reported for language and communication outcome measures used across India and Pakistan; however, there were unclear connections made with adaptation recommendations and whether these were used to adapt the outcome measures used. Given that outcome measures were administered in different languages, it is vital that authors describe how the measures were adapted, or the very least, translated for use with their population.

3.4.2 Psychometric properties

No psychometric details were shared about the CSBS-DP in its use with Indian and Pakistani children with ASD (Rahman et al., 2016). No psychometric properties were reported for the Communication DEALL Developmental Checklist when used with Indian children with ASD who were between 2 and 6 years of age. The DCMA was reported to have excellent inter-rater reliability for parental synchrony (Pakistan, $r=0.92$; India, $r=0.90$), child initiations (Pakistan, $r=0.84$; India, $r=0.58$, increased to 0.98), and mutual shared attention (Pakistan, $r=0.98$; India, $r=0.98$) for one study conducted in Pakistan and India (Rahman et al., 2016). These psychometric properties were cited by another study as support for use in their own study and indicated that the DCMA was sensitive to treatment change (Divan et al., 2019). This latter study also reported excellent inter-rater reliability, Parent acts, $r=0.90$; Child communication initiations, $r=0.93$; Mutual shared attention, $r=0.96$ (Divan et al., 2019). Psychometric properties for the ESCS were reported by the study authors (Chiang et al., 2016). The authors reported inter-rater reliabilities for two behavioral measures from the ESCS (Alternate gaze, $r=0.94$; Pointing, $r=0.81$). No psychometric details were shared about the MacArthur

Communicative Development Inventory in its use with Indian and Pakistani children with ASD (Rahman et al., 2016). Overall, some psychometric properties were shared for some language and communication outcome measures that reflected the racial/ethnic and linguistic diversity of the study samples. However, some studies did not include or reference any psychometric properties for the language and communication outcome measures, even when using a standardized tool (e.g., MacArthur Communicative Development Inventory).

3.5 Outcomes measures: Social and emotional skills

Outcomes across the social and emotional domains were captured by eight distinct tools that were used with children and youth (2–17 years) with ASD across three studies. These studies took place across three countries (Israel, Malaysia, and Taiwan) and included a total of 105 children and youth. The eight tools included: Contextual Assessment of Social Skills (Ratto, Turner-Brown, Rupp, Mesibov, & Penn, 2011), Empathy Quotient (Baron-Cohen & Wheelwright, 2004), Loneliness and Social Dissatisfaction Questionnaire (Asher, Hymel, & Renshaw, 1984), Parent-child Interaction (Kasari, Gulsrud, Wong, Kwon, & Locke, 2010), Quality of Socialization Questionnaire (Laugeson, Frankel, Mogil, & Dillon, 2009), Social Responsiveness Scale-2 (Constantino & Gruber, 2012), Social Skills Improvement System (SSIS; Gresham & Elliott, 2008), and the Test of Adolescent Social Skills Knowledge (Laugeson & Frankel, 2010).

3.5.1 Cultural and linguistic adaptation

The Contextual Assessment of Social Skills, Empathy Quotient, Loneliness and Social Dissatisfaction Questionnaire, Quality of Socialization Questionnaire, Social Responsiveness Scale-2, and the Test of Adolescent Social Skills Knowledge were all used in Israel to evaluate youth with ASD between 12 and 17 years of age (Rabin et al., 2018). Although the authors shared that the intervention, PEERS, had been culturally and linguistically adapted through an iterative process (e.g., adaptations with original publishers, feedback from stakeholders), the authors did not report whether any of these measures were culturally or linguistically adapted for their sample. Furthermore, the authors described that the intervention was implemented in Hebrew. However, the authors did not explicitly mention whether the measures were also administered in Hebrew, although it is assumed. The Parent-child Interaction measure was administered in

Taiwan to children with ASD who were between 2 and 4 years of age. The authors described that the Parent-child Interaction procedures followed those outlined by Kasari et al. (2010) where parents were instructed to play with a standard set of toys (e.g., dolls, puzzles, blocks). However, there was no discussion by the authors regarding any cultural or linguistic adaptations made to the procedures. Although the translation of instructions to play may be simple, the nature of how play is described can be quite varied across cultural groups (Haight, Wang, Fung, Williams, & Mintz, 1999). The SSIS was used by researchers in Malaysia (Ong et al., 2021) and Israel (Rabin et al., 2018) to evaluate children and youth with ASD (7–17 years of age). Despite the diverse contexts, this measure was used in, neither author included details about the cultural or linguistic adaptation of the measure. Overall, some discussion was included by the authors on the cultural adaptations used for the interventions; however, this discussion was not applied to outcome measures included as part of the studies. Studies should include detailed information about cultural and linguistic adaptations, especially when conducted in a setting that differs from the original validation study of the outcome measures.

3.5.2 Psychometric properties

Rabin et al. (2018) reported on the psychometric properties of their outcome measures. The Contextual Assessment of Social Skills, an observational measure of conversational skills, had an average inter-rater agreement ($r = 0.86$) and adequate internal consistency ($\alpha = 0.84$) for the current study at baseline. The Empathy Quotient was reported as having adequate internal consistency for Israeli youth with ASD ($\alpha = 0.82$; Rabin et al., 2018). The Loneliness and Social Dissatisfaction Questionnaire had adequate internal consistency ($\alpha = 0.80$) for their sample of Israeli youth with ASD. The Quality of Socialization Questionnaire was reported to have adequate internal consistency for the parent version ($\alpha = 0.79$) and the adolescent version ($\alpha = 0.72$). The Social Responsiveness Scale-2 had excellent internal consistency for parents ($\alpha = 0.94$) and teachers ($\alpha = 0.92$). No psychometric information was provided regarding the Test of Adolescent Social Skills Knowledge. No other psychometric properties were reported (Rabin et al., 2018). The Parent-child Interaction was coded by two separate raters. Chiang et al. (2016) reported psychometric properties for the parent-child interaction coding (Unengaged/Other engagement, $r = 0.98$; Object engagement, $r = 0.94$; Child-initiated supported joint engagement, $r = 0.86$; Parent-initiated joint engagement, $r = 0.88$; child-initiated coordinated joint engagement, $r = 0.85$; Parent-initiated coordinated joint engagement, $r = 0.92$). The SSIS was used in two studies across two regions: Israel and Malaysia. Ong et al. (2021) indicated that the scale reliability coefficients were adequate for the parent form ($\alpha = 0.88$) in their study of Malaysian children with ASD. Rabin et al. (2018) reported similar psychometric properties for their use of the measure in Israel for parent report ($\alpha = 0.86$) and the teacher report ($\alpha = 0.91$). Overall, psychometric properties were more consistently reported for social and emotional skills outcomes across the reviewed studies, including separate properties by reporters and raters from their respective samples. Additional data on the validity of outcome measures should be reported for the specific cultural and linguistic groups.

4. Discussion

To date, numerous reviews have been published describing the complexities that arise when evaluating outcomes for children and youth with DD (Howell, Bradshaw, & Langdon, 2021; Imms et al., 2016; Steinhausen, Mohr Jensen, & Lauritsen, 2016; Stolte, Hodgetts, & Smith, 2016; Thurm, Kelleher, & Wheeler, 2020). However, much of this research has not evaluated whether outcomes for children and youth with DD are culturally responsive or relevant. This chapter highlighted several critical issues for culturally responsive measurement of outcomes, namely, defining and measuring meaningful outcomes, addressing language issues, and ensuring accessibility of outcome measures. Our literature review revealed a broad range of outcome measures used globally with children and youth who have DD. However, many studies included proximal outcomes or outcomes directly targeted by the intervention or program. It is not clear from the studies described whether these proximal outcomes were meaningful for the child and family. Fewer studies examined distal outcomes or outcomes across more extended periods of time. The limited types of outcomes included may reflect differences between studies that focused solely on the research vs evaluating interventions or programs within community settings. For example, McConachie et al. (2015) found in their systematic review of ASD outcome measures that researchers primarily concentrated on the goals of the intervention, the external validity of the tool, and the measurement properties. In contrast, providers and educators focused on face validity and test-retest reliability.

We reported on 17 studies that used 30 different outcome measures with children and youth with DD across racially/ethnically and linguistically diverse backgrounds. We found that the most consistent psychometric properties reported for outcome measures were internal consistency and inter-rater reliability, primarily for measures that focused on behavioral coding. These psychometric properties were reported for 16 outcome measures. Only five studies mentioned using outcome tools in other languages, although some we had to infer based on the information provided (Bordini et al., 2020; Divan et al., 2019; Feitosa et al., 2017; Habib-Hasan et al., 2020; Rahman et al., 2016). Details on the linguistic adaptations and translations were limited. Only three studies (Bordini et al., 2020; Feitosa et al., 2017; Rahman et al., 2016) reported that the outcome measures were culturally adapted, a finding consistent with systematic reviews on outcome measures that neglect to comment on the utility of these outcome measures for racially/ethnically and linguistically diverse children and youth with DD (Askari et al., 2015; Schaaf, Carroll, Waskie, Dumont, & Ridgway, 2021). Schaaf et al. (2021) evaluated performance-based outcome measures that captured daily living skills and socialization among children with ASD and identified measures that met quality indicators. These included the availability of subscales and total scores, ability to detect change or group differences, feasibility in terms of administration time, and use of standardized norms for the specified age range. The authors identified two outcome measures that met their criteria (Assessment of Motor and Process Skills and the Evaluation of Social Interact—2nd edition); however, these measures may not capture the daily living skills and socialization of children and youth with DD from diverse cultural and linguistic backgrounds. For example, Ratto et al. (2016) found that Black youth with ASD had greater daily living skills when compared to White youth with ASD based on parent report. Other studies have also identified cross-cultural differences in parent-reported socialization behaviors (e.g., participating in social games, using social gestures, recognizing emotions) which may impact whether measuring socialization skills within one context would be comparable to a distinct cultural context (Matson et al., 2017).

Although not discussed in this scoping review, we recognize that adaptations may not always happen locally, but rather on a global scale. For example, assessment measures may be created in one country (e.g., Spain) and then exported to another country with a similar language profile (e.g., Mexico). This process may also be appealing for researchers and providers who work with immigrant communities. Although these methods can increase the availability and accessibility of outcome measures, caution is necessary. Even though the language foundations may be similar, local and regional dialects may shift the terminology used when describing certain conditions. This can also impact the use of metaphors or other abstract language in the measures. Furthermore, Bhui et al. (2003) called attention to acculturation as a potential issue when using measures developed in one country or region and then exported to another region.

The paucity of research on outcomes for children and youth with DD from diverse racial/ethnic and linguistic backgrounds is not a new issue or even an isolated issue in DD research. Most research is not culturally responsive, even among language interventions for typically developing children (Larson et al., 2020). Therefore, language intervention research may not reflect outcomes or support evidence-based practices for children and youth from diverse racial/ethnic and linguistic backgrounds. Several efforts are underway to increase the accessibility of linguistically appropriate and meaningful outcome measures for use with DD (e.g., Malawi Developmental Assessment Tool, Gladstone et al., 2010). It is essential that, at a minimum, researchers recognize and acknowledge the limitations of findings when they do not include measures that have considered diverse perspectives. Best practices suggest that careful consideration should be taken by researchers in selecting measures, translating them, and culturally adapting them. These best practices begin with researchers reporting information about the demographic characteristics of their samples, the languages included in the procedures, and any cultural adaptations made, even if minor when publishing their work. Transparency of this information is critical to ensure that engage in culturally responsive research.

4.1 Implications for future research

In this paper, we reviewed a sampling of research studies that have examined outcomes for children and youth with DD from racially/ethnically and linguistically diverse communities. Future research should include a systematic review of child outcomes that have been used with these communities and the status of each outcome on language translation, cultural adaptations, and psychometric properties. A systematic review would provide the field with a listing of measures researchers may consider and what cultural considerations have been made. One of the reasons that measures have not been assessed for cultural equivalence and then culturally adapted is that it involves a separate research project for each measure examined and corresponding funding to conduct the study. Large sample sizes are needed to examine psychometric properties adequately. Incentives for researchers to do this work are minimal; it is more expedient and encouraged to utilize existing measures that have been established. Albeit, they have been primarily established on White or European populations. Additionally, the field needs more diverse researchers who have expertise in these communities and these kinds of adaptations and who may be more likely to focus on these critical issues. Additional support for researchers is needed to truly create a more inclusive and culturally and linguistically responsive array of research tools.

5. Conclusions

In this paper, we reviewed intervention studies conducted with culturally and linguistically diverse populations and reported on the outcome measures they used to assess progress. We only focused on strengths-based rather than deficit-focused outcomes. We found that the vast majority of studies utilized existing outcome measures that were developed and established in the United States or Europe. Some studies included diverse populations but were conducted entirely in English. Studies conducted with participants who spoke different languages (other than English) or in other countries did not, for the most part, report on how outcome measures were translated. Only three studies reported using a culturally adapted outcome measure. Few studies reported psychometric properties of the outcome measures used with diverse populations, even when the original development of the measures was primarily from English-speaking countries. Future research should identify important outcomes for diverse populations and ensure that measures for these outcomes are culturally and linguistically sound.

References

Abbeduto, L., Berry-Kravis, E., Sterling, A., Sherman, S., Edgin, J. O., McDuffie, A., et al. (2020). Expressive language sampling as a source of outcome measures for treatment studies in fragile X syndrome: Feasibility, practice effects, test-retest reliability, and construct validity. *Journal of Neurodevelopmental Disorders*, *12*(1), 10. https://doi.org/10.1186/s11689-020-09313-6.

Achenbach, T. M., & Rescorla, L. A. (2001). Manual for ASEBA school-age forms & profiles. In *Families* Research Center for Children, Youth, and Families.

Ainsworth, M. (1977). Attachment theory and its utility in cross-cultural research BT—Culture and infancy. In P. H. Leiderman, S. R. Tulkin, & A. Rosenfield (Eds.), *Variations in the human experience* Academic Press.

Ainsworth, M., Blehar, M. C., Waters, E., & Wall, S. (1978). Patterns of attachment: A psychological study of the strange situation. In *Patterns of attachment: A psychological study of the strange situation* Lawrence Erlbaum.

Aldred, C., Green, J., Emsley, R., & McConachie, H. (2012). Brief report: Mediation of treatment effect in a communication intervention for pre-school children with autism. *Journal of Autism and Developmental Disorders*, *42*(3), 447–454. https://doi.org/10.1007/s10803-011-1248-3.

Asher, S. R., Hymel, S., & Renshaw, P. D. (1984). Loneliness in children. *Child Development*, *55*(4), 1456–1464. https://doi.org/10.2307/1130015.

Askari, S., Anaby, D., Bergthorson, M., Majnemer, A., Elsabbagh, M., & Zwaigenbaum, L. (2015). Participation of children and youth with autism spectrum disorder: A scoping review. *Review Journal of Autism and Developmental Disorders*, *2*(1), 103–114. https://doi.org/10.1007/s40489-014-0040-7.

Baron-Cohen, S., & Wheelwright, S. (2004). The empathy quotient: An investigation of adults with asperger syndrome or high functioning autism, and normal sex differences. *Journal of Autism and Developmental Disorders*, *34*(2), 163–175. https://doi.org/10.1023/B:JADD.0000022607.19833.00.

Bayley, N. (2006). *Bayley scales of infant and toddler development* (3rd ed.). Harcourt.

Berry-Kravis, E. M., Hessl, D., Abbeduto, L., Reiss, A. L., Beckel-Mitchener, A., & Urv, T. K. (2013). Outcome measures for clinical trials in fragile X syndrome. *Journal of Developmental and Behavioral Pediatrics*, *34*, 508–522. https://doi.org/10.1097/DBP.0b013e31829d1f20.

Bhui, K., Mohamud, S., Warfa, N., Craig, T. J., & Stansfeld, S. A. (2003). Cultural adaptation of mental health measures: Improving the quality of clinical practice and research. *The British Journal of Psychiatry: the Journal of Mental Science*, *183*, 184–186. https://doi.org/10.1192/bjp.183.3.184.

Bordini, D., Paula, C. S., Cunha, G. R., Caetano, S. C., Bagaiolo, L. F., Ribeiro, T. C., et al. (2020). A randomised clinical pilot trial to test the effectiveness of parent training with video modelling to improve functioning and symptoms in children with autism spectrum disorders and intellectual disability. *Journal of Intellectual Disability Research*, *64*(8), 629–643.

Brookman-Frazee, L., Roesch, S., Chlebowski, C., Baker-Ericzen, M., & Ganger, W. (2019). Effectiveness of training therapists to deliver an individualized mental health intervention for children with asd in publicly funded mental health services: A cluster randomized clinical trial. *JAMA Psychiatry*, *76*(6), 574–583. https://doi.org/10.1001/jamapsychiatry.2019.0011.

Bruininks, R. H., & Bruininks, B. D. (2005). *Bruininks-Oseretsky test of motor proficiency*. NCS Pearson, Inc.

Chiang, C.-H., Chu, C.-L., & Lee, T.-C. (2016). Efficacy of caregiver-mediated joint engagement intervention for young children with autism spectrum disorders. *Autism*, *20*(2), 172–182. https://doi.org/10.1177/1362361315575725.

Constantino, J. N., & Gruber, C. P. (2012). *Social responsiveness scale: SRS-2*. Western Psychological Services.

de Assis, T. R. S., Forlin, E., Bruck, I., Antoniuk, S. A., & dos Santos, L. H. C. (2008). Quality of life of children with cerebral palsy treated with botulinum toxin: Are well-being measures appropriate? *Arquivos de Neuro-Psiquiatria*, *66*(3B), 652–658. https://doi.org/10.1590/s0004-282x2008000500009.

Divan, G., Hamdani, S. U., Vajartkar, V., Minhas, A., Taylor, C., Aldred, C., et al. (2015). Adapting an evidence-based intervention for autism spectrum disorder for scaling up in resource-constrained settings: The development of the PASS intervention in South Asia. *Global Health Action*, *8*(1), 27278. https://doi.org/10.3402/gha.v8.27278.

Divan, G., Vajaratkar, V., Cardozo, P., Huzurbazar, S., Verma, M., Howarth, E., et al. (2019). The feasibility and effectiveness of PASS Plus, a lay health worker delivered comprehensive intervention for autism spectrum disorders: Pilot RCT in a rural low and middle income country setting. *Autism Research, 12*(2), 328–339. https://doi.org/10.1002/aur.1978.

DuBay, M., & Watson, L. R. (2019). Translation and cultural adaptation of parent-report developmental assessments: Improving rigor in methodology. *Research in Autism Spectrum Disorders, 62*, 55–65. https://doi.org/10.1016/j.rasd.2019.02.005.

Esbensen, A. J., Hooper, S. R., Fidler, D., Hartley, S. L., Edgin, J., D'Ardhuy, X. L., et al. (2017). Outcome measures for clinical trials in down syndrome. *American Journal on Intellectual and Developmental Disabilities, 122*(3), 247–281. https://doi.org/10.1352/1944-7558-122.3.247.

Eyberg, S. M., & Pinctus, D. (1999). *Eyberg child behvaiour inventory and Sutter-Eyberg student behavior inventory-revised; professional manual*. Psychological Assessment Resources.

Fannin, D. K. (2017). Reporting of underrepresented populations in autism treatment studies across 25 years. *Clinical Archives of Communication Disorders, 2*(3), 250–263. https://doi.org/10.21849/cacd.2017.00129.

Feitosa, L. C., Muzzolon, S. R. B., Rodrigues, D. C. B., de S Crippa, A. C., & Zonta, M. B. (2017). The effect of adapted sports in quality of life and biopsychosocial profile of children and adolescents with cerebral palsy. *Revista Paulista de Pediatria, 35*(4), 429–435. https://doi.org/10.1590/1984-0462/;2017;35;4;00001.

Felix, V. G., Mena, L. J., Ostos, R., & Maestre, G. E. (2017). A pilot study of the use of emerging computer technologies to improve the effectiveness of reading and writing therapies in children with Down syndrome. *British Journal of Educational Technology, 48*(2), 611–624. https://doi.org/10.1111/bjet.12426.

Fenson, L., Marchman, V. A., Thal, D. J., Reznick, J. S., & Bates, E. (2007). *MacArthur-Bates communicative development inventories: User's guide and technical manual* (2nd ed.). Brookes Publishing Co.

Frankel, F., & Mintz, J. (2008). Measuring the quality of play dates. In *UCLA parenting and children's friendship program*UCLA Jane & Terry Semel Institute for Neuroscience & Human Behavior.

Gioia, G. A., Espy, K. A., & Isquith, P. K. (2002). *Behavior rating inventory of executive function, preschool version*. Psychological Assessment Resources.

Gioia, G. A., Isquith, P. K., Guy, S. C., & Kenworthy, L. (2000). *BRIEF: Behavior rating inventory of executive function*. Psychological Assessment Resources.

Gladstone, M., Lancaster, G. A., Umar, E., Nyirenda, M., Kayira, E., van den Broek, N. R., et al. (2010). The Malawi developmental assessment tool (MDAT): The creation, validation, and reliability of a tool to assess child development in rural African settings. *PLoS Medicine*, 7(5). https://doi.org/10.1371/journal.pmed.1000273.

Green, J., Charman, T., McConachie, H., Aldred, C., Slonims, V., & Howlin, P. (2010). Parent-mediated communication focused treatment in children with autism (PACT): A randomized controlled trial. *Lancet, 375*, 2152–2160. https://doi.org/10.1016/S0140-6736(10)60587-9.

Gresham, F. M., & Elliott, S. N. (2008). *Social skills improvement system: Rating scales manual*. Pearson Education.

Gross, D., Fogg, L., Young, M., Ridge, A., Cowell, J., Sivan, A., et al. (2007). Reliability and validity of the Eyberg Child Behavior Inventory with African-American and Latino parents of young children. *Research in Nursing & Health, 30*(2), 213–223. https://doi.org/10.1002/nur.20181.

Haataja, L., Mercuri, E., Regev, R., Cowan, F., Rutherford, M., Dubowitz, V., et al. (1999). Optimality score for the neurologic examination of the infant at 12 and 18 months of age. *The Journal of Pediatrics, 135*(2 Pt. 1), 153–161. https://doi.org/10.1016/s0022-3476(99)70016-8.

Habib-Hasan, Z., Sheikh, M. S., Hoodbhoy, Z., Azam, I., & O'Neil, M. (2020). Early intervention physical therapy using "Parent Empowerment Program" for children with Down syndrome in Pakistan: A feasibility study. *Journal of Pediatric Rehabilitation Medicine, 13*(3), 233–240. https://doi.org/10.3233/PRM-190605.
Haight, W. L., Wang, X. L., Fung, H. H., Williams, K., & Mintz, J. (1999). Universal, developmental, and variable aspects of young children's play: A cross-cultural comparison of pretending at home. *Child Development, 70*(6), 1477–1488. https://doi.org/10.1111/1467-8624.00107.
Hawkins, M., Cheng, C., Elsworth, G. R., & Osborne, R. H. (2020). Translation method is validity evidence for construct equivalence: Analysis of secondary data routinely collected during translations of the Health Literacy Questionnaire (HLQ). *BMC Medical Research Methodology, 20*(1), 130. https://doi.org/10.1186/s12874-020-00962-8.
Haynes, R. J., & Sullivan, E. (2001). The Pediatric Orthopaedic Society of North America pediatric orthopaedic functional health questionnaire: An analysis of normals. *Journal of Pediatric Orthopedics, 21*(5), 619–621.
Howell, M., Bradshaw, J., & Langdon, P. E. (2021). A systematic review of behaviour-related outcome assessments for children on the autism spectrum with intellectual disabilities in education settings. *Review Journal of Autism and Developmental Disorders*, 67–91. https://doi.org/10.1007/s40489-020-00205-y.
Hu, X., Wang, M., & Fei, X. (2012). Family quality of life of Chinese families of children with intellectual disabilities. *Journal of Intellectual Disability Research: JIDR, 56*(1), 30–44. https://doi.org/10.1111/j.1365-2788.2011.01391.x.
Imms, C., Adair, B., Keen, D., Ullenhag, A., Rosenbaum, P., & Granlund, M. (2016). 'Participation': A systematic review of language, definitions, and constructs used in intervention research with children with disabilities. *Developmental Medicine and Child Neurology, 58*(1), 29–38. https://doi.org/10.1111/dmcn.12932.
International Consortium for Health Outcomes Measurement (ICHOM). (2021). *Autism spectrum disorder: Data collection reference guide.* International Consortium for Health Outcomes Measurement.
International Test Commission. (2017). *ITC guidelines for translating and adapting tests* (2nd ed.). International Test Commission.
Jansen-van Vuuren, J., Nuri, R. P., Nega, A., Batorowicz, B., Lysaght, R., & Aldersey, H. M. (2022). Family quality of life for families of children with disabilities in African contexts: A scoping review. *Quality of Life Research, 31*, 1289–1307. https://doi.org/10.1007/s11136-021-02994-z.
Karanth, P. (2007). *Communication DEALL developmental checklists.* The Com DEALL Trust.
Karanth, P., Shaista, S., & Srikanth, N. (2010). Efficacy of communication DEALL—An indigenous early intervention program for children with autism spectrum disorders. *The Indian Journal of Pediatrics*, 77(9), 957–962. https://doi.org/10.1007/s12098-010-0144-8.
Karino, C. A., Laros, J. A., & De Jesus, G. R. (2011). Evidências de validade convergente do SON-R 2½-7[a] com o WPPSI-III e WISC-III. *Psicologia: Reflexão e Crítica, 24*(4), 621–629. https://doi.org/10.1590/S0102-79722011000400001.
Kasari, C., Gulsrud, A. C., Wong, C., Kwon, S., & Locke, J. (2010). Randomized controlled caregiver mediated joint engagement intervention for toddlers with autism. *Journal of Autism and Developmental Disorders, 40*(9), 1045–1056. https://doi.org/10.1007/s10803-010-0955-5.
Keeling, L. A., Spiridigliozzi, G. A., Hart, S. J., Baker, J. A., Jones, H. N., & Kishnani, P. S. (2017). Challenges in measuring the effects of pharmacological interventions on cognitive and adaptive functioning in individuals with Down syndrome: A systematic review. *American Journal of Medical Genetics. Part A, 173*(11), 3058–3066. https://doi.org/10.1002/ajmg.a.38416.

Kelleher, B. L., & Wheeler, A. C. (2020). Introduction to special issue on outcome measures for IDD: Where we have been, where we are now, and where we are heading. *American Journal on Intellectual and Developmental Disabilities, 125*(6), 413–417. https://doi.org/10.1352/1944-7558-125.6.413.

Koly, K. N., Martin-Herz, S. P., Islam, M. S., Sharmin, N., Blencowe, H., & Naheed, A. (2021). Parent mediated intervention programmes for children and adolescents with neurodevelopmental disorders in South Asia: A systematic review. *PLoS One, 16*(3 March). https://doi.org/10.1371/journal.pone.0247432.

Laros, J. A., Reis, R. F., & Tellegen, P. J. (2010). Indicações da validade convergente do teste não-verbal de inteligência SON-R 2½-7[A]. *Avaliação Psicológica, 9*(1), 43–52.

Larson, A. L., Cycyk, L. M., Carta, J. J., Hammer, C. S., Baralt, M., Uchikoshi, Y., et al. (2020). A systematic review of language-focused interventions for young children from culturally and linguistically diverse backgrounds. *Early Childhood Research Quarterly, 50*, 157–178. https://doi.org/10.1016/j.ecresq.2019.06.001.

Laugeson, E. A., & Frankel, F. (2010). *Social skills for teenagers with developmental and autism spectrum disorders: The PEERS® treatment manual.* Routledge.

Laugeson, E. A., Frankel, F., Mogil, C., & Dillon, A. R. (2009). Parent-assisted social skills training to improve friendships in teens with autism spectrum disorders. *Journal of Autism and Developmental Disorders, 39*, 596–606. https://doi.org/10.1007/s10803-008-0664-5.

Liao, C.-Y., Ganz, J. B., Vannest, K. J., Wattanawongwan, S., Pierson, L. M., Yllades, V., et al. (2021). Caregiver involvement in communication intervention for culturally and linguistically diverse families with individuals with ASD and IDD: A systematic review of cross-cultural research. *Review Journal of Autism and Developmental Disorders.* https://doi.org/10.1007/s40489-021-00288-1.

Magaña, S., Dababnah, S., Xu, Y., Garcia Torres, M., Rieth, S. R., Corsello, C., et al. (2021). Cultural adaptations of a parent training program for families of children with ASD/IDD: Parents taking action. In N. R. Riggs, & B. Rigles (Eds.), *Vol. 61. Prevention science and research in intellectual and developmental disabilities* (pp. 263–300). Academic Press. https://doi.org/10.1016/bs.irrdd.2021.07.005.

Magaña, S., Lopez, K., Salkas, K., Iland, E., Morales, M. A., Garcia Torres, M., et al. (2019). A randomized waitlist-control group study of a culturally tailored parent education intervention for Latino parents of children with ASD. *Journal of Autism and Developmental Disorders*, 250–262. https://doi.org/10.1007/s10803-019-04252-1.

Maldonado, B. N., Chandna, J., & Gladstone, M. (2019). A systematic review of tools used to screen and assess for externalising behaviour symptoms in low and middle income settings. *Global Mental Health (Cambridge, England), 6*, e13. https://doi.org/10.1017/gmh.2019.11.

Matson, J. L., Matheis, M., Burns, C. O., Esposito, G., Venuti, P., Pisual, E., et al. (2017). Examining cross-cultural differences in autism spectrum disorder: A multinational comparison from Greece, Italy, Japan, Poland, and the United States. *European Psychiatry, 42*, 70–76. https://doi.org/10.1016/j.eurpsy.2016.10.007.

McConachie, H., Livingstone, N., Morris, C., Beresford, B., Le Couteur, A., Gringras, P., et al. (2018). Parents suggest which indicators of progress and outcomes should be measured in young children with autism spectrum disorder. *Journal of Autism and Developmental Disorders, 48*(4), 1041–1051. https://doi.org/10.1007/s10803-017-3282-2.

McConachie, H., Parr, J. R., Glod, M., Hanratty, J., Livingstone, N., Oono, I. P., et al. (2015). Systematic review of tools to measure outcomes for young children with autism spectrum disorder. *Health Technology Assessment, 19*(41), 1–538. https://doi.org/10.3310/hta19410.

McLeod, S., & Verdon, S. (2014). A review of 30 speech assessments in 19 languages other than english. *American Journal of Speech-Language Pathology, 23*(4), 708–723. https://doi.org/10.1044/2014_AJSLP-13-0066.

Meral, B. F., Cavkaytar, A., Turnbull, A. P., & Wang, M. (2013). Family quality of life of Turkish families who have children with intellectual disabilities and autism. *Research and Practice for Persons with Severe Disabilities, 38*(4), 233–246. https://doi.org/10.1177/154079691303800403.

Miles, B., Nierengarten, M., & Nearing, R. (1988). A review of the eleven most often-cited assessment instruments used in adapted physical education. *Clinical Kinesiology, 42*(2), 33–41.

Mullen, E. M. (1995). *Mullen scales of early learning*. American Guidance Service Inc.

Mundy, P., Delgado, C., Block, J., Venezia, M., Hogan, A., & Seibert, J. (2003). *A manual for the abridged early social communication scales (ESCS)*. University of Miami, Psychology Department.

Novak, I., Morgan, C., Adde, L., Blackman, J., Boyd, R. N., Brunstrom-Hernandez, J., et al. (2017). Early, accurate diagnosis and early intervention in cerebral palsy: Advances in diagnosis and treatment. *JAMA Pediatrics, 171*(9), 897–907. https://doi.org/10.1001/jamapediatrics.2017.1689.

Ong, S. Y., Roslan, S., Ahmad, N. A., Ayub, A. F. M., Ping, C. L., Zaremohzzabieh, Z., et al. (2021). A mixed-methods evaluation of parent-assisted children's friendship training to improve social skills and friendship quality in children with autism in Malaysia. *International Journal of Environmental Research and Public Health, 18*(5), 2566. https://doi.org/10.3390/ijerph18052566.

Parladé, M. V., Weinstein, A., Garcia, D., Rowley, A. M., Ginn, N. C., & Jent, J. F. (2020). Parent–child interaction therapy for children with autism spectrum disorder and a matched case-control sample. *Autism, 24*(1), 160–176. https://doi.org/10.1177/1362361319855851.

Rabin, S. J., Israel-Yaacov, S., Laugeson, E. A., Mor-Snir, I., & Golan, O. (2018). A randomized controlled trial evaluating the Hebrew adaptation of the PEERS® intervention: Behavioral and questionnaire-based outcomes. *Autism Research, 11*(8), 1187–1200. https://doi.org/10.1002/aur.1974.

Rahman, A., Divan, G., Hamdani, S. U., Vajaratkar, V., Taylor, C., Leadbitter, K., et al. (2016). Effectiveness of the parent-mediated intervention for children with autism spectrum disorder in south Asia in India and Pakistan (PASS): A randomised controlled trial. *The Lancet Psychiatry, 3*(2), 128–136. https://doi.org/10.1016/S2215-0366(15)00388-0.

Rahman, S. A., & Rahman, A. (2010). Efficacy of virtual reality-based therapy on balance in children with Down syndrome. *World Applied Sciences Journal, 10*(3), 254–261.

Ratto, A. B., Anthony, B. J., Kenworthy, L., Armour, A. C., Dudley, K., & Anthony, L. G. (2016). Are non-intellectually disabled black youth with ASD less impaired on parent report than their white peers? *Journal of Autism and Developmental Disorders, 46*(3), 773–781. https://doi.org/10.1007/s10803-015-2614-3.

Ratto, A. B., Turner-Brown, L., Rupp, B. M., Mesibov, G. B., & Penn, D. L. (2011). Development of the contextual assessment of social skills (CASS): A role play measure of social skill for individuals with high-functioning autism. *Journal of Autism and Developmental Disorders, 41*(9), 1277–1286. https://doi.org/10.1007/s10803-010-1147-z.

Reynolds, C. R., & Kamphaus, R. W. (2004). *Behavior assessment system for children, second edition (BASC-2) manual*. American Guidance Service.

Rudan, I., Chopra, M., Kapiriri, L., Gibson, J., Ann Lansang, M., Carneiro, I., et al. (2008). Setting priorities in global child health research investments: Universal challenges and conceptual framework. *Croatian Medical Journal, 49*(3), 307–317. https://doi.org/10.3325/cmj.2008.3.307.

Russell, D., Palisano, R., Walter, S., Rosenbaum, P., Gemus, M., Gowland, C., et al. (1998). Evaluating motor function in children with Down syndrome: Validity of the GMFM. *Developmental Medicine and Child Neurology, 40*(10), 693–701. https://doi.org/10.1111/j.1469-8749.1998.tb12330.x.

Russell, D. C., van Heerden, R., van Vuuren, S., Venter, A., & Joubert, G. (2016). The impact of the "Developmental Resource Stimulation Programme" (DRSP) on children with Down syndrome. *South African Journal of Occupational Therapy, 46*, 33–40.

Schaaf, R. C., Carroll, A., Waskie, E. C., Dumont, R. L., & Ridgway, E. (2021). Choosing Performance-based outcome measures of daily living skills and socialization for clinical trials in autistic children. *The American Journal of Occupational Therapy, 75*(6), 7506205060. https://doi.org/10.5014/ajot.2021.044602.

Scheibel, G., Zane, T. L., & Zimmerman, K. N. (2022). An economic evaluation of emerging and ineffective interventions: Examining the role of cost when translating research into practice. *Exceptional Children, 00144029211073522*, 245–262. https://doi.org/10.1177/00144029211073522.

Siller, M., Hutman, T., & Sigman, M. (2013). A parent-mediated intervention to increase responsive parental behaviors and child communication in children with ASD: A randomized clinical trial. *Journal of Autism and Developmental Disorders, 43*(3), 540–555. https://doi.org/10.1007/s10803-012-1584-y.

Siller, M., Swanson, M., Gerber, A., Hutman, T., & Sigman, M. (2014). A parent-mediated intervention that targets responsive parental behaviors increases attachment behaviors in children with ASD: Results from a randomized clinical trial. *Journal of Autism and Developmental Disorders, 44*(7), 1720–1732. https://doi.org/10.1007/s10803-014-2049-2.

Simpson, H. A. (2021). Forming strong cultural identities in an intersecting space of indigeneity and autism in Canada, the United States, Australia, and New Zealand. *AlterNative: An International Journal of Indigenous Peoples, 17*(3), 416–424. https://doi.org/10.1177/11771801211039274.

Soto, S., Linas, K., Jacobstein, D., Biel, M., Migdal, T., & Anthony, B. J. (2015). A review of cultural adaptations of screening tools for autism spectrum disorders. *Autism, 19*(6), 646–661. https://doi.org/10.1177/1362361314541012.

Sparrow, S. S., Balla, D., & Cicchetti, D. (1984). *Vineland adaptive behavior scales: Survey form manual*. American Guidance Service.

Sparrow, S. S., Cicchetti, D. V., & Balla, D. A. (2005). *Vineland adaptive behavior scales* (2nd ed.). AGS Publishing.

Sparrow, S. S., Cicchetti, D. V., & Balla, D. A. (2008). Vineland adaptive behavior scales. In S. Stein, & K. F. Widaman (Eds.), *Vineland-II* (2nd ed.). NCS Pearson, Inc.

Sparrow, S. S., Cicchetti, D. V., & Saulnier, C. A. (2016). *Vineland adaptive behavior scales* (3rd ed.). Pearson.

Steinbrenner, J. R., McIntyre, N., Rentschler, L. F., Pearson, J. N., Luelmo, P., Jaramillo, M. E., et al. (2022). Patterns in reporting and participant inclusion related to race and ethnicity in autism intervention literature: Data from a large-scale systematic review of evidence-based practices. *Autism*. https://doi.org/10.1177/13623613211072593. 13623613211072592.

Steinhausen, H.-C., Mohr Jensen, C., & Lauritsen, M. B. (2016). A systematic review and meta-analysis of the long-term overall outcome of autism spectrum disorders in adolescence and adulthood. *Acta Psychiatrica Scandinavica, 133*(6), 445–452. https://doi.org/10.1111/acps.12559.

Stolte, M., Hodgetts, S., & Smith, V. (2016). A critical review of outcome measures used to evaluate the effectiveness of comprehensive, community based treatment for young children with ASD. *Research in Autism Spectrum Disorders, 23*, 221–234. https://doi.org/10.1016/j.rasd.2015.12.009.

Tann, C. J., Kohli-Lynch, M., Nalugya, R., Sadoo, S., Martin, K., Lassman, R., et al. (2021). Surviving and thriving early intervention for neonatal survivors with developmental disability in Uganda. *Infants and Young Children, 34*(1), 17–32. https://doi.org/10.1097/IYC.0000000000000182.

Thurm, A., Kelleher, B., & Wheeler, A. (2020). Outcome measures for core symptoms of intellectual disability: state of the field. *American Journal on Intellectual and Developmental Disabilities, 125*(6), 418–433. https://doi.org/10.1352/1944-7558-125.6.418.

Tomlinson, M., Yasamy, M. T., Emerson, E., Officer, A., Richler, D., & Saxena, S. (2014). Setting global research priorities for developmental disabilities, including intellectual disabilities and autism. *Journal of Intellectual Disability Research, 58*(12), 1121–1130. https://doi.org/10.1111/jir.12106.

Trembath, D., Westerveld, M., & Shellshear, L. (2016). Assessing spoken language outcomes in children with ASD: A systematic review. *Current Developmental Disorders Reports, 3*(1), 33–45. https://doi.org/10.1007/s40474-016-0068-8.

van Widenfelt, B. M., Treffers, P. D. A., de Beurs, E., Siebelink, B. M., & Koudijs, E. (2005). Translation and cross-cultural adaptation of assessment instruments used in psychological research with children and families. *Clinical Child and Family Psychology Review, 8*(2), 135–147. https://doi.org/10.1007/s10567-005-4752-1.

Vanegas, S. B., Magaña, S., Zeng, W., & Pavon, C. (2021). Decision making and culturally diverse individuals with IDD and their families: A call for research. In I. Khemka, & L. Hickson (Eds.), *Decision making by individuals with intellectual and developmental disabilities: Integrating research into practice* (pp. 221–251). Springer International Publishing. https://doi.org/10.1007/978-3-030-74675-9_10.

West, E. A., Travers, J. C., Kemper, T. D., Liberty, L. M., Cote, D. L., McCollow, M. M., et al. (2016). Racial and ethnic diversity of participants in research supporting evidence-based practices for learners with Autism Spectrum Disorder. *Journal of Special Education, 50*(3), 151–163. https://doi.org/10.1177/0022466916632495.

Wetherby, A., & Prizant, B. (2003). *Communication and symbolic behavior scales*. Brookes: Paul H.

Witwer, A. N., & Lecavalier, L. (2007). Autism screening tools: An evaluation of the Social Communication Questionnaire and the Developmental Behaviour Checklist-Autism Screening Algorithm. *Journal of Intellectual and Developmental Disability, 32*(3), 179–187. https://doi.org/10.1080/13668250701604776.

CHAPTER FOUR

Distress and challenging behavior in people with profound or severe intellectual disability and complex needs: Assessment of causes and evaluation of intervention outcomes

Chris Oliver[a], Katherine Ellis[b], Georgie Agar[a], Stacey Bissell[a], Justin Cheuk Yin Chung[a], Hayley Crawford[c], Effie Pearson[d], Kelly Wade[a], Jane Waite[d], Debbie Allen[e], Lucy Deeprose[f], Georgina Edwards[d], Lauren Jenner[f], Breanne Kearney[g], Lauren Shelley[d], Kayla Smith[c], Hayley Trower[c], Dawn Adams[h], Louise Daniel[i], Laura Groves[a,j], Mary Heald[k], Jo Moss[f], Caroline Richards[a], Rachel Royston[l], Joanne Tarver[d], Alice Welham[m], Lucy Wilde[n], and Kate Woodcock[o]

[a]School of Psychology, University of Birmingham, Birmingham, United Kingdom
[b]Clinical, Educational and Health Psychology, University College London, London, United Kingdom
[c]Mental Health and Wellbeing Unit, Division of Health Sciences, Warwick Medical School, University of Warwick, Coventry, United Kingdom
[d]School of Psychology, College of Health and Life Sciences, Aston University, Birmingham, United Kingdom
[e]School of Psychology, University of Wolverhampton, Wolverhampton, United Kingdom
[f]School of Psychology, University of Surrey, Guildford, United Kingdom
[g]Institute of Cognitive Neuroscience, University College London, London, United Kingdom
[h]Autism Centre of Excellence, Griffith University, Queensland, Australia
[i]Specialist Assessment Service, University Hospitals Birmingham NHS Foundation Trust, Birmingham, United Kingdom
[j]Department of Neuroscience, Psychology and Behaviour, University of Leicester, Leicester, United Kingdom
[k]Learning Disability Service, Lancashire and South Cumbria NHS Foundation Trust, Preston, United Kingdom
[l]Division of Psychiatry, University College London, London, United Kingdom
[m]School of Psychology, University of Leicester, Leicester, United Kingdom
[n]School of Psychology and Counselling, Open University, Milton Keynes, United Kingdom
[o]Centre for Applied Psychology and the Institute for Mental Health, School of Psychology, University of Birmingham, Birmingham, United Kingdom

Contents

International Review of Research in Developmental Disabilities, Volume 62
ISSN 2211-6095
https://doi.org/10.1016/bs.irrdd.2022.05.004

Abstract

Previously, we have proposed that there are nine domains that warrant assessment when intervening to decrease challenging behavior and\or increase well-being in people with profound or severe intellectual disability and complex needs. These domains are: pain and discomfort, sensory sensitivity, anxiety and low mood, sleep, emotional dysregulation, cognitive difference, learned or functional behaviors, and expressive communication. In this article we: (1) identify specific challenging behaviors that might be influenced by these domains, (2) describe the relationship between these domains and the specified challenging behaviors, (3) identify assessments for each domain and (4) describe interactions between the domains. Our aim in this article is to provide practitioners with a framework for assessment and to stimulate debate about the domains that are demonstrably important when considering challenging behavior and well-being in people with profound or severe intellectual disability and complex needs.

1. Introduction

Recently, we published an article in which we described nine domains that influence the well-being and challenging behavior of people with profound or severe intellectual disability and complex needs (Oliver et al., 2020). The domains we described were: pain and discomfort, sensory sensitivity, anxiety and low mood, sleep, emotional dysregulation, cognitive difference, learned or functional behaviors, and expressive communication. We also proposed that each domain has an immediate impact on quality of life for the person with profound or severe intellectual disability and complex needs, in areas such as health, community presence, dignity, relationships, choice and competence, and hence warrants assessment. Our aim was to bring these domains to the attention of researchers, parents, carers and practitioners for the purpose of guiding assessment. We also developed a practical checklist of the domains to ensure that each was considered at regular reviews or when trying to improve well-being or reduce challenging behavior (Oliver et al., 2020). In the current article, we develop the rationale for this approach further, and recommend assessments that might be used to determine the importance of each domain for any individual with profound or severe intellectual disability and complex needs.

We have chosen to focus on people with profound or severe intellectual disability and complex needs specifically, as opposed to all people with intellectual disability, because the characteristics of this group have clear implications for understanding and assessing the domains of importance and hence formulation and intervention. Generally, people with severe or profound intellectual disability will evidence significant delay in cognitive development and adaptive behavior and consequently are likely to be non- or minimally verbal. In addition, people with profound or severe intellectual disability are likely to have: (1) physical or sensory impairments, (2) co-occurring conditions, such as autism spectrum disorder (ASD) and/or Attention-Deficit Hyperactivity Disorder and (3) neurological conditions such as epilepsy. This imperfect description of complex needs captures the diversity of presentation and a spectrum of difference recognizable to practitioners, parents and carers. Importantly, the description does not include challenging behavior or distress that are each associated with profound or severe intellectual disability and complex needs but are not inevitable and consequently should not define the group.

Concerns about well-being, which may arise as a result of observed distress or challenging behavior, are common reasons for referral to services and a feature of regular reviews. Compromised cognitive development, adaptive behavior and expressive communication all affect an individual's experience of, and capacity to describe, causes of distress or the reasons for behavior. Often, the distress and behaviors described do not readily lend themselves to diagnostic taxonomy used for people of typical development, because the person characteristics described above influence the form, expression and interpretation of distress or behavior. For example, a common emotional state such as anxiety may present differently in the presence of specific person characteristics, impeding identification and appropriate interpretation of the person's distress. Misattribution of the cause of distress and behavior is common, with description often conflated with explanation (e.g., self-injury is common in severe intellectual disability and so is explained by severe intellectual disability). Similarly, one component of a behavioral phenotype of a syndrome (such as self-injury) can erroneously be assumed to be inevitable in that syndrome, as opposed to being caused by a specific modifiable characteristic or experience (such as pain), also associated with the syndrome. Finally, many established assessments of possible causes of distress and specific challenging behaviors may not be appropriate for people with profound or severe intellectual disability and complex needs, because they have been developed for and normed on the typically developing population or people with mild or moderate intellectual disability. For these reasons, the process of assessment is often heavily reliant on observation and proxy reports with validity potentially compromised.

When stipulating areas of concern for any individual and hypothesizing possible causes or influences, it is important to use clear and well-defined terms. Regarding areas of concern for care-givers, terms that are commonly used, such as "challenging behavior," are vague and imprecise. For each individual, the behaviors being considered should be stipulated clearly prior to assessment, formulation and intervention. In Table 1, we propose a list of specific behaviors, with working definitions, that fall under the umbrella term 'challenging behavior' and are often cause for concern in this group. This list can be used to identify which behaviors should form the focus of an assessment. The list consists of behaviors that are: (1) quantifiable by observation, and (2) likely to have a demonstrable deleterious impact on the person showing the behavior and/or on others in the person's life, in terms of injury, health, dignity, relationships and quality of life (e.g., community presence, participation, choice). The list is derived from the Challenging Behavior Interview (Oliver et al., 2003) which enables quantification of different parameters of specified behaviors, such as frequency, duration, injury, disruption, impact on participation and restriction. Individual profiles differ both within and between behaviors and consequently the goals of any intervention may differ depending on the behavior. We propose the use of this modified list in the assessment process when a specified challenging behavior is identified as the focus for assessment and intervention.

Table 1 Definitions of specified challenging behaviors.

Behavior	Definition	Examples and notes
Self-Injury	Non-accidental behaviors producing temporary marks or reddening of the skin or cause bruising, bleeding or other temporary or permanent tissue damage.	Self-biting, head banging, head-punching or slapping, removing hair, self-scratching, body hitting, eye poking or pressing.
Pica	Eating inedible substances.	Eating paper, leaves, rotten food.
Physical aggression	A non-accidental, physical act involving physical contact with another person likely to result in pain or distress.	Punching, pushing, kicking, tripping, pulling hair, scratching, throwing objects, using objects as weapons, grabbing clothing.
Verbal aggression	Verbal statements that are likely to induce fear or distress.	Threats, insults.
Emotional outburst	Explosive episodes of specified challenging behaviors with sudden onset in combination with signs of physiological arousal. Episodes are 'out of the blue' or disproportionate to the cause, and the person cannot calm themselves or be calmed.	Physiological arousal indicated by facial flushing, excessive salivation. This behavior should be noted alongside other specified challenging behaviors when the physiological arousal is also evident.
Disruption and destruction of property or the environment	A non-accidental physical act which results in disruption or superficial or substantial damage to any property or the environment.	Tearing or chewing own clothing, tearing newspapers, notes, books, breaking windows or furniture, throwing or tipping furniture, slamming doors, pulling pictures from walls, spoiling a meal, throwing objects, knocking objects to the floor.

Continued

Table 1 Definitions of specified challenging behaviors.—cont'd

Behavior	Definition	Examples and notes
Anal poking	Insertion of objects, fingers or hand into the anus.	
Inappropriate negative vocalizations	Vocalizations that are not identifiable as intentional communicative acts and indicate a negative emotional state.	Shouting, screaming, repetitive groaning or moaning, growling.
Inappropriate removal of clothing	Removing clothing to the point at which there is an unacceptable degree of exposure given the social setting.	Stripping when others are present but not for washing, bathing, use of the toilet, changing clothing or going to bed.
Inappropriate or unacceptable sexual behavior	A sexual act which is inappropriate to the social setting and/or the relationship between the participants.	Masturbation when others are present. Inappropriate kissing and touching. Any physical, sexual contact which is rejected or unwanted.
Smearing	Non-accidental, inappropriate and repeated wiping of feces, saliva or mucus with the hand.	
Self-induced vomiting and regurgitation	Vomiting which is induced by inserting the fingers or hand into the mouth or throat. Regurgitating and re-swallowing vomit.	

In this article, we use the term "distress" to capture a presentation that is indicative of a negative state as indicated by facial expression, vocalizations, agitation, and related behaviors. In this context, distress is indicative of compromised well-being. Identifying these areas of concern specifically ensures that there is clarity regarding what the assessment process seeks to account for, what should be appraised in terms of severity to establish a baseline and what should change if an intervention is effective.

For a specified challenging behavior or distress, we propose that nine areas should be assessed to inform formulation. Seven of these domains refer to person characteristics or states. These are: pain and discomfort, sensory sensitivity, anxiety and low mood, sleep, emotional outbursts, cognitive difference, and social differences. The two remaining domains are points of immediate interaction between the person and their (usually social) environment: learned or functional behavior, and communication. We have deliberately omitted other domains that are broader environmental variables, such as parental stress and material resources, as the evidence for these having a direct causal role for specified challenging behavior in those with profound or severe intellectual disability is less than that for the total group of people with intellectual disability. The nine identified domains can be direct causes of behavior or distress, or can moderate or mediate the relationship between another domain and a specified challenging behavior or distress.

Identification of a domain (e.g., sensory sensitivity) as influencing distress or challenging behavior (e.g., episodes of aggression) does not mean that changing the person characteristic or state that might define the domain should necessarily be the focus of intervention. Although in some instances, for example where distress or challenging behavior is influenced by pain and discomfort, this is clearly beneficial. Instead, it indicates that the deleterious outcome from the interaction between the environment and that person characteristic should be mitigated by considering a range of strategies such as environmental modifications (broadly defined), enhancing skills and communication, and accommodation. For sensory sensitivity to sounds, an example is the use of ear defenders, or reducing or changing the level and other properties of sounds, or ensuring there is effective expressive communication for the person to indicate that sounds are aversive.

We have selected these nine domains because there is evidence, at least at the level of proof of principle, that they are relevant to the outcomes of distress and/or specified challenging behaviors. Much of this evidence is derived from our studies of specific behaviors and distress in people with genetic syndromes that cause intellectual disability. This strategy enabled us to: (1) identify groups at high risk for specified behaviors or distress (e.g., Agar et al., 2021; Arron, Oliver, Moss, Berg, & Burbidge, 2011; Powis & Oliver, 2014), (2) identify and evaluate associations between likely causes and outcomes within syndrome groups (e.g., Waite, 2012; Waite, Beck, Powis, & Oliver, in press; Woodcock, Oliver, & Humphreys, 2011), (3) use syndrome groups in contrast studies of likely causes to partially account for the variability typically evident in people with profound or severe intellectual disability and complex needs (e.g., Crawford et al., 2020; Trickett, Heald, Oliver, & Richards, 2018; Wilde et al., 2017) and (4) evaluate the relationship between a purported cause and outcome in new groups (e.g., Eden, de Vries, Moss, Richards, & Oliver, 2014; Richards, Davies, & Oliver, 2017).The wider group of people with profound or severe intellectual disability and complex needs will include a significant proportion of people with genetic and other causes of intellectual disability but also those for whom cause has yet to be identified. At this stage, given proof of principle, we believe it is possible and beneficial to generalize our findings beyond those syndrome groups for which we have direct evidence.

Arguably, the next stage in the research process should be to evaluate if a purported cause and an outcome are associated in the way we propose, using large scale case-control trials or randomized controlled trials. This is important to do but too slow to produce useful results within a reasonable time when there is such modest progress in this field. One strategy employed in intervention research for challenging behavior is randomized controlled trials of combined interventions, for which substantial evidence is already available for specified behaviors. These interventions are applied to heterogeneous groups across numerous behaviors and conditions of varied cause, with broad assessment of ambiguously defined outcomes. The results have inevitably confirmed positive outcomes demonstrated in previous research with modest and incremental gains in efficacy or effectiveness. More refined studies of single interventions that focus on specified behaviors with shared cause using well-defined homogenous groups are warranted. However, given the broad range of likely causes and the numbers of participants with shared characteristics that need to be recruited for such studies, the delay in making likely effective interventions available for this group conferred by randomized controlled trial methodology is unacceptable. A step change is needed to move from confirmation to innovation. For this reason, we describe here an assessment strategy based on research at the level of proof of principle.

The research process we used has generated a raft of findings that might be generalized to the wider population of people with profound or severe intellectual disability and complex needs regardless of the cause of intellectual disability. Critically, the research has shown that the likely causes of specified challenging behaviors and distress can be established at an individual level and that if this can be achieved then the interventions (broadly defined) are usually readily available. Therefore, the most important task is identifying the proximal cause(s) of specified challenging behavior(s) and distress at the level of the individual, as opposed to developing new interventions. This means developing an assessment process that can be applied in service settings to guide formulation and then intervention. As noted above, the research required to evaluate such a protocol and corresponding interventions is substantial and there is a pressing need to move more quickly. Consequently, in this article we describe an assessment strategy for people with profound or severe intellectual disability and complex needs for use in applied settings that can be adopted by practitioners. Our broad aims are to provide this resource to practitioners and to stimulate research into the use of assessment protocols in this field.

The specific aims of this article are to describe: (1) the nine domains that influence specified challenging behaviors and/or distress, (2) the problems associated with assessment of domains, (3) methods of assessment, their properties and information on administration and (4) the importance of domains to specified outcomes and their relationship to other domains.

2. The nine domains that influence distress and specified challenging behaviors

2.1 Pain and discomfort

2.1.1 Background and importance

Pain in people with intellectual disability is under-researched and consequently not well-recognized or treated (Breau & Burkitt, 2009). This is primarily due to the problems associated with establishing the presence of pain in individuals whose effective reporting of internal states is compromised. Additional challenges are conferred by wider societal beliefs about pain insensitivity or indifference, complex presentations of pain and diagnostic overshadowing (Barney et al., 2020). The available published literature indicates that pain is likely to be grossly underestimated in this group (Barney et al., 2020), and that people with intellectual disability are at greater risk of developing painful disorders than their typically developing peers

(Bottos & Chambers, 2006). The identification and treatment of pain in people with intellectual disability is paramount for relieving discomfort and distress, addressing the health problems that cause pain and reducing specific challenging behaviors. There is a self-evident argument regarding quality of life.

Health problems that cause pain that are more common in people with intellectual disability include gastro-esophageal reflux, otitis media, constipation, and dental caries (Böhmer et al., 1999; Böhmer, Taminiau, Klinkenberg-Knol, & Meuwissen, 2001; Bosch, Van Dyke, Milligan Smith, & Poulton, 1997; Hartman, Gilles, McComas, Danov, & Symons, 2008; Taylor, Rush, Hetrick, & Sandman, 1993). Additionally, discomfort can arise with physical disability that limits self-initiated mobility. Given the high proportion of people with specific syndromes in this population, health conditions associated with these syndromes are more likely. Examples are: gastro-esophageal reflux in Cornelia de Lange, Cri du Chat and Smith-Magenis syndromes; otitis media in fragile X, Down and Williams syndromes; and tumors in tuberous sclerosis complex.

There is a complex relationship between pain and specified challenging behaviors. Clearly, self-injury can result in pain, but evidence suggests that experiencing pain increases the risk of self-injury. When children are ill, there are higher levels of self-injury and aggression (Carr & Owen-DeSchryver, 2007) compared to when they are well. Furthermore, evidence shows that when painful health conditions are treated, specified challenging behaviors decrease (Bosch et al., 1997; Carr & Blakeley-Smith, 2006) and specified challenging behaviors fluctuate with improvements and deterioration in health. Finally, behaviors such as self-injury are associated with compromised health (Richards et al., 2017).

2.1.2 Assessment methods

Given the subjective nature of pain, self-report is the gold standard for assessment in adults and children as young as three years old (Royal College of Nursing, 2009). Effective self-report requires an understanding of the concept of pain, the ability to identify and label internal states and a method of communicating to others an accurate description of the nature and location of pain. Even the measures commonly used to support this process, such as visual analogue scales, number scales, or scales with facial images, require an understanding of magnitude and serial order alongside physical ability (Fanurik, Koh, Harrison, Conrad, & Tomerlin, 1998). Given that individuals with severe and complex needs may have difficulties in these areas, as well as having communication impairments prohibiting them reporting pain, self-report cannot be depended upon as a reliable method of assessment for this population.

Observation of behaviors potentially indicative of pain is used increasingly in clinical and research settings. However, indicators of pain, such as crying, may not be pain specific (Breau, McGrath, Camfield, & Finley, 2002) and other evidence of potentially painful health conditions and changes in behavior, sleep and appetite, are informative. Assessments of behaviors that are associated with pain are outlined in Table 2. Measures such as the Face, Legs, Activity, Cry, Consolability (FLACC; Voepel-Lewis et al., 1997) guide observers towards behaviors likely to indicate pain and require little in the way of preparation or personalization to be effective. Other measures, such as the Individualized Numeric Rating Scale (INRS; Solodiuk & Curley, 2003), are designed to be personalized and require preparation before use. In either case, best practice is to note change in behavior that is otherwise unexplained.

2.1.3 Assessment strategy

If pain is thought to be transient and recurrent, then the FLACC, for example, for a set period of time (e.g., 10 min) is useful for structured observation. Additionally, a record of specific behaviors observed is informative to aid reliability across observers. Ideally, observation takes place when the person is well and healthy, and then repeated when painful health conditions are identified or suspected. Brief videos at these times are informative for clinicians. Comparison between the "healthy" and "unhealthy" presentations can help to develop a shared perception of the person's "pain signature" (e.g., two lines in the middle of the forehead combined with vocalizations and a body defense posture), and can mitigate diagnostic overshadowing. The FLACC can also be used over a period of a few days to establish a baseline level of behavior before intervention or the use of analgesics if pain is suspected but the cause unknown. A decrease in behavior following administration of analgesics would suggest underlying pain. Individuals who are showing behaviors suggestive of pain should always undergo a thorough health assessment with a particular focus on health difficulties that are more common in people with intellectual disability. As part of the assessment, clinicians should rule out health difficulties associated with the etiology of intellectual disability. Arguably, a health assessment should be conducted prior to any other assessments or interventions. Finally, pain can go unrecognized for many years, so even if there is a long history of specified

Table 2 Assessments of pain and discomfort.

Measures	Domains assessed	Appropriateness for profound and severe intellectual disability	Notes
Face, Legs, Activity, Crying, Consolability (FLACC; Voepel-Lewis, Shayevitz, & Malviya, 1997)	Five domains: Face; Legs; Activity; Crying; Consolability.	Established	Quick to use and easy to learn for parents or clinicians without prior knowledge of the person being assessed.
Non - Communicating Child Pain Checklist Revised (NCCPC-R; Breau et al., 2002)	Seven domains: Vocal; Social; Facial; Activity; Body and Limbs; Physiological; Eating/Sleeping.	Established	Designed for use by parents or clinicians and can be used by people without prior knowledge of the child and/or their usual behaviors.
Pediatric Pain Profile (PPP; Hunt et al., 2004)	Behaviors not scored in specific domains.	Established	Much more in depth tool useful for building an individual profile and monitoring change. Potentially less appropriate for brief assessments.
Children's Hospital East Ontario Pain Scale (CHEOPS; McGrath et al., 1985)	Six domains: Cry; Facial; Verbal; Torso; Touch; Legs.	Probable	Not designed for children with ID but widely used and does not require verbal communication or rating from child.
Individualized Numeric Rating Scale (INRS; Solodiuk & Curley, 2003)	Points are populated by behaviors specific to that child.	Established	Requires good knowledge of the individual and their personal pain related behaviors in setting up of the tool. Once set-up could be used by professionals or clinicians with limited prior knowledge of the individual being scored.
Disability Distress Awareness Tool (DisDAT; Regnard et al., 2007)	Includes: Appearance; Vocal Signs; Habits and Mannerisms; Posture and Observations. Selected behaviors scored depending on impact on day.	Established	Assesses broader distress behaviors including those that may be related to pain. Although it does not produce a specific pain score it can help families and/or teams become more aware of developing patterns of distress which could indicate underlying pain.

challenging behaviors or compromised well-being, pain and discomfort should always be considered and assessed.

2.2 Sensory sensitivity

2.2.1 Background and importance

Sensory modulation refers to the ability to translate sensory input effectively and efficiently into behavior graded relative to the degree, nature, or intensity of the sensory information (Miller, Anzalone, Lane, Cermak, & Osten, 2007). Sensory modulation differences include hyperreactivity, hypo-reactivity and sensory seeking behavior. Hyperreactivity is characterized by an increased awareness and sensitivity to sensory stimuli, whereas hypo-reactivity is characterized by reduced sensitivity (Miller-Kuhaneck, Henry, Glennon, & Mu, 2007). Sensory seeking behavior is an intense interest or craving of sensory experiences (Ben-Sasson et al., 2009). Sensory modulation differences are common in individuals with intellectual disability, including those with rare genetic syndromes, although most research has focused on autistic populations (Engel-Yeger, Hardal-Nasser, & Gal, 2011). Importantly, evidence suggests that those with severe-profound intellectual disability show more extreme sensory modulation patterns compared to those with mild intellectual disability (Engel-Yeger et al., 2011). Sensory modulation differences are associated with several emotional and behavioral outcomes. For example, autistic individuals with severe to profound intellectual disability who show hypo-reactivity to sensory input are more likely to show irritability, aggression, and self-injury (Gonthier, Longuépée, & Bouvard, 2016).

2.2.2 Assessment methods

Although sensory modulation differences form part of the diagnostic criteria for autism, gold standard assessments for autism (e.g., Autism Diagnostic Observation Schedule [ADOS-2]; Lord et al., 2012) do not have a strong focus on sensory processing. Furthermore, sensory modulation is rarely assessed routinely in individuals with neurodevelopmental conditions and particularly those with more severe intellectual disability. Best practice is that assessments should collate information from multiple sources (Schaaf & Lane, 2015). As for pain and discomfort, informant report has the inevitable problem of reliance on informants' interpretations of behavior and experience. Whilst there are several assessment measures that explore sensory modulation differences, these are mostly developed for autistic populations, with few developed for use with individuals with intellectual disability

(Burns, Dixon, Novack, & Granpeesheh, 2017). Proxy report questionnaire measures are the most used (Burns et al., 2017; Dunn, 1999, 2014) with a paucity of sensory modulation assessments using behavioral observation (Burns et al., 2017; Siper, Kolevzon, Wang, Buxbaum, & Tavassoli, 2017). Physiological measures of electrodermal activity, salivary cortisol and heart rate have been used in autistic populations (Bitsika, Sharpley, Andronicos, Agnew, & Mills, 2015; Corbett, Schupp, Levine, & Mendoza, 2009; Schoen, Miller, Brett-Green, & Nielsen, 2009; Woodard et al., 2012) but may not be tolerable for individuals who have tactile hypersensitivities. There is a need for further studies utilizing a multi-method approach to assessing sensory modulation differences in individuals with complex needs (Burns et al., 2017; Yeung & Thomacos, 2020).

Assessments are outlined in Table 3. The Sensory Experiences Questionnaire- 3rd edition (SEQ-3; Baranek, David, Poe, Stone, & Watson, 2006), the Sensory Processing Assessment for Young Children (SPA; Baranek, 1999) and the Sensory Assessment for Neurodevelopmental Disorders (SAND; Siper et al., 2017) are validated for people with intellectual disability. These assessments provide detailed profiles of sensory modulation patterns and the modalities in children. The SEQ additionally identifies the contexts (social/non-social) in which sensory behaviors emerge. This detailed level of information may inform hypotheses on the neurobiological and environmental causes of sensory modulation differences. The SEQ is an informant report that has been found to have good internal consistency and test-retest reliability (Baranek et al., 2006; Little et al., 2011) and provides clinical cut-off scores useful for screening. The SPA and SAND are direct observational assessments of behavioral responses to sensory stimuli. The SAND has been shown to have strong internal consistency, reliability, and convergent validity with the Short Sensory Profile (SSP) (Siper et al., 2017). The SPA is not standardized and has limited psychometric data available (Jorquera-Cabrera, Romero-Ayuso, Rodriguez-Gil, & Triviño-Juárez, 2017) but has been shown to have robust test-retest reliability (Baranek et al., 2013).

2.2.3 Assessment strategy

Assessment strategies typically utilize informant reports with formal and informal observations of behaviors in response to sensory stimuli (Jorquera-Cabrera et al., 2017). Hypersensitive individuals may find direct assessments distressing and informant reports may be more ethical if they

Table 3 Assessments of sensory sensitivity.

Measures	Domains assessed	Appropriateness for profound and severe intellectual disability	Notes
Informant report			
Sensory Profile 1 and 2, Short Sensory Profile (SP; SP-2; Dunn, 1999, 2014)	Sensory domains: auditory, visual, tactile, oral, movement, body position Sensory subtypes: low registration, sensory seeking, sensory avoiding, sensory sensitivity	Probable	Parent/caregiver report. Development based on research on over 1000 children, including children with disabilities, ADHD, and autism. Not all questions may be appropriate for individuals with ID, especially on adolescent/adult form. Moderate convergent validity with SPM.
Sensory Experiences Questionnaire (SEQ) versions 1.0, 2.0, 2.1, 3.0 (Baranek, 1999; Baranek et al., 2006)	Sensory domains: tactile, auditory, visual, gustatory/olfactory, vestibular/proprioceptive Sensory subtypes: hypo- and hyperresponsiveness in social and non-social contexts	Probable	Parent/caregiver report. Standardized using autistic populations and populations with developmental delay. Good convergent validity with Sensory Processing Assessment for Young Children (SPA).
Sensory Processing Measure (SPM; Miller-Kuhaneck et al., 2007; Parham & Ecker, 2007)	Sensory domains: visual, auditory, tactile, vestibular, proprioception touch Sensory subtypes: sensory over/ under-responsivity, sensory seeking, praxis Subscales: social participation, vision, hearing, touch, body awareness, balance and motion, total sensory systems	Probable	Parent/caregiver/teacher report. Considers multiple contexts with separate forms for home and school environments and social participation. Not standardized on ID populations: some questions may not be suitable for ID populations. Limited information on sensory modulation subtypes.
Touch Inventory for elementary school-aged children (TIE); Touch Inventory for Preschoolers (TIP; Royeen & Fortune, 1990; Royeen, 1987)	Sensory domain: tactile Sensory subtype- hyper-responsivity	Unknown	Specifically focuses on tactile over-responsivity when applicable. TIE: Not appropriate for children with severe or profound ID due to child self-report form (IQ of at least 80 required) or physical disabilities. TIP with caregiver/teacher informant may be utilized.

Continued

Table 3 Assessments of sensory sensitivity.—cont'd

Measures	Domains assessed	Appropriateness for profound and severe intellectual disability	Notes
Direct observation			
Sensory Processing Assessment for Young Children (SPA; Baranek, 1999)	Sensory domains: tactile, auditory, visual Sensory subtypes/subscales: hyper/hypo-responsivity, sensory seeking, sensory habituation. Assesses for stereotyped behaviors.	Established	Play-based observational assessment. Designed for ID populations. Appropriate for those who use few or no words as does not rely on language. Does not include all sensory domains, e.g., gustatory, olfactory, vestibular, proprioceptive. Designed to be used in combination with SEQ. Weak-moderate convergent validity with SEQ. Difficult to administer without training from author.
Tactile defensiveness and discrimination test- Revised (TDDT-R)	Sensory domains: tactile Sensory subtypes/subtests: tactile discrimination, sensory seeking, sensory hyper-responsivity, orienting/habituation	Established	Play-based tasks designed for children with developmental delay. Appropriate for non-verbal and ID populations. Scored based on observable behavioral reactions (presence and intensity) to light touch stimuli and tactile experiences. Only assesses tactile processing. Validated with children with autism, fragile X syndrome, and other developmental disabilities (Baranek et al., 2002; Boyd et al., 2010; Watson et al., 2011). Not standardized. Weak to moderate convergent validity with TIP (Baranek & Berkson, 1994).
Mixed direct observation and information report			
Sensory Integration Inventory - Revised for Individuals with Developmental Disabilities (Reisman & Hanschu, 1992)	Sensory domains: tactile, vestibular, proprioceptive, general reactions Subtests: Provides additional information on self-stimulating or self-injurious behaviors	Established	Developed for developmental disability populations. Dichotomous scoring of presence or absence of behavior. Screens out individuals who demonstrate behaviors for reasons other than sensory challenges. No psychometric data available; not standardized. Requires clinician to interpret results by indicating patterns in behaviors.

Sensory Assessment for Neurodevelopmental Disorders (SAND; Siper et al., 2017)	Sensory domains: auditory, visual, tactile Sensory subtypes: hyper/hypo-reactivity, reactivity, sensory seeking	Established	Assessment of non-verbal, observable behavior. Appropriate for those who use few or no words as does not rely on verbal ability. Does not include all sensory domains, e.g., gustatory, olfactory, vestibular, proprioceptive. Moderate-strong convergent validity with Short Sensory Profile.
Sensory Over-responsivity (SensOR) Scales; SensOR Inventory (Schoen, Miller, & Green, 2008)	Sensory domains: visual, auditory, gustatory, olfactory, tactile, vestibular, proprioceptive Sensory subtype: sensory over-responsivity	Probable	Examiner evaluation based on behavioral responses to various sensory stimuli. Some items of direct assessment require following verbal directions but can mostly be administered nonverbally. Informant report filled out by parent/caregiver. Not standardized on ID populations. Does not capture under-responsivity, praxis or postural challenges in ID. Significant concurrent validity with SSP.
Sensory Processing Scale Assessment (SPS) Version 1.0, 2.0 (Schoen et al., 2008; Schoen, Miller, & Sullivan, 2014)	Sensory domains: visual, auditory, tactile, vestibular, proprioceptive, gustatory, olfactory Sensory subtypes: sensory modulation	Unknown	Play-based examiner-administered items are scored based on behavioral observations across three time periods (during the activity, after the activity ($\leq$15 s), and during the transition to the next activity). Parent/caregiver rating scale included. Some items may require following verbal directions. Not standardized or developed for ID populations. Limited psychometric data: lacks comparison to other assessments. Increased ecological validity with observations in naturalistic settings.

provide sufficient information. The availability of sensory modulation assessments and referral to Occupational Therapists are variable and, in some countries, may only be offered to those with a mental health or autism diagnosis.

2.3 Anxiety and low mood

2.3.1 Background and importance

Anxiety is characterized by apprehension, worry and/or "nervousness" which includes psychological, behavioral and somatic changes, such as hyperarousal (Cooray & Bakala, 2005). Low mood and anhedonia are core symptoms of depression, with the latter very difficult to establish in people with severe intellectual disability (Ross & Oliver, 2003). Both anxiety and low mood are common in individuals with intellectual disability, with children with intellectual disability two to three times more likely to develop anxiety than the typically developing population (Crawford, Waite, & Oliver, 2017; Green, Berkovits, & Baker, 2015; Maïano et al., 2018; Royston, Howlin, Waite, & Oliver, 2017; Whitney, Shapiro, Peterson, & Warschausky, 2019). Anxiety and low mood are both associated with lower quality of life for autistic people and those with intellectual disabilities (e.g., Adams, Clark, & Keen, 2019; Olatunji, Cisler, & Tolin, 2007; Rapaport, Clary, Fayyad, & Endicott, 2005; van Steensel, Bögels, & Dirksen, 2012).

2.3.2 Assessment methods

As for other domains, assessments typically rely on self-report for which an individual is required to identify, label, and effectively communicate internal states and emotions to others, an often ineffective mode of assessment for individuals with intellectual disability (Appleton, Roberts, & Simpson, 2019; Flynn et al., 2017). Observations of behavior are considered more appropriate but bring other difficulties to assessment due to the complex behavior profile of individuals with intellectual disability and co-occurring conditions (Appleton et al., 2019). Establishing the etiology of behaviors and identifying which are indicative of anxiety and low mood can be challenging; for example, behavioral indicators of anxiety can present similarly to those of autism or pain (Edwards et al., 2022; Flynn et al., 2017). Finally, atypical triggers for anxiety and atypical anxiety symptomatology are reported in the literature, yet there are few reliable and valid assessments that consider these (Crawford et al., 2020; Flynn et al., 2017; Kerns et al., 2014).

Informant-report questionnaires are the most widely used and include questionnaires developed for typically developing groups (e.g., Spence Child Anxiety Scale; Spence, 1999), those with intellectual disability (e.g., Anxiety, Depression and Mood Scale (ADAMS), Esbensen, Rojahn, Aman, & Ruedrich, 2003; Mood, Interest and Pleasure Questionnaire (MIPQ), Ross & Oliver, 2003), and questionnaires developed specifically for populations with neurodevelopmental conditions (e.g., Parent-Rated Anxiety Scale for ASD; Scahill et al., 2019) (See Table 4). Informant-report interviews are also available and have the advantage of probing and assessment of behavioral overlap (Simonoff et al., 2008). Structured observations of fearfulness and anxious behavior provide another form of assessment including the Anxiety Dimensional Observation Scale (Anx-DOS; Mian et al., 2015) and physiological and behavioral observation measures are increasingly becoming available. Examples include the Physiological Measure of Subjective Wellbeing (Vos, De Cock, Petry, Van Den Noortgate, & Maes, 2010) and the Social Anxiety and Motivation Rating Scale (Crawford et al., 2020). Future research is needed to explore the psychometric properties and utility of these measures for people with profound or severe intellectual disability.

2.3.3 Assessment strategy

The assessment process typically involves first ruling out alternative explanations for behavioral change. Developmental history and baseline behavior can indicate whether anxiety and low mood items have been endorsed on informant measures due to overlap with indicators of autism. A functional behavior assessment can identify the anxiety or mood related antecedents and consequences of behaviors, increasing or reducing support for a formulation of anxiety or low mood. For example, if specific challenging behaviors occur alongside physiological signs of arousal and are reliably followed by escape or avoidance of situations, this could indicate anxiety as motivation (Moskowitz et al., 2013). Even when a stepwise assessment process is followed, it is often unclear whether anxiety and/or low mood are present, due to atypical presentations (Cooper & Collacott, 1996; Edwards et al., 2022). In some instances, response to treatment may be a necessary indicator that the assessment is accurate.

Questionnaires and interviews are relatively low cost, require limited resources, with fewer ethical concerns, but the initial process of gathering information and questionnaires on anxiety and low mood benefits from careful planning. Questionnaires often require informants to rate over a

Table 4 Assessments of anxiety and low mood.

Measures	Domains assessed	Appropriateness for profound and severe intellectual disability	Notes
Informant report			
Aberrant Behavior Checklist (ABC; Aman & Singh, 1985)	Irritability, agitation and crying, Lethargy/social withdrawal, Stereotypic behavior, Hyperactivity/noncompliance, Inappropriate speech	Established	Parent/caregiver report. Developed for use in people with a range of ID.
Anxiety, Depression and Mood Scale (ADAMS; Esbensen et al., 2003)	Mania/hyperactivity, Depressed mood, Social avoidance, General anxiety, Obsessive/compulsive	Established	Parent/caregiver report. Developed for use in people with a range of ID.
Child and Adolescent Psychiatric Assessment (CAPA; Simonoff et al., 2008)	Depressive disorders, Attention-deficit/hyperactivity disorder, Oppositional defiant disorder, Conduct disorder, Anxiety disorders	Established	Parent/caregiver report, but self-report questionnaire is also available. Developed for use in typically developing children aged 9–17 years, but has been used in children with ID (e.g., Baker & Skuse, 2005; Simonoff et al., 2013).
Diagnostic Assessment of the Severely Handicapped (DASH-II; Matson, Gardner, Coe, & Sovner, 1991)	Stereotypies and tics, Self-injurious behavior, Pervasive developmental disorders, Organic syndromes, Anxiety, Depression/mood, Mania, Schizophrenia, Elimination disorders, Eating disorders, Sleep disorders, Sexual disorders, Impulse control and other miscellaneous behaviors	Established	Parent/caregiver report. Developed for use in people with severe and profound ID.
Glasgow Anxiety Scale for People with an Intellectual Disability (GAS-ID) Mindham & Espie, 2003)	Worries, Specific fears, Physiological symptoms	Unknown	Self-report questionnaire. Developed for use in adults with mild to moderate ID.

Mood, Interest and Pleasure Questionnaire (MIPQ; Ross & Oliver, 2003)	Mood; Interest and pleasure	Established	Informant report. Developed for use in people with a range of ID.
Parent-Rated Anxiety Scale for ASD (PRAS-ASD; Scahill et al., 2019)	Anxiety severity	Established	Parent/caregiver report. Developed for use in autistic children with a range of ID.
Reiss Screen for Maladaptive Behavior (Reiss, 1988)	Aggressive behavior, Autistic symptoms, Psychosis, Paranoia, Depression (behavioral signs), Depression (physical signs), Dependent personality disorder, Avoidant behavior	Established	Parent/caregiver report. Developed for use in adolescents and adults with a range of ID.
Spence Children's Anxiety Scale (SCAS; Spence, 1999)	Separation anxiety, Social phobia, Obsessive-compulsive disorder, Panic disorder/agoraphobia, Personal injury fears, Generalized anxiety	Probable	Parent/caregiver report, but self-report questionnaire is also available. Developed for use in typically developing children, but has been used in autistic children and children with rare genetic syndromes associated with ID with some evidence of psychometric properties (e.g., Crawford et al., 2017; Glod et al., 2017).
Direct Observation			
Anxiety Dimensional Observation Scale (Anx-DOS; Mian, Carter, Pine, Wakschlag, & Briggs-Gowan, 2015)	Mystery jar (novelty/uncertainty), Spider (novelty/present threat), Bell (startle/uncertainty), Separation (separation distress)	Probable	Situational presses directly administered. Developed for use in typically developing children aged 3–6 years, but has been used in minimally verbal autistic children with some evidence of psychometric properties (Muskett, 2020).
Social Anxiety and Motivation Rating Scale (SAMS; Crawford et al., 2020)	No social interaction, Voluntary social interaction, Required social interaction, Performance	Probable	Social presses directly administered. Specifically designed for people with ID.

specific period, so consideration should be given as to when it is best to collect that data and whether to collect data simultaneously or consecutively across different environments. Assessments of change in symptoms may be particularly problematic for those in supported living accommodation where family members or consistent carers may not be available as informants.

Time should be invested in exploring assessment data across informants, settings, and time. Each informant can provide information and insight on a different area or aspect of an individual's life, so differences between informants should not be interpreted as a problem, but as a way to understand the impact of environments, time, or systems (Adams, Young, Simpson, & Keen, 2019; De Los Reyes et al., 2015). It is important to consider the profile of symptoms reported as well as the meaning of any numerical score; a stable score on a questionnaire does not necessarily mean a stable profile of symptoms, and changes in score may be due a change in the number or frequency of symptoms.

2.4 Poor sleep

2.4.1 Background and importance

The term 'poor sleep' encompasses both specific sleep disorders (such as insomnia, sleep-related breathing disorders, parasomnias) and differences in the timing, duration and/or quality of sleep. Meta-analyses suggest that sleep quality is poorer in individuals with intellectual disability (Surtees, Oliver, Jones, Evans, & Richards, 2018), with some sleep disorders more common in certain genetic syndromes than others (Agar et al., 2021). Poor sleep is also persistent in the majority of children and adults with profound or severe intellectual disability and complex needs (Kieman & Alborz, 1996; Quine, 1991).

2.4.2 Assessment methods

The sleep assessments to consider depend on the nature of the suspected sleep problem (see Table 5). These range from informant-based measures, such as sleep diaries and questionnaires, to direct measures of sleep/wake cycles and sleep architecture, such as actigraphy, pulse oximetry and polysomnography. The utility of an assessment, particularly direct measures, may or may not be appropriate for an individual depending on a number of factors and considerations.

Informant-based measures provide a subjective assessment of sleep, limited by the informant's proximity to the person overnight and the

Table 5 Assessments of sleep.

Measures	Domains assessed	Appropriateness for profound and severe intellectual disability	Notes
Informant based assessment			
Modified Simonds and Parraga Sleep Questionnaire (MSPSQ; Simonds & Parraga, 1982; Wiggs & Stores, 1996)	Total score and seven subscales: Bedtime Resistance, Sleep Onset Delay, Night Waking, Sleep Anxiety, Parasomnias, Sleep-Disordered Breathing and Daytime Sleepiness.	Established	Validated for use in individuals with developmental disorders, includes broader information about sleeping environment. Both total and subscale scores correlate significantly with corresponding scores on the CSHQ.
Children's Sleep Habits Questionnaire (CSHQ; Owens, Spirito, & McGuinn, 2000)	Total score and eight subscales: Bedtime Resistance, Sleep Onset Delay, Sleep Duration, Night Wakings, Sleep Anxiety, Parasomnias, Sleep-Disordered Breathing and Daytime Sleepiness.	Unknown	Not validated for use in individuals with developmental disorders, though has been used in individuals with Down syndrome (Esbensen & Hoffman, 2018). Widely used in typical pediatric literature, comparative data available; version for pre-school and school aged children.
Brief Infant Sleep Questionnaire-Revised (BISQ-R; Sadeh, 2004; Mindell, Gould, Tikotzy, Leichman, & Walters, 2019)	Total score and three subscales: Infant Sleep, Parent Perception and Parent Sleep-related Behaviors.	Unknown	Not validated for use in individuals with developmental disorders; designed for use with infants only. Widely used in typical pediatric literature, comparative data available. Strongly correlated with actigraphy and daily sleep logs.

Continued

Table 5 Assessments of sleep.—cont'd

Measures	Domains assessed	Appropriateness for profound and severe intellectual disability	Notes
Sleep Disturbance Scale for Children (SDSC; Bruni et al., 1996)	Total score and six subscales: Disorders of Initiating and Maintaining Sleep, Sleep Breathing Disorders, Disorders of Arousal/ Nightmares, Sleep Wake Transition Disorders, Disorders of Excessive Somnolence, Sleep Hyperhydrosis.	Unknown	Not validated for use in individuals with developmental disorders. Widely used in typical pediatric literature, comparative data available.
Sleep Diary (Various, see examples available online, e.g., see Cerebra sleep guide https://cerebra.org.uk/wp-content/uploads/2020/03/sleep-guide-june19-low-res.pdf)	Typically includes: Bed Time, Wake Up Time, Time Taken to Fall Asleep, Number, Timing and Duration of Night Wakings, Individual/Caregiver Behavior.	Widely used	Not a standardized or validated assessment tool. Is used widely in individuals with developmental disorders and additional, complex needs. Useful when used in conjunction with actigraphy. Subject to recall bias and relies heavily on caregiver availability.

Direct observations			
Polysomnography	Typically includes: Total Sleep Time, Wake After Sleep Onset, Sleep Onset Latency, Sleep Efficiency, Arousal Index and Sleep Staging. May also include apnea-hypopnea index, oxygen saturation levels and periodic limb movement index.	Variable	Invasive, difficult to tolerate, requires a substantial change to typical sleeping environment; not easily accessible. Tolerability will depend on several individual factors. May not be appropriate for some individuals. 'Gold standard' especially for identifying sleep related breathing and movement disorders; allows examination of sleep staging. Test-retest reliability modest in assessment of adult obstructive sleep apnea; no data available in relation to ID.
Pulse oximetry	Standard parameters measured by pulse oximetry are based on the blood oxygen saturation level (SpO2). This includes mean SpO2, minimum SpO2, the oxyhemoglobin desaturation index (ODI) as a measure of decreased oxygen saturation below threshold, basal oxygen saturations, length of time with oxygen saturation $<90\%$, and average number of desaturations per hour.	Variable	Tolerability will depend on a number of individual factors. May not be appropriate for some individuals. May have limited utility for aspects relating to sleep disordered breathing or obstructive sleep apnea if not used in conjunction with sleep diaries or polysomnography. Has been used in clinical and home settings with pediatric populations and individuals with Down syndrome (Hill et al., 2018). Analysis relies on trained interpretation.

Continued

Table 5 Assessments of sleep.—cont'd

Measures	Domains assessed	Appropriateness for profound and severe intellectual disability	Notes
Actigraphy	Typically includes: Bed Time, Get Up Time, Time in Bed, Total Sleep Time, Wake After Sleep Onset, Sleep Onset Latency, Sleep Efficiency. Can also derive measures of sleep fragmentation and longest period of sleep before wake.	Variable	Good evidence of concurrent validity with PSG in Down syndrome and Angelman syndrome (Esbensen, Hoffman, Stansberry, & Shaffer, 2018; (Goldman, Bichell, Surdyka, & Malow, 2012). Easily tolerated by some individuals with developmental disorders; appropriateness of use will depend on a number of individual factors. Reasonably easy to access in terms of comparative cost. Needs to be completed alongside a sleep diary, for the purpose of accurate data 'cleaning' and interpretation.

informant's ability to recall specific details. Despite these constraints, informant-based assessments can be a useful screening tool to inform priorities. Sleep diaries are freely available and are typically completed for a minimum of 2 weeks. Sleep questionnaires such as the Modified Simmons and Parraga Sleep Questionnaire (MSPSQ; Simonds & Parraga, 1982; Wiggs & Stores, 1996), the Children's Sleep Habits Questionnaire (CSHQ; Owens et al., 2000 and see Esbensen & Hoffman, 2018) and the Sleep Disturbance Scale for Children (SDSC; Bruni et al., 1996) are useful screening tools for symptoms associated with sleep disorders, as well as notable sleep difficulties, such as sleep anxiety and bedtime resistance. These questionnaires generate total scores that discriminate between clinical and control samples (Bruni et al., 1996; Johnson, Turner, Foldes, Malow, & Wiggs, 2012). However, only the MSPSQ is validated for use in individuals with intellectual disability. In addition, clinicians may consider using the Brief Infant Sleep Questionnaire (BISQ; Sadeh, 2004) to assess sleep timing, the sleep environment and interactions between caregivers and infants (0–36 months) overnight. Understanding these aspects of sleep ecology may allude to potential causal factors that underpin poor sleep.

Direct measures such as actigraphy, pulse oximetry and polysomnography provide more objective assessment of sleep parameters indicative of poor sleep such as reduced sleep efficiency. Actigraphy uses wearable accelerometers to record movement as a proxy for sleep and wake. Typically, actigraphs are worn around the wrist or ankle for at least 1 week to record habitual sleep patterns in the home environment. These habitual patterns are useful for assessing potential circadian rhythm disorders as well as night by night variability in sleep parameters. As a movement sensor, actigraphy may overestimate sleep and underestimate wake if an individual is lying still but not actually asleep (Van de Water, Holmes, & Hurley, 2011). Therefore, it is critical that a sleep diary is completed by the caregiver at the same time as the actigraphy assessment, and that the actigraphy data are 'cleaned' according to a standardized protocol in order to remove artifact (Acebo et al., 1999). A pulse oximeter detects how well the blood is oxygenated via a clip device usually attached to the finger. Pulse oximetry is a particularly useful assessment when obstructive sleep apnea or sleep disordered breathing are suspected, in young children and in genetic syndromes such as Down syndrome (Burke et al., 2016). Overnight pulse oximetry has particular utility as a screening tool for sleep disordered breathing when routine access to polysomnography is not feasible or readily accessible. Polysomnography is a comprehensive overnight sleep study using electroencephalography, electromyography, electrooculography and, in some cases, electrocardiography and measures of breathing. This may be conducted at home or in a sleep laboratory or hospital over one or two nights. Polysomnography is the "gold standard" sleep assessment for typically developing individuals and is particularly indicated for diagnosis of breathing and movement related disorders (Pandi-Perumal, Spence, & BaHammam, 2014). Polysomnography also provides an insight into sleep staging and architecture, which may support identification of specific types of parasomnias. However, many individuals with intellectual disability are not able to tolerate the invasive procedures of a polysomnography study, and even when the assessment is tolerated it is unlikely to result in a typical night's sleep for the individual. In contrast, actigraphy is generally well tolerated by people with intellectual disability, particularly if strategies such as systematic desensitization and the use of dummy watches are employed to mitigate sensory sensitivity (Esbensen et al., 2018).

2.4.3 Assessment strategy

As an initial strategy, caregivers are advised to keep a sleep diary for 2 weeks and complete a sleep questionnaire at home. If caregivers are concerned about parasomnias or sleep related breathing difficulties, use of at-home video monitoring may also be helpful. Following this initial assessment, clinicians will need to guide the assessment process towards the identification of a specific sleep disorder or issue with sleep timing, quality, or duration. This may include the use of actigraphy to assess circadian rhythm sleep/wake disorders or polysomnography to diagnose sleep-related breathing or movement disorders. Additional monitoring may also be required to assess potential causes of poor sleep, including the use of pulse oximetry to assess overnight breathing and oxygen saturation of the blood, and mats or alarms to monitor potential seizure activity. Finally, the use of video monitoring and/or standardized pain assessment should be used to rule out pain that compromises sleep through overnight observations (e.g., Agar, Oliver, Trickett, Licence, & Richards, 2020).

2.5 Emotional dysregulation

2.5.1 Background and importance

The most likely significant driver of emotional outbursts is emotional dysregulation (see Manning et al., 2016) and we propose that the presence of emotional outbursts indicate that more general emotional dysregulation should be considered. Emotional outbursts are explosive episodes of specified challenging behavior with sudden onset *in combination with* signs of physiological arousal (e.g., facial flushing, excessive salivation). Episodes occur in response to a range of distressing antecedents and setting events, or are "out of the blue" or disproportionate to the cause, and the person cannot calm themselves or be calmed (Cressey, Oliver, Crawford, & Waite, 2019; Tunnicliffe, Woodcock, Bull, Oliver, & Penhallow, 2014). Episodes are typically characterized by individuals losing control, with the patterns of behavior, including specified challenging behaviors, varying within and across individuals (Acker, Knight, & Knott, 2018; Chung, Mevorach, & Woodcock, 2022).

We identify emotional outbursts as both a specified challenging behavior (in Table 1) and an influence on other challenging behaviors and distress. We would argue that it is important to differentiate specified challenging behaviors that occur without evidence of high levels of physiological arousal from emotional outbursts. The latter can be decreased by physiological intervention alone, such as vagal nerve stimulation (Manning et al., 2016, 2019), indicating physiological arousal as central to the behavioral outcomes. Additionally, emotional outbursts are a cause of distress given the observation of significant remorse for outbursts reported by people with Prader-Willi syndrome (Tunnicliffe et al., 2014).

Outbursts are common in people with profound or severe intellectual disability and complex needs (Lowe et al., 2007; Myrbakk & Tetzchner, 2008), and have significant negative implications for the well-being of people who experience outbursts and those around them (Acker et al., 2018; Montaque, Dallos, & McKenzie, 2018; Ryan, 2010). Terms such as 'temper outbursts' and 'tantrums' have been commonly used in previous literature, but caregivers report these to be stigmatizing and inaccurate (Chung, Mevorach, & Woodcock, 2022). Emotional outbursts are typically assumed to manifest from emotion dysregulation, but this etiological relationship is only meaningful if it can account for the variability in the contexts that can cause outbursts within and across individuals with intellectual disability.

2.5.2 Assessment methods

The current means of assessing outbursts are outlined in Table 6. The primary assessment method relies on informant-report measures, such as questionnaires, interviews, and behavior diaries, to produce an overview of an individual's outbursts in terms of impact (e.g., frequency, duration, severity, intensity of outbursts) and the associated contexts. However, the

Table 6 Assessments of emotional dysregulation.

Measures	Domains assessed	Appropriateness for profound and severe intellectual disability	Notes
Informant report			
Developmental Behavior Checklist (Einfeld & Tonge, 1995)	Disruptive Behavior, Self-Absorbed, Communication Disturbance, Anxiety, Social Relating	Established	Extensive normative data available. Not all subscales are relevant to emotional dysregulation.
Child Behavior Checklist (Achenbach & Rescorla, 2001)	Anxious/Depressed, Withdrawn/Depressed, Somatic Complaints, Social Problems, Thought Problems, Attention Problems, Rule-Breaking Behavior, Aggressive Behavior	Probable	Home and School versions. Extensive normative data available. Not all subscales are relevant to emotional dysregulation.
Multidimensional Assessment of Preschool Disruptive Behavior (Wakschlag et al., 2012, 2014)	Temper Loss Noncompliance Aggression Low Concern for Others	Unknown	Includes estimate of outburst severity.
Emotional Outburst Questionnaire (Chung, Mevorach, & Woodcock, 2022)	Characteristics of most severe outbursts Characteristics of least severe outbursts General characteristics of outbursts	Probable	Focusses on precise description of emotional outburst specific to the person being assessed.

Emotional outburst caregiver interview (Tunnicliffe et al., 2014)	Description of outbursts Antecedents and setting events Intervention strategies used	Probable	Parent or caregiver informant.
Emotional outburst behavior diary (Bull, Oliver, Tunnicliffe, & Woodcock, 2015; Bull, Oliver, & Woodcock, 2017)	Description of outbursts Antecedents and setting events Behaviors before and after outbursts	Probable	Parent/caregiver report. Individualized description of sequences of emotional indicators and behaviors.
Direct observation			
(Bull et al., 2017; Bull, Oliver, Callaghan, & Woodcock, 2015; Woodcock et al., 2011)	Outburst-related behaviors Antecedents	Established	Presence of unfamiliar observers may alter the behavior of individuals and caregivers.
Physiological recording			
(Bull, Oliver, Callaghan, & Woodcock, 2015)	Heart rate Physical activity	Unknown	May not be tolerated well. Record of context is important for interpretation.

development of measures for outbursts is currently at a nascent stage, such that further investigation will be required to establish the measures as valid, reliable, and sensitive to change.

2.5.3 Assessment strategy

As indicated in Table 6, assessment strategies for emotional dysregulation are comparatively new, reflecting emerging interest in emotional outbursts as a form of challenging behavior that can be differentiated from other behaviors by the presence of observable indicators of a strong emotional state. An appropriate assessment strategy involves questionnaire methods, usually a specific subscale of a broader assessment (see Table 6), followed by direct observation to identify indicators of a strong emotional state. The latter can be achieved by brief videos recorded by parents or carers.

2.6 Cognitive difference

2.6.1 Background and importance

The term "cognitive difference" is used here to refer to specific cognitive differences underpinned by compromised performance of aspects of Executive Functions (EFs) that cannot be accounted for by degree of intellectual disability. Executive functions are cognitive processes involved in the control and regulation of thoughts, behaviors, and emotions (Miyake & Friedman, 2012). Core EFs include inhibition (the ability to suppress behavior), cognitive flexibility ("set-shifting" or "task-switching"; the ability to switch the focus of attention to adapt and respond appropriately to changing demands and situations) and working memory (the ability to hold in mind and manipulate information to complete tasks; Miyake & Friedman, 2012).

Delayed executive development and difficulties with specific elements of EF are common in individuals with intellectual disability (e.g., Numminen et al., 2000; Pennington & Ozonoff, 1996; Spaniol & Danielsson, 2022). Dissociations in profiles of EF capacities and distinct developmental trajectories for specific EFs are also evidenced within and between rare syndrome groups (Cornish, Scerif, & Karmiloff-Smith, 2007; Landry, Russo, Dawkins, Zelazo, & Burack, 2012; Reid, Moss, Nelson, Groves, & Oliver, 2017; Woodcock, Oliver, & Humphreys, 2009a). For example, more pronounced cognitive flexibility and inhibition difficulties in Cornelia de Lange syndrome when compared to Down syndrome, and greater difficulties with cognitive flexibility, verbal memory and inhibition in Down syndrome compared to Williams syndrome (Costanzo et al., 2013; Reid et al., 2017).

2.6.2 Assessment methods

There are few gold standard assessment batteries of EFs for individuals with more severe intellectual disabilities and the tasks that exist often have limitations. Some neuropsychological tasks that have been designed for young typically developing children have been adapted and/or piloted with individuals with ID, e.g., Battery of Executive Function for Intellectual Disabilities (BEF-ID; Waite, 2012; Waite, Beck, Heald, Powis, & Oliver, 2016). Neuropsychological tasks typically assess EF indirectly based on task performance, however, performance on these tasks is often underpinned by multiple EF components and therefore clinicians and researchers have difficulty concluding whether poor performance indicates a specific or general EF difficulty (the 'task impurity' problem; Miyake, Emerson, & Friedman, 2000). Other difficulties are that tasks rely on verbal language, either to understand task instructions or to generate a response, or do not have appropriate normative data to aid interpretation. Individuals with intellectual disability may also encounter additional difficulties with tasks designed for typically developing populations, such as compromised motor and language development that may impact task performance (Fidler & Lanfranchi, 2022). The ecological validity of EF tasks has also been questioned. Despite these difficulties, there are examples of neuropsychological assessments being employed to demonstrate differing EF profiles in intellectual disability groups (Landry et al., 2012; Woodcock et al., 2009a).

Informant-report measures of EF behavioral manifestations are available and eliminate some of the confounding factors of neuropsychological tasks, such as comprehension of instructions or floor effects (Pulina, Vianello, & Lanfranchi, 2019). These informant-based measures also have improved ecological validity compared to direct assessments (Toplak, West, & Stanovich, 2013). Despite this, there are issues regarding interpretation of these measures because what is considered normal for one informant may be appraised differently by another.

Informant-report questionnaires of EFs have been applied with intellectual disability populations (see Table 7), including the Behavior Rating Inventory of Executive Function 2nd Edition (BRIEF-2; Gioia et al., 2015) and the preschool version for young children (BRIEF-P; Gioia et al., 2003). The BRIEF is appropriate for use in intellectual disability populations and shows sensitivity for identifying difficulties and profiles in some syndrome groups (e.g., Down and Williams syndromes; Csumitta, Stephan, LaQuaglia, Miller, & Lee, 2022; Greiner de Magalhães, Pitts, & Mervis, 2022). An additional strength is that the BRIEF enables evaluation of EF impairments based on age and gender based normative data.

Table 7 Assessments of cognitive difference.

Measures	Domain assessed	Appropriateness for profound and severe intellectual disability	Notes
Informant-report			
Behavior Rating Inventory of Executive Function (BRIEF; Gioia, Isquith, Guy, & Kenworthy, 2000, 2015)	Eight clinical scales (Inhibit, Shift, Emotional Control, Initiate, Working Memory, Plan/Organize, Organization of Materials, Monitor). The clinical scales form two broader Indexes (Behavioral Regulation and Metacognition) and an overall score, the Global Executive Composite.	Probable	Parent/caregiver/teacher-report. Has been used in ID populations and genetic syndromes associated with ID. Normative data based on age and gender, with separate normative tables for parent and teacher forms; provide T scores, percentiles and 90% confidence intervals for four developmental age groups by gender.
Behavior Rating Inventory for Executive Function – Preschool (BRIEF-P; Gioia, Andrews Epsy, & Isquith, 2003)	Five clinical scales (Inhibit, Shift, Emotional Control, Working Memory, Plan/Organize). The clinical scales form three broad indexes (Inhibitory Self-Control, Flexibility, and Emergent Metacognition) and an overall score, the Global Executive Composite.	Probable	Single rating form suitable for parent/caregiver/teacher report. Normative data based on age and gender, with separate normative tables for parent and teacher forms; provide T scores, percentiles and 90% confidence intervals for four developmental age groups by gender.
Comprehensive Executive Functioning Inventory (CEFI; Naglieri & Goldstein, 2013)	Full scale score alongside nine subscales: Attention, Emotion Regulation, Flexibility, Inhibitory Control, Initiation, Organization, Planning, Self-Monitoring, Working Memory. A Consistency Index, Negative Impression and Positive Impression score can be calculated.	Probable	Parent/caregiver/teacher report. Developed for use in children and adolescents aged 5–18 years. Some evidence of internal reliability and test-retest reliability in individuals with ASD (Naglieri & Goldstein, 2013).

The Dysexecutive Behavior Questionnaire for Children (DEX-C; Emslie, Wilson, Burden, Nimmo-Smith, & Wilson, 2003)	Three subscales: Behavioral, Cognitive and Social/Emotional.	Unknown	Should be completed by someone who knows the child well, such as a parent, family member, teacher or care worker.
Learning, Executive, and Attention Functioning scale (LEAF; Castellanos, Kronenberger, & Pisoni, 2018)	Eleven subscales reflecting memory, learning and reasoning skills closely related to EF: comprehension and conceptual learning, factual memory, attention, processing speed, visual-spatial organization, sustained sequential processing, working memory, novel problem solving, mathematics skills, basic reading skills, written expression skills.	Unknown	Normative scores not yet available.
Repetitive Behavior Questionnaire (RBQ; Moss, Oliver, Arron, Burbidge, & Berg, 2009)	Five subscales (stereotyped behaviors, compulsive behaviors, repetitive use of language, restricted preferences, and insistence on sameness behaviors).	Established	Clinical cut-off scores available at item, subscale, and full-scale level. Specifically designed for use in people with rare genetic syndromes associated with ID. Suitable for use with verbal and non-verbal individuals. Behaviors occurring 'once a day' or 'more than once a day' considered to be of clinical significance.
Children's Routines Inventory (Evans et al., 1997)	Designed to assess compulsive-like behaviors. Two subscales: 'Just right' behavior and repetitive/insistence on sameness behaviors.	Probable	Has been used in individuals with Prader-Willi and fragile X syndromes (e.g., Haig & Woodcock, 2017; Woodcock et al., 2009a; Woodcock, Oliver, & Humphreys, 2009b).

Continued

Table 7 Assessments of cognitive difference.—cont'd

Measures	Domain assessed	Appropriateness for profound and severe intellectual disability	Notes
The Activity Questionnaire (TAQ; Burbidge et al., 2010)	Three subscales (Overactivity, Impulsivity and Impulsive Speech).	Established	Contains clinical cut off scores for the overactivity and impulsivity subscales which are considered to indicate abnormally high scores. Developed for use in children and adults with a range of ID. Suitable for use with verbal and non-verbal, and mobile and non-mobile individuals.
Intolerance of Uncertainty Scale – Parent Report (Rodgers, Freeston, South, Wigham, & Boulter, 2012)	Assessment of intolerance to uncertainty (cognitive construct) through examination of emotional, cognitive, and behavioral response to uncertainty.	Probable	Parent/caregiver report. Has been used in ASD samples with some evidence of psychometric properties (Boulter, Freeston, South, & Rodgers, 2013; Chamberlain et al., 2013).
Responses to Uncertainty and Low Environmental Structure (RULES; Sanchez et al., 2017)	Examination of child response to uncertainty and low environmental structure.	Probable	Developed for use in typically developing children aged 3–10 years.
Direct assessment			
The Battery of Executive Function for Intellectual Disabilities (BEF-ID; Waite, 2012; Waite et al., 2016)	Inhibition, working memory, attention/set-shifting, emotion regulation.	Probable	The BEF-ID has been administered in a group of 262 neurotypical children aged 3 to 7.5 years and a group of individuals with Rubinstein-Taybi syndrome. Includes a number of tasks appropriate for a range of developmental ages (15 months upwards).

Simon Spatial Interference Task (Woodcock et al., 2009a; adapted from Simon, 1969)	Response inhibition and task-switching.	Unknown	Has been administered in individuals with Prader-Willi and fragile X syndromes (e.g., Woodcock et al., 2009a).
Test of everyday attention for children (Manly, Robertson, Anderson, & Nimmo-Smith, 1999)	Shifting, Inhibition, Attention (Selective, Divided, Sustained, Attentional Control via several subtests)	Unknown	Not appropriate to test EF below mental age of 6 years.
Behavioral Assessment of Dysexecutive Syndrome - Children (BADS-C; Emslie et al., 2003)	Six tests assessing global executive functioning constructs (planning, organizing, switching/shifting, cognitive estimation, monitoring and inhibition).	Unknown	Designed for use in children aged 8–16 years with neurodevelopmental disorders such as Pervasive Development Disorder, Attention Deficit Hyperactive Disorder (ADHD) and Traumatic Brain Injury. Normative data available: 8 age groups, 3 ability bands, age-scaled scores and percentile ranks. Not appropriate for individuals with more severe ID, however, the BADS-C has been used in adults with mild to moderate ID (e.g., Willner, Bailey, Parry, & Dymond, 2010).
The Hayling and Brixton Tests (Burgess & Shallice, 1997)	Inhibition and Cognitive Flexibility.	Unknown	Requires verbal ability.

Examples of informant report questionnaires that assess behaviors associated with compromised EF include the Repetitive Behavior Questionnaire (RBQ; Moss et al., 2009) and The Activity Questionnaire (TAQ; Burbidge et al., 2010), which assess behavioral manifestations of cognitive inflexibility and impulsivity respectively. These measures were developed for use in genetic syndrome populations with a range of intellectual disabilities and are suitable for both non-verbal and verbal individuals.

In some genetic syndromes neuroimaging techniques, such as functional magnetic resonance imaging (fMRI), have been used in combination with neuropsychological tasks to assess brain functioning in relation to EF abilities. However, in isolation from neuropsychological tasks, neuroimaging techniques have limited ability to contribute to assessment of EF and are often poorly tolerated.

2.6.3 Assessment strategy

Employing a range of assessment measures is important to capture a comprehensive picture of EF (e.g., neuropsychological tasks and informant-report questionnaire measures). Given floor and ceiling effects on EF tasks, utilizing several tasks that cover a wide developmental range can be helpful along with a general measure of cognitive functioning to aid interpretation. Although it is difficult to obtain a pure measure of an EF, employing measures of working memory, inhibition and cognitive flexibility together can aid interpretation (e.g., to rule out that poor performance on an inhibition task is not due to forgetting the rules due to poor working memory). It is not uncommon for informant report and direct assessment measures to align poorly, consequently clinicians may need to conduct observations of the individual in their everyday context and clinical interviews to gather a detailed understanding of the person's presenting difficulties when interpreting the EF scores.

2.7 Social difference

2.7.1 Background and importance

The term 'social functioning' is used here to refer to a range of social abilities and preferences that contribute to the successful navigation of social interaction. It includes differences in social behavior that are central to the diagnosis of ASD, as well as broader aspects of day-to-day social interaction that are not autism specific, such as motivation for and enjoyment of social interaction, and social avoidance. Social functioning is to some extent inherent in the conceptualization of severe intellectual disability, with evaluation of day-to-day social abilities being one of several core components used to assess an individual's global adaptive functioning (American Psychological Association, 2013).

2.7.2 Assessment methods

Table 8 provides an overview of assessment tools. Most assessments relevant to this domain are designed for screening for and diagnosing ASD specifically. However, these standardized tools lack sensitivity and specificity when used in the context of co-occurring intellectual disability, particularly in genetic syndromes with distinct profiles of autistic traits (Thurm, Farmer, Salzman, Lord, & Bishop, 2019). The Social Communication Questionnaire (Rutter et al., 2003) is one of few informant questionnaires with good discrimination between autism and intellectual disability but there is evidence that psychometric properties are compromised for some genetic syndromes (Moss, Howlin, & Oliver, 2011). For diagnosis, the ADOS-2 (Lord et al., 2012) has good diagnostic validity and reliability across abilities but might be compromised for those with the most severe disability (Moss et al., 2011). Other common standardized tools assess adaptive social skills (e.g., Vineland Adaptive Behavior Scales 3rd edition, Sparrow et al., 2016). These measures are frequently used during diagnosis, have good reliability and validity, cover a wide age range of skills (0–89 years) and enable assessment of change over development or in response to intervention.

Typically, only broad clinical cut-off scores are used in assessment, simply for the purpose of diagnosis. However, these fail to describe more subtle profiles of strengths and challenges- information which could guide more targeted support. Fine grained scoring systems of autistic traits (e.g., in the ADOS-2) allow more in-depth evaluation of social functioning not restricted by diagnostic boundaries. However, such approaches often lack sufficient normative data for those with more severe intellectual disability. Adaptations of standardized screening measures for specific genetic syndromes with atypical autistic trait profiles indicate better specificity and sensitivity within these populations (Kidd et al., 2020). For example, the shortened form of the SRS-2 appears to have better validity for Phelan-McDermid syndrome than the long form (Gergoudis et al., 2020). Recent development of informant reports (Moss et al., 2016), standardized behavioral observation paradigms (Hall, DeBernardis, & Reiss, 2006; Hessl, Glaser, Dyer-Friedman, & Reiss, 2006; Nelson, Crawford, Reid, Moss, & Oliver, 2017; Roberts et al., 2009) and accompanying observational rating

Table 8 Assessments of social difference.

Measures	Domains assessed	Appropriateness for profound and severe intellectual disability	Notes
Informant report			
Adaptive Behavior Assessment (ABAS-3; Harrison & Oakland, 2015)	Assess adaptive skills within the social domain: (social and leisure subscales)	Established	Parent/caregiver report. Designed for diagnosing and evaluating individuals with developmental disabilities. Norm-referenced scaled scores available for each subscale based on a large representative of the US population including those with and without an ID. Wide age range enables evaluation of change across time (0–89 years).
Assessment of Social Competence (ASC; Meyer et al., 1985)	Eleven dimensions (initiate, self-regulate, follow rules, provide positive reinforcement, provide negative feedback, obtain cues, offer assistance, accept assistance, indicate preference, cope with negatives, and terminate).	Established	Parent/caregiver report Designed for all levels of functioning but Meyer, Cole, McQuarter, and Reichle (1990) used it on a sample of individuals with moderate - severe ID, with good reliability). Ceiling effect when used on young adults (ages it can be used on may be limited, suitable for 7–21 years)
Matson Evaluation of Social Skills for individuals with severe mental retardation (MESSIER; Matson, 1995)	Positive verbal, Positive non-verbal, General positive, Negative verbal, Negative non-verbal, General negative	Established	Parent/caregiver report. Designed specifically for adults with severe and profound ID. Cut-off scores available (Matson & Boisjoli, 2008). Overlap with other constructs, e.g., challenging behavior. Very broad categories (positive or negative).

Sociability Questionnaire for people with Intellectual Disabilities (SQID; Oliver et al., 2021)	Sociability, social anxiety Social contexts (receive interaction, ongoing interaction, initiate interaction, group interaction) Interaction with familiar/ unfamiliar person Selective mutism	Probable	Parent/caregiver report. Designed for ID populations. Enables assessment of verbal and non-verbal individuals. Assessment of behaviors across wide range of contexts. Sensitive to wide range and heterogeneous social profiles. Lack of normative data.
Social Communication Questionnaire (SCQ; Rutter, Bailey, & Lord, 2003)	Communication and Reciprocal Social interaction autistic-related traits	Probable	Parent/caregiver report.
Social Responsiveness Questionnaire second edition (SRS-2, Constantino & Gruber, 2012)	Social awareness, social cognition, social communication, social motivation autistic-related traits	Probable	Parent/caregiver report. Preschool (2.5–4.5 years), School-age (4–18 years) and Adult (19 years and older) forms available. Some validation of first edition in mild to moderate ID but not severe/profound ID.
Vineland Adaptive Behavior Scale 3rd edition (Vineland-3; Sparrow, Cicchetti, & Saulnier, 2016)	Assesses adaptive abilities in the Socialization domain (interpersonal relationships, play and leisure, and coping skills subscales)	Established	Parent/caregiver report. Designed for diagnosing and evaluating individuals with developmental disabilities. Normative data available from birth to from birth to 90 years. Good ecological validity - what individuals actually use in day-to-day life, their functional/adaptive ability.

Continued

Table 8 Assessments of social difference.—cont'd

Measures	Domains assessed	Appropriateness for profound and severe intellectual disability	Notes
Direct Observation			
Autism Diagnostic Observation Schedule, Second Edition (ADOS-2; Lord et al., 2012)	Communication and Reciprocal Social interaction autistic-related traits	Probable	Considered the 'gold standard' semi-structured observational assessment of autism spectrum disorder. Include five modules – Toddler (12–30 months old, pre-verbal/single words), module 1 (31 months and older, pre-verbal/single words), module 2 (phrase speech), module 3 (child/adolescent, fluent speech), module 4 (adolescent/adult, fluent speech). Requires formal training. Some validation in people mild to moderate ID but not severe to profound ID.
Child Sociability Rating Scale (CSRS; Oliver et al., 2021)	Behavioral indicators of social enjoyment (negative affect, social anxiety, social avoidance, nature of physical contact, positive affect, social responsiveness), social motivation (motivation for adult interaction, spontaneous initiation of interaction, spontaneous initiation of physical contact, focus of child attention) and social interaction skills (social-communication, eye contact)	Probable	Direct observation of operationally defined behaviors. Does not require special training. Can be applied across a range of social settings, both naturalistic and experimental, with familiar and unfamiliar individuals. Sensitive to phenotypic differences between genetic syndromes. Not validated against a typical developing sample. No validated clinical cut-off scores.

Social anxiety and social motivation scale (SAMS; Crawford et al., 2020)	Behavioral indicators of social anxiety (Gaze, Vocal Length, Time to First Utterance, Avoidance of Social Interaction, Discomfort, Negative Emotional Affect) and social motivation (Positive Emotional Affect, Focus of Attention, Social Responsiveness, Socially Motivated Initiation of Interaction)	Probable	Direct observation of operationally defined behaviors. Does not require special training. Can be applied across a range of social settings, both naturalistic and experimental, with familiar and unfamiliar individuals. Sensitive to phenotypic differences between genetic syndromes. Not validated against a typical developing sample. No validated clinical cut-off scores. Suitable for verbal and non-verbal individuals but currently only been applied to verbal participants.

scales (Crawford et al., 2020) focus on non-autism specific behaviors, and have shown to be sensitive to subtle but important differences in a range of domains including social engagement, motivation and anxiety across different social contexts. However, currently these measures lack normative data.

2.7.3 Assessment strategy

Questionnaires can provide quick measures of broad profiles of social difficulties whereas clinical interviews provide in-depth information on current behavior and developmental history. Direct observation places demands on the person with intellectual disability but yields more objective social profiles. However, the reliability of coders needs to be established and maintained. Some may find direct assessments with unfamiliar individuals and high social demands stressful and engage in attention-escape maintained behaviors (Rispoli, Ninci, Neely, & Zaini, 2014).

Autism assessment should be considered, given the high prevalence of autism traits among those with severe intellectual disability and some genetic syndromes (LaMalfa, Lassi, Bertelli, Salvini, & Placidi, 2004; Richards, Jones, Groves, Moss, & Oliver, 2015). Autism can increase the likelihood of challenging behavior in those with intellectual disability due to additional communication difficulties (Absoud, Wake, Ziriat, & Hassiotis, 2019) and is associated with compromised social and physical wellbeing (Arias et al., 2018). It is important to recognize that some social differences may benefit from similar clinical and educational support strategies primarily developed for autistic people and an ASD diagnosis may provide wider access to services.

2.8 Learned or functional behavior

2.8.1 Background and importance

For the specified challenging behaviors listed in the Table 1, there is substantial evidence that people can learn to show these behaviors when particular types of social circumstances or sensory conditions are present, and that these behaviors are then reinforced and so become more likely to occur under the same conditions in the future. When this is the case, these behaviors are often referred to as learned or functional. The empirical evidence that these behaviors can be learned comes from studies manipulating the level and type of social interaction and available sensory input, reducing the reward following the behavior or reward competing behaviors. In each case concomitant changes in the behavior indicate the behavior is likely to be learned. Less robust evidence that behaviors are learned comes from establishing a chain of behavior from an antecedent or trigger before the behavior, the behavior itself and a response that is likely to be rewarding or reinforcing.

There are three basic mechanisms of reward: 1) positive social reinforcement. This typically takes the form of attention from others or access to activities or tangible items such as food, drink, etc., 2) negative social reinforcement, typically the removal of demands to do something but could also be the removal of someone from a situation they find aversive or anxiety provoking, and 3) either positive or negative sensory reinforcement. Examples are perceived light from eye pressing and scratching an itch respectively.

2.8.2 Assessment methods

The possibility that a behavior is learned and functional should always be evaluated. Throughout this process it is important to consider individual forms of behavior (e.g., self-injury, aggression) separately until there is evidence that they serve the same function. The main approach to assessment is to evaluate if there is a meaningful association between events prior to and following the behavior. Five types of assessment seek to establish the sequence of events surrounding an episode of behavior: interview, charts, questionnaires, scatter and probability plots, and natural observations (see Table 9). The most widely used assessment is an informal but structured interview with someone who has seen a number of episodes of the behavior. Two types of charts, Antecedent-Behavior-Consequence (ABC) and Settings-Trigger-Action-Results (STAR), are completed after episodes of behavior are seen and provide a narrative account of the sequence of events and hence possible antecedents and consequences. Questionnaires such as the Motivation Assessment Scale (Durand & Crimmins, 1988) and the Questionnaire About Behavioral Function (Matson & Vollmer, 1995; Paclawskyj et al., 2000) focus more on the antecedents to behavior and the overall likelihood of behavior given environmental events, and have scoring protocols. Scatter and probability plots are completed based on the direct observation of the frequency of behavior when given environmental conditions are present and generate indices of the relationship between antecedents and behavior. Finally, direct natural observations involve systematically defining and recording events with either informal or calculated analysis of the relationship between antecedents and the consequences of behavior. A sixth strategy, experimental functional analysis,

Table 9 Assessments of learned and functional behavior.

Measures	Domains assessed	Appropriateness for profound and severe intellectual disability	Notes
Informant Report			
Motivational Assessment Scale (MAS; Durand & Crimmins, 1988)	Assesses social and non-social hypotheses for behavior. Attention (social positive reinforcement), Tangible (social positive reinforcement), Escape (social negative reinforcement), Sensory (non-social reinforcement)	Established	Parent/caregiver rating scale. Developed for people with ID across the range of abilities. Robust reliability and validity.
Questions About Behavioral Function (QABF; Matson & Vollmer, 1995; Paclawskyj, Matson, Rush, Smalls, & Vollmer, 2000)	Assesses social, non-social and physical hypotheses for behavior. Attention (social positive reinforcement), Tangible (social positive reinforcement), Demand (social negative reinforcement), Non-social (automatic reinforcement), Physical (pain).	Established	Parent/caregiver rating scale. Developed for people with ID across the range of abilities. Robust reliability and validity.
Direct Observation			
Scatterplot (Touchette, MacDonald, & Langer, 1985)	The frequency of a behavior of interest is recorded over time (hours, days, weeks). Typically the presence or absence of the behavior of interest is recorded for specified time intervals. Establishing the temporal distribution of a behavior can be used to schedule future observations efficiently and identify general 'high frequency' or 'behavior present' periods which may relate to particular activities that occur at those times.	Established	Parents, teachers, caregivers and/or professionals can conduct an ABC assessment in school, home or in the community. Developed for people with ID across the range of abilities. Limited reliability and validity data.

(ABC: Antecedents, Behaviors & Consequences; Groden, 1989) (STAR: Settings, Triggers, Actions & Results; Zarkowska & Clements, 1994)	Detailed narrative descriptions of the antecedents and consequences of behavior(s) of interest are recorded. The topography, frequency, duration, physical effects of the behavior are described.	Established	Parents, teachers, caregivers and/or professionals can conduct an ABC assessment in school, home or in the community. Developed for people with ID across the range of abilities.
Sequential analysis (Emerson et al., 1996)	Involves recording the sequence of occurrence of behaviors of interest, antecedent and consequent events. Conditional probabilities are calculated: a) for the behavior of interest given a particular antecedent and b) for particular consequences given the occurrence of a particular behavior.	Established	Conducted by researchers or professionals with experience of using observational methods and software.
Direct Observation (Structured / Experimental)			
Experimental Functional Analysis (Carr & Durand, 1985; Iwata, Dorsey, Slifer, Bauman, & Richman, 1982)	Considered the gold standard in functional behavioral assessment. A series of analogue / experimental conditions in which antecedent and consequent events (known to commonly play a role in the maintenance of challenging behaviors in individuals with an ID) are experimentally manipulated to test hypotheses surrounding the cause / maintenance of an individual's behavior. Social and non-social hypotheses can be tested. The frequency / duration of behaviors of interest is observed under analogue test conditions such as: (1) attention or low attention and (2) tangibles (social positive reinforcement), (3) demand or difficult tasks (social negative reinforcement), (4) alone (non-social reinforcement) in comparison to (5) free play (control condition). Analogue conditions are repeated a number of times in rapid succession.	Established	Conducted under the supervision of a professional with experience of assessing and conducting interventions with individuals with a severe ID (due to the ethical / safety issues associated with this method). Brief functional analyses (Northrup et al., 1991) comprise of shorter sessions for a set number of repetitions regardless of response differentiation.

Continued

Table 9 Assessments of learned and functional behavior.—cont'd

Measures	Domains assessed	Appropriateness for profound and severe intellectual disability	Notes
Structured Descriptive Assessment (SDA; Anderson & Long, 2002)	Similar to functional analysis but only antecedents are manipulated and consequences are free to vary. Antecedent conditions typically include those known to be associated with challenging behavior in individuals with an ID such a: (a) Attention delivery/deprivation (b) Tangible delivery/deprivation (c) Prompt (or demands) / prompt removal Rates / duration of behaviors of interest are compared across test and control conditions to inform hypotheses about the functions of behavior.	Established	Conducted under the supervision of a professional with experience of assessing and conducting interventions with individuals with a severe ID (due to the ethical / safety issues associated with this method).

differs from these five strategies because there is systematic manipulation of the probable antecedents and consequences of behavior to establish empirically an effect on the rate or duration of a behavior. Various methods have been developed to reduce ethical concerns and increase sampling, including brief analogues and structured descriptive assessments.

2.8.3 Assessment strategy

Assessment methods differ in terms of the resources required (expertise of the practitioner, time and physical resources), the capacity for sampling possible influences and episodes of the behavior, ethical and safety issues, and reliability and validity of the methods. Table 9 describes the variability across strategies regarding these dimensions. Broadly, as the reliability and validity of methods increase, so do the ethical and safety concerns and the demand on resources with a corresponding loss of the capacity for sampling possible influences. These differences across assessment strategies indicate that a combination of strategies is likely to be beneficial. The decision on the combination used can be guided by key questions about the complete process:

1. Are all the likely possible learned functions considered across environments? Including atypical and idiosyncratic functions.
2. Are interactions between functions and other domains considered? For example, the effects of poor sleep, pain, sensory sensitivity, low mood and anxiety on demand escape behavior; impulsivity on tangible reward.
3. Has the behavior been directly observed by the practitioner to establish levels of safety and distress that will inform intervention decisions?
4. Have communicative and other behaviors that reliably precede or co-occur with episodes of challenging behaviors been described or observed?
5. Does the assessment process minimize ethical concerns, maximize safety and well-being whilst generating sufficiently robust information to inform interventions?

Given these key questions, it is likely that the process of assessment will involve interview (Q1, Q2 and Q3), either charts or questionnaires (Q1), and direct natural observation or experimental functional analysis (Q1, Q3 and Q4) within a hypothesis driven framework. This combination will help strike a balance between the need to sample across influences and combinations of influences to inform interventions, whilst minimizing concerns about distress and safety (Q5).

2.9 Communication

2.9.1 Background and importance

Communicating with others enables choice and control over environments, impacts on the ability to form and maintain relationships, and influences all aspects relating to quality of life and emotional well-being (García, Díez, Wojcik, & Santamaría, 2020; Petry, Maes, & Vlaskamp, 2005; Smith et al., 2020). Communication can be divided into receptive and expressive abilities; receptive communication is how information is interpreted and understood, expressive communication is how thoughts, feelings, needs and desires are expressed. Communication skills in individuals with severe and complex needs can be further defined as pre-symbolic, symbolic, and verbal (Boardman, Bernal, & Hollins, 2014), with symbolic communication determined according to an individual's use and understanding of pictures, photographs, gestures and signs. In terms of verbal ability, 66% of individuals with severe intellectual disability were described as pre-linguistic or minimally verbal and 6% communicated using multiple non-echolalic words (Snell et al., 2010). There is an extensive literature documenting the relationship between expressive communication and behaviors such as self-injury and aggression.

2.9.2 Assessment methods

People with severe to profound intellectual disability mostly communicate at the pre-linguistic stage of communication, which many norm-referenced, standardized assessments do not directly or comprehensively measure (Brady et al., 2012). This problem is further compounded by people with complex needs being more likely to use unconventional, idiosyncratic forms of communication or more likely to evidence sensory differences and motor impairments that are difficult to measure within a formal standardized assessment context (Chadwick, Buell, & Goldbart, 2019). As such, individuals may be reliant on others to interpret their pre-symbolic forms of communication, such as gestures, facial expressions, and body language (Coupe-O'Kane & Goldbart, 1998). The use of informant report or direct assessment should be selected based on purpose, context and need. A summary of specific assessment tools appropriate for severe to profound intellectual disability populations is outlined in Table 10, with a focus on both general and expressive communication skills. More in-depth reviews on approaches and considerations to communication assessment are also available (Chadwick et al., 2019; Ogletree & Price, 2018).

Table 10 Assessments of communication.

Measures	Domains assessed	Appropriateness for profound and severe intellectual disability	Notes
Informant report measures			
Inventory of Potential Communicative Acts (IPCA; Sigafoos et al., 2000)	Questions ask how a child communicates according to 10 distinct pragmatic functions. Under each general function, specific communicative exemplars are assessed.	Established	Original field testing with 30 children with developmental disabilities indicated good agreement between parents and teachers (Sigafoos et al., 2000). Developed for use in ID populations with severe communication impairment. Not a formal or standardized assessment. Interview-based assessment (also in questionnaire format).
Pre-Verbal Communication Schedule (PVCS; Kiernan & Reid, 1987)	Eight subscale scores evaluate how the person uses his/her means of communication and 2 direct test subscale items evaluate imitation skills based on motor imitation and understanding.	Established	Good inter-rater reliability data for the schedule items in study with 48 individuals with ID. Most items were reported to have >0.70 agreement (Kiernan & Reid, 1987). Developed to measure functional use of communication in children with ID. Parent survey – now out of print.
Communication Matrix (Rowland, 2004)	Organized into seven levels of communicative competence. Looks at four major reasons to communicate (refusal, obtainment, social interaction, provide/seek information).	Probable	Original matrix developing according to communication in typically developing infants. Has been used to measure communication in individuals with severe ID and with people using unaided/aided AAC devices.

Continued

Table 10 Assessments of communication.—cont'd

Measures	Domains assessed	Appropriateness for profound and severe intellectual disability	Notes
Checklist of Communication Competencies (Triple C; Bloomberg, West, Johnson, & Iacono, 2009)	Assesses for observations of behavior according to five levels: unintentional passive, unintentional active, intentional informal, basic symbolic, and established symbolic.	Established	Checklist of behaviors designed to be completed by support staff of adults with ID, and severe, complex needs. Not suitable for adults who communicate using more than 50 words, signs or symbols. Items do not take into account functional impairments such as sensory impairments or medication side effects. Measure completed by two caregivers across different environments, over a 1–2 week period.
Direct observations			
Communication and Symbolic Behavior Scales Developmental Profile (CSBS-DP; Wetherby & Prizant, 2002)	Consists of communication and symbolic rating scales grouped into seven "clusters". Three measures of communication: a one-page Infant-Toddler Checklist, a four-page Caregiver Questionnaire; and a Behavior Sample, which is a face-to-face evaluation of the child interacting with a parent present.	Unknown	Developed as a screening tool to identify children who may present with developmental delay or disability. Validated for use with children aged up to 6 years, but is not validated with older children or adolescents with severe ID. Includes both informant report and observational components. Must be administered in a professional setting with trained clinician.

Communication Complexity Scale (CCS; Brady et al., 2012, 2018)	The CCS encompasses three levels of early expressive communication behaviors: preintentional and intentional non-symbolic communication (gestures, eye gaze, vocalizations) and early intentional communication (speech, signs or symbols).	Established	Developed and validated with children and adults with intellectual, developmental or multiple disabilities, including autism, motor and visual impairments. Minimum of 12 different scripted communication opportunities to elicit communication (e.g., stopping a desired activity, presenting a choice between two objects). Only tested in structured (scripted) contexts with specific focus on behavior regulation. Intended use currently for research and practice as opposed to clinical use.

Informant report provides a good overview of the individual's repertoire and current communicative abilities, particularly in relation to idiosyncrasies across a range of environments and situations. However, it is difficult to identify and interpret pre-linguistic communication skills via informant report in comparison to more overt communication skills such as word production (Eadie et al., 2010). Parental variability in reporting within a research context is also an important consideration (Crais & Ogletree, 2016). Examples of appropriate informant report measures for individuals communicating at a pre-linguistic level include: the Inventory of Potential Communicative Acts (IPCA; Sigafoos et al., 2000), the Pre-Verbal Communication Schedule (PVCS; Kiernan & Reid, 1987), the Communication Matrix (Rowland, 2004) and the Checklist of Communication Competencies (Triple C; Bloomberg et al., 2009).

Direct observations can examine the influence of the environment on communication, as well as providing more detail about the subtleties of communication skills. Observations can either be structured or naturalistic depending on the context of assessment, with strengths and limitations to both approaches. Structured observations provide a standardized model of assessment and are therefore more beneficial in research contexts. Examples of structured direct assessments for severe to profound intellectual disability populations include: the Communication and Symbolic Behavior Scales Developmental Profile (CSBS-DP; Wetherby & Prizant, 2002) and the Communication Complexity Scale (CCS; Brady et al., 2012). In contrast, naturalistic observations are less resource and time intensive and may be more informative in clinical contexts. The biggest overall limitation of direct observations is the increased likelihood of missing communicative abilities within the short window of opportunity. The familiarity versus novelty of the observation setting and the familiarity of the communication partner can all influence the demonstration of communicative abilities, with greater familiarity yielding better results (Crais & Ogletree, 2016; Iverson, Capirci, & Caselli, 1994; Lewedag, Oller, & Lynch, 1994).

2.9.3 Assessment strategy

The selection of assessments, and subsequent development of an assessment strategy, may need to be tailored according to an individual's specific needs, their learning environment, and the precise rationale for assessment. As previously noted, pain, anxiety, sensory experiences, visual or hearing impairments, and the presentation of behavior need to be considered within a communicative context. From a research perspective, particular practical and ethical considerations include: the selection of appropriate settings and assessments, the availability and validity of assessments and demand on both individuals and their families. Detailed assessment across multiple settings and contexts is important to determine the accuracy of communication passports; a tool for supporting people who need help to communicate important information about themselves, particularly their communication strengths and needs. Within clinical settings, additional systemic factors may impact on the precise assessment framework and strategy selected by clinicians, including the availability of particular assessments, clinician training, clinical guidelines (e.g., NICE guidance in the UK) and resources available within a particular service. It is important to highlight the use of checklists and unpublished/adapted assessments in clinical practice, which can be informative and necessary depending on individual profile (Chadwick et al., 2019).

The overall goal of assessment is to determine how an individual communicates to inform strategies for intervention and support (Johnson et al., 2012). Assessment should be an iterative and dynamic process repeated across the lifespan to capture changes in presentation and need, which is particularly important when considering the introduction and effectiveness of augmentative and alternative communication (AAC) devices (Sigafoos, O'Reilly, Lancioni, & Sutherland, 2014). Communication partners and speech and language therapists are of critical importance within the assessment strategy, and a person-centered, multidisciplinary approach to assessment and intervention is key (Boardman et al., 2014; Chadwick et al., 2019; Goldbart, Chadwick, & Buell, 2014). This is important because communication may vary in different contexts. Familiarity in relation to the assessment setting and availability of familiar caregivers and professionals can influence the demonstration of communicative abilities, with greater familiarity yielding greater levels of communication. Therefore, multiple methods of assessment with multiple people will provide the most accurate overall picture of an individual's communicative strengths and needs.

3. The relationship between domains

As noted previously, when addressing challenging behavior and distress in people with profound or severe intellectual disability and complex needs, the combination of compromised expressive communication and atypical presentation of many conditions is a significant barrier to assessment and intervention selection. In addition to these problems, the accumulation of the number of the domains that influence challenging behavior or distress in any individual, and the moderating or mediating effects of domains on other domains compounds the complexity of clinical formulation. In this section we identify the influences of domains on specified challenging behaviors and the interactions between domains.

3.1 Pain and discomfort

In pediatric populations with physical disabilities and sleep disorders, pain exacerbates poor sleep (Allen, Graef, Ehrentraut, Tynes, & Crabtree, 2016; Hemmingsson, Stenhammar, & Paulsson, 2009). Similarly, in children with intellectual disability, those experiencing pain have shorter sleep duration and more sleep problems than children not experiencing pain (Breau & Camfield, 2011). In other populations, pain is associated with anxiety, which can influence social behavior more generally and increase the motivation for learned or functional behaviors.

3.2 Sensory sensitivity

There is a strong association between sensory processing and anxiety, and particularly auditory hypersensitivity and anxiety in autism (MacLennan, Rossow, & Tavassoli, 2021) and rare genetic syndromes, such as Williams syndromes (Royston et al., 2020). Sensory modulation differences can affect sleep, potentially due to sensitivity to background noise and bedsheets. Specifically, hypersensitivity to touch accounts for substantial variation in parent-reported sleep disturbance in autistic children (Tzischinsky et al., 2018). Finally, sensory sensitivity can interact with learned or functional behavior by increasing the motivation for escape behaviors and behaviors that lead to access to preferred sensory stimuli.

3.3 Anxiety and low mood

Anxiety and/or low mood in the typically developing population are associated with poor sleep, social difference, and pain, with research increasingly establishing the importance of these links for individuals with intellectual disability (e.g., Whitney et al., 2019). Anxiety and low mood have an impact on the wider family. For example, parents of autistic children with higher levels of anxiety report lower quality of life for both children and parents (Adams, Clark, & Simpson, 2020). The domains associated with anxiety and/or low mood are associated in complex and multi-directional ways. For example, poor sleep may be both a cause and an effect of anxiety and/or low mood, and poor sleep may also affect parents/caregivers, and thus contribute to anxiety more widely within the family system. Anxiety and low mood can also increase the motivation for learned or functional specific challenging behaviors. For example, social anxiety can increase the likelihood of escape motivated behaviors in social settings.

3.4 Poor sleep

Poor sleep can increase rates of anxiety and underpin low mood (Alvaro, Roberts, & Harris, 2013; Baglioni et al., 2011). Sleep disturbance has also been linked to high levels of irritability, impulsive behavior and emotional outbursts (Didden, Korzilius, Aperlo, Overloop, & Vries, 2002). In individuals with intellectual disability and complex needs, difficulties with sleep may be exacerbated by pain from under-detected and under-treated health conditions (Agar et al., 2020), especially in those who are not able to self-report pain. These include, but are not limited to, constipation, gastro-esophageal reflux, respiratory tract infections, otitis media, and dental caries (Hartshorne et al., 2009; Mannion, Leader, & Healy, 2013; Weckwerth et al., 2016). As noted above, sensory sensitivity to specific aspects of the sleeping environment (e.g., a label in the pajamas, the texture of bedclothing) or anxiety around falling asleep or being separated from a caregiver may also make it more difficult for individuals to settle to sleep (Cortesi, Giannotti, Ivanenko, & Johnson, 2010). Finally, elevated rates of sociability may make individuals more likely to seek caregiver input at bedtime and overnight that requires a caregiver response, particularly when there are overnight safety or health-related concerns (Agar et al., 2022; Agar, Oliver, & Richards, 2022). This in turn can reinforce cycles of learned behavior around caregiver presence at sleep onset, which can result in difficulties with settling and night waking (Didden, Sigafoos, & Lancioni, 2011).

3.5 Emotional dysregulation

Emotional outbursts can be triggered by environmental events that are experienced as aversive due to specific cognitive difference (Tunnicliffe et al., 2014; Woodcock et al., 2009a). For example, emotional outbursts in response to expectations or changes in routine in individuals with Prader-Willi syndrome are associated with a specific impairment in task-switching, such that the demands of change may overwhelm individuals and trigger emotional outbursts when emotion dysregulation is present

(Woodcock et al., 2009a, 2009b; Woodcock et al., 2011). There is some evidence that this same relationship between cognitive difference and emotional outbursts might hold for individuals with other neurodevelopmental conditions (Miller, Ragozzino, Cook, Sweeney, & Mosconi, 2015). Anxiety can be evoked by environmental events, and autistic adolescents have described how anxiety could become overwhelming and consequently escalate into outbursts (Acker et al., 2018; Cressey et al., 2019; Tunnicliffe et al., 2014).

Sensory stimuli have been reported to be direct antecedents of emotional outbursts, likely related to individual differences in sensory processing (Acker et al., 2018; Duignan & Connell, 2015; Ryan, 2010). It has been hypothesized that the demands from background sensory stimuli may interfere with the ability of individuals with sensory sensitivity to regulate their emotions across a wide range of seemingly unrelated contexts (Chung, Mevorach, & Woodcock, 2022). Individuals who are sensitive to social demands may be more likely to perceive social situations as threatening or lacking in safety, which has been hypothesized to lead to the experience of outbursts in these unsafe contexts (e.g., in public; Chung et al., 2022). Conversely, some people may be socially motivated to suppress their emotions in these unsafe contexts (e.g., to maintain social desirability), which may result in an increase in negative emotions that can escalate into outbursts when individuals return to a safe environment (e.g., at home; Chung et al., 2022).

3.6 Cognitive difference

Associations have been identified between specific cognitive difference and behavioral outcomes. Examples are: compromised inhibitory control and impulsivity (Burbidge et al., 2010; Young et al., 2009), cognitive inflexibility and adherence to routines/insistence on sameness (Woodcock et al., 2009a, 2009b), and compromised working memory with repetitive questioning (Walley & Donaldson, 2005; Wigren & Hansen, 2005). These associations can underpin and influence specific challenging behaviors, distress and/or anxiety (Furniss & Biswas, 2012; Woodcock et al., 2009b). For example, impulsivity is a robust risk marker for more severe and persistent self-injurious and/or aggressive behavior in people with intellectual disability generally and in specific populations, e.g., tuberous sclerosis complex, fragile X syndrome (Crawford, Karakatsani, Singla, & Oliver, 2019; Wilde et al., 2018). Compromised cognitive flexibility can contribute to self-injury, aggressive or destructive behaviors alongside emotional outbursts, if there are unexpected or undesired changes to routines or plans (e.g., temper outbursts in Prader-Willi syndrome; Woodcock et al., 2009a, 2009b). However, similar EF difficulties might lead to varying behavioral presentations across syndromes. For example, cognitive inflexibility and associated adherence to routines occurs in Prader-Willi and fragile X syndromes but these difficulties are associated with severe anxiety in fragile X rather than emotional outbursts (Woodcock et al., 2009b).

3.7 Social difference

Reduced social functioning is associated with poorer quality of life (Arias et al., 2018) and compromised mental health (Cervantes & Matson, 2015). Autism characteristics are reported in at least 40% of individuals with an intellectual disability (LaMalfa et al., 2004) and over half of autistic individuals have an associated intellectual disability (Charman et al., 2011; Loomes, Hull, & Mandy, 2017). Those with a genetic syndrome associated with intellectual disability are at least 10 times more likely to show autistic traits compared to the general population (Richards et al., 2015). Increased prevalence of autism in genetic syndrome populations has been argued to be caused by associated intellectual disability, which inhibits the capacity for cognitive compensation, allowing independently "inherited" autistic traits to manifest (Skuse, 2007). However, research indicates varying prevalence and phenotypic differences in autism traits and broader social profiles across genetic syndromes with comparable levels of intellectual disability (Moss & Howlin, 2009). Examples include higher levels of social motivation seen in Williams, Angelman, Smith-Magenis and Down syndromes (Horsler & Oliver, 2006, Oliver et al., 2007, Wilde, Mitchell, & Oliver, 2016) and social anxiety, selective mutism, extreme shyness in Cornelia de Lange and fragile X syndromes (Moss et al., 2016). These profiles appear driven by distinct etiological pathways, and vary in developmental trajectory (Ellis, Oliver, Stefanidou, Apperly, & Moss, 2020).

The importance of social differences to specified challenging behaviors and other domains lies primarily in motivation for learned and functional behaviors. In Angelman and Smith-Magenis syndromes a strong preference for social contact can drive specified challenging behaviors such as self-injury and aggression when the behaviors are maintained by access to social contact (Oliver et al., 2013). Similarly, it is likely that the poor sleep evident in these syndromes might contribute to social signaling following night-time waking in each of these syndromes, a problem likely exacerbated by impulsivity downstream from a cognitive difference in these syndromes. Social difference might also be underpinned by social anxiety, and hence related to anxiety, in Cornelia de Lange and fragile X syndromes. There is also an association between social initiation and EF problems in Cornelia de Lange syndrome that might drive the social anxiety (Reid et al., 2017).

3.8 Learned or functional behavior

All other domains evidence a possible influence on learned and functional behaviors. Arguably, 'pain gate' theory could explain why a self-injurious act occurs in response to pain (i.e. by the transient reduction (negative reinforcement by gating) of pain). The behavior initially caused by pain could then become learned or functional. A second mechanism is increased motivation for a learned behavior. For example, the demands that trigger a functional behavior, can be made more aversive if someone is in pain, sleep deprived or experiencing anxiety. Additionally, if people experience sensory sensitivity, then sensory stimuli can trigger a behavior that is reinforced by escape from that sensation. A similar argument can be made for anxiety provoking stimuli or disruption to routines if these are strongly preferred and a strong motivation for social contact can increase the likelihood of attention-maintained behaviors when attention levels are low. Finally, if expressive communication is compromised, then functional behaviors that are socially reinforced can serve a substitute pragmatic communicative purpose.

3.9 Communication

Due to the emphasis on self-report for the diagnosis of most health conditions, individuals who are non-verbal are at significant risk for undiagnosed and untreated painful physical health conditions (McGuire, Daly, & Smyth, 2010; Symons, Harper, McGrath, Breau, & Bodfish, 2009). Several studies have highlighted the association between low levels of communication or verbal ability and behaviors such as self-injury and aggression (Danquah et al., 2009; Matson, Boisjoli, & Mahan, 2009; Schroeder et al., 2014). The persistence of self-injury is particularly associated with low levels of verbal communication in autistic people (Richards, Moss, Nelson, & Oliver, 2016), and may persist over time when pain, sensory overload, discomfort or distress are experienced (Kern et al., 2006). In individuals at the pre-linguistic stage, it is difficult for the communication partner to interpret internal experiences or states such as pain, anxiety or low mood (Summers et al., 2017).

The ability to communicate should be considered with attention to sensory difficulties, particularly visual and hearing impairments, that are more prevalent in intellectual disability populations (Carvill & Marston, 2002; Van den Broek, Janssen, & Van Ramshorst, 2006). Sensory and social differences can both have an impact on an individual's ability to interact and process information within a communicative environment (Hoevenaars-van den Boom, Antonissen, Knoors, & Vervloed, 2009; Kiani et al., 2019). For example, individuals with sensory difficulties may find imitation, facial perception, visual focus and auditory distractions challenging within a social exchange (Lueck, Dutton, & Chokron, 2019). A variable profile of communication difficulties is associated with social difference such as autism and depends on level of intellectual disability, with joint attention deficits, delays in expressive language, limited gesture use, and echolalic speech commonly described (Prelock & Nelson, 2012).

4. Conclusions

In this article we have outlined nine domains that we argue are important to focus on and assess when addressing the well-being and behavior of people with profound or severe intellectual disability and complex needs. For each domain we have indicated the importance of that domain for distress and behavior, the available methods of assessment, an assessment strategy, and interactions with other domains. The domains were selected because their relevance and importance for well-being and behavior had been established, at least to the level of proof of principle. Additionally, each domain typically is difficult to assess, might have an unusual presentation, is often overlooked or eclipsed, or is mistakenly identified. We argue that given there is proof of principle, available targeted interventions (for the most part) and the possibility that a domain can drive detrimental outcomes, then there is value in assessing each domain. We have also tried to avoid omitting a domain because it is difficult or resource demanding to assess. These challenges must be met. Our aims in this article are to stimulate debate about this broader approach to assessment and intervention for specified challenging behaviors and distress, and to alert practitioners to the rationale to assessing all domains and the methods available to do so.

There are other domains that are associated with well-being and specified challenging behaviors that we have omitted, such as caregiver mental health and the micro- and macro- social-environmental context. These were omitted because either they are unlikely to have a presentation different from than that typically seen or because intervention is not under the immediate control of a practitioner. Other areas, for example excessive appetite for food, were omitted because, although these are associated with well-being and specified challenging behaviors, they are very uncommon, except in specific syndromes. We are sure that the list of domains will change as new evidence becomes available and the value of the list is evaluated. Such changes would be welcome, this is a starting point.

The overall assessment process for the domains is divided into a surveillance or checklist phase followed by a direct assessment phase. We have described the checklist in a previous article (see Oliver et al., 2020) and this has the purpose of ensuring that each domain is actively considered, preferably jointly by caregivers and practitioners, and priorities for assessment established. We have described the possible direct assessments of each domain in this article. We have deliberately avoided strong recommendations and protocol like procedures because local context, knowledge and experience should inform complex decision making and the research literature is not yet strong enough to inform the overall process. The strategy is more one of empowering and informing decision making than establishing rigid pathways.

There are some recommendations that we would make for using the screening tool and the assessment information most effectively. First, it is important to consider all domains equally, regardless of any initial impression of their likely relevance. Second, it is important to repeat the screen at intervals as the assessment and intervention process unfolds. Third, domains should be considered in the order described above. There are two reasons for this. There is, arguably, a greater ethical imperative regarding pain and discomfort, hence it is first. Additionally, knowledge of each of the first seven domains will inform the functional analysis of learned behavior and the relative importance of specific expressive communicative behaviors, and consequently the priorities for established interventions, such as functional communication training, hence these are last. Fourth, when using the screen it is important to be aware of cognitive biases in any decision-making process, such as seeking confirmation rather than contradiction. Formal assessment can aid this. Fifth, we propose that interventions or guidelines to address communication and existing or potential reinforcement of behavior should always be implemented. Clearly, these recommendations should be modified as future research reveals the importance of each domain to the outcomes of well-being and specified challenging behaviors, the nature of interactions between domains and the utility of the overall strategy in applied settings.

References

Absoud, M., Wake, H., Ziriat, M., & Hassiotis, A. (2019). Managing challenging behaviour in children with possible learning disability. *BMJ*, *365*. https://doi.org/10.1136/bmj.l1663.

Acebo, C., Sadeh, A., Seifer, R., Tzischinsky, O., Wolfson, A. R., Hafer, A., et al. (1999). Estimating sleep patterns with activity monitoring in children and adolescents: How many nights are necessary for reliable measures? *Sleep*, *22*(1), 95–103. https://doi.org/10.1093/sleep/22.1.95.

Achenbach, T. M., & Rescorla, L. A. (2001). *Manual for ASEBA school-age forms and profiles*. University of Vermont, Research Center for Children, Youth, & Families.

Acker, L., Knight, M., & Knott, F. (2018). 'Are they just gonna reject me?' Male adolescents with autism making sense of anxiety: An interpretative phenomenological analysis. *Research in Autism Spectrum Disorders*, *56*, 9–20. https://doi.org/10.1016/j.rasd.2018.07.005.

Adams, D., Clark, M., & Keen, D. (2019). Using self-report to explore the relationship between anxiety and quality of life in children on the autism spectrum. *Autism Research*, *12*(10), 1505–1515. https://doi.org/10.1002/aur.2155.

Adams, D., Clark, M., & Simpson, K. (2020). The relationship between child anxiety and the quality of life of children, and parents of children, on the autism spectrum. *Journal of Autism and Developmental Disorders*, *50*(5), 1756–1769. https://doi.org/10.1007/s10803-019-03932-2.

Adams, D., Young, K., Simpson, K., & Keen, D. (2019). Parent descriptions of the presentation and management of anxiousness in children on the autism spectrum. *Autism*, *23*(4), 980–992. https://doi.org/10.1177/1362361318794031.

Agar, G., Brown, C., Sutherland, D., Coulborn, S., Oliver, C., & Richards, C. (2021). Sleep disorders in rare genetic syndromes: A meta-analysis of prevalence and profile. *Molecular Autism*, *12*(1), 1–17. https://doi.org/10.1186/s13229-021-00426-w.

Agar, G., Bissell, S., Wilde, L., Over, N., Williams, C., Richards, C., et al. (2022). Caregivers' experience of sleep management in Smith–Magenis syndrome: A mixed-methods study. *Orphanet Journal of Rare Diseases*, *17*(1), 1–15. https://doi.org/10.1186/s13023-021-02159-8.

Agar, G., Oliver, C., & Richards, C. (2022). Direct assessment of overnight parent-child proximity in children with behavioural insomnia: Extending models of operant and classical conditioning. *Behavioural Sleep Medicine*.

Agar, G., Oliver, C., Trickett, J., Licence, L., & Richards, C. (2020). Sleep disorders in children with Angelman and Smith-Magenis syndromes: The assessment of potential causes of disrupted settling and night time waking. *Research in Developmental Disabilities*, *97*, 103555. https://doi.org/10.1016/j.ridd.2019.103555.

Allen, J. M., Graef, D. M., Ehrentraut, J. H., Tynes, B. L., & Crabtree, V. M. (2016). Sleep and pain in pediatric illness: A conceptual review. *CNS Neuroscience & Therapeutics*, *22*(11), 880–893. https://doi.org/10.1111/cns.12583.

Alvaro, P. K., Roberts, R. M., & Harris, J. K. (2013). A systematic review assessing bidirectionality between sleep disturbances, anxiety, and depression. *Sleep*, *36*(7), 1059–1068. https://doi.org/10.5665/sleep.2810.

Aman, M. G., & Singh, N. N. (1985). Aberrant behavior checklist manual. *Slosson Educational* (Publications).
American Psychological Association. (2013). *Diagnostic and statistical manual of mental disorders* (5th). American Psychiatric Publishing.
Anderson, C. M., & Long, E. S. (2002). Use of a structured descriptive assessment methodology to identify variables affecting problem behavior. *Journal of Applied Behavior Analysis, 35*(2), 137–154. https://doi.org/10.1901/jaba.2002.35-137.
Appleton, H., Roberts, J., & Simpson, K. (2019). How is anxiety identified and diagnosed in individuals with autism spectrum disorder and intellectual disability? A scoping review. *Journal of Mental Health Research in Intellectual Disabilities, 12*(3–4), 152–175. https://doi.org/10.1080/19315864.2019.1679299.
Arias, V. B., Gómez, L. E., Morán, M. L., Alcedo, M. A., Monsalve, A., & Fontanil, Y. (2018). Does quality of life differ for children with autism spectrum disorder and intellectual disability compared to peers without autism? *Journal of Autism and Developmental Disorders, 48*, 123–136. https://doi.org/10.1007/s10803-017-3289-8.
Arron, K., Oliver, C., Moss, J., Berg, K., & Burbidge, C. (2011). The prevalence and phenomenology of self-injurious and aggressive behaviour in genetic syndromes. *Journal of Intellectual Disability Research, 55*(2), 109–120. https://doi.org/10.1111/j.1365-2788.2010.01337.x.
Baglioni, C., Battagliese, G., Feige, B., Spiegelhalder, K., Nissen, C., Voderholzer, U., et al. (2011). Insomnia as a predictor of depression: A meta-analytic evaluation of longitudinal epidemiological studies. *Journal of Affective Disorders, 135*(1–3), 10–19. https://doi.org/10.1016/j.jad.2011.01.011.
Baker, K. D., & Skuse, D. H. (2005). Adolescents and young adults with 22qll deletion syndrome: Psychopathology in an at-risk group. *The British Journal of Psychiatry, 186*(2), 115–120. https://doi.org/10.1192/bjp.186.2.115.
Baranek, G. T. (1999). *Sensory Experiences Questionnaire (SEQ)*. Unpublished manuscript, University of North Carolina at Chapel Hill.
Baranek, G. T., & Berkson, G. (1994). Tactile defensiveness in children with developmental disabilities: Responsiveness and habituation. *Journal of Autism and Developmental Disorders, 24*(4), 457–471. https://doi.org/10.1007/bf02172128.
Baranek, G. T., Chin, Y. H., Greiss Hess, L. M., Yankee, J. G., Hatton, D. D., & Hooper, S. R. (2002). Sensory processing correlates of occupational performance in children with fragile X syndrome: Preliminary findings. *American Journal of Occupational Therapy, 56*(5), 538–546. https://doi.org/10.5014/ajot.56.5.538.
Baranek, G. T., David, F. J., Poe, M. D., Stone, W. L., & Watson, L. R. (2006). Sensory experiences questionnaire: Discriminating sensory features in young children with autism, developmental delays, and typical development. *Journal of Child Psychology and Psychiatry and Allied Disciplines, 47*(6). https://doi.org/10.1111/j.1469-7610.2005.01546.x.
Baranek, G. T., Watson, L. R., Boyd, B. A., Poe, M. D., David, F. J., & McGuire, L. (2013). Hyporesponsiveness to social and nonsocial sensory stimuli in children with autism, children with developmental delays, and typically developing children. *Development and Psychopathology, 25*(2). https://doi.org/10.1017/S0954579412001071.
Barney, C. C., Anderon, R. D., Defrin, R., Genik, L. M., McGuire, B. E., & Symons, F. J. (2020). Challenges in pain assessment and management among individuals with intellectual and developmental disabilities. *Pain Reports, 5*(4), e821. https://doi.org/10.1097/PR9.0000000000000822.
Ben-Sasson, A., Hen, L., Fluss, R., Cermak, S. A., Engel-Yeger, B., & Gal, E. (2009). A meta-analysis of sensory modulation symptoms in individuals with autism spectrum disorders. *Journal of Autism and Developmental Disorders, 39*(1), 1–11. https://doi.org/10.1007/s10803-008-0593-3.

Bitsika, V., Sharpley, C. F., Andronicos, N. M., Agnew, L. L., & Mills, R. (2015). Which aspects of sensory features are associated with elevated cortisol concentrations in boys with autism spectrum disorder? *Journal of Developmental and Physical Disabilities*, *27*, 661–675. https://doi.org/10.1007/s10882-015-9442-4.

Bloomberg, K., West, D., Johnson, H., & Iacono, T. (2009). *Triple C: Checklist of communication competencies*. Box Hill, Victoria: Scope. Revised Edition.

Boardman, L., Bernal, J., & Hollins, S. (2014). Communicating with people with intellectual disabilities: A guide for general psychiatrists. *Advances in Psychiatric Treatment*, *20*(1), 27–36. https://doi.org/10.1192/apt.bp.110.008664.

Böhmer, C. J. M., Niezen-de Boer, M. C., Klinkenberg-Knol, E. C., Devillé, W. L. J. M., Nadorp, J. H. S. M., & Meuwissen, S. G. M. (1999). The prevalence of gastroesophageal reflux disease in institutionalized intellectually disabled individuals. *The American Journal of Gastroenterology*, *94*(3), 804–810. https://doi.org/10.1111/j.1572-0241.1999.00854.x.

Böhmer, C. J. M., Taminiau, J. A. J. M., Klinkenberg-Knol, E. C., & Meuwissen, S. G. M. (2001). The prevalence of constipation in institutionalized people with intellectual disability. *Journal of Intellectual Disability Research*, *45*(3), 212–218. https://doi.org/10.1046/j.1365-2788.2001.00300.x.

Bosch, J., Van Dyke, D. C., Milligan Smith, S., & Poulton, S. (1997). Role of medical conditions in the exacerbation of self injurious behavior: An exploratory study. *Mental Retardation*, *35*(2), 124–130. https://doi.org/10.1352/0047-6765(1997)035<0124:ROMCIT>2.0.CO;2.

Bottos, S., & Chambers, C. T. (2006). The epidemiology of pain in developmental disabilities. In I. T. F. Oberlander, & F. J. Symons (Eds.), *Pain in children & adults with developmental disabilities* (pp. 67–87). Paul H Brookes Publishing Co.

Boulter, C., Freeston, M., South, M., & Rodgers, J. (2013). Intolerance of uncertainty as a framework for understanding anxiety in children and adolescents with autism spectrum disorders. *Journal of Autism and Developmental Disorders*. https://doi.org/10.1007/s10803-013-2001-x.

Boyd, B. B., Baranek, G. T., Sideris, J., Poe, M. D., Watson, L. R., Patten, E., & Miller, H. (2010). Sensory features and repetitive behaviors in children with autism and developmental delays. *Autism Research*, *3*(2), 78–87. https://doi.org/10.1002/aur.124.

Brady, N. C., Fleming, K., Swinburne Romine, R., Holbrook, A., Muller, K., & Kasari, C. (2018). Concurrent validity and reliability for the Communication Complexity Scale. *American Journal of Speech-Language Pathology*, *27*(1), 237–246. https://doi.org/10.1044/2017_AJSLP-17-0106.

Brady, N. C., Fleming, K., Thiemann-Bourque, K., Olswang, L., Dowden, P., Saunders, M. D., et al. (2012). Development of the communication complexity scale. *American Journal of Speech-Language Pathology*, *21*(1), 16–28. https://doi.org/10.1044/1058-0360(2011/10-0099).

Breau, L. M., & Burkitt, C. (2009). Assessing pain in children with intellectual disabilities. *Pain Research and Management*, *14*(2), 116–120. https://doi.org/10.1155/2009/642352.

Breau, L. M., & Camfield, C. S. (2011). Pain disrupts sleep in children and youth with intellectual and developmental disabilities. *Research in Developmental Disabilities*, *32*(6), 2829–2840. https://doi.org/10.1016/j.ridd.2011.05.023.

Breau, L. M., McGrath, P. J., Camfield, C. S., & Finley, G. A. (2002). Psychometric properties of the non-communicating children's pain checklist-revised. *Pain*, *99*(1–2), 349–357. https://doi.org/10.1016/s0304-3959(02)00179-3.

Bruni, O., Ottaviano, S., Guidetti, V., Romoli, M., Innocenzi, M., Cortesi, F., et al. (1996). The sleep disturbance scale for children (SDSC) construct ion and validation of an instrument to evaluate sleep disturbances in childhood and adolescence. *Journal of Sleep Research*, *5*(4), 251–261. https://doi.org/10.1111/j.1365-2869.1996.00251.x.

Bull, L. E., Oliver, C., Callaghan, E., & Woodcock, K. A. (2015). Increased exposure to rigid routines can lead to increased challenging behavior following changes to those routines. *Journal of Autism and Developmental Disorders*, *45*(6), 1569–1578. https://doi.org/10.1007/s10803-014-2308-2.

Bull, L. E., Oliver, C., Tunnicliffe, P. L., & Woodcock, K. A. (2015). An informant report behavior diary for measuring temper outbursts in an intervention setting. *Journal of Developmental and Physical Disabilities*, *27*(4), 489–504. https://doi.org/10.1007/s10882-015-9429-1.

Bull, L. E., Oliver, C., & Woodcock, K. A. (2017). Signalling changes to individuals who show resistance to change can reduce challenging behaviour. *Journal of Behavior Therapy and Experimental Psychiatry*, *54*, 58–70. https://doi.org/10.1016/j.jbtep.2016.06.006.

Burbidge, C., Oliver, C., Moss, J., Arron, K., Berg, K., Hill, L., et al. (2010). The association between repetitive behaviours, impulsivity and hyperactivity in people with intellectual disability. *Journal of Intellectual Disability Research*, *54*(12), 1078–1092. https://doi.org/10.1111/j.1365-2788.2010.01338.x.

Burgess, P. W., & Shallice, T. (1997). *The Hayling and Brixton tests*. Edmonds, England: Thames Valley Test Company Bury St.

Burke, R. M., Maxwell, B., Hunter, C., Graham, D., O'Donoghue, D., & Shields, M. D. (2016). Night-to-night variation of pulse oximetry in children with sleep-disordered breathing. *Archives of Disease in Childhood*, *101*(12), 1095–1099. https://doi.org/10.1136/archdischild-2015-308981.

Burns, C. O., Dixon, D. R., Novack, M., & Granpeesheh, D. (2017). A systematic review of assessments for sensory processing abnormalities in autism spectrum disorder. *Review Journal of Autism Developmental Disorders*, *4*, 209–224. https://doi.org/10.1007/s40489-017-0109-1.

Carr, E. G., & Blakeley-Smith, A. (2006). Classroom intervention for illness-related behavior in children with developmental disabilities. *Behavior Modification*, *30*(6), 901–924. https://doi.org/10.1177/0145445506290080.

Carr, E. G., & Durand, V. M. (1985). Reducing behavior problems through functional communication training. *Journal of Applied Behavior Analysis*, *18*(2), 111–126. https://doi.org/10.1901/jaba.1985.18-111.

Carr, E. G., & Owen-DeSchryver, J. S. (2007). Physical illness, pain, and problem behavior in minimally verbal people with developmental disabilities. *Journal of Autism and Developmental Disorders*, *37*(3), 413–424. https://doi.org/10.1007/s10803-006-0176-0.

Carvill, S., & Marston, G. (2002). People with intellectual disability, sensory impairments and behaviour disorder: A case series. *Journal of Intellectual Disability Research*, *46*(3), 264–272. https://doi.org/10.1046/j.1365-2788.2002.00400.x.

Castellanos, I., Kronenberger, W. G., & Pisoni, D. B. (2018). Questionnaire-based assessment of executive functioning: Psychometrics. *Applied Neuropsychology: Child*, 7(2), 93–109.

Cervantes, P. E., & Matson, J. L. (2015). Comorbid symptomology in adults with autism spectrum disorder and intellectual disability. *Journal of Autism and Developmental Disorders*, *45*(12), 3961–3970. https://doi.org/10.1007/s10803-015-2553-z.

Chadwick, D., Buell, S., & Goldbart, J. (2019). Approaches to communication assessment with children and adults with profound intellectual and multiple disabilities. *Journal of Applied Research in Intellectual Disabilities*, *32*(2), 336–358. https://doi.org/10.1111/jar.12530.

Chamberlain, P. D., Rodgers, J., Crowley, M. J., White, S. E., Freeston, M. H., & South, M. (2013). A potentiated startle study of uncertainty and contextual anxiety in adolescents diagnosed with autism spectrum disorder. *Molecular Autism*, *4*(31). http://www.molecularautism.com/content/4/1/31.

Charman, T., Jones, C. R., Pickles, A., Simonoff, E., Baird, G., & Happé, F. (2011). Defining the cognitive phenotype of autism. *Brain Research*, *1380*, 10–21. https://doi.org/10.1016/j.brainres.2010.10.075.

Chung, J. C. Y., Mevorach, C., & Woodcock, K. A. (2022). Establishing the transdiagnostic contextual pathways of emotional outbursts. *Scientific Reports*, *12*, 7414. https://doi.org/10.1038/s41598-022-11474-4.

Cooper, S., & Collacott, R. A. (1996). Depressive episodes in adults with learning disabilities. *Irish Journal of Psychological Medicine*, *13*(3), 105–113. https://doi.org/10.1017/S0790966700002664.

Cooray, S., & Bakala, A. (2005). Anxiety disorders in people with learning disabilities. *Advances in Psychiatric Treatment*, *11*(5), 355–361. https://doi.org/10.1192/apt.11.5.355.

Corbett, B. A., Schupp, C. W., Levine, S., & Mendoza, S. (2009). Comparing cortisol, stress, and sensory sensitivity in children with autism. *Autism Research*, *2*(1), 39–49. https://doi.org10.1002/aur.64.

Cornish, K., Scerif, G., & Karmiloff-Smith, A. (2007). Tracing syndrome-specific trajectories of attention across the lifespan. *Cortex*, *43*(6), 672–685. https://doi.org/10.1016/s0010-9452(08)70497-0.

Cortesi, F., Giannotti, F., Ivanenko, A., & Johnson, K. (2010). Sleep in children with autistic spectrum disorder. *Sleep Medicine*, *11*(7), 659–664. https://doi.org/10.1016/j.sleep.2010.01.010.

Costanzo, F., Varuzza, C., Menghini, D., Addona, F., Gianesini, T., & Vicari, S. (2013). Executive functions in intellectual disabilities: A comparison between Williams syndrome and down syndrome. *Research in Developmental Disabilities*, *34*, 1770–1780. https://doi.org/10.1016/j.ridd.2013.01.024.

Coupe-O'Kane, J., & Goldbart, J. (1998). *Communication before speech: Development and assessment*. Taylor & Francis.

Crais, E., & Ogletree, B. T. (2016). Prelinguistic communication development. In *Prelinguistic and minimally verbal communicators on the autism spectrum* (pp. 9–32). Singapore: Springer.

Crawford, H., Moss, J., Groves, L., Dowlen, R., Nelson, L., Reid, D., et al. (2020). A behavioural assessment of social anxiety and social motivation in fragile X, Cornelia de Lange and Rubinstein-Taybi syndromes. *Journal of Autism and Developmental Disorders*, *50*(1), 127–144. https://doi.org/10.1007/s10803-019-04232-5.

Crawford, H., Karakatsani, E., Singla, G., & Oliver, C. (2019). The persistence of self-injurious and aggressive behavior in males with fragile X syndrome over 8 years: A longitudinal study of prevalence and predictive risk markers. *Journal of Autism and Developmental Disorders*, *49*(7), 2913–2922. https://doi.org/10.1007/s10803-019-04002-3.

Crawford, H., Waite, J., & Oliver, C. (2017). Diverse profiles of anxiety related disorders in fragile X, Cornelia de Lange and Rubinstein-Taybi syndromes. *Journal of Autism and Developmental Disorders*, *47*(12), 3728–3740. https://doi.org/10.1007/s10803-016-3015-y.

Cressey, H., Oliver, C., Crawford, H., & Waite, J. (2019). Temper outbursts in Lowe syndrome: Characteristics, sequence, environmental context and comparison to Prader–Willi syndrome. *Journal of Applied Research in Intellectual Disabilities*, *32*(5), 1216–1227. https://doi.org/10.1111/jar.12613.

Csumitta, K. D., Stephan, C. M., LaQuaglia, R. I., Miller, E., & Lee, N. R. (2022). Updated profiles of everyday executive function in youth with down syndrome using the BRIEF-2. *Journal of Intellectual Disability Research*, *66*(1–2), 68–80. https://doi.org/10.1111/jir.12879.

Danquah, A., Limb, K., Chapman, M., Burke, C., Flood, A., Gore, S., et al. (2009). An investigation of the factors predictive of continued self-injurious behaviour in an intellectual disability service. *Journal of Applied Research in Intellectual Disabilities, 22*, 395–399. https://doi.org/10.1111/j.1468-3148.2008.00470.x.

De Los Reyes, A., Augenstein, T. M., Wang, M., Thomas, S. A., Drabick, D. A., Burgers, D. E., et al. (2015). The validity of the multi-informant approach to assessing child and adolescent mental health. *Psychological Bulletin, 141*(4), 858. https://doi.org/10.1037/a0038498.

Didden, R., Korzilius, H. P. L. M., Aperlo, B. V., Overloop, C. V., & Vries, M. D. (2002). Sleep problems and daytime problem behaviours in children with intellectual disability. *Journal of Intellectual Disability Research, 46*(7), 537–547. https://doi.org/10.1016/j.jad.2011.01.011.

Didden, R., Sigafoos, J., & Lancioni, G. E. (2011). Unmodified extinction for childhood sleep disturbance. In *Behavioral treatments for sleep disorders* (pp. 257–263). Academic Press.

Duignan, M., & Connell, J. (2015). Living with autistic spectrum disorders: Families, homes and the disruption of space. *Geographical Research, 53*(2), 199–210. https://doi.org/10.1111/1745-5871.12112.

Dunn, W. (1999). *The sensory profile: User's manual.* Psychological Corporation.

Dunn, W. (2014). *The sensory profile 2 manual.* Pearson.

Durand, M. V., & Crimmins, D. B. (1988). Identifying the variables maintaining self-injurious behavior. *Journal of Autism and Developmental Disorders, 18*(1), 99–117. https://doi.org/10.1007/BF02211821.

Eadie, P. A., Ukoumunne, O., Skeat, J., Prior, M. R., Bavin, E., Bretherton, L., et al. (2010). Assessing early communication behaviours: Structure and validity of the communication and symbolic behaviour scales—Developmental profile (CSBS-DP) in 12-month-old infants. *International Journal of Language & Communication Disorders, 45*(5), 572–585. https://doi.org/10.3109/13682820903277944.

Eden, K., de Vries, P. J., Moss, J., Richards, C., & Oliver, C. (2014). Self-injury and aggression in tuberous sclerosis complex; cross syndrome comparison and associated risk markers. *Journal of Neurodevelopmental Disorders, 6*, 1–11.

Edwards, G., Tarver, J., Shelley, L., Bird, M., Hughes, J., Crawford, H., et al. (2022). Utilising interview methodology to inform the development of new clinical assessment tools for anxiety in autistic individuals who speak few or no words. *Journal of Autism and Developmental Disorders*. https://doi.org/10.1007/s10803-022-05509-y.

Einfeld, S. L., & Tonge, B. J. (1995). The developmental behavior checklist: The development and validation of an instrument to assess behavioral and emotional disturbance in children and adolescents with mental retardation. *Journal of Autism and Developmental Disorders, 25*(2), 81–104. https://doi.org/10.1007/BF02178498.

Ellis, K., Oliver, C., Stefanidou, C., Apperly, I., & Moss, J. (2020). An observational study of social interaction skills and behaviours in Cornelia de Lange, fragile X and Rubinstein-Tabyi syndromes. *Journal of Autism and Developmental Disorders, 50*(11), 4001–4010. https://doi.org/10.1007/s10803-020-04440-4.

Emerson, E., Reeves, D., Thompson, S., Henderson, D., Robertson, J., & Howard, D. (1996). Time-based lag sequential analysis and the functional assessment of challenging behavior. *Journal of Intellectual Disability Research, 40*(3), 260–274. https://doi.org/10.1111/j.1365-2788.1996.tb00629.x.

Emslie, H., Wilson, F. C., Burden, V., Nimmo-Smith, I., & Wilson, B. A. (2003). Behavioural assessment of the Dysexecutive syndrome for children (BADS-C). *Child Neuropsychology, 13*, 539–542.

Engel-Yeger, B., Hardal-Nasser, R., & Gal, E. (2011). Sensory processing dysfunctions as expressed among children with different severities of intellectual developmental disabilities. *Research in Developmental Disabilities, 32*(5), 1770–1775. https://doi.org/10.1016/j.ridd.2011.03.005.

Esbensen, A. J., & Hoffman, E. K. (2018). Impact of sleep on executive functioning in school-age children with Down syndrome. *Journal of Intellectual Disability Research, 62*(6), 569–580. https://doi.org/10.1111/jir.12496.

Esbensen, A. J., Hoffman, E. K., Stansberry, E., & Shaffer, R. (2018). Convergent validity of actigraphy with polysomnography and parent reports when measuring sleep in children with down syndrome. *Journal of Intellectual Disability Research, 62*(4), 281–291. https://doi.org/10.1111/jir.12464.

Esbensen, A. J., Rojahn, J., Aman, M. G., & Ruedrich, S. (2003). Reliability and validity of an assessment instrument for anxiety, depression, and mood among individuals with mental retardation. *Journal of Autism and Developmental Disorders, 33*(6), 617–629. https://doi.org/10.1023/b:jadd.0000005999.27178.55.

Evans, D. W., Leckman, J. F., Carter, A., Reznick, J. S., Henshaw, D., King, R. A., et al. (1997). Ritual, habit and perfectionism: The prevalence and development of compulsive-like behaviour in normal young children. *Child Development, 68*(1), 58–68. https://doi.org/10.1111/j.1467- 8624.1997.tb01921.x.

Fanurik, D., Koh, J. L., Harrison, R. D., Conrad, T. M., & Tomerlin, C. (1998). Pain assessment in children with cognitive impairment. *Clinical Nursing Research*, 7(2), 103–124. https://doi.org/10.1177/105477389800700202.

Fidler, D. J., & Lanfranchi, S. (2022). Executive function and intellectual disability: Innovations, methods and treatment. *Journal of Intellectual Disability Research, 66*(1–2), 1–8. https://doi.org/10.1111/jir.12906.

Flynn, S., Vereenooghe, L., Hastings, R. P., Adams, D., Cooper, S. A., Gore, N., et al. (2017). Measurement tools for mental health problems and mental well-being in people with severe or profound intellectual disabilities: A systematic review. *Clinical Psychology Review, 57*, 32–44. https://doi.org/10.1016/j.cpr.2017.08.006.

Furniss, F., & Biswas, A. B. (2012). Recent research on aetiology, development and phenomenology of self-injurious behaviour in people with intellectual disabilities: A systematic review and implications for treatment. *Journal of Intellectual Disability Research, 56*(5), 453–475. https://doi.org/10.1111/j.1365-2788.2012.01534.x.

García, J. C., Díez, E., Wojcik, D. Z., & Santamaría, M. (2020). Communication support needs in adults with intellectual disabilities and its relation to quality of life. *International Journal of Environmental Research and Public Health, 17*(20), 7370. https://doi.org/10.3390/ijerph17207370.

Gergoudis, Weinberg, A., Templin, J., Farmer, C., Durkin, A., Weissman, J., et al. (2020). Psychometric study of the social responsiveness scale in Phelan–McDermid syndrome. *Autism Research, 13*(8), 1383–1396. https://doi.org/10.1002/aur.2299.

Gioia, G. A., Andrews Epsy, K., & Isquith, P. K. (2003). *BRIEF-P: Behavior rating inventory of executive function– Preschool version, professional manual.* Psychological Assessment Resources.

Gioia, G., Isquith, P., Guy, S. C., & Kenworthy, L. (2000). Behavior rating inventory of executive function. *Child Neuropsychology, 6*, 235–238.

Gioia, G. A., Isquith, P. K., Guy, S. C., & Kenworthy, L. (2015). *BRIEF-2: Behavior rating inventory of executive function: Professional manual.* Psychological Assessment Resources.

Glod, M., Creswell, C., Waite, P., Jamieson, R., McConachie, H., South, M. D., et al. (2017). Comparisons of the factor structure and measurement invariance of the Spence Children's anxiety scale-parent version in children with autism spectrum disorder and typically developing children. *Journal of Autism and Developmental Disorders, 47*, 3834–3846. https://doi.org/10.1007/s10803-017-3118-0.

Goldbart, J., Chadwick, D., & Buell, S. (2014). Speech and language therapists' approaches to communication intervention with children and adults with profound and multiple learning disability. *International Journal of Language & Communication Disorders, 49*(6), 687–701. https://doi.org/10.1111/1460-6984.12098.

Goldman, S. E., Bichell, T. J., Surdyka, K., & Malow, B. A. (2012). Sleep in children and adolescents with Angelman syndrome: Association with parent sleep and stress. *Journal of Intellectual Disability Research*, *56*(6), 600–608. https://doi.org/10.1111/j.1365-2788.2011.01499.x.

Gonthier, C., Longuépée, L., & Bouvard, M. (2016). Sensory processing in low-functioning adults with autism spectrum disorder: Distinct sensory profiles and their relationships with behavioral dysfunction. *Journal of Autism and Developmental Disorders*, *46*(9), 3078–3089. https://doi.org/10.1007/s10803-016-2850-1.

Green, S. A., Berkovits, L. D., & Baker, B. L. (2015). Symptoms and development of anxiety in children with or without intellectual disability. *Journal of Clinical Child and Adolescent Psychology*, *44*(1), 137–144. https://doi.org/10.1080/15374416.2013.873979.

Greiner de Magalhães, C., Pitts, C. H., & Mervis, C. B. (2022). Executive function as measured by the behavior rating inventory of executive Function-2: Children and adolescents with Williams syndrome. *Journal of Intellectual Disability Research*, *66*(1–2), 94–107. https://doi.org/10.1111/jir.12858.

Groden, G. (1989). A guide for conducting a comprehensive behavioral analysis of a target behavior. *Journal of Behavior Therapy and Experimental Psychiatry*, *20*, 163–169. https://doi.org/10.1016/0005-7916(89)900049-8.

Haig, E. L., & Woodcock, K. A. (2017). Rigidity in routines and the development of resistance to change in individuals with Prader–Willi syndrome. *Journal of Intellectual Disability Research*, *61*(5), 488–500. https://doi.org/10.1111/jir.12368.

Hall, DeBernardis, M., & Reiss, A. (2006). Social escape behaviors in children with fragile X syndrome. *Journal of Autism and Developmental Disorders*, *36*(7), 935–947. https://doi.org/10.1007/s10803-006-0132-z.

Harrison, P., & Oakland, T. (2015). *Adaptive behavior assessment system* (3rd ed.). Torrance: Western Psychological Services.

Hartman, E. C., Gilles, E., McComas, J. J., Danov, S. E., & Symons, F. J. (2008). Clinical observation of self-injurious behavior correlated with changes in scalp morphology in a child with congenital hydrocephalus. *Journal of Child Neurology*, *23*(9), 1062–1065.

Hartshorne, T. S., Heussler, H. S., Dailor, A. N., Williams, G. L., Papadopoulos, D., & Brandt, K. K. (2009). Sleep disturbances in CHARGE syndrome: Types and relationships with behavior and caregiver well-being. *Developmental Medicine & Child Neurology*, *51*(2), 143–150. https://doi.org/10.1111/j.1469-8749.2008.03146.x.

Hemmingsson, H., Stenhammar, A. M., & Paulsson, K. (2009). Sleep problems and the need for parental night-time attention in children with physical disabilities. *Child: Care Health and Development*, *35*, 89–95. https://doi.org/10.1111/j.1365-2214.2008.00907.x.

Hessl, Glaser, B., Dyer-Friedman, J., & Reiss, A. L. (2006). Social behavior and cortisol reactivity in children with fragile X syndrome: Social behavior and cortisol in fragile X. *Journal of Child Psychology and Psychiatry*, *47*(6), 602–610. https://doi.org/10.1111/j.1469-7610.2005.01556.x.

Hill, C. M., Elphick, H. E., Farquhar, M., Gringras, P., Pickering, R. M., Kingshott, R. N., et al. (2018). Home oximetry to screen for obstructive sleep apnoea in Down syndrome. *Archives of Disease in Childhood*, *103*(10), 962–967. https://doi.org/10.1136/archdischild-2017-314409.

Hoevenaars-van den Boom, M. A. A., Antonissen, A. C. F. M., Knoors, H., & Vervloed, M. P. J. (2009). Differentiating characteristics of deafblindness and autism in people with congenital deafblindness and profound intellectual disability. *Journal of Intellectual Disability Research*, *53*(6), 548–558. https://doi.org/10.1111/j.1365-2788.2009.01175.x.

Horsler, K., & Oliver, C. (2006). Environmental influences on the behavioral phenotype of Angelman syndrome. *American Journal of Mental Retardation : AJMR*, *111*(5), 311–321. https://doi.org/10.1352/0895-8017(2006)111[311:EIOTBP]2.0.CO;2.

Hunt, A., Goldman, A., Seers, K., Crichton, N., Mastroyannopoulou, K., Moffat, V., & Brady, M. (2004). Clinical validation of the paediatric pain profile. *Developmental Medicine & Child Neurology, 46*(1), 9–18. https://doi.org/10.1111/j.1469-8749.2004.tb00428.x.

Iverson, J. M., Capirci, O., & Caselli, M. C. (1994). From communication to language in two modalities. *Cognitive Development, 9*, 23–43. https://doi.org/10.1016/0885-2014(94)90018-3.

Iwata, B. A., Dorsey, M. F., Slifer, K. J., Bauman, K. E., & Richman, G. S. (1982). Toward a functional analysis of self-injury. *Analysis and Intervention in Developmental Disabilities, 2*, 3–20. https://doi.org/10.1901/jaba.1994.27-197.

Johnson, C. R., Turner, K. S., Foldes, E. L., Malow, B. A., & Wiggs, L. (2012). Comparison of sleep questionnaires in the assessment of sleep disturbances in children with autism spectrum disorders. *Sleep Medicine, 13*(7), 795–801. https://doi.org/10.1016/j.sleep.2012.03.005.

Jorquera-Cabrera, S., Romero-Ayuso, D., Rodriguez-Gil, G., & Triviño-Juárez, J. M. (2017). Assessment of sensory processing characteristics in children between 3 and 11 years old: A systematic review. *Frontiers in Pediatrics, 5*(57). https://doi.org/10.3389/fped.2017.00057.

Kern, J. K., Trivedi, M. H., Garver, C. R., Grannemann, B. D., Andrews, A. A., Savla, J. S., et al. (2006). The pattern of sensory processing abnormalities in autism. *Autism : The International Journal of Research and Practice, 10*(5), 480–494. https://doi.org/10.1177/1362361306066564.

Kerns, C. M., Kendall, P. C., Berry, L., Souders, M. C., Franklin, M. E., Schultz, R. T., et al. (2014). Traditional and atypical presentations of anxiety in youth with autism spectrum disorder. *Journal of Autism and Developmental Disorders, 44*(11), 2851–2861. https://doi.org/10.1007/s10803*014*2141-7.

Kiani, R., Bhaumik, S., Tyrer, F., Bankart, J., Miller, H., Cooper, S., et al. (2019). The relationship between symptoms of autism spectrum disorder and visual impairment among adults with intellectual disability. *Autism Research, 12*, 1411–1422.

Kidd, S. A., Berry-Kravis, E., Choo, T. H., Chen, C., Esler, A., Hoffman, A., et al. (2020). Improving the diagnosis of autism spectrum disorder in fragile X syndrome by adapting the social communication questionnaire and the social responsiveness scale-2. *Journal of Autism and Developmental Disorders, 50*, 3276–3295. https://doi.org/10.1007/s10803-019-04148-0.

Kieman, C., & Alborz, A. (1996). Persistence and change in challenging and problem behaviours of young adults with intellectual disability living in the family home. *Journal of Applied Research in Intellectual Disabilities, 9*(3), 181–193. https://doi.org/10.1111/j.1468-3148.1996.tb00108.x.

Kiernan, C., & Reid, B. (1987). *Pre-verbal communication schedule.* Windsor: NFER-NELSON.

LaMalfa, G., Lassi, S., Bertelli, M., Salvini, R., & Placidi, G. F. (2004). Autism and intellectual disability: A study of prevalence on a sample of the Italian population. *Journal of Intellectual Disability Research, 48*(3), 262–267. https://doi.org/10.1111/j.1365-2788.2003.00567.x.

Landry, O., Russo, N., Dawkins, T., Zelazo, P. D., & Burack, J. A. (2012). The impact of verbal and nonverbal development on executive function in down syndrome and Williams syndrome. *Journal on Developmental Disabilities, 18*(2), 26.

Lewedag, V. L., Oller, D. K., & Lynch, M. P. (1994). Infants' vocalization patterns across home and laboratory environments. *First Language, 14*(40, Pt 1), 49–65. https://doi.org/10.1177/014272379401404204.

Little, L. M., Freuler, A. C., Houser, M. B., Guckian, L., Carbine, K., David, F. J., et al. (2011). Psychometric validation of the sensory experiences questionnaire. *American Journal of Occupational Therapy, 65*(2). https://doi.org/10.5014/ajot.2011.000844.

Loomes, R., Hull, L., & Mandy, W. (2017). What is the male-to-female ratio in autism Spectrum disorder? A systematic review and Meta-analysis. *Journal of the American Academy of Child and Adolescent Psychiatry*, *56*(6), 466–474. https://doi.org/10.1016/j.jaac.2017.03.013.

Lord, C., Rutter, M., DiLavore, P. C., Risi, S., Gotham, K., & Bishop, S. (2012). *Autism diagnostic observation schedule, second edition (ADOS-2) manual.* Western Psychological Services.

Lowe, K., Allen, D., Jones, E., Brophy, S., Moore, K., & James, W. (2007). Challenging behaviours: Prevalence and topographies. *Journal of Intellectual Disability Research*, *51*(8), 625–636. https://doi.org/10.1111/j.1365-2788.2006.00948.x.

Lueck, A. H., Dutton, G. N., & Chokron, S. (2019). Profiling children with cerebral visual impairment using multiple methods of assessment to aid in differential diagnosis. In *Vol. 31. Seminars in pediatric neurology* (pp. 5–14). WB Saunders.

MacLennan, K., Rossow, T., & Tavassoli, T. (2021). The relationship between sensory reactivity, intolerance of uncertainty and anxiety subtypes in preschool-age autistic children. *Autism*, *25*(8), 2305–2316. https://doi.org/10.1177/13623613211016110.

Maïano, C., Coutu, S., Tracey, D., Bouchard, S., Lepage, G., Morin, A., et al. (2018). Prevalence of anxiety and depressive disorders among youth with intellectual disabilities: A systematic review and meta-analysis. *Journal of Affective Disorders*, *236*, 230–242. https://doi.org/10.1016/j.jad.2018.04.029.

Manly, T., Robertson, I. H., Anderson, V., & Nimmo-Smith, I. (1999). *The test of everyday attention (TEA-CH).* Bury St. Edmunds, England: Thames Valley Test Company.

Manning, K. E., Beresford-Webb, J. A., Aman, L. C. S., Ring, H. A., Watson, P. C., Porges, S. W., et al. (2019). Transcutaneous vagus nerve stimulation (t-VNS): A novel effective treatment for temper outbursts in adults with Prader-Willi syndrome indicated by results from a non-blind study. *PLoS One*, *14*(12), e0223750. https://doi.org/10.1371/journal.pone.0223750.

Manning, K. E., McAllister, C. J., Ring, H. A., Finer, N., Kelly, C. L., Sylvester, K. P., et al. (2016). Novel insights into maladaptive behaviours in Prader-Willi syndrome: Serendipitous findings from an open trial of vagus nerve stimulation. *Journal of Intellectual Disability Research*, *60*(2), 149–155. https://doi.org/10.1111/jir.12203.

Mannion, A., Leader, G., & Healy, O. (2013). An investigation of comorbid psychological disorders, sleep problems, gastrointestinal symptoms and epilepsy in children and adolescents with autism spectrum disorder. *Research in Autism Spectrum Disorders*, 7(1), 35–42. https://doi.org/10.1016/j.rasd.2012.05.002.

Matson, J. L. (1995). *The Matson evaluation of social skills for individuals with severe retardation.* Baton Rouge, LA: Scientific Publishers Inc.

Matson, J. L., & Boisjoli, J. A. (2008). Cutoff scores for the Matson evaluation of social skills for individuals with severe retardation (MESSIER) for adults with intellectual disability. *Behavior Modification*, *32*(1), 109–120. https://doi.org/10.1177/0145445507307466.

Matson, J. L., Boisjoli, J. A., & Mahan, S. (2009). The relation of communication and challenging behaviors in infants and toddlers with autism Spectrum disorders. *Journal of Developmental and Physical Disabilities*, *21*, 253–261.

Matson, J. L., Gardner, W. I., Coe, D. A., & Sovner, R. (1991). A scale for evaluating emotional disorders in severely and profoundly retarded persons: Developmental of the diagnostic assessment for the severely handicapped (DASH-II). *Research in Developmental Disabilities*, *18*, 457–469.

Matson, J. L., & Vollmer, T. R. (1995). *User's guide: Questions about behavioral function (QABF).* Scientific Publishers, Inc.

McGrath, P. J., Johnson, G., Goodman, J. T., Schillinger, J., Dunn, J., & Chapman, J. (1985). CHEOPS: A behavioral scale for rating postoperative pain in children. In H. L. Fields, R. Dubner, & F. Cervero (Eds.), *9. Advances in pain research and therapy* (pp. 395–402). Raven Press.

McGuire, B. E., Daly, P., & Smyth, F. (2010). Chronic pain in people with an intellectual disability: Under-recognised and under-treated? *Journal of Intellectual Disability, 54*, 240–245. https://doi.org/10.1111/j.1365-2788.2010.01254.x.

Meyer, L. H., Cole, D. A., McQuarter, R., & Reichle, J. (1990). Validation of the assessment of social competence (ASC) for children and Young adults with developmental disabilities. *Journal of the Association for Persons with Severe Handicaps, 15*(2), 57–68. https://doi.org/10.1177/154079699001500201.

Meyer, L. H., Reichle, J., McQuarter, R., Cole, D., Vandercook, T., Evans, I., et al. (1985). *Assessment of social competence (ASC): A scale of social competence functions*. Minneapolis: University of Minnesota Consortium Institute.

Mian, N. D., Carter, A. S., Pine, D. S., Wakschlag, L. S., & Briggs-Gowan, M. J. (2015). Development of a novel observational measure for anxiety in young children: The anxiety dimensional observation scale. *Journal of Child Psychology and Psychiatry, and Allied Disciplines, 56*(9), 1017–1025. https://doi.org/10.1111/jcpp.12407.

Miller, L. J., Anzalone, M. E., Lane, S. J., Cermak, S. A., & Osten, E. T. (2007). Concept evolution in sensory integration: A proposed nosology for diagnosis. *The American Journal of Occupational Therapy, 61*(2), 135–140. https://doi.org/10.5014/ajot.61.2.135.

Miller, H. L., Ragozzino, M. E., Cook, E. H., Sweeney, J. A., & Mosconi, M. W. (2015). Cognitive set shifting deficits and their relationship to repetitive behaviors in autism spectrum disorder. *Journal of Autism and Developmental Disorders, 45*(3), 805–815. https://doi.org/10.1007/s10803-014-2244-1.

Miller-Kuhaneck, H., Henry, D. A., Glennon, T. J., & Mu, K. (2007). Development of the sensory processing measure-school: Initial studies of reliability and validity. *American Journal of Occupational Therapy, 61*(2). https://doi.org/10.5014/ajot.61.2.170.

Mindell, J. A., Gould, R. A., Tikotzy, L., Leichman, E. S., & Walters, R. M. (2019). Norm-referenced scoring system for the brief infant sleep questionnaire–revised (BISQ-R). *Sleep Medicine, 63*, 106–114.

Mindham, J., & Espie, C. A. (2003). Glasgow anxiety scale for people with an intellectual disability (GAS-ID): Development and psychometric properties of a new measure for use with people with mild intellectual disability. *Journal of Intellectual Disability Research, 47*(1), 22–30. https://doi.org/10.1046/j.1365-2788.2003.00457.x.

Miyake, A., Emerson, M. J., & Friedman, N. P. (2000). Assessment of executive functions in clinical settings: Problems and recommendations. *Seminars in Speech and Language, 21*(2), 169–183. https://doi.org/10.1055/s-2000-7563.

Miyake, A., & Friedman, N. P. (2012). The nature and organization of individual differences in executive functions: Four general conclusions. *Current Directions in Psychological Science, 21*(1), 8–14. https://doi.org/10.1177/0963721411429458.

Montaque, I., Dallos, R., & McKenzie, B. (2018). "It feels like something difficult is coming back to haunt me": An exploration of 'meltdowns' associated with autistic spectrum disorder from a parental perspective. *Clinical Child Psychology and Psychiatry, 23*(1), 125–139. https://doi.org/10.1177/1359104517730114.

Moskowitz, L. J., Mulder, E., Walsh, C. E., McLaughlin, D. M., Zarcone, J. R., Proudfit, G. H., et al. (2013). A multimethod assessment of anxiety and problem behavior in children with autism spectrum disorders and intellectual disability. *American Journal on Intellectual and Developmental Disabilities, 118*(6), 419–434. https://doi.org/10.1352/1944.7558.118.6.419.

Moss, J., & Howlin, P. (2009). Autism spectrum disorders in genetic syndromes: Implications for diagnosis, intervention and understanding the wider autism spectrum disorder population. *Journal of Intellectual Disability Research, 53*(10), 852–873. https://doi.org/10.1111/j.1365-2788.2009.01197.xx.

Moss, J., Howlin, P., & Oliver, C. (2011). The assessment and presentation of autism spectrum disorder and associated characteristics in individuals with severe intellectual disability and genetic syndromes. In J. A. Burack, R. M. Hodapp, G. Iarocci, & E. Zigler (Eds.), *The Oxford handbook of intellectual disability and development* Oxford University Press. https://doi.org/10.1093/oxfordhb/9780195305012.013.0018.

Moss, J., Nelson, L., Powis, L., Waite, J., Richards, C., & Oliver, C. (2016). A comparative study of sociability in Angelman, Cornelia de Lange, fragile X, down and Rubinstein Taybi syndromes and autism spectrum disorder. *American Journal on Intellectual and Developmental Disabilities, 121*(6), 465–486. https://doi.org/10.1352/1944-7558-121.6.465.

Moss, J., Oliver, C., Arron, K., Burbidge, C., & Berg, K. (2009). The prevalence and phenomenology of repetitive behaviour in genetic syndromes. *Journal of Autism and Developmental Disorders, 39*(4), 572–588. https://doi.org/10.1007/s10803-008-0655-6.

Muskett, A. E. (2020). *Feasibility of anxieyt assessment for children with minimally-verbal autism (doctoral dissertation)*. https://vtechworks.lib.vt.edu/handle/10919/5534.

Myrbakk, E., & Tetzchner, S. V. (2008). The prevalence of behavior problems among people with intellectual disability living in community settings? *Journal of Mental Health Research in Intellectual Disabilities, 1*(3), 205–222. https://doi.org/10.1080/19315860802115607.

Naglieri, J. A., & Goldstein, S. (2013). *Comprehensive executive function inventory*. North Tonawanda, NY: Multi-Health Systems.

Nelson, L., Crawford, H., Reid, D., Moss, J., & Oliver, C. (2017). An experimental study of executive function and social impairment in Cornelia de Lange syndrome. *Journal of Neurodevelopmental Disorders, 9*(1), 33. https://doi.org/10.1186/s11689-017-9213-x.

Numminen, H., Service, E., Ahonen, T., Korhonen, T., Tolvanen, A., Patja, K., et al. (2000). Working memory structure in intellectual disability. *Journal of Intellectual Disability Research, 44*(5), 579–590. https://doi.org/10.1046/j.1365-2788.2000.00279.x.

Ogletree, B. T., & Price, J. R. (2018). Nonstandardized evaluation of emergent communication in individuals with severe intellectual disabilities: Exploring existing options and proposing innovations. *Advances in Neurodevelopmental Disorders, 2*(1), 38–48. https://doi.org/10.1007/s41252-017-0043-3.

Olatunji, B. O., Cisler, J. M., & Tolin, D. F. (2007). Quality of life in the anxiety disorders: A meta-analytic review. *Clinical Psychology Review, 27*(5), 572–581. https://doi.org/10.1016/j.cpr.2007.01.015.

Oliver, C., Adams, D., Allen, D., Bull, L., Heald, M., Moss, J., et al. (2013). Causal models of clinically significant behaviors in Angelman, Cornelia de Lange, Prader-Willi and Smith-Magenis syndromes. *International Review of Research in Developmental Disabilities, 44*, 167–211.

Oliver, C., Adams, D., Allen, D., Crawford, H., Heald, M., Moss, J., et al. (2020). The behaviour and wellbeing of children and adults with severe intellectual disability and complex needs: The be-well checklist for carers and professionals. *Paediatrics and Child Health, 30*(12), 416–424. https://doi.org/10.1016/j.paed.2020.09.003.

Oliver, C., Horsler, K., Berg, K., Bellamy, G., Dick, K., & Griffiths, E. (2007). Genomic imprinting and the expression of affect in Angelman syndrome: What's in the smile? *Journal of Child Psychology and Psychiatry, 48*(6), 571–579. https://doi.org/10.1111/j.1469-7610.2007.01736.x.

Oliver, C., McClintock, K., Hall, S., Smith, M., Dagnan, D., & Stenfert-Kroese, B. (2003). Assessing the severity of challenging behaviour: Psychometric properties of the challenging behaviour interview. *Journal of Applied Research in Intellectual Disabilities, 16*(1), 53–61. https://doi.org/10.1046/j.1468-3148.2003.00145.x.

Oliver, C., Royston, R., Crawford, H., Moss, J., Waite, J., Adams, D., et al. (2021). *Informant assessments of behaviour and affect for people with intellectual disability (V2)*. University of Birmingham.

Owens, J. A., Spirito, A., & McGuinn, M. (2000). The Children's sleep habits questionnaire (CSHQ): Psychometric properties of a survey instrument for school-aged children. *Sleep, 23*(8), 1043–1052. https://doi.org/10.1093/sleep/23.8.1d.

Paclawskyj, T. R., Matson, J. L., Rush, K. S., Smalls, Y., & Vollmer, T. R. (2000). Questions about behavioral function (QABF): A behavioral checklist for functional assessment of aberrant behavior. *Research in Developmental Disabilities, 21*, 223–229. https://doi.org/10.1016/s0891-4222(00)00036-6.

Pandi-Perumal, S. R., Spence, D. W., & BaHammam, A. S. (2014). Polysomnography: An overview. In *Primary care sleep medicine* (pp. 29–42). Springer.

Parham, L. D., & Ecker, C. (2007). *Sensory processing measure (SPM): Manual.* Western Psychological Services.

Pennington, B. F., & Ozonoff, S. (1996). Executive functions and developmental psychopathology. *Journal of Child Psychology and Psychiatry, 37*(1), 51–87. https://doi.org/10.1111/j.1469-7610.1996.tb01380.x.

Petry, K., Maes, B., & Vlaskamp, C. (2005). Domains of quality of life of people with profound multiple disabilities: The perspective of parents and direct support staff. *Journal of Applied Research in Intellectual Disabilities, 18*(1), 35–46. https://doi.org/10.1111/j.1468-3148.2004.00209.x.

Powis, L., & Oliver, C. (2014). The prevalence of aggression in genetic sydnromes: A review. *Research in Developmental Disabilities, 35*(5), 1051–1071. https://doi.org/10.1016/j.ridd.01.033.

Prelock, P. J., & Nelson, N. W. (2012). Language and communication in autism: An integrated view. *Pediatric Clinics of North America, 59*(1), 129–145. https://doi.org/10.1016/j.pcl.2011.10.008.

Pulina, F., Vianello, R., & Lanfranchi, S. (2019). Cognitive profiles in individuals with down syndrome. In *Vol. 56. International review of research in developmental disabilities* (pp. 67–92). Academic Press.

Quine, L. (1991). Sleep problems in children with mental handicap. *Journal of Intellectual Disability Research, 35*(4), 269–290. https://doi.org/10.1111/j.1365-2788.1991.tb00402.x.

Rapaport, M. H., Clary, C., Fayyad, R., & Endicott, J. (2005). Quality-of-life impairment in depressive and anxiety disorders. *American Journal of Psychiatry, 162*(6), 1171–1178. https://doi.org/10.1176/appi.ajp.162.6.1171.

Regnard, C., Reynolds, J., Watson, B., Matthews, D., Gibson, L., & Clarke, C. (2007). Understanding distress in people with severe communication difficulties: Developing and assessing the Disability Distress Assessment Tool (DisDAT). *Journal of Intellectual Disability Research, 51*(4), 277–292. https://doi.org/10.1111/j.1365-2788.2006.00875.x.

Reid, D., Moss, J., Nelson, L., Groves, L., & Oliver, C. (2017). Executive functioning in Cornelia de Lange syndrome: Domain asynchrony and age-related performance. *Journal of Neurodevelopmental Disorders, 9*(1), 1–12. https://doi.org/10.1186/s1689-017-9208-7.

Reisman, J., & Hanschu, B. (1992). *Sensory integration inventory – Revised for individuals with developmental disabilities.* PDP Press.

Reiss, S. (1988). *Reiss screen for maladaptive behavior: Test manual. Vol. 1988.* IDS Publishing Corporation.

Richards, C., Davies, L., & Oliver, C. (2017). Predictors of self-injurious behavior and self-restraint in autism spectrum disorder: Towards a hypothesis of impaired behavioral control. *Journal of Autism and Developmental Disorders, 47*, 701–713. https://doi.org/10.1007/s10803-016-3000-5.

Richards, C., Jones, C., Groves, L., Moss, J., & Oliver, C. (2015). Prevalence of autism spectrum disorder phenomenology in genetic syndromes: A systematic review and meta-analysis. *Lancet Psychiatry, 2*(10), 909–916. https://doi.org/10.1016/S2215-0366(15)00376-4.

Richards, C., Moss, J., Nelson, L., & Oliver, C. (2016). Persistence of self-injurious behaviour in autism spectrum disorder over three years: A prospective cohort study of risk markers. *Journal of Neurodevelopmental Disorders*, *8*, 21. https://doi.org/10.1186/s11689-016-9153-x.

Rispoli, M., Ninci, J., Neely, L., & Zaini, S. (2014). A systematic review of trial-based functional analysis of challenging behavior. *Journal of Developmental and Physical Disabilities*, *26*, 271–283. https://doi.org/10.1007/s10882-013-9363-z.

Roberts, et al. (2009). Autistic behavior in boys with fragile X syndrome: Social approach and HPA-axis dysfunction. *Journal of Neurodevelopmental Disorders*, *1*(4), 283–291. https://doi.org/10.1007/s11689-009-9028-5.

Rodgers, J., Freeston, M., South, M., Wigham, S., & Boulter, C. (2012). Intolerance of uncertainty: Its relevance to autism spectrum disorder. In *British Association of Behavioural and Cognitive Psychotherapy Annual Meeting, Leeds, UK*.

Ross, E., & Oliver, C. (2003). Preliminary analysis of the psychometric properties of the mood, interest & pleasure questionnaire (MIPQ) for adults with severe and profound learning disabilities. *The British Journal of Clinical Psychology*, *42*(Pt 1), 81–93. https://doi.org/10.1348/014466503762842039.

Rowland, C. (2004). *Communication matrix*. Oregon Health & Science University.

Royal College of Nursing. (2009). Clinical guideline for the recognition and assessment of acute pain in children. *Royal College of Nursing*. www.rcn.org.uk/development/practice/pain.

Royeen, C. B. (1987). TIP-touch inventory for preschoolers. *Physical & Occupational Therapy in Pediatrics*, 7(1), 29–40. https://doi.org/10.1080/J006v07n01_04.

Royeen, C. B., & Fortune, J. C. (1990). Touch inventory for elementary-school-aged children. *The American Journal of Occupational Therapy : Official Publication of the American Occupational Therapy Association*, *44*(2). https://doi.org/10.5014/ajot.44.2.155.

Royston, R., Oliver, C., Howlin, P., Dosse, A., Armitage, P., Moss, J., et al. (2020). The profiles and correlates of psychopathology in adolescents and adults with Williams, fragile X and Prader-Willi syndromes. *Journal of Autism and Developmental Disorders*, *50*(3), 893–903. https://doi.org/10.1007/s10803-019-04317-1.

Royston, R., Howlin, P., Waite, J., & Oliver, C. (2017). Anxiety disorders in Williams syndrome contrasted with intellectual disability and the general population: A systematic review and meta-analysis. *Journal of Autism and Developmental Disorders*, *47*(12), 3765–3777. https://doi.org/10.1007/s10803-016-2909-z.

Rutter, M., Bailey, A., & Lord, C. (2003). *The social communication questionnaire*. Western Psychological Services.

Ryan, S. (2010). "Meltdowns", surveillance and managing emotions; going out with children with autism. *Health and Place*, *16*(5), 868–875. https://doi.org/10.1016/j.healthplace.2010.04.012.

Sadeh, A. (2004). A brief screening questionnaire for infant sleep problems: Validation and findings for an internet sample. *Pediatrics*, *113*(6), e570–e577. https://doi.org/10.1542/peds.113.6.e570.

Sanchez, A. L., Cornacchio, D., Chou, T., Leyfer, O., Coxe, S., Pincus, D., et al. (2017). Development of a scale to evaluate young children's responses to uncertainty and low environmental structure. *Journal of Anxiety Disorders*, *45*, 17–23. https://doi.org/10.1016/j.janxdis.2016.11.006.

Scahill, L., Lecavalier, L., Schultz, R. T., Evans, A. N., Maddox, B., Pritchett, J., et al. (2019). Development of the parent-rated anxiety scale for youth with autism Spectrum disorder. *Journal of the American Academy of Child & Adolescent Psychiatry*, *58*(9), 887–896. https://doi.org/10.1016/j.jaac.2018.10.016.

Schaaf, R. C., & Lane, A. E. (2015). Toward a best-practice protocol for assessment of sensory features in ASD. *Journal of Autism and Developmental Disorders*, *45*(5), 1380–1395. https://doi.org/10.1007/s10803-014-2299-z.

Schoen, S. A., Miller, L. J., Brett-Green, B. A., & Nielsen, D. M. (2009). Physiological and behavioral differences in sensory processing: A comparison of children with autism spectrum disorder and sensory modulation disorder. *Frontiers in Integrative Neuroscience, 3*, 1–11. https://doi.org/10.3389/neuro.07.029.2009.

Schoen, S. A., Miller, L. J., & Green, K. E. (2008). Pilot study of the sensory over-responsivity scales: Assessment and inventory. The American Journal of Occupational Therapy, 62(4), 393–406. https://dx.doi.org/https://doi.org/10.5014/ajot.62.4.393.

Schoen, S. A., Miller, L. J., & Sullivan, J. C. (2014). Measurement in sensory modulation: The sensory processing scale assessment. *The American Journal of Occupational Therapy, 68*(5), 522–530. https://psycnet.apa.org/doi/10.5014/ajot.2014.012377.

Schroeder, S. R., Marquis, J. G., Reese, R. M., Richman, D. M., Mayo-Ortega, L., Oyama-Ganiko, R., et al. (2014). Risk factors for self-injury, aggression, and stereotyped behavior among young children at risk for intellectual and developmental disabilities. *American Journal on Intellectual and Developmental Disabilities, 119*(4), 351–370. https://doi.org/10.1352/1944-7558-119.4.351.

Sigafoos, J., Woodyatt, G., Keen, D., Tait, K., Tucker, M., Roberts-Pennell, D., et al. (2000). Identifying potential communicative acts in children with developmental and physical disabilities. *Communication Disorders Quarterly, 21*(2), 77–86. https://doi.org/10.1177/152574010002100202.

Sigafoos, J., O'Reilly, M. F., Lancioni, G. E., & Sutherland, D. (2014). Augmentative and alternative communication for individuals with autism spectrum disorder and intellectual disability. *Current Developmental Disorders Reports, 1*(2), 51–57. https://doi.org/10.1007/s40474-013-00007-x.

Simon, J. R. (1969). Reactions toward the source of stimulation. *Journal of Experimental Psychology, 81*(1), 174. https://psycnet.apa.org/doi/10.1037/h0027448.

Simonds, J. F., & Parraga, H. (1982). Prevalence of sleep disorders and sleep behaviors in children and adolescents. *Journal of the American Academy of Child & Adolescent Psychiatry, 21*(4), 383–388. https://doi.org/10.1016/S0002-7138(09)60942-0.

Simonoff, E., Pickles, A., Charman, T., Chandler, S., Loucas, T., & Baird, G. (2008). Psychiatric disorders in children with autism spectrum disorders: Prevalence, comorbidity, and associated factors in a population-derived sample. *Journal of the American Academy of Child & Adolescent Psychiatry, 47*(8), 921–929. https://doi.org/10.1097/CHI.0b013e318179964f.

Simonoff, E., Taylor, E., Baird, G., Bernard, S., Chadwick, O., Liang, H., et al. (2013). Randomized controlled double-blind trial of optimal dose methylphenidate in children and adolescents with severe attention deficit hyperactivity disorder and intellectual disability. *Journal of Child Psychology and Psychiatry, 54*(5), 527–535. https://doi.org/10.1111/j.1469-7610.2012.02569.x.

Siper, P. M., Kolevzon, A., Wang, A. T., Buxbaum, J. D., & Tavassoli, T. (2017). A clinician-administered observation and corresponding caregiver interview capturing DSM-5 sensory reactivity symptoms in children with ASD. *Autism Research: Official Journal of the International Society for Autism Research, 10*(6), 1133–1140. https://doi.org/10.1002/aur.1750.

Skuse, D. H. (2007). Rethinking the nature of genetic vulnerability to autistic spectrum disorders. *Trends in Genetics : TIG, 23*(8), 387–395. https://doi.org/10.1016/j.tig.2007.06.003.

Smith, M., Manduchi, B., Burke, É., Carroll, R., McCallion, P., & McCarron, M. (2020). Communication difficulties in adults with intellectual disability: Results from a national cross-sectional study. *Research in Developmental Disabilities, 97*. https://doi.org/10.1016/j.ridd.2019.103557.

Snell, M. E., Brady, N., McLean, L., Ogletree, B. T., Siegel, E., Sylvester, L., et al. (2010). Twenty years of communication intervention research with individuals who have severe intellectual and developmental disabilities. *American Journal on Intellectual and Developmental Disabilities, 115*(5), 364–380. https://doi.org/10.1353/1944-7558-115-5.364.

Solodiuk, J., & Curley, M. A. Q. (2003). Pain assessment in nonverbal children with severe cognitive impairments: The individualized numeric rating scale (INRS). *Journal of Pediatric Nursing, 18*(4), 295–299. https://doi.org/10.1016/S0882-5963(03)00090-3.

Spaniol, M., & Danielsson, H. (2022). A meta-analysis of the executive function components inhibition, shifting, and attention in intellectual disabilities. *Journal of Intellectual Disability Research, 66*(1–2), 9–31. https://doi.org/10.1111/jir.12878.

Sparrow, S. S., Cicchetti, D. V., & Saulnier, C. A. (2016). *Vineland adaptive behaviour scales.* Third Edition PsychCorp.

Spence, S. H. (1999). *Spence children's anxiety scale (parent version).* University of Queensland.

Summers, J., Shahrami, A., Cali, S., D'Mello, C., Kako, M., Palikucin-Reljin, A., et al. (2017). Self-injury in autism spectrum disorder and intellectual disability: Exploring the role of reactivity to pain and sensory input. *Brain Sciences,* 7(11), 140. https://doi.org/10.3390/brainsci7110140.

Surtees, A. D., Oliver, C., Jones, C. A., Evans, D. L., & Richards, C. (2018). Sleep duration and sleep quality in people with and without intellectual disability: A meta-analysis. *Sleep Medicine Reviews, 40,* 135–150. https://doi.org/10.10016/j.smrv.2017.11.003.

Symons, F. J., Harper, V. N., McGrath, P. J., Breau, L. M., & Bodfish, J. W. (2009). Evidence of increase non-verbal behavioral signs of pain in adults with neurodevelopmental disorders and chronic self-injury. *Research in Developmental Disabilities, 30,* 521–528. https://doi.org/10.1016/j.ridd.2008.07.012.

Taylor, D. V., Rush, D., Hetrick, W. P., & Sandman, C. A. (1993). Self-injurious behavior within the menstrual cycle of women with mental retardation. *American Journal on Mental Retardation, 97*(6), 659–664.

Thurm, A., Farmer, C., Salzman, E., Lord, C., & Bishop, S. (2019). State of the field: Differentiating intellectual disability from autism spectrum disorder. *Frontiers in Psychiatry, 10,* 526. https://doi.org/10.3389/fpsyt.2019.00526.

Toplak, M. E., West, R. F., & Stanovich, K. E. (2013). Practitioner review: Do performance-based measures and ratings of executive function assess the same construct? *Journal of Child Psychology and Psychiatry, 54,* 131–143.

Touchette, P. E., MacDonald, R. F., & Langer, S. N. (1985). A scatter plot for identifying stimulus control of problem behavior. *Journal of Applied Behavior Analysis, 18*(4), 343–351. https://doi.org/10.1901/jaba.1985.18-343.

Trickett, J., Heald, M., Oliver, C., & Richards, C. (2018). A cross-syndrome cohort comparison of sleep disturbance in children with Smith-Magenis syndrome, Angelman syndrome, autism spectrum disorder and tuberous sclerosis complex. *Journal of Neurodevelopmental Disorders, 10*(1), 1–14. https://doi.org/10.1186/s11689-018-9226-0.

Tunnicliffe, P., Woodcock, K., Bull, L., Oliver, C., & Penhallow, J. (2014). Temper outbursts in Prader-Willi syndrome: Causes, behavioural and emotional sequence and responses by carers. *Journal of Intellectual Disability Research, 58*(2), 134–150. https://doi.org/10.1111/jir.12010.

Tzischinsky, O., Meiri, G., Manelis, L., Bar-Sinai, A., Flusser, H., Michaelovski, A., et al. (2018). Sleep disturbances are associated with specific sensory sensitivities in children with autism. *Molecular Autism, 9*(1), 22. https://doi.org/10.1186/s13229-018-0206-8.

Van den Broek, E. G., Janssen, C. G. C., & Van Ramshorst, T. (2006). Visual impairments in people with severe and profound multiple disabilities: An inventory of visual functioning. *Journal of Intellectual Disability Research, 50*(6), 470–475. https://doi.org/10.1111/j.1365-2788.2006.00804.x.

Van de Water, A. T., Holmes, A., & Hurley, D. A. (2011). Objective measurements of sleep for non-laboratory settings as alternatives to polysomnography–a systematic review. *Journal of Sleep Research*, *20*, 183–200. https://doi.org/10.1111/j.1365-2869.2009.00814.x.

van Steensel, F. J., Bögels, S. M., & Dirksen, C. D. (2012). Anxiety and quality of life: Clinically anxious children with and without autism spectrum disorders compared. *Journal of Clinical Child & Adolescent Psychology*, *41*(6), 731–738. https://doi.org/10.1080/15374416.2012.698725.

Voepel-Lewis, T., Shayevitz, J. R., & Malviya, S. (1997). The FLACC: A behavioral scale for scoring postoperative pain in young children. *Pediatric Nursing*, *23*(3), 293–297.

Vos, P., De Cock, P., Petry, K., Van Den Noortgate, W., & Maes, B. (2010). Do you know what I feel? A first step towards a physiological measure of the subjective well-being of persons with profound intellectual and multiple disabilities. *Journal of Applied Research in Intellectual Disabilities*, *23*(4), 366–378. https://doi.org/10.1111/j.1468-3148.2010.00553.x.

Waite, J. (2012). *The behavioural and cognitive phenotype of Rubinstein-Taybi syndrome [Doctoral Thesis, University of Birmingham]*. University of Birmingham eTheses Repository.

Waite, J., Beck, S. R., Heald, M., Powis, L., & Oliver, C. (2016). Dissociation of cross-sectional trajectories for verbal and visuo-spatial working memory development in Rubinstein-Taybi syndrome. *Journal of Autism and Developmental Disorders*, *46*(6), 2064–2071. https://doi.org/10.1007/s10803-016-2736-2.

Waite, J. Beck, S., Powis, L., Oliver, C. (in press). The Executive function account of repetitive behavior: Evidence from Rubinstein-Taybi syndrome. American Journal on Intellectual and Developmental Disabilities.

Wakschlag, L. S., Briggs-Gowan, M. J., Choi, S. W., Nichols, S. R., Kestler, J., Burns, J. L., et al. (2014). Advancing a multidimensional, developmental spectrum approach to preschool disruptive behavior. *Journal of the American Academy of Child and Adolescent Psychiatry*, *53*(1), 82–96.e3. https://doi.org/10.1016/j.jaac.2013.10.011.

Wakschlag, L. S., Choi, S. W., Carter, A. S., Hullsiek, H., Burns, J., McCarthy, K., et al. (2012). Defining the developmental parameters of temper loss in early childhood: Implications for developmental psychopathology. *Journal of Child Psychology and Psychiatry and Allied Disciplines*, *53*(11), 1099–1108. https://doi.org/10.1111/j.1469-7610.2012.02595.x.

Walley, R. M., & Donaldson, M. D. C. (2005). An investigation of executive function abilities in adults with Prader–Willi syndrome. *Journal of Intellectual Disability Research*, *49*(8), 613–625. https://doi.org/10.1111/j.1365-2788.2005.00717.x.

Watson, L. R., Patten, E., Baranek, G. T., Poe, M., Boyd, B. A., Freuler, A., et al. (2011). Differential associations between sensory response patterns and language, social, and communication measures in children with Autism or other developmental disabilities. *Journal of Speech, Language, and Hearing Research*, *54*(6), 1562–1576. https://doi.org/10.1044/1092-4388(2011/10-0029.

Weckwerth, S. A. M., Weckwerth, G. M., Ferrairo, B. M., Chicrala, G. M., Ambrosio, A. M. B., Toyoshima, G. H. L., et al. (2016). Parents' perception of dental caries in intellectually disabled children. *Special Care in Dentistry*, *36*(6), 300–306. https://doi.org/10.1111/scd.12191.

Wetherby, A. M., & Prizant, B. M. (2002). *Communication and symbolic behavior scales: Developmental profile*. Paul H Brookes Publishing.

Whitney, D. G., Shapiro, D. N., Peterson, M. D., & Warschausky, S. A. (2019). Factors associated with depression and anxiety in children with intellectual disabilities. *Journal of Intellectual Disability Research*, *63*(5), 408–417. https://doi.org/10.1111/jir.12583.

Wiggs, L., & Stores, G. (1996). Severe sleep disturbance and daytime challenging behaviour in children with severe learning disabilities. *Journal of Intellectual Disability Research*, *40*(6), 518–528.

Wigren, M., & Hansen, S. (2005). ADHD symptoms and insistence on sameness in Prader-Willi syndrome. *Journal of Intellectual Disability Research*, *49*(6), 449–456. https://doi.org/10.1111/j.1365-2788.2005.00690.x.

Wilde, L., Eden, K., de Vries, P., Moss, J., Welham, A., & Oliver, C. (2017). Self-injury and aggression in adults with tuberous sclerosis complex: Frequency, associated person characteristics, and implications for assessment. *Research in Developmental Disabilities*, *64*, 119–130. https://doi.org/10.1016/j.ridd.2017.03.007.

Wilde, L., Mitchell, A., & Oliver, C. (2016). Differences in social motivation in children with Smith–Magenis syndrome and down syndrome. *Journal of Autism and Developmental Disorders*, *46*(6), 2148–2159. https://doi.org/10.1007/s10803-016-2743-3.

Wilde, L., Wade, K., Eden, K., Moss, J., de Vries, P. J., & Oliver, C. (2018). Persistence of self-injury, aggression and property destruction in children and adults with tuberous sclerosis complex. *Journal of Intellectual Disability Research*, *62*(12), 1058–1071. https://doi.org/10.1111/jir.12472.

Willner, P., Bailey, R., Parry, R., & Dymond, S. (2010). Evaluation of executive functioning in people with intellectual disabilities. *Journal of Intellectual Disability Research*, *54*(4), 366–379. https://doi.org/10.1111/j.1365-2788.2010.01249.x.

Woodard, C. R., Goodwin, M. S., Zelazo, P. R., Aube, D., Scrimgeour, M., Ostholthoff, T., et al. (2012). A comparison of autonomic, behavioral, and parent-report measures of sensory sensitivity in young children with autism. *Research in Autism Spectrum Disorders*, *6*(3), 1234–1246. https://doi.org/10.1016/j.rasd.2012.03.012.

Woodcock, K. A., Oliver, C., & Humphreys, G. W. (2009a). Task switching deficits and repetitive behavior in genetic neurodevelopmental disorders: Data from children with Prader-Willi syndrome chromosome 15 q11-q13 deletion and boys with fragile-X syndrome. *Cognitive Neuropsychology*, *26*(2), 172–194. https://doi.org/10.1080/02643290802685921.

Woodcock, K. A., Oliver, C., & Humphreys, G. W. (2009b). Associations between repetitive questioning, resistance to change, temper outbursts and anxiety in Prader-Willi and fragile-X syndromes. *Journal of Intellectual Disability Research*, *53*(3), 265–278. https://doi.org/10.1111/j.1365-2788.2008.01122.x.

Woodcock, K. A., Oliver, C., & Humphreys, G. W. (2011). The relationship between specific cognitive impairment and behaviour in Prader-Willi syndrome. *Journal of Intellectual Disability Research*, *55*(2), 152–171. https://doi.org/10.1111/j.1365-2788.2010.01368.x.

Yeung, L. H. J., & Thomacos, N. (2020). Assessments of sensory processing in infants and children with autism spectrum disorder between 0–12 years old: A scoping review. *Research in Autism Spectrum Disorders*, *72*. https://doi.org/10.1016/j.rasd.2020.101517.

Young, S. E., Friedman, N. P., Miyake, A., Willcutt, E. G., Corley, R. P., Haberstick, B. C., et al. (2009). Behavioral disinhibition: Liability for externalizing spectrum disorders and its genetic and environmental relation to response inhibition across adolescence. *Journal of Abnormal Psychology*, *118*(1), 117–130. https://doi.org/10.1037/a0014657.

Zarkowska, E., & Clements, J. (1994). *Problem behaviour and people with severe learning disabilities: the S.T.A.R. approach* (2nd ed.). Chapman and Hall.

Further reading

Brady, N. C., Bruce, S., Goldman, A., Erickson, K., Mineo, B., Ogletree, B. T., et al. (2016). Communication services and supports for individuals with severe disabilities: Guidance

for assessment and intervention. *American Journal on Intellectual and Developmental Disabilities, 121*(2), 121–138. https://doi.org/10.1352/1944-7558-121.2.121.
Johnson, H., Watson, J., Iacono, T., Bloomberg, K., & West, D. (2012). Assessing communication in people with severe-profound disabilities: Co-constructing competence. *Journal of Clinical Practice in Speech-Language Pathology, 14*(2), 64–68.
Sharpley, C. F., Andronicos, N. M., Agnew, L. L., & Mills, R. (2015). Which aspects of sensory features are associated with elevated cortisol concentrations in boys with an autism spectrum disorder? *Journal of Developmental and Physical Disabilities, 27*(5), 661–675. https://doi.org/10.1007/s10882-015-9442-4.
Siegel, D. J., & Bryson, T. P. (2021). *The power of showing up*. Ballantine Books.

CHAPTER FIVE

Considerations for measuring individual outcomes across contexts in Down syndrome: Implications for research and clinical trials

Anna J. Esbensen[a,b], Emily K. Schworer[a], Deborah J. Fidler[c], and Angela John Thurman[d]

[a]Division of Developmental and Behavioral Pediatrics, Cincinnati Children's Hospital Medical Center, Cincinnati, OH, United States
[b]Department of Pediatrics, University of Cincinnati College of Medicine, Cincinnati, OH, United States
[c]Human Development and Family Studies, Colorado State University, Fort Collins, CO, United States
[d]University of California Davis Health, MIND Institute and Department of Psychiatry and Behavioral Sciences, Sacramento, CA, United States

Contents

International Review of Research in Developmental Disabilities, Volume 62
ISSN 2211-6095
https://doi.org/10.1016/bs.irrdd.2022.05.005

Abstract

Individuals with Down syndrome (DS) are increasingly involved in clinical trials that target developmental outcomes, like cognition and behavior. The increased focus on treatment in DS has led to ongoing discussions regarding the selection of outcome measures using syndrome-informed criteria. This discourse is warranted as clinical trials can fail if the outcome measures selected are inappropriate for individuals with DS or do not take into account the behavioral phenotype commonly associated with DS. This review focuses on the challenges present in the measurement of outcomes in DS, with a specific focus on considerations made in evaluating cognitive, language, and behavioral/psychopathology outcomes. This review also provides a summary of recommendations for assessment of outcomes in these domains as well as recommendations for future research. The impact of physical health and assessment psychometrics on the measurement of outcomes is also reviewed.

1. Introduction

Individuals with intellectual and developmental disabilities, including Down syndrome (DS), are increasingly being included in research, intervention studies, and clinical trials. Recent efforts have been initiated by the National Institutes of Health INCLUDE (INvestigation of Co-occurring conditions across the Lifespan to Understand Down syndromE) Project to support care and quality of life in individuals with DS by focusing research on new treatments, large cohorts, and clinical trials. In addition, there are refocused calls for improving developmental, social, and vocational outcomes for individuals with DS across the lifespan, with a specific interest in understanding the behavioral and health phenotype of individuals with DS, and the impact of co-occurring conditions on adaptation and outcomes (Esbensen et al., 2017; Gardiner et al., 2010; McCabe, Hickey, & McCabe, 2011). Driven by these new initiatives for DS research, understanding the heterogeneous development of the behavioral and health phenotypes of individuals with DS has even greater importance as this information has substantial implications for evaluating individual outcomes and the impact of interventions.

Research findings from Trisomy 21 mouse models and studies of the derived benefits of nutritional compounds (i.e., folic acid) have spurred examination of existing pharmaceutical compounds that have the potential to improve cognition and language in individuals with DS (Heller et al., 2003; Heller et al., 2006; Kishnani et al., 2010; Mircher et al., 2020). The number of pharmaceutical clinical trials in DS has doubled in the last decade, with 17 trials from 2000 to 2010 and 36 from 2011 to 2021. To date, many clinical trials have not met with successful outcomes. It is difficult to identify the reason clinical trials have failed. For example, the investigated pharmaceutical compounds may be ineffective for the targeted purpose or the selected age range and/or length of the trial may not be appropriate for detecting effects. Outcome measures have also been identified as a key hurdle in clinical trials, with specific challenges relating to assessments that are prone to floor effects, inappropriate for participants' ability levels, insensitive or unreliable, or limited by overlap in measurement demands (e.g., cognitive and language measures) that confound interpretation of performance.

Other factors also further complicate the interpretation of clinical trial findings. Indeed, clinical trials are finding that the pharmaceutical compounds demonstrated efficacy in only some individuals with DS, such as in the discontinued Roche trial (Moyer, 2021). Moreover, this problem is exacerbated because many individuals with DS may be excluded from trials due to their limited cognitive or communication skills, co-occurring behavioral or psychological conditions, or physical health features (d'Ardhuy et al., 2015; Kishnani et al., 2010). Although excluding individuals with DS with limited cognitive and communication skills may ensure that all participants can complete the study protocol, it can also exclude the individuals that may be most amenable to improvement from a pharmaceutical compound. In addition, physical health (e.g., motor skills, hearing, vision) is known to impact the expression of cognitive and language abilities. Study designs with extensive exclusionary criteria are problematic, as they then lead to pharmaceutical interventions that could appear successful but are only effective for a subset of individuals with DS.

To avoid these pitfalls, clinical researchers must anticipate measurement challenges and rely on experts in DS to inform the selection of measures that will not restrict eligibility criteria. Expert guidance should be based on our most accurate understanding of phenotypic characteristics associated with DS at different stages of the lifespan, accounting for a wide range of cognitive presentations and the potential for co-occurring conditions. Doing so will ensure equity in research and the development of interventions for individuals with DS. Preparing for clinical trials by addressing these areas will also increase the likelihood of accurate clinical trial results and reduce the risk of false negative/Type 2 error (i.e., treatment effects occurred, but were not captured and reported). This paper highlights current challenges to clinical outcome measurement among individuals with DS that may contribute to potential false negative trial findings, summarizes key considerations for measurement of these outcomes emphasizing the phenotypic profile associated with DS, and offers recommendations for subsequent research. We also summarize progress in outcome measure evaluation in DS and provide future directions for growth in this area to complement the advances in clinical trials for this population.

2. Challenges to measurement of individual outcomes in Down syndrome

DS is associated with a probabilistic behavioral phenotype consisting of relative challenges in cognition, language, and specific behavioral or physical health outcomes (Chapman & Hesketh, 2000; Daunhauer et al., 2014; Dykens, Hodapp, & Finucane, 2000; Esbensen & MacLean, 2017; Pulina, Vianello, & Lanfranchi, 2019). Despite reported group-level patterns of delays in each of these areas, there is substantial within-group variability in outcomes for individuals with DS (Karmiloff-Smith et al., 2016). The heterogeneity within the behavioral and cognitive phenotypes, as well as with associated co-occurring health conditions, presents a complex set of challenges for reliably and validly measuring outcomes among individuals with DS. Thus, it is important that outcome measures be specifically evaluated for use in this population. Researchers have identified very few empirically evaluated, psychometrically sound outcome measures appropriate for use in clinical trials with individuals with DS (Esbensen et al., 2017) or with populations with significant communication limitations and concomitant support needs.

In evidence-based research and practice, outcome measures are required to assess an individual's current status, often for the purposes of establishing if there is a change with intervention. Assessments can be performance-based, self-report, observer-report, or clinician-report. To reduce bias, outcome measures need to be reliable, valid, sensitive to change over time, and show variability across individuals (Berry-Kravis et al., 2013; Esbensen et al., 2017). They need to be relevant to the research questions being asked, feasible and acceptable to the individual or study design, replicable, and decided upon prior to initiating an intervention. Whenever possible, measures should be designed to allow for responses using different modes of communication, cognitive levels, and adaptive abilities.

In general, the selection of measures for assessing individual outcomes depends on the purpose of the evaluation. In clinical contexts, providers have some flexibility with the selection of measures specific to one individual and their clinical presentation. However, in research contexts, decisions about measures need to be made based on the overall sample to be evaluated. It is therefore important for the tools utilized to be appropriate and valid for a broader range of phenotypic presentations. Because of the dearth of psychometrically sound outcome measures for individuals with DS, inclusion and exclusion criteria for a study have been used to align the study population with the tools available. Thus, the identification and development of outcome measures that are psychometrically appropriate for use in individuals with DS will be critical for ensuring equity in research.

In the selection of outcome measures, it is also important to consider how measures selected align with the mechanisms of the intervention. Oftentimes, outcome measures are selected to capture the dimensions that are hypothesized to be directly targeted by the intervention. However, there are benefits to including outcome measures that are hypothesized to have secondary or downstream impacts from the intervention, or that may have moderating impacts on the primary outcome of the intervention. Therefore, the selection of outcome measures for a treatment study in DS should not only be informed by the increased likelihood of specific phenotypic patterns of strength and challenge, but also the larger landscape of daily living and the potential for a targeted treatment to have broader effects in broader dimensions of functioning.

3. Assessment considerations based on the phenotypic profile associated with Down syndrome

Several decades of research on phenotypic outcomes associated with DS have made it possible to select outcome measures in more advanced, phenotype-informed ways. In this section, we summarize key recommendations for the selection of measures of cognition, communication, and behavior (Chapman & Hesketh, 2000; Dykens et al., 2000; Esbensen & MacLean, 2017; Pulina et al., 2019). Each recommendation is geared toward reducing measurement error, eliminating interpretational confounds, and capturing treatment effects with accuracy. Table 1 provides a summary of representative examples of measures aligned with the domains of cognition, language, and behavior/psychopathology.

Table 1 Representative examples of measures within the domains of cognition, language, and behavior/psychopathology.

Domain	Measure	Age range
Cognition (IQ)	KBIT-2	4–90 years
	SB-5	2–85 + years
	Leiter-3	3–75 + years
Cognition (subtests)	DAS-II Recognition of Pictures	2.5–17 years
	NEPSY-II (Visuomotor Precision, Word Generation)	VP 5–12 years WG 5–16 years
	RBANS List Learning	12–89 years
	WISC-V Picture Span	6–16 years
Cognition (computer testing)	CANTAB (Paired Associates Learning, Intra-Extra Dimensional Set-Shift, Spatial Span, Simple Reaction Time)	4 years and older
	NIH-TCB	3–85 years
Cognition (parent-report)	BRIEF/BRIEF-2	Preschool 2–5 years School-age 5–18 years Adult 18–90 years
	OMQPF	5–16 years
Language	Expressive Language Sampling	6–23 years
	CELF-P	3–6 years
	RBANS Picture Naming & Semantic Fluency	12–89 years
Behavior/ Psychopathology	CBCL	Preschool 1.5–5 years School-age 6–18 years Adult 18–59 years
	SCQ	4 years and older
	SRS/SRS-2	Preschool 2.5–4.5 years School-age 4–18 years Adult 19 years and older

Note: KBIT-2 = Kaufman Brief Intelligence Test, second edition; SB-5 = Stanford-Binet, fifth edition; CANTAB = Cambridge Neuropsychological Testing Automated Battery; NIH-TCB = National Institutes of Health–Toolbox Cognitive Battery; BRIEF = Behavior Rating Inventory of Executive Function; OMQPF = Observer Memory Questionnaire-Parent Form; DAS-II = Differential Ability Scales, second edition; RBANS = Repeatable Battery for the Assessment of Neuropsychological Status; WISC-V = Wechsler Intelligence Scale for Children, fifth edition; CELF-P = Clinical Evaluation of Language Fundamentals Preschool; CBCL = Child Behavior Checklist; SCQ = Social Communication Questionnaire; SRS = Social Responsiveness Scale.

3.1 Cognition

DS is associated with relative strengths in visual processing, visuospatial short-term memory, visuo-constructive abilities, and imitation that co-exist with documented general intellectual disability (Gathercole & Alloway, 2006; Hodapp et al., 1992; Kanno & Ikeda, 2002; Klein & Mervis, 1999; Zoia, Pelamatti, & Rumiati, 2004). Relative weaknesses are noted in working and long-term memory (Fidler, Most, & Philofsky, 2008; Hodapp & Dykens, 2004). Moreover, there is a great deal of heterogeneity among individuals with DS in terms of phenotypic presentation. Although most children with DS demonstrate cognitive delays during early childhood, the degree of delay observed can vary greatly from one child to another (Grieco, Pulsifer, Seligsohn, Skotko, & Schwartz, 2015). This heterogeneity is observed throughout the lifespan and has important implications for the selection of outcome measures. To have a full representation of individuals with DS in a given treatment study, the measures selected must capture performances across a wide range of cognitive skill levels.

Furthermore, because the rate of learning is slower in DS than it is for their peers without disabilities, the differential between performances among people with and without DS increases with chronological age. Nonetheless, for most individuals cognitive skills do indeed progress throughout childhood and into early adulthood (Couzens, Cuskelly, & Haynes, 2011). This development is then followed by a period of stability in cognitive and functional ability from early to middle adulthood. The risk of dementia then dramatically increases after age 50 (Hawkins, Eklund, James, & Foose, 2003). Prior to 40 years of age, the risk of dementia is around 9% (Strydom et al., 2010). This risk increases to 17% for 50- to 54-year-olds, 32% for 55- to 59-year-olds, and 50% to 60% for adults with DS over 60 years of age (Coppus et al., 2006; Holland, Hon, Huppert, & Stevens, 2000; Zigman, Schupf, Sersen, & Silverman, 1996). Because there are lifespan-related features associated with cognitive performance in DS, measure selection must also be informed by developmental phase, chronological age, and risk for age-related decline.

3.1.1 Selection of measures

To adequately capture within-DS heterogeneity in cognitive abilities, measures should be designed to assess a wide range of ability levels (Karmiloff-Smith et al., 2016). For example, although the physical signs of dementia (plaques and tangles) appear in early adulthood and are present in most adults with DS, not all adults exhibit the clinical presentation of dementia, reinforcing that measures in adulthood be able to measure a wide variety of functioning (Jack et al., 2013). This heterogeneity also has implications for measuring individual outcomes as adults transition from non-dementia status to the onset of dementia symptoms. Thus, it is critical that measures are selected with a broad scale of possible scores that can evaluate a wide range of performances within the same measure.

It is also important to select outcome measures that are appropriate for the range of chronological ages of participants in a given study. Measures that are designed for use with adolescents and adults in the general population may assess complex informational processing skills and therefore lead to floor effects when used in individuals with DS. At the same time, it is important to not overlook the maturational needs of individuals with DS. For example, when working with adults with DS, although child/adolescent measures may be more developmentally appropriate in some cases, it is important to consider how the lives of adults differ from school-age children and adapt measures accordingly. For example, one might modify questions that consider interaction at school to interactions within the workplace. Establishing a balance between questions that capture the appropriate cognitive developmental level while also including chronological age-appropriate contextual factors is an important challenge for best practices in measure selection in DS.

3.1.2 Interpreting assessment outcomes

When interpreting assessment outcomes, it is often the case that assessments with psychometric properties based on individuals of the same chronological age as an individual with DS will comprise test items that are too difficult for individuals with DS. At the same time, tests with more developmentally appropriate items for individuals with DS may have normative information based on younger individuals and will preclude the ability to derive standardized scores. Scoring based on developmental age has also been implemented, however, rigorous evaluation of this scoring method has not yet been completed.

3.1.3 Capturing longitudinal change

When evaluating cognitive skills over time, measures need to be sensitive to both growth and decline. Developmental gains are expected in younger individuals. However, because the rate of growth in individuals with DS is generally slower than it is for individuals with typical development, a large portion of individuals with DS may earn a score at floor level (i.e., the lowest score for the measure's norms), thus making it impossible to describe the heterogeneity and/or developmental improvements in these individuals. On the Kaufman Brief Intelligence Test, second edition (KBIT-2), 37% of a sample of children with DS had standard IQ scores at the floor of the measure (Edgin et al., 2017; Kaufman & Kaufman, 2004). Raw scores had lower rates of floor effects (5–9% of participants) but do not provide insight into performance relative to chronological age expectations. These findings of problems with floor effects on the KBIT-2 have been replicated and highlight the need for choosing IQ measures that are better able to capture the heterogeneity observed among individuals with DS (Schworer, Esbensen et al., 2021). Because of the co-occurrence of dementia in adults with DS, it is also important that measures consider the potential decline in cognitive functioning. Without selection of appropriate outcome measures, results from intervention studies or clinical evaluations may be difficult to interpret, and null findings could result from inadequate outcome measures, rather than from the ineffectiveness of the treatment.

3.1.4 Cognition measurement recommendations

Because of the degree of challenge experienced by most individuals with DS in cognitive domains and their corresponding targets for pharmaceutical and behavioral intervention, measures of cognition are at the forefront of outcome measure validation efforts. Significant progress has been made for measurement of overall IQ with the use of deviation scores on the Stanford-Binet, fifth edition (SB-5) (Roid, 2003; Sansone et al., 2014). Most assessments of intelligence, such as the SB-5, yield IQ scores that traditionally have a lower bound of 40. Because a substantial number of individuals with DS will perform at or below this lower bound, using traditional methods of generating IQ scores masks meaningful variability in cognitive performance. One way to resolve these problems uses deviation *Z*-score methods. These methods use descriptive statistics of subtest raw scores for each age band within the standardized sample to generate a deviation *Z*-score that provides a more accurate comparison of participant performance relative to performance in the standardization sample (Sansone et al., 2014). Deviation *Z*-scores have been developed for the SB-5 as well as specifically with individuals with DS using the Wechsler Intelligence Scale for Children, 4th edition (WISC-IV) (Pezzuti et al., 2018; Sansone et al., 2014). This deviation scoring technique eliminates floor effects found using traditional IQ scores and, unlike raw scores, provides an index of cognitive performance relative to chronological age expectations (Roid, 2003; Sansone et al., 2014). For example, traditional scaled scores on the SB-5 are likely to show a flat profile for individuals with intellectual disability (with scores of 1 across cognitive subdomains). Rather than grouping all raw scores of 0–13 into one scaled score category of 1, deviation scoring methods capture relative strengths and weaknesses among cognitive subdomains. A child with scaled scores of 1 on both Nonverbal Fluid Reasoning and Verbal Knowledge could have deviation scores of −2.33 on Nonverbal Fluid Reasoning and −5.45 on Verbal Knowledge, demonstrating relative strengths in nonverbal skills and challenges with verbal abilities. Without the floor effects on IQ measures typically found in populations with intellectual disability, it is possible to describe the cognitive abilities of study participants with DS more accurately.

Another, more long-term approach to resolve the issue of floor effects would be to appeal to publishers to extend the lower limit of traditional IQ scores when establishing test norms. For example, the Leiter-3 has a lower normed floor than other IQ assessments (lower bound of 30), and it showed minimal floor effects in a sample of adolescents and adults with DS (1% at floor) (d'Ardhuy et al., 2015). Based on these features, it has been recommended for study designs that require nonverbal IQ testing.

Another important recent innovation in outcome measure work in DS involves psychometric evaluation of specific candidate measures to determine their appropriateness for specific age groups of individuals with DS. Recent validation work has been conducted with the Arizona Cognitive Test Battery (ACTB), which was developed by Edgin et al. (2010) to assess hippocampal, prefrontal, and cerebellar brain regions in DS (Edgin et al., 2010; Edgin et al., 2017). Measures were examined over a 3-month test-retest period in children and adults with DS (Edgin et al., 2017). Results of this work demonstrated that certain ACTB tasks were promising, particularly those assessing cerebellar functioning [the Cambridge Neuropsychological Testing Automated Battery (CANTAB) Simple Reaction Time, and the NEPSY Visuomotor Precision task (Edgin et al., 2017)]. Yet the tasks assessing hippocampal functioning demonstrated mixed results, with the CANTAB Paired Associates Learning generating variable performance on test-retest reliability and practice effects, and the CANTAB Intra-Extra Dimensional Set-Shift presenting concerns for floor effects (53%) and inadequate test-retest reliability (Intraclass correlation coefficient [ICC] <0.50). Another outcome measure from the ACTB is the CANTAB Spatial Span forward which demonstrates good test-retest reliability ICC > 0.70 for the total score, but poor psychometric properties for the error measure (Edgin et al., 2017). This adequate test-retest reliability was replicated in adolescents with DS (ICC = 0.67; d'Ardhuy et al., 2015), however, test-retest reliability indices were lower for adults (ICC = 0.55; (d'Ardhuy et al., 2015). There also was a trend toward practice effects identified (Edgin et al., 2017), suggesting a need for alternate versions of the measure.

Beyond the ACTB, additional efforts have been made to identify the most psychometrically sound measures for evaluating cognition in DS. In one study, candidate outcome measures for treatment studies in DS were examined over a 6-month period among adolescents and adults with DS. This study demonstrated good test-retest reliability (ICC = 0.64–0.69) for the Repeatable Battery for the Assessment of Neuropsychological Status (RBANS) List Learning in both adolescents and adults with DS (d'Ardhuy et al., 2015). In another study, a set of working memory clinical assessments was evaluated in children and adolescents with DS (Schworer, Esbensen et al., 2021). Specific measures that met most psychometric criteria (i.e., measure completion of ≥80%, test-retest reliability ICC ≥ 0.75, and nonsignificant practice effects) included the SB-5 Working Memory (verbal and nonverbal), the Differential Ability Scales, second edition (DAS-II) Recognition of Pictures, and the WISC-V Picture Span. On each of these measures, raw or ability scores generally had better psychometrics than standard scores and floor effects were below 20% in the sample (Schworer, Esbensen et al., 2021).

Evaluations of cognitive measures have also included computerized programs. The National Institutes of Health Toolbox Cognitive Battery (NIH-TCB) includes measures of working memory, episodic memory, processing speed, inhibitory control, cognitive flexibility, oral reading, and receptive vocabulary, and offers developmental extensions that support feasibility in the assessment of individuals with intellectual disabilities (Hessl et al., 2016; Shields et al., 2020). Feasibility is the percentage of children examined that can complete the task to yield a valid score. In recent evaluations of the set of measures, feasibility ranged from 66 to 92% in children and adolescents with DS and fragile X syndrome (Hessl et al., 2016) and 61 to 99% in DS specifically (Shields et al., 2020). Further, the collective set of NIH-TCB tasks had variable feasibility for children with a mental age of three and 4 years, with feasibility increasing as mental age increased (Hessl et al., 2016; Shields et al., 2020). Overall, test-retest reliability, construct validity, and ecological validity results were promising for use of these computerized measures in future clinical trials (Hessl et al., 2016; Shields et al., 2020).

Parent questionnaires are highly feasible and informant measures of executive function and memory have been evaluated for children and adults with DS (d'Ardhuy et al., 2015; Esbensen et al., 2019). The Behavior Rating Inventory of Executive Function (BRIEF) and Observer Memory Questionnaire-Parent Form (OMQPF) were found to be psychometrically reliable in children and adolescents with DS (d'Ardhuy et al., 2015; Esbensen et al., 2019; Schworer, Voth, Hoffman, & Esbensen, 2022). Specifically, the BRIEF generally demonstrates acceptable to excellent internal consistency ($\alpha > 0.70$), and the OMQPF had moderate test-retest reliability (ICC = 0.70, 0.76). The BRIEF-Preschool was used by d'Ardhuy et al. (2015) and was not found to be appropriate for adults with DS but was recommended for adolescents.

Note: Cognitive outcome measures have also been investigated for utility in detecting decline in cognitive skills related to the onset of Alzheimer's disease in adults with DS. The progress and challenges associated with measuring cognitive decline are reviewed in Fleming et al in this volume (Fleming et al., 2022).

3.1.5 Future directions for cognitive measurement

To support the appropriate selection of cognitive outcome measures, a greater understanding of the natural history of cognitive development in individuals with DS is needed. While the field has made advances in evaluating a variety of measures associated with several cognitive constructs, there is a need to evaluate additional cognitive constructs in greater detail to support the selection of outcome measures for future clinical trials, particularly for the earlier phases of the lifespan (Esbensen et al., 2017). Though studies above have addressed the psychometric properties of measures that assess cognition in older children, adolescents, and adults with DS, there is very little empirical work examining the psychometric properties of measures of early cognition in this population. In addition, it is important to investigate the best approaches to scoring standardized assessments when they are used out of the norming age range. Research is needed to (a) understand how non-standardized scoring impacts interpretation, and (b) to develop normative data based on individuals with DS where appropriate. Out of range scoring may also be calculated based on developmental level, but as observed with d'Ardhuy, this may not always be appropriate. Thus, we need a greater understanding of when, or for what age ranges, it is suitable to score standardized measures based on an individual's developmental level.

3.2 Language

Children with DS experience delays in meeting language milestones across most language domains, including phonology, vocabulary, grammar, and pragmatics (Martin, Klusek, Estigarribia, & Roberts, 2009; McDuffie & Abbeduto, 2009; Thurman & del Hoyo Soriano, 2021). Moreover, the degree of delay observed in language skills is often greater in individuals with DS than it is in individuals with other intellectual disability conditions (Chapman, 2006; del Hoyo Soriano, Thurman, & Abbeduto, 2018; Finestack & Abbeduto, 2010; Finestack, Sterling, & Abbeduto, 2013; Thurman et al., 2021).

Importantly, areas of relative strength and challenge are often observed across language domains. Receptive skills are often more advanced than expressive skills, pragmatic skills are generally more advanced than other structural language skills (e.g., vocabulary and syntax), and vocabulary skills are generally more advanced than syntactic skills (e.g., (Abbeduto, McDuffie, Thurman, & Kover, 2016). However, even when considering one of these areas (e.g., receptive vocabulary, nonverbal communication), patterns of strength and challenge may be observed (Fidler, Philofsky, Hepburn, & Rogers, 2005; Finestack et al., 2013; Hahn, Loveall, Savoy, Neumann, & Ikuta, 2018; Phillips, Loveall, Channell, & Conners, 2014). Nonetheless, great variability also exists in absolute skill levels across individuals. The expressive language abilities of older children and adults with DS vary from limited speech to syntactically complex utterances (Finestack & Abbeduto, 2010; Klein & Mervis, 1999). Delays in language skills are a substantial barrier to independence for individuals with DS. Thus, treatments that support language development are of high priority.

3.2.1 Selection of measures

When measuring language skills specifically, once again it is important to consider the range of possible scores that can be achieved on a language measure and the extent to which floor effects and restricted range can impact overall findings. Moreover, whenever possible, measures that allow for the use of a range of communication styles should be utilized to ensure that individuals with DS with severe speech impairments can be included.

In particular, assessments that rely on verbal instructions and responses may be of limited utility for individuals who use alternative modes of communication. The assessment of language skills specifically, or skills in other domains (e.g., executive functioning), may be supported by allowing participants to use Augmentative and Alternative Communication (AAC), or forms of communication other than oral speech. In these instances, within instructions or participant responses, unaided (e.g., facial expressions, gestures, or sign language) or aided AAC (e.g., pictures, objects, or other AAC applications) may strengthen communication effectiveness until spoken language is acquired. Although off-standardization procedures may provide insight into useful supports that can generalize to other contexts (e.g., home, school, vocational settings), a deviation from assessment procedures presents a confound when using norming data for comparison. If used, these off-standardization assessment methods warrant documenting and reporting.

3.2.2 Interpreting assessment outcomes

For accurate interpretation of language assessments, it is again important to consider both age and developmental level. An assessment may be developmentally appropriate for an individual's language level, but chronological age-related issues may arise. Though an assessment normed on chronologically younger children without disabilities may offer the possibility of careful evaluation of language gains in an intervention study, the topical content of that assessment may be developmentally inappropriate for older individuals, which can prohibit its use.

3.2.3 Capturing longitudinal change

Language assessment measures in DS should be sensitive to both growth and decline in order to detect developmental gains as well as regression in adolescence and cognitive/language decline in adulthood. Capturing growth and change in this area should also consider the specific language stage (e.g., preverbal, single words, word combinations) and developmental level of a child or adult with DS. Indicators of progress in language development vary across each language stage, with increases in frequency and types of prelinguistic communicative forms (e.g., vocalizations, gestures) preceding increases in frequency and types of lexical and grammatical forms. Because of the slower rate of language development in DS relative to peers with typical development, language stage is particularly important to consider in investigations of change over time. Moreover, language is also sensitive to changes in related neurocognitive systems and these relations may change across development. For example, in early development, language dysfluencies are likely to increase as children begin to produce longer and more complex sentences (Zackheim & Conture, 2003); in contrast, in later stages of development, increases in language dysfluencies may be an indicator of cognitive declines (Faroqi-Shah et al., 2020).

3.2.4 Language measurement recommendations

To date, many measures have been used to assess language in individuals with DS; however, more research is still needed to fully understand the psychometric properties of these assessments when used in individuals with DS (Esbensen et al., 2017). Nonetheless, progress has been made. As mentioned earlier, use of deviation scores has significantly improved measurement of IQ in individuals with DS; with these procedures, verbal knowledge scores from the SB-5 are no longer subject to floor effects, thereby providing accurate measurements of the performance in individuals with DS relative to their chronologically-matched peers with typical development (Roid, 2003; Sansone et al., 2014).

In addition, new data are available considering the feasibility and psychometric properties of utilizing Expressive Language Sampling (ELS) as a procedure for generating spoken language outcome measures for individuals with DS (Thurman et al., 2021). More specifically, when utilizing ELS procedures to measure spoken language skills in children and young adults with DS, the procedures were considered feasible and yielded variables for measuring expressive vocabulary, syntax, and intelligibility that were psychometrically valid (Thurman et al., 2021). All three measures were found to demonstrate strong construct validity. That is, they were significantly correlated with other variables designed to measure the same construct (i.e., demonstrating convergent validity), and they were not associated, or associated to a lesser extent, with variables designed to measure dissimilar constructs (i.e., demonstrating discriminant validity). In addition, all three scores demonstrated test-retest stability, with minimal practice effects and strong test-retest reliability (ICCs: 0.79–0.93) observed across the 4-week interval considered. The authors reported that noncompliance rates for these procedures were most likely for youth with more limited cognitive and linguistic skills (i.e., youth under 12 years of age who earned abbreviated IQ age-equivalent scores from the SB-5 less than 4 years, 9 months, and demonstrated phrase-level speech or less); for youth who did not meet all of these criteria, noncompliance rates were 5% or less. Although data are still pending regarding the extent to which language variables derived from ELS procedures are sensitive to change in individuals with DS, preliminary data considering the utility of these procedures in youth without disabilities (Channell, Loveall, Conners, Harvey, & Abbeduto, 2018) and in small samples of youth with DS (Conners, Tungate, Abbeduto, Merrill, & Faught, 2018; del Hoyo Soriano, Thurman, Harvey, Kover, & Abbeduto, 2020) suggest these measures are sensitive to change over time.

D'Ardhuy et al. (2015) considered the utility of three additional measures of language performance in adolescents and adults with DS: (1) Clinical Evaluation of Language Fundamentals Preschool – 2 (CELF-P) Word Classes subtest (Wiig, Secord, & Semel, 2004) raw scores, (2) RBANS Picture Naming subtest raw scores and (3) RBANS Semantic Fluency subtest raw scores (d'Ardhuy et al., 2015). With regard to the CELF-P, although acceptable test-retest reliability was observed in adolescents (receptive ICC: 0.63, expressive ICC: 0.71) and adults with DS (receptive ICC: 0.68, expressive ICC: 0.69), along with associations with IQ, significant associations were not observed with age (d'Ardhuy et al., 2015). There was also some evidence of a ceiling effect for receptive scores on the CELF-P for individuals with DS. The RBANS Picture Naming did not show adequate test-retest reliability (ICC = 0.50, 0.53) for adolescents and adults across a 6-month interval, yet scores were associated with IQ. Results showed that the RBANS Semantic Fluency subtest demonstrated acceptable test-retest reliability across a 6-month interval in adults with DS, with an ICC of 0.73 and no practice effects; scores were also associated with IQ. RBANS Semantic Fluency scores were observed to decline with time. Moreover, the RBANS Semantic Fluency score has been found to distinguish patients with Alzheimer's Disease from a comparison sample of adults matched on age, education, and gender who were not diagnosed with dementia (Duff et al., 2008). A similar semantic verbal fluency task (NEPSY-II Word Generation) has also been shown to have adequate feasibility (74–85%), moderate test-retest reliability (ICC = 0.72–0.75), and negligible practice effects in a sample of youth with DS (Smeyne et al., in press). More data on the developmental trajectory of this score across adolescence into adulthood for individuals with DS is required to help validate the utility of this measure as an indicator of cognitive decline in DS.

3.2.5 Future directions for language measurement

To further characterize the feasibility and utility of language outcome measures, it would be helpful for future studies considering the psychometric adequacy of language outcome measures to also consider the influences of language level and age on psychometric properties. Indeed, as an individual transitions across language stages (e.g., preverbal, first words, word combinations), differences in the rate and indicators of growth are likely to be observed. For example, an individual who is using gestures and vocalizations, but not yet words, to communicate does not have the foundational skills necessary to participate in a semantic fluency test. In addition, a greater understanding of the developmental trajectories of language measures across the lifespan is needed to determine the extent to which present measures are sensitive to both developmental growth and the cognitive decline observed in adulthood for many individuals with DS. Thus, identifying language measures that are multifaceted and appropriate across the lifespan is of critical need.

3.3 Behavior and psychopathology

At the group level, individuals with DS tend to demonstrate strengths in specific social skills (e.g., eye gaze, facial displays, social interactions) and have generally fewer behavioral concerns in comparison to peers with matched levels of intellectual disability (Fidler & Nadel, 2007). Nonetheless, when compared to the general population, or even some other individuals with intellectual and developmental disability, higher rates of common behavioral symptoms are present, including noncompliance, inattention, and wandering (Dykens et al., 2000; Mantry et al., 2008). In addition, despite areas of relative strength in social relatedness, social cognition and communication can be areas of challenge for many individuals with DS (Abbeduto et al., 2016; Channell, 2020). Risk for attention deficit hyperactivity disorder (ADHD) and autism spectrum disorder (ASD) is also elevated in children with DS, in comparison to both peers without disabilities and peers with intellectual disability (Dekker & Koot, 2003; DiGuiseppi et al., 2010; Ekstein, Glick, Weill, Kay, & Berger, 2011; Froehlich et al., 2007).

3.3.1 Selection of measures

The preponderance of behavior measures used in DS research rely on informant-report, often a parent, teacher, or caregiver. Similar to the selection of measures of cognition and language, measures of behavior warrant selection for their appropriateness to the age and developmental level of the individual. One must also consider whether the measure of behavior has been developed for individuals with typical development, or individuals with intellectual disability, and whether normative data are needed or available for the study.

When evaluating symptoms of psychopathology, there are options to use proxy-report or self-report measures. One challenge with proxy-report measures involves difficulties inferring thoughts and feelings of another individual, such as worries or delusional thoughts. However, self-report approaches pose challenges as well, including the need to ensure that the measure is developmentally appropriate in both item wording and in response options. Self-report of these dimensions is dependent upon the theory of mind and vocabulary skills that make it possible to characterize one's own mental states. For example, an adult with DS may not fully understand what "depressed" means and it may be necessary to ask more concrete questions about their behaviors. Instead, interviewers may ask the individual with DS if they feel sad or the frequency they have cried in the past week or month. Having pictures of people displaying different emotions available may also help individuals with DS describe their feelings and emotions. Additionally, if using an AAC speech-output device, it would be necessary for some individuals with DS to have access to pictures, buttons, or keys to support their expression of emotions and mental states. However, these challenges with assessing symptoms of psychopathology using self-report are not unique to DS, and are reviewed in detail elsewhere (Finlay & Lyons, 2001).

3.3.2 Interpretation of assessment outcomes

It is important to understand the variety of symptom presentations that may exist in DS and how they impact the interpretation of behavioral and psychopathological constructs being measured in DS. Self-talk and having imaginary friends are common among individuals with DS and can be present throughout the lifespan (Patel, Wolter-Warmerdam, Leifer, & Hickey, 2018). While it is normative for individuals with DS to engage in self-talk, changes in the level of self-talk (volume, intensity) may be an indicator of stress or loneliness (McGuire & Chicoine, 2006). Thus, if measuring reactions to a stressor, intensity of self-talk (and not just frequency or presence) is important to consider. In the general population, measurement of self-talk is often included in measures of psychoses and hallucinations. Thus, care is warranted in evaluating outcome measures to ensure that they are not erroneously labeling a developmentally appropriate behavior in DS as a symptom of psychopathology.

3.3.3 Capturing longitudinal change

Assessments of behavior and psychopathology are developed for different purposes. Measures of behavior are likely to give an indication of behaviors present at that time. The sensitivity of behavior measures to capture change over time among individuals with DS is expected to be adequate but has yet to be established with empirical studies. However, measures of psychopathology appropriate for individuals with intellectual and developmental disabilities are generally developed for diagnostic purposes rather than for assessing change over time. For making a clinical diagnosis, these measures assess symptoms over a specified period (i.e., 6 months). As a result, both the item wording on the measure for diagnostic purposes and the length of time assessed by the measure may contribute to the measure being insensitive to change over time in shorter assessment intervals of a clinical trial (i.e., change in the last week/month).

3.3.4 Behavior and psychopathology measurement recommendations

Attention to the measurement of behaviors and psychopathology in DS is needed for the success of future clinical trials that target these domains or those with primary outcomes in other domains. Validation of clinical measures for use in future treatment trials will be critical for determining whether measures presently used in the general population are appropriate for use in individuals with DS. For example, early ASD surveillance has become the standard of care in the general pediatric population, with widely used measures that screen for early social-communicative and repetitive behavior features. However, many of the currently available measures include items that are generally considered to be part of the phenotypic profile associated with DS, such as communication delays. An important future direction for improving early detection of risk for ASD in DS, as well as for measuring responses to ASD treatments, will be to distinguish between those features that are unique to the co-occurrence of DS and ASD, and which features are more generally observed among people with DS, regardless of their ASD status. Similar concerns can be raised regarding the diagnosis and detection of co-occurring ADHD (Esbensen et al., 2021).

Parent-report measures of behavior and psychopathology are feasible and show some evidence of reliability for this population. For example, the Child Behavior Checklist (CBCL) was determined to be a good screening tool for global behavioral concerns (internalizing, externalizing, total score) in DS, although reliability and validity were variable across individual subscales with caution warranted if using the Anxious/Depressed, Somatic Complaints, and Thought Problems subscales (Esbensen et al., 2018). Another parent-report measure, the Social Communication Questionnaire (SCQ), is commonly used as a screening tool for ASD and in pilot data appears appropriate for children and adolescents with DS (Magyar, Pandolfi, & Dill, 2012).

The SCQ demonstrated good sensitivity and specificity to detect ASD, along with high convergent validity with the Autism Diagnostic Interview-Revised (Magyar et al., 2012). The Social Responsiveness Scale (SRS) has also been described as appropriate for describing ASD symptoms in children, adolescents, and adults with DS (Channell, 2020; Channell et al., 2015; Schworer, Hoffman, et al., 2021). However, convergence was not found between the SRS-2 and direct assessments of social cognition (Schworer, Hoffman, et al., 2021). Therefore, parent-report may be assessing a different application of social skills compared to what is measured in the laboratory. For all measures of ASD, further research is needed to understand what modifications may be warranted when diagnosing ASD among individuals with DS.

3.3.5 Future directions for behavior and psychopathology measurement

There is a need for new measures to assess the common behavioral concerns and the probabilistic DS behavioral phenotype, as well as to understand the developmental trajectories of symptom profiles (Patel et al., 2018). Several key DS-related behavioral concerns are often inadequately captured in currently available measures of behavior, including wandering, noncompliance, self-stimulatory behaviors, insistence on sameness, social boundaries, and excessive self-talk (Capone, Goyal, Ares, & Lannigan, 2006; Feeley & Jones, 2008; McGuire & Chicoine, 2006; Patel et al., 2018; Stein, 2016). Increased efforts to develop and validate self-report measures of psychopathology are also necessary. As noted above, there are specific questions in the intersection between developmental science and diagnostic assessment that must be answered in order to improve our measurement of symptomatology of co-occurring conditions, like ASD and ADHD. There is currently no comprehensive account of the early emergence of ASD in the context of early development in DS, and no means to distinguish between early phenotypic features associated with DS and early indicators of risk for ASD. Similarly, we are beginning to learn more about the early forms of cognitive control in infants with DS (Schworer, Fidler, & Daunhauer, 2021; Schworer et al., 2022), but at this time, no link has been made between variability in infant cognitive control presentation and later co-occurrence of ADHD. Until these issues are addressed, current measures of behavior or psychopathology may not detect, or may improperly detect areas of concern. As a result, individuals with DS may not be identified to receive effective treatment or may receive inappropriate treatment.

4. Impact of physical health on assessment of outcomes

4.1 Medical conditions

The expression of cognitive and language phenotypes in DS can be strongly influenced by co-occurring health conditions. Many such conditions exist in DS. Congenital heart defects and sleep apnea affect approximately half of individuals with DS, negatively impact cognition and language performance, and account for within-syndrome variability in developmental outcomes and adaptation in this population (Breslin et al., 2014; Bull & Genetics, 2011; Shott, 2006; Visootsak et al., 2011). Children with DS are at greater risk for childhood acute lymphoblastic leukemia, which has been demonstrated to impact the developmental trajectory of children with typical development (Bull & Genetics, 2011). Children with DS are also at higher risk for gastrointestinal conditions, hypothyroidism, and other conditions that impact development and individual outcomes (Bull & Genetics, 2011; McCarron, Gill, McCallion, & Begley, 2005). Thus, consideration of co-occurring health conditions is required when selecting measures and when interpreting outcomes. One also needs to appropriately control for changes in co-occurring medical conditions/symptoms when interpreting behavioral, cognitive, or language outcome measures, particularly in studies evaluating change over time.

Co-occurring medical conditions are important to consider for their impact on measuring outcomes and the interpretation of assessment outcomes, particularly when evaluating change in previously reviewed mental health outcomes. Symptomatically, several medical conditions present similarly to depression and thus may impact measurement of depressive symptoms (Esbensen, 2010). Symptoms of hypothyroidism may present as lethargy and decreased interest in activities. Sleep apnea symptoms may present as fatigue, irritability, and lack of interest in activities. Symptoms of menopause or pain can also present as decreased activity. When interpreting mental health outcomes, similar concerns with overlapping symptom presentation of medical (such as thyroid, gastrointestinal, respiratory) and mental health conditions are important to consider.

4.2 Motor skills

Decisions regarding the selection of outcome measures should also consider motor skills and coordination to ensure the accurate assessment of a target cognitive or behavioral dimension. Motor skills are often impaired in individuals with DS, both due to low muscle tone and difficulties with balance and coordination. Additional difficulties are often noted with motor planning, motor control, and muscle strength (Frank & Esbensen, 2015; Winders, 2013). Early in development, in particular, motoric responses may be the sole modality for cognitive and communication assessments. For example, to assess early planning and problem-solving, infants with DS may be required to pull on a cloth to obtain an object out of reach (Schworer et al., 2020) and toddlers with DS may be required to retrieve objects manually from within a container (Fidler et al., 2005). Later in development, fine motor coordination may impact assessment of processing speed when the task requires use of paper and pencil. This also applies to iPad tasks that require participants to select responses on a touch screen (Hessl et al., 2016; Shields et al., 2020). In each of these cases, motor challenges may interfere with the valid measurement of cognition in the form of problem-solving and goal-directed behavior. Evaluation of motor presentation prior to the use of these measures is critical for the accurate interpretation of cognitive and communication assessments that use manipulatives or require motoric responses in people with DS throughout the lifespan.

Interestingly, despite challenges with aspects of motor development, the use of manipulatives facilitates learning in individuals with DS and thus facilitates performance on individual outcome measures (Buckley & Johnson-Glenberg, 2008; Wolpert, 2001). This evidence applies to virtual and tangible manipulatives, as both varieties are shown to effectively support learning in children with other developmental disabilities, such as ASD (Bouck, Satsangi, Doughty, & Courtney, 2014). One important assessment strategy, therefore, may be the use of manipulatives to increase interest in the task, motivation, and performance on individual outcome measures.

Though a great deal of emphasis is placed on the role of fine motor skills in the assessment of cognition or communication, gross motor skills may also limit participants' ability to move about in assessment environments. On the Autism Diagnostic Observation Schedule, second edition (ADOS-2), for example, the evaluation of social initiations, and other critical social behaviors can be confounded by a child's ability to ambulate. Showing an object to a caregiver or examiner by bringing it to them, for example, is an important joint attention initiation behavior. While accommodations are possible for participants with fine and gross motor challenges, motor abilities are important to consider when designing a study to reduce unintended confounds to outcome measure performance due to variability in motor skills.

4.3 Vision and hearing

Individuals with DS are at elevated risk for visual and hearing impairments (Esbensen & MacLean, 2017). In childhood, individuals with DS are often in need of corrective lenses for nearsightedness, farsightedness, or astigmatism. Strabismus, a misalignment of the eyes, and cataracts are common in individuals with DS, with the risk for cataracts most common in childhood and the risk increasing with early aging. Vision impairments have direct implications for outcome measurement, as many assessments have a visual component to prompts and may have broader implications for cognitive functioning for adults with DS (Krinsky-McHale et al., 2014). Middle ear infections increase the risk for conductive hearing loss in childhood and children with hearing loss and DS are at greater risk for language delays than children with DS and no hearing loss (Laws & Hall, 2014). In adulthood, hearing impairments, especially high-frequency sensorineural hearing impairments, generally onset earlier than in the general population (Buchanan, 1990). As few adults with hearing loss use hearing devices, and most caregivers are unaware of hearing loss, hearing impairments have significant implications for understanding the developmental trajectory of aging adults with DS and measuring individual outcomes (Van Buggenhout et al., 1999).

4.4 Recommendations and future directions for addressing the impact of physical health on outcome measures

Despite the advances that have been made in the evaluation of cognitive and communication outcome measures presented in previous sections, there are large gaps in our current understanding of how co-occurring health conditions impact measure selection. In future outcome measures validation research, researchers should evaluate whether medical conditions, motor abilities, and/or vision and hearing impairments interact with the psychometric properties of candidate measures. This entails collecting normative or natural history data to delineate the different trajectories of development for children with or without a specific medical condition. Until such data are available, clinical trial designs are recommended to randomize participants by medical conditions or account for co-occurring medical conditions in statistical analyses.

Additional evaluation should take into account common vision and hearing challenges to determine whether procedures involving visual or auditory stimuli should be presented during assessments. Larger stimuli or pictures may be needed. Vision and hearing screenings may be critical prior to participation in a research study and studies may benefit from procedures that ensure whether glasses and hearing aids should be used throughout the study. A quiet room may be needed for assessments or have the option of augmented volume. Measurement of individual outcomes that do not account for vision and hearing can produce skewed or inaccurate data. Support for accommodations of motor abilities may also be needed. In instances where manipulatives are small, having larger options could allow for outcome measures to be accessible for children with a greater range of motor skills.

5. Additional assessment considerations in Down syndrome

5.1 Phenotypic profile associated with Down syndrome: Impact on performance

Appropriate measurement tools for treatment studies in DS must reliably measure a wide range of presentations (co-occurring medical and psychiatric conditions) and developmental and language levels. This is necessary to capture the full range of ability levels among individuals with DS with validity. In addition, a skill of interest may be influenced by performance in another developmental domain or co-occurring condition. For example, most individuals with DS experience difficulties with working memory; thus, the working memory demands associated with a range of cognitive, language, and behavioral tasks may limit their performance and contribute to floor effects. Similarly, limitations in attention may significantly impact performances on cognitive outcome measures. Thus, beyond the selection of specific measures, clinical trial assessment visits should consider the use of shorter administration times to reduce study burden, produce greater interest in the testing, and ultimately facilitate greater compliance with the evaluation.

In addition, because language skills play a key role in social development, cognitive development, and academic achievement, it is vital that language also be considered when considering outcome measure selection in other domains. Most outcome measures, regardless of the domain of interest, rely on a person's ability to comprehend verbal task instructions and the ability to formulate a verbal response (Edgin et al., 2010). For example, if an individual with DS fails to respond to an item because they do not have the appropriate language skills to provide a response, it can be difficult for the clinician or examiner to disentangle challenges in language skills from challenges within a given domain of interest, leading to the potential for scores that inaccurately represent the true ability level of the individual. That is, comprehension of the task and ability to respond will impact task compliance and task completion and thus, are both essential to obtain valid and reliable measures of the behavior of interest.

5.2 Interaction between performance and assessment context

When evaluating outcomes to measure, yet another factor to consider is the context and environment in which the assessment is administered. Child assessments may take place at home, at school, in a research lab, clinic, or other environments. Each of these contexts can have an impact on outcomes that are measured. In some contexts, the measurement may be more natural and thus findings more generalizable. For example, a child may be more comfortable being evaluated at home or in their classroom or being evaluated by a familiar teacher or instructor. A child who uses an AAC device may be more likely to use the device at school where they were taught how to use the device than in a research lab or even at home, where their parents might successfully understand their speech or other forms of communication. In other contexts, study control and standardization may be greater, but may also introduce novel examiners, which may impede the generalizability of findings or compliance of the individual completing the task. Pre-testing may be beneficial to reduce any variance from working with novel tasks and examiners, and to increase participant familiarity with task demands. Depending on which outcomes are being measured, context may also impact selection of outcome measures. For example, if studying expressive language, it is important to consider the use of standardized measures of language as well as language produced in more naturalistic contexts, as they capture different components of how language changes over time.

Another important aspect of the interaction between performance and context is monitoring the participant's attention levels and attention to the task. While computerized testing provides the opportunity for standardization and automatic scoring, this type of testing might be hindered by the relatively short attention span and the social nature of individuals with DS if the tasks are less motivating or too long. If computerized testing is used, tablet administration is argued to be more motivating and simpler than keyboard/mouse tasks (Hessl et al., 2016). Further, the amount of experience an individual with DS has with computers and technology may impact testing using these modalities.

5.3 Assessment psychometric properties

5.3.1 Floor effects

As mentioned earlier, features of the phenotypic profile associated with DS can contribute to floor effects. When measures are selected that were developed for the general population, there is a chance of having a high rate of floor effects when administered to an individual with DS. Scores at the floor are particularly important to understand further to ensure appropriate interpretation. Individuals may score at the floor of a measure due to task difficulty, due to noncompliance with the task, due to difficulty with understanding task instructions, or due to other demands of the task. It is important to be monitoring whether a child is considering their response options before responding to track engagement with the activity.

Certain tasks lend themselves to unreliable scores due to acquiescence or chance. For instance, memory tasks that rely on recognition or placement of chips on a grid may result in correct responses due to chance (Schworer, Voth, et al., 2022). Thus, it is important to monitor if an individual with DS is creating a pattern, or selecting the same corner on subsequent presentations, to best understand if their score is a true reflection of their performance. Understanding how the same score can be generated from different scenarios is important when deciding which data to include in a research study or a clinical evaluation, and in interpreting outcome measures and reporting findings.

The concern with floor effects may also be especially important with regards to other skills of interest among individuals with DS, such as language ability or working memory. Floor effects can dramatically undermine the evaluation of an intervention as they restrict the range for demonstrating change in performance (Hessl et al., 2016). Thus, selection of raw scores or alternate forms of calculating standard scores are often necessary (Hessl et al., 2009).

5.3.2 Validity

The phenotypic trajectory associated with DS also can have implications for accurate and valid measurement of specific constructs of interest. Measurement of cognition, for example, often requires verbal responses.

List learning tasks have been frequently used in studies of adults with DS, wherein auditory input is recalled verbally (i.e., verbal recall). However, the increased expressive language challenges that are observed in many individuals with DS may compromise the validity of such a memory assessment. The confound of a verbal response serves as a filter through which such a memory assessment must be interpreted, and the "impurity" of the task makes interpretability of any performance challenging. To address this issue of compromised validity, it is recommended that measures are selected that minimize expressive language demands, reduce the complexity of motor demands, and preserve motivation for engagement as best as possible. It is also recommended that receptive language demands are reduced as well, with clear instructions and modified teaching trials to ensure participant understanding of a task prior to administration.

5.3.3 Reliability and practice effects

Other important psychometric properties essential for establishing the utility of assessments in DS include test-retest reliability and practice effects. Essential information can be determined by establishing if scores are consistent across short testing intervals (test-retest reliability) and if scores change with multiple administrations (practice effects). Many factors influence test-retest reliability and practice effects including the difficulty of the measure, motivation, examiner effects, testing time of day, and the testing environment. Evidence for a measure's reliability established using normative data of primarily individuals with typical development does not guarantee that same reliability in scores of individuals with DS. Both test-retest reliability and practice effects can influence how scores are interpreted and ultimately the findings reported from behavioral or pharmaceutical interventions. To date, there has been some variation in specific "acceptable" psychometrics for these indices. Moving forward, it will be important to demonstrate consistency across studies for suitable test-retest reliability and practice effects for evaluation of measures in DS research. For studies involving multiple visits, it is necessary to determine if the same examiner is needed to improve consistency across intervals. It is also necessary to evaluate other measures in a battery, to determine if these measures could impact practice effects or improve performance. For example, if "cat" is a target word on a list memory task, the animal should be avoided in measures administered prior to the memory task as this repetition may increase the likelihood that the word would be remembered.

5.4 Informant report

Depending on the nature of the outcome of interest, measures can be obtained from parents, teachers, siblings, clinicians, or other informants. Each rater completes rating forms based on their own perspective and experiences with an individual with DS. As a result of viewing individuals in different contexts, abundant literature demonstrates low interrater reliability across raters in the general population, especially when rating behaviors (Achenbach, McConaughy, & Howell, 1987). However, low interrater reliability does not negate the value of collecting information across multiple informants or contexts. Diverging evaluations, such as between a teacher and a parent, can potentially shed light on differing behavior presentations in different settings (Daunhauer et al., 2014), or may point to different baseline comparisons for one set of evaluators versus another (Esbensen et al., 2021). Thus, understanding the influence of different raters or contexts on selected outcome measures does have value.

5.5 Study eligibility

The requirements and types of measures chosen for a study may have implications for those selected to be included in a study. Excluding participants who are minimally verbal for a study that has multiple verbal indicators could be justified, however, the effects of exclusion need to be considered. While the use of verbal tasks is at times warranted, it is important to consider how verbal measures restrict the range of individuals eligible for a study. In the example of verbal requirements for a study, researchers should be cautious as not to only create treatments for a subset of individuals with DS. Inclusion criteria in previous studies have had minimum Vineland Adaptive Behavior score requirements to participate (>55) (Kishnani et al., 2010). Although it is reasonable for a study to have a minimum adaptive level, it is equally important to design studies with appropriate outcome measures that would allow for broader inclusion criteria.

6. Summary of future directions for measuring outcomes

In the US, individuals with DS currently have access to early intervention programs, inclusive education practices, post-secondary educational opportunities, and vocational opportunities at greater rates than earlier generations (Roizen, 2013). They are benefiting from advances in medicine and health care that are associated with substantial gains in longevity. As a result, it is important to accurately measure the outcomes of these opportunities and therapies. As the field develops new pharmaceutical and clinical interventions, there is a critical need to identify sensitive outcome measures that are likely to detect treatment changes in important domains among all individuals with DS. Selection of outcome measures and how current assessment challenges are addressed has important implications for capturing intervention effects and ultimately allows a greater number of individuals with DS to benefit from clinical and research programs.

Acknowledgment

Authors have no conflicts of interest to disclose. This manuscript was prepared with support from the *Eunice Kennedy Shriver* National Institute of Child Health and Human Development of the National Institutes of Health (R01 HD074346 PI Abbeduto; R01 HD093654 PI Thurman; R01 HD093754 PI Esbensen; R01 HD099150 [& R01 HD099150-S] PI Fidler; R21 HD101000 PI Fidler; R61 HD100934 MPI Esbensen/Froehlich; P50 HD103526 PI Abbeduto).

References

Abbeduto, L., McDuffie, A., Thurman, A., & Kover, S. (2016). In *Vol. 50. Language development in individuals with intellectual and developmental disabilities: From phenotypes to treatments International Review of Research in Developmental Disabilities* (pp. 71–118). Elsevier.

Achenbach, T. M., McConaughy, S. H., & Howell, C. T. (1987). Child/adolescent behavioral and emotional problems: Implications of cross-informant correlations for situational specificity. *Psychological Bulletin, 101*(2), 213–232.

Berry-Kravis, E., Hessl, D., Abbeduto, L., Reiss, A. L., Beckel-Mitchener, A., Urv, T. K., et al. (2013). Outcome measures for clinical trials in fragile X syndrome. *Journal of Developmental and Behavioral Pediatrics, 34*(7), 508.

Bouck, E. C., Satsangi, R., Doughty, T. T., & Courtney, W. T. (2014). Virtual and concrete manipulatives: A comparison of approaches for solving mathematics problems for students with autism spectrum disorder. *Journal of Autism and Developmental Disorders, 44*(1), 180–193. https://doi.org/10.1007/s10803-013-1863-2.

Breslin, J., Spanò, G., Bootzin, R., Anand, P., Nadel, L., & Edgin, J. O. (2014). Obstructive sleep apnea syndrome and cognition in down syndrome. *Developmental Medicine & Child Neurology, 56*(7), 657–664.

Buchanan, L. H. (1990). Early onset of presbyacusis in down syndrome. *Scandinavian Audiology, 19*(2), 103–110.

Buckley, S., & Johnson-Glenberg, M. (2008). Increasing literacy learning for individuals with down syndrome and fragile X syndrome. In J. Roberts, R. Chapman, & S. Warren (Eds.), *Speech and language development and intervention in down syndrome and fragile X syndrome* Paul H. Brookes.

Bull, M. J., & Genetics, C. O. (2011). Health supervision for children with down syndrome. *Pediatrics, 128*(2), 393–406. https://doi.org/10.1542/peds.2011-1605.

Capone, G., Goyal, P., Ares, W., & Lannigan, E. (2006). Neurobehavioral disorders in children, adolescents, and young adults with down syndrome. *American Journal of Medical Genetics Part C: Seminars in Medical Genetics, 142*(3), 158–172.

Channell, M. M. (2020). The social responsiveness scale (SRS-2) in school-age children with down syndrome at low risk for autism spectrum disorder. *Autism & Developmental Language Impairments*, *5*, 2396941520962406.
Channell, M. M., Loveall, S. J., Conners, F. A., Harvey, D. J., & Abbeduto, L. (2018). Narrative language sampling in typical development: Implications for clinical trials. *American Journal of Speech-Language Pathology*, *27*(1), 123–135.
Channell, M. M., Phillips, B. A., Loveall, S. J., Conners, F. A., Bussanich, P. M., & Klinger, L. G. (2015). Patterns of autism spectrum symptomatology in individuals with down syndrome without comorbid autism spectrum disorder. *Journal of Neurodevelopmental Disorders*, *7*(1), 1–9.
Chapman, R. (2006). Language learning in down syndrome: The speech and language profile compared to adolescents with cognitive impairment of unknown origin. *Down Syndrome Research and Practice*, *10*(2), 61–66.
Chapman, R. S., & Hesketh, L. J. (2000). Behavioral phenotype of individuals with down syndrome. *Mental Retardation and Developmental Disabilities Research Reviews*, *6*(2), 84–95.
Conners, F. A., Tungate, A. S., Abbeduto, L., Merrill, E. C., & Faught, G. G. (2018). Growth and decline in language and phonological memory over two years among adolescents with down syndrome. *American Journal on Intellectual and Developmental Disabilities*, *123*(2), 103–118.
Coppus, A., Evenhuis, H., Verberne, G. J., Visser, F., Van Gool, P., Eikelenboom, P., et al. (2006). Dementia and mortality in persons with Down's syndrome. *Journal of Intellectual Disability Research*, *50*(10), 768–777.
Couzens, D., Cuskelly, M., & Haynes, M. (2011). Cognitive development and down syndrome: Age-related change on the Stanford-Binet test. *American Journal on Intellectual and Developmental Disabilities*, *116*(3), 181–204.
d'Ardhuy, X. L., Edgin, J. O., Bouis, C., de Sola, S., Goeldner, C., Kishnani, P., et al. (2015). Assessment of cognitive scales to examine memory, executive function and language in individuals with down syndrome: Implications of a 6-month observational study. *Frontiers in Behavioral Neuroscience*, *9*, 300.
Daunhauer, L. A., Fidler, D. J., Hahn, L., Will, E., Lee, N. R., & Hepburn, S. (2014). Profiles of everyday executive functioning in young children with down syndrome. *American Journal on Intellectual and Developmental Disabilities*, *119*(4), 303–318. https://doi.org/10.1352/1944-7558-119.4.303.
Dekker, M. C., & Koot, H. M. (2003). DSM-IV disorders in children with borderline to moderate intellectual disability. I: Prevalence and impact. *Journal of the American Academy of Child & Adolescent Psychiatry*, *42*(8), 915–922.
del Hoyo Soriano, L., Thurman, A. J., & Abbeduto, L. (2018). Specificity: A phenotypic comparison of communication-relevant domains between youth with down syndrome and fragile X syndrome. *Frontiers in Genetics*, *9*, 424.
del Hoyo Soriano, L., Thurman, A. J., Harvey, D., Kover, S. T., & Abbeduto, L. (2020). Expressive language development in adolescents with down syndrome and fragile X syndrome: Change over time and the role of family-related factors. *Journal of Neurodevelopmental Disorders*, *12*(1), 1–18.
DiGuiseppi, C., Hepburn, S., Davis, J. M., Fidler, D. J., Hartway, S., Lee, N. R., et al. (2010). Screening for autism spectrum disorders in children with down syndrome: Population prevalence and screening test characteristics. *Journal of Developmental and Behavioral Pediatrics*, *31*(3), 181–191. https://doi.org/10.1097/DBP.0b013e3181d5aa6d.
Duff, K., Clark, H. J. D., O'Bryant, S. E., Mold, J. W., Schiffer, R. B., & Sutker, P. B. (2008). Utility of the RBANS in detecting cognitive impairment associated with Alzheimer's disease: Sensitivity, specificity, and positive and negative predictive powers. *Archives of Clinical Neuropsychology*, *23*(5), 603–612.

Dykens, E. M., Hodapp, R. M., & Finucane, B. M. (2000). *Genetics and mental retardation syndromes: A new look at behavior and interventions*. Paul H Brookes Publishing.
Edgin, J. O., Anand, P., Rosser, T., Pierpont, E. I., Figueroa, C., Hamilton, D., et al. (2017). The arizona cognitive test battery for down syndrome: Test-retest reliability and practice effects. *American Journal on Intellectual and Developmental Disabilities*, *122*(3), 215–234.
Edgin, J. O., Mason, G. M., Allman, M. J., Capone, G. T., DeLeon, I., Maslen, C., et al. (2010). Development and validation of the Arizona cognitive test battery for down syndrome. *Journal of Neurodevelopmental Disorders*, *2*, 149–164.
Ekstein, S., Glick, B., Weill, M., Kay, B., & Berger, I. (2011). Down syndrome and attention-deficit/hyperactivity disorder. *Journal of Child Neurology*, *26*, 1290–1295.
Esbensen, A. J. (2010). Health conditions associated with aging and end of life of adults with down syndrome. *International Review of Research in Mental Retardation*, *39*, 107–126.
Esbensen, A. J., Epstein, J. N., Vincent, L. B., Kamimura-Nishimura, K., Wiley, S., Angkustsiri, K., et al. (2021). Comparison of attention-deficit hyperactivity disorder in typically developing children and children with down syndrome. *Journal of Developmental & Behavioral Pediatrics.*.
Esbensen, A. J., Hoffman, E. K., Shaffer, R., Chen, E., Patel, L., & Jacola, L. (2018). Reliability of parent report measures of behaviour in children with down syndrome. *Journal of Intellectual Disability Research*, *62*(9), 785–797. https://doi.org/10.1111/jir.12533.
Esbensen, A. J., Hoffman, E. K., Shaffer, R., Chen, E., Patel, L., & Jacola, L. (2019). Reliability of informant-report measures of executive functioning in children with down syndrome. *American Journal on Intellectual and Developmental Disabilities*, *124*(3), 220–233. https://doi.org/10.1352/1944-7558-124.3.220.
Esbensen, A. J., Hooper, S. R., Fidler, D., Hartley, S. L., Edgin, J. O., d'Ardhuy, X. L., et al. (2017). Outcome measures for clinical trials in down syndrome. *American Journal on Intellectual and Developmental Disabilities*, *122*(3), 247–281.
Esbensen, A. J., & MacLean, W. (2017). Down syndrome. In M. L. Wehmeyer, I. Brown, M. Percy, K. A. Shogren, & W. L. A. Fung (Eds.), *A comprehensive guide to intellectual and developmental disabilities* (2nd Edition). Brookes: Paul H.
Faroqi-Shah, Y., Treanor, A., Ratner, N. B., Ficek, B., Webster, K., & Tsapkini, K. (2020). Using narratives in differential diagnosis of neurodegenerative syndromes. *Journal of Communication Disorders*, *85*, 105994.
Feeley, K., & Jones, E. (2008). Strategies to address challenging behaviour in young children with down syndrome. *Down Syndrome Research and Practice*, *12*(2), 153–163.
Fidler, D., Most, D., & Philofsky, A. (2008). The down syndrome behavioural phenotype: Taking a developmental approach. *Down Syndrome Research and Practice*, *12*(3), 37–44.
Fidler, D., & Nadel, L. (2007). Education and children with down syndrome: Neuroscience, development, and intervention. *Mental Retardation and Developmental Disabilities Research Reviews*, *13*(3), 262–271.
Fidler, D. J., Philofsky, A., Hepburn, S. L., & Rogers, S. J. (2005). Nonverbal requesting and problem-solving by toddlers with down syndrome. *American Journal on Mental Retardation*, *110*(4), 312–322.
Finestack, L. H., & Abbeduto, L. (2010). Expressive language profiles of verbally expressive adolescents and young adults with down syndrome or fragile X syndrome. *Journal of Speech, Language, and Hearing Research*, *53*(5), 1334–1348.
Finestack, L. H., Sterling, A. M., & Abbeduto, L. (2013). Discriminating down syndrome and fragile X syndrome based on language ability. *Journal of Child Language*, *40*(1), 244–265.
Finlay, W. M., & Lyons, E. (2001). Methodological issues in interviewing and using self-report questionnaires with people with mental retardation. *Psychological Assessment*, *13*(3), 319.

Fleming, V., Hom, C. L., Clare, I. C. H., Hurd-Thomas, S. L., Krinsky-McHale, S., Handen, B. L., et al. (2022). Cognitive outcome measures for tracking Alzheimer's disease in down syndrome. *International Review of Research in Developmental Disabilities.*

Frank, K., & Esbensen, A. (2015). Fine motor and self-care milestones for individuals with down syndrome using a retrospective chart review. *Journal of Intellectual Disability Research, 59*, 719–729.

Froehlich, T. E., Lanphear, B. P., Epstein, J. N., Barbaresi, W. J., Katusic, S. K., & Kahn, R. S. (2007). Prevalence, recognition, and treatment of attention-deficit/hyperactivity disorder in a national sample of US children. *Archives of Pediatrics & Adolescent Medicine, 161*(9), 857–864.

Gardiner, K. J., Herault, Y., Lott, I. T., Antonarakis, S. E., Reeves, R. H., & Dierssen, M. (2010). Down syndrome: From understanding the neurobiology to therapy. *The Journal of Neuroscience, 30*(45), 14943–14945.

Gathercole, S. E., & Alloway, T. P. (2006). Practitioner review: Short-term and working memory impairments in neurodevelopmental disorders: Diagnosis and remedial support. *Journal of Child Psychology and Psychiatry, 47*(1), 4–15.

Grieco, J., Pulsifer, M., Seligsohn, K., Skotko, B., & Schwartz, A. (2015). Down syndrome: Cognitive and behavioral functioning across the lifespan. *American Journal of Medical Genetics Part C: Seminars in Medical Genetics.*

Hahn, L. J., Loveall, S. J., Savoy, M. T., Neumann, A. M., & Ikuta, T. (2018). Joint attention in down syndrome: A meta-analysis. *Research in Developmental Disabilities, 78*, 89–102.

Hawkins, B. A., Eklund, S. J., James, D. R., & Foose, A. K. (2003). Adaptive behavior and cognitive function of adults with down syndrome: Modeling change with age. *Intellectual and Developmental Disabilities, 41*(1).

Heller, J. H., Spiridigliozzi, G. A., Crissman, B. G., Sullivan, J. A., Eells, R. L., Li, J. S., et al. (2006). Safety and efficacy of rivastigmine in adolescents with down syndrome: A preliminary 20-week, open-label study. *Journal of Child and Adolescent Psychopharmacology, 16*(6), 755–765.

Heller, J. H., Spiridigliozzi, G. A., Sullivan, J. A., Doraiswamy, P. M., Krishnan, R. R., & Kishnani, P. S. (2003). Donepezil for the treatment of language deficits in adults with down syndrome: A preliminary 24-week open trial. *American Journal of Medical Genetics Part A, 116*(2), 111–116.

Hessl, D., Nguyen, D. V., Green, C., Chavez, A., Tassone, F., Hagerman, R. J., et al. (2009). A solution to limitations of cognitive testing in children with intellectual disabilities: The case of fragile X syndrome. *Journal of Neurodevelopmental Disorders, 1*(1), 33.

Hessl, D., Sansone, S. M., Berry-Kravis, E., Riley, K., Widaman, K. F., Abbeduto, L., et al. (2016). The NIH toolbox cognitive battery for intellectual disabilities: Three preliminary studies and future directions. *Journal of Neurodevelopmental Disorders, 8*(1), 35.

Hodapp, R., & Dykens, E. (2004). Genetic and behavioural aspects: Application to maladaptive behavior and cognition. In J. Rondal, R. Hodapp, S. Soresi, E. Dykens, & L. Nota (Eds.), *Intellectual disabilities: Genetics, behaviour and inclusion* (pp. 13–48). Whurr.

Hodapp, R., Leckman, J., Dykens, E., Sparrow, S., Zelinsky, D., & Ort, S. (1992). K-ABC profiles in children with fragile X syndrome, down syndrome, and nonspecific mental retardation. *American Journal on Mental Retardation, 97*(1), 39–46.

Holland, A., Hon, J., Huppert, F., & Stevens, F. (2000). Incidence and course of dementia in people with Down's syndrome: Findings from a population-based study. *Journal of Intellectual Disability Research, 44*(2), 138–146.

Jack, C. R., Knopman, D. S., Jagust, W. J., Petersen, R. C., Weiner, M. W., Aisen, P. S., et al. (2013). Tracking pathophysiological processes in Alzheimer's disease: An updated hypothetical model of dynamic biomarkers. *The Lancet Neurology, 12*(2), 207–216. https://doi.org/10.1016/S1474-4422(12)70291-0.

Kanno, K., & Ikeda, Y. (2002). Word-length effect in verbal short-term memory in individuals with Down's syndrome. *Journal of Intellectual Disability Research, 46*(8), 613–618.

Karmiloff-Smith, A., Al-Janabi, T., D'Souza, H., Groet, J., Massand, E., Mok, K., et al. (2016). The importance of understanding individual differences in Down syndrome. *F1000Research*, 5.

Kaufman, A. S., & Kaufman, N. L. (2004). *Kaufman brief intelligence test–second edition (KBIT-2)*. Circle Pines, MN: American Guidance Service.

Kishnani, P. S., Heller, J. H., Spiridigliozzi, G. A., Lott, I., Escobar, L., Richardson, S., et al. (2010). Donepezil for treatment of cognitive dysfunction in children with down syndrome aged 10–17. *American Journal of Medical Genetics Part A, 152*(12), 3028–3035.

Klein, B. P., & Mervis, C. B. (1999). Contrasting patterns of cognitive abilities of 9-and 10-year-olds with Williams syndrome or down syndrome. *Developmental Neuropsychology, 16*(2), 177–196.

Krinsky-McHale, S. J., Silverman, W., Gordon, J., Devenny, D. A., Oley, N., & Abramov, I. (2014). Vision deficits in adults with down syndrome. *Journal of Applied Research in Intellectual Disabilities, 27*(3), 247–263. https://doi.org/10.1111/jar.12062.

Laws, G., & Hall, A. (2014). Early hearing loss and language abilities in children with down syndrome. *International Journal of Language & Communication Disorders, 49*(3), 333–342. https://doi.org/10.1111/1460-6984.12077.

Magyar, C. I., Pandolfi, V., & Dill, C. A. (2012). An initial evaluation of the social communication questionnaire for the assessment of autism spectrum disorders in children with down syndrome. *Journal of Developmental and Behavioral Pediatrics, 33*(2), 134–145. https://doi.org/10.1097/DBP.0b013e318240d3d9.

Mantry, D., Cooper, S. A., Smiley, E., Morrison, J., Allan, L., Williamson, A., et al. (2008). The prevalence and incidence of mental ill-health in adults with down syndrome. *Journal of Intellectual Disability Research, 52*(2), 141–155.

Martin, G. E., Klusek, J., Estigarribia, B., & Roberts, J. E. (2009). Language characteristics of individuals with down syndrome. *Topics in Language Disorders, 29*(2), 112–132.

McCabe, L. L., Hickey, F., & McCabe, E. R. (2011). Down syndrome: Addressing the gaps. *Journal of Pediatrics, 159*(4), 525–526.

McCarron, M., Gill, M., McCallion, P., & Begley, C. (2005). Health co-morbidities in ageing persons with down syndrome and Alzheimer's dementia. *Journal of Intellectual Disability Research, 49*(7), 560–566.

McDuffie, A., & Abbeduto, L. (2009). Language disorders in children with mental retardation of genetic origin: Down syndrome, fragile X syndrome, and Williams syndrome. In *Handbook of child language disorders* (pp. 44–66).

McGuire, D., & Chicoine, B. (2006). Mental wellness in adults with down syndrome. *Woodbine*..

Mircher, C., Sacco, S., Bouis, C., Gallard, J., Pichot, A., Le Galloudec, E., et al. (2020). Thyroid hormone and folinic acid in young children with down syndrome: The phase 3 ACTHYF trial. *Genetics in Medicine, 22*(1), 44–52.

Moyer, A. (2021). *Too good to be true: Reflections on a down syndrome clinical trial*. Johns Hopkins Medicine. Retrieved 8/5 from https://biomedicalodyssey.blogs.hopkinsmedicine.org/2021/03/too-good-to-be-true-reflections-on-a-down-syndrome-clinical-trial/.

Patel, L., Wolter-Warmerdam, K., Leifer, N., & Hickey, F. (2018). Behavioral characteristics of individuals with down syndrome. *Journal of Mental Health Research in Intellectual Disabilities, 11*(3), 221–246.

Pezzuti, L., Nacinovich, R., Oggiano, S., Bomba, M., Ferri, R., La Stella, A., et al. (2018). Beyond the floor effect on the WISC-IV in individuals with down syndrome: Are there cognitive strengths and weaknesses? *Journal of Intellectual Disability Research, 62*(7), 593–603.

Phillips, B. A., Loveall, S. J., Channell, M. M., & Conners, F. A. (2014). Matching variables for research involving youth with down syndrome: Leiter-R versus PPVT-4. *Research in Developmental Disabilities, 35*(2), 429–438.

Pulina, F., Vianello, R., & Lanfranchi, S. (2019). Cognitive profiles in individuals with down syndrome. In *International Review of Research in Developmental Disabilities: Vol. 56* (pp. 67–92). Elsevier.

Roid, G. H. (2003). *Stanford-binet intelligence scales (SB5)*. Riverside.

Roizen, N. (2013). Down syndrome. In M. Batshaw, N. Roizen, & G. R. Lotrecchiano (Eds.), *Children with disabilities* (7th ed., pp. 307–318). Paul H Brookes.

Sansone, S. M., Schneider, A., Bickel, E., Berry-Kravis, E., Prescott, C., & Hessl, D. (2014). Improving IQ measurement in intellectual disabilities using true deviation from population norms. *Journal of Neurodevelopmental Disorders, 6*(1), 1–15.

Schworer, E. K., Esbensen, A. J., Fidler, D. J., Beebe, D. W., Carle, A., & Wiley, S. (2021). Evaluating working memory outcome measures for children with down syndrome. *Journal of Intellectual Disability Research*. https://doi.org/10.1111/jir.12833.

Schworer, E. K., Fidler, D. J., & Daunhauer, L. A. (2021). Early regulatory skills and social communication development in infants with down syndrome. *Brain Sciences, 11*(2), 208.

Schworer, E. K., Fidler, D., Kaur, M., Needham, A., Prince, M., & Daunhauer, L. (2020). Goal-directed action planning in infants with down syndrome. *Journal of Intellectual Disability Research, 64*(9), 713–724.

Schworer, E. K., Fidler, D. J., Kaur, M., Needham, A., Prince, M. A., & Daunhauer, L. A. (2022). Infant precursors of executive function in down syndrome. *Journal of Intellectual Disability Research, 66*, 108–120. https://doi.org/10.1111/jir.12824.

Schworer, E. K., Hoffman, E. K., & Esbensen, A. J. (2021). Psychometric evaluation of social cognition and behavior measures in children and adolescents with down syndrome. *Brain Sciences, 11*(7). https://doi.org/10.3390/brainsci11070836.

Schworer, E. K., Voth, K., Hoffman, E., & Esbensen, A. (2022). Short-term memory outcome measures: Psychometric evaluation and performance in youth with down syndrome. *Research in Developmental Disabilities, 120*, 104147.

Shields, R. H., Kaat, A. J., McKenzie, F. J., Drayton, A., Sansone, S. M., Coleman, J., et al. (2020). Validation of the NIH toolbox cognitive battery in intellectual disability. *Neurology, 94*(12), e1229–e1240.

Shott, S. (2006). Down syndrome: Common otolaryngologic manifestations. *American Journal of Medical Genetics Part C: Seminars in Medical Genetics, 142C*, 131–140.

Smeyne, C., Esbensen, A. J., Schworer, E., Belizaire, S., Hoffman, E., Beebe, D., et al. (2022). *Evaluating verbal fluency outcome measures for children with down syndrome.* American Journal on Intellectual and Developmental Disabilities.

Stein, D. (2016). *Supporting positive behavior in children and teens with down syndrome*. Woodbine House.

Strydom, A., Shooshtari, S., Lee, L., Raykar, V., Torr, J., Tsiouris, J., et al. (2010). Dementia in older adults with intellectual disabilities—Epidemiology, presentation, and diagnosis. *Journal of Policy and Practice in Intellectual Disabilities,* 7(2), 96–110.

Thurman, A., & del Hoyo Soriano, L. (2021). Down syndrome. In L. Cummings (Ed.), *Pragmatic language disorders: Complex and underserved populations* (pp. 99–128). Springer Nature.

Thurman, A. J., Edgin, J. O., Sherman, S. L., Sterling, A., McDuffie, A., Berry-Kravis, E., et al. (2021). Spoken language outcome measures for treatment studies in down syndrome: Feasibility, practice effects, test-retest reliability, and construct validity of variables generated from expressive language sampling. *Journal of Neurodevelopmental Disorders, 13*(1), 1–17.

Van Buggenhout, G., Trommelen, J., Schoenmaker, A., De Bal, C., Verbeek, J., Smeets, D., et al. (1999). Down syndrome in a population of elderly mentally retarded patients:

Genetic-diagnostic survey and implications for medical care. *American Journal of Medical Genetics, 85*(4), 376–384.

Visootsak, J., Mahle, W. T., Kirshbom, P. M., Huddleston, L., Caron-Besch, M., Ransom, A., et al. (2011). Neurodevelopmental outcomes in children with down syndrome and congenital heart defects. *American Journal of Medical Genetics Part A, 155*(11), 2688–2691.

Wiig, E., Secord, W. A., & Semel, E. (2004). *Clinical evaluation of language fundamentals—Preschool, (CELF Preschool-2)*. San Antonio, TX: Harcourt Assessment.

Winders, P. (2013). *Gross motor skills for children with down syndrome. In*. Bethesda, MD: Woodbine House.

Wolpert, G. (2001). What general educators have to say about successfully including students with down syndrome in their classes. *Journal of Research in Childhood Education, 16*(1), 28–38.

Zackheim, C. T., & Conture, E. G. (2003). Childhood stuttering and speech disfluencies in relation to children's mean length of utterance: A preliminary study. *Journal of Fluency Disorders, 28*(2), 115–142.

Zigman, W. B., Schupf, N., Sersen, E., & Silverman, W. (1996). Prevalence of dementia in adults with and without down syndrome. *American Journal on Mental Retardation*.

Zoia, S., Pelamatti, G., & Rumiati, R. I. (2004). Praxic skills in down and mentally retarded adults: Evidence for multiple action routes. *Brain and Cognition, 54*(1), 7–17.

CHAPTER SIX

Cognitive outcome measures for tracking Alzheimer's disease in Down syndrome

Victoria Fleming[a,b], Christy L. Hom[c], Isabel C.H. Clare[d], Shemaya L. Hurd-Thomas[d], Sharon Krinsky-McHale[e], Benjamin Handen[f], and Sigan L. Hartley[a,b]

[a]Waisman Center, University of Wisconsin-Madison, Madison, WI, United States
[b]School of Human Ecology, University of Wisconsin-Madison, Madison, WI, United States
[c]Department of Psychiatry and Human Behavior, University of California, Irvine School of Medicine, Orange, CA, United States
[d]Department of Psychiatry, University of Cambridge, Cambridge, United Kingdom
[e]New York State Institute for Basic Research in Developmental Disabilities, Staten Island, NY, United States
[f]Department of Psychiatry, University of Pittsburgh, Pittsburgh, PA, United States

Contents

Abstract

Down syndrome (DS) is now viewed as a genetic type of Alzheimer's disease (AD), given the near-universal presence of AD pathology in middle adulthood and the elevated risk for developing clinical AD in DS. As the field of DS prepares for AD clinical intervention trials, there is a strong need to identify cognitive measures that are specific and sensitive to the transition from being cognitively stable to the prodromal (e.g., Mild Cognitive

International Review of Research in Developmental Disabilities, Volume 62
ISSN 2211-6095
https://doi.org/10.1016/bs.irrdd.2022.05.006

Impairment—Down syndrome) and clinical AD (e.g., Dementia) stages of the disease in DS. It is also important to determine cognitive measures that map onto biomarkers of early AD pathology during the transition from the preclinical to the prodromal stage of the disease, as this transition period is likely to be targeted and tracked in AD clinical trials. The present chapter discusses the current state of research on cognitive measures that could be used to screen/select study participants and as potential outcome measures in future AD clinical trials with adults with DS. In this chapter, we also identify key challenges that need to be overcome and questions that need to be addressed by the DS field as it prepares for AD clinical trials in the coming years.

Abbreviations

DS Down syndrome
AD Alzheimer's disease
Aβ amyloid beta
APP amyloid precursor protein
AT[N] amyloid, tau, neurodegeneration

1. Introduction

Down syndrome (DS) is a developmental disability caused by a full or partial extra copy of chromosome 21 (Korenberg et al., 1994). Complete triplication of chromosome 21 occurs in approximately 95% of DS cases. Other less common forms of DS include translocation (4% of DS cases), in which the extra copy of chromosome 21 attaches to another chromosome, and mosaicism (1% of DS cases), which involves only some cells containing three copies of chromosome 21 and other cells being euploid (Irum et al., 2021). DS is the most common known genetic cause of intellectual disability and has an estimated incidence of 1 in 691 live births in the US (Mai et al., 2019) and 1 in 1000 to 1100 worldwide (World Health Organization, 2018). Individuals with DS have a physical phenotype consisting of shortened extremities, poor muscle tone, flat nasal bridge, and a large tongue (Bhattacharyya, Sanyal, & Bhattacharyya, 2018). Individuals with DS also share a behavioral phenotype consisting of intellectual disability, language impairments especially in expressive language (Abbeduto, Warren, & Conners, 2007), and mental health problems and maladaptive behaviors including restlessness, inattention, and anxiety (Hodapp & Fidler, 2021).

Adults with DS are also at increased risk for Alzheimer's disease (AD) and experience an earlier age of AD onset than adults without DS (e.g., Zigman &

Lott, 2007). The early hallmark features of AD brain pathology, including the accumulation of amyloid-beta (Aβ), are near-universally present in DS by age 40 years (Fortea et al., 2021; Head, Powell, Gold, & Schmitt, 2012; Lao et al., 2017). It is estimated that over half of adults with DS exhibit AD dementia by 55 years of age (Rubenstein, Hartley, & Bishop, 2020) and this rises to 88–100% after age 65 years (Mann & Esiri, 1989). AD has been identified as the proximate cause of death in 70% of cases of adults with DS (Hithersay et al., 2019; McCarron et al., 2017). These findings have led researchers to view DS as a genetically-determined form of AD, similar to the autosomal dominant form of AD (Fortea et al., 2020).

The high risk of AD in DS is posited to be due to the triplication of the amyloid precursor protein (APP) gene located on chromosome 21 (e.g., Prasher et al., 1998; Wiseman et al., 2015). There is excess production of Aβ due to increased APP expression and proteolytic processing. With age, Aβ accumulates into intracellular plaques, which is an early event in the cascade of AD pathology (Jack et al., 2013). Thus, the triplication of the APP gene is considered to be sufficient to cause the elevated rate of AD in DS. Indeed, in a recent case report, an adult with DS who had partial trisomy of chromosome 21 that did not involve the triplication of the *APP* gene, did not exhibit elevated AD pathology (Doran et al., 2017). Other genes located on chromosome 21 are posited to modify and/or contribute to the effects of increased APP expression through mechanisms such as oxidative stress and inflammation (Fortea et al., 2021). Genes on chromosomes other than 21, including those shown to alter the risk of AD in non-DS populations (e.g., Giri, Zhang, & Lü, 2016; Rossini et al., 2020), may also alter the timing of AD in DS. Although findings are mixed (Kim, Basak, & Holtzman, 2009; Yamazaki, Zhao, Caulfield, Liu, & Bu, 2019), the apoliprotein E (APOE) gene has been associated with an earlier age of AD-related cognitive decline and increased Aβ deposition in DS (e.g., Prasher et al., 2008; Vilaplana et al., 2020).

2. Unfolding of AD pathology and symptomology in DS

The unfolding of AD pathology in DS occurs over many decades (Fig. 1). Aβ and synaptojanin 1 begin accumulating within enlarged endosomes and lysosomes as early as the embryonic stage (e.g., Flores-Aguilar et al., 2020; Martini et al., 2020). Intracellular Aβ, within endosomes, can lead to mitochondrial dysfunction and oxidative damage throughout the developmental period (Benejam et al., 2020). By early adulthood,

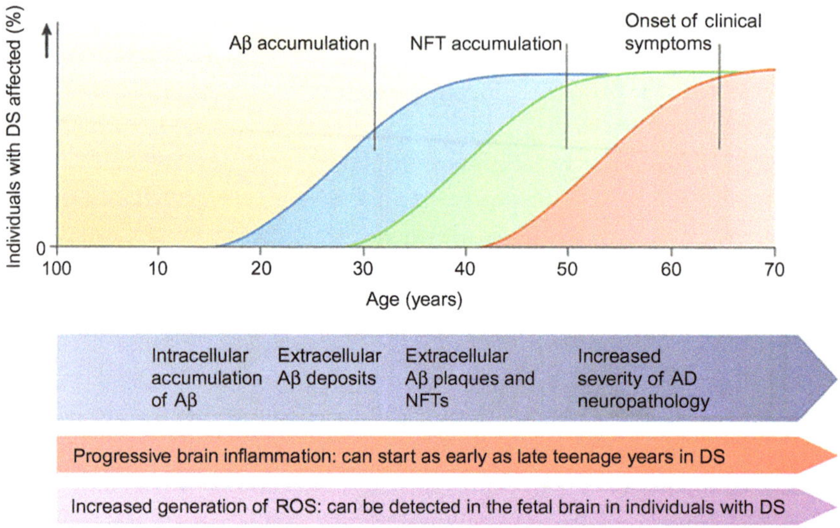

Fig. 1 Hypothetical model of Alzheimer's disease from birth to 70 years in Down syndrome from Lott and Head (2019).

individuals with DS evidence decreased cerebral spinal fluid (CSF) Aβ concentrations (Dekker, Fortea, Blesa, & De Deyn, 2017; Fortea et al., 2020), that correspond to fibrilized Aβ plaques in the brain (Jennings et al., 2015; Montoliu-Gaya, Strydom, Blennow, Zetterberg, & Ashton, 2021). Elevated levels of tau protein are evident as individual with DS age into their mid-30s (Fortea et al., 2020). By the mid-40s, tau is hyperphosphorylated, leading to neurofibrillary tangles (Schöll et al., 2019; Startin et al., 2019), increased plasma neurofilament light protein (NfL), an indication of neuroinflammation (Fortea et al., 2018), and decreased brain glucose metabolism and hippocampal volume (e.g., Teipel & Hampel, 2006; Wisniewski, Wisniewski, & Wen, 1985). White matter degeneration has been linked to other AD pathology and observed in individuals with DS in their 40s and 50s (e.g., Bazydlo et al., 2021; Lin et al., 2016). Overall, the pattern of unfolding AD pathology observed in DS has overlap with what has been theorized using the Aβ cascade hypothesis (e.g., Karran, Mercken, & De Strooper, 2011) and modeled using the amyloid, tau, neurodegeneration (AT[N])biomarker framework (Jack et al., 2016) with the autosomal dominant AD population (e.g., Fortea et al., 2021; Lott & Head, 2019; Rafii, 2020).

Similar to autosomal dominant and late onset AD, there is a long preclinical phase in DS, where AD-related pathological changes have occurred but clinical AD symptomology is not present (e.g., Fortea et al., 2020;

Head & Ances, 2020; Lott & Head, 2019). During this preclinical stage, adults with DS continue to be "cognitively stable," meaning that their cognitive functioning remains intact with no more than normative aging-related changes. The cognitively stable stage is then followed by the transition into a "prodromal" stage, where initially mild and subtle declines in cognition and functioning occur at a level beyond normative aging. The term mild cognitive impairment (MCI) has been used to describe this intermediate stage between being cognitively stable and clinically-significant AD dementia in the DS population and in other AD populations. Finally, the 'AD dementia' stage involves marked impairments in cognitive and functional ability.

Studies indicate a median age of clinical status of AD dementia ranging from approximately 50 to 58 years in adults with DS (e.g. Knox et al., 2021; Rubenstein et al., 2020; Sinai et al., 2018) with transition to the prodromal stage reported to occur around age 50 to 53 years (Fortea et al., 2020). However, there is considerable variability in the age of onset of the prodromal stage and clinical AD dementia in DS. Some studies report that up to 55% of adults with DS exhibit clinical AD dementia by age 49 years, while other studies indicate that 15% to 77% may not exhibit clinical AD dementia until their 60s (Holland, Hon, Huppert, & Stevens, 2000; Lai & Williams, 1989; Tyrrell et al., 2001). A variety of factors are thought to drive this variability including genes such as APOE (Fortea et al., 2020), co-occurring physical health conditions (Lao et al., 2020), and lifestyle (e.g., Mihaila et al., 2019). As for survival, the median survival time from clinical AD dementia to death in adults with DS has been reported to be 3.8 years, which is half as long as what has been reported for late onset and autosomal dominant forms of AD (Sinai et al., 2018). However, there is a need for more longitudinal studies to fully understand the course of prodromal AD in DS.

Given the high risk for AD in DS, developing interventions that can delay or prevent the onset of AD-related pathology and cognitive decline is of high importance to the field of DS. Due to this critical need, the National Institutes of Health have funded several studies aimed at establishing biomarkers of AD pathology in DS and understanding their association with AD-related cognitive decline and dementia. Funded studies include the Alzheimer's Biomarkers Consortium of Down syndrome (ABC-DS), which involves a collaboration between eight primary research sites located across the United States and one in the United Kingdom. Inherent in this effort is the aim of establishing feasible, reliable, and valid measures that can track AD-related cognitive declines in adults with DS. Similar large-scale efforts aimed at identifying valid measures of cognitive declines occurring in the progression of AD in DS are underway both in the United States and other countries, including, the LuMIND-International Down Syndrome Community (LuMIND-IDSC)led Longitudinal Investigation for Enhancing Down Syndrome Research (LIFE-DSR) Study and Down Syndrome—Clinical Trial Network (DS-CTN), London Down Syndrome Consortium (LonDownS) and the Down Alzheimer Barcelona Neuroimaging Initiative. Recent efforts to launch large data management and portals (e.g., NIH-funded Data Coordinating Center for INCLUDE projects) are also underway and will allow DS researchers to combine and analyze data on common cognitive measures across studies.

With the identification of feasible, valid, and sensitive measures for tracking AD-related cognitive decline in adults with DS, the field will be primed to support clinical AD trials, such as the efforts that are underway in the Trial-Ready-Down Syndrome (TRC-DS; https://clinicaltrials.gov/ct2/show/NCT04165109) study. These future AD clinical trials in DS are likely to be aimed at early AD pathology, including Aβ or tau accumulation, and are likely to focus on individuals in the "cognitively stable" and/or "preclinical" stage. Thus, having established measures of early cognitive decline that align with biomarkers of AD during the preclinical stage may be especially important for screening and identifying participants for these clinical trials and for monitoring intervention effectiveness across time.

3. Challenges in assessing cognition and dementia in DS

Direct assessments of cognitive decline and dementia symptoms, however, can be challenging with adults with DS. Otherwise healthy adults with DS (i.e., prior to the onset of AD-related cognitive decline) generally score on standardized measures of IQ in the mild (IQ: 50–69) to moderate (IQ: 35–49) intellectual range and evidence adaptive functioning impairments in-line with this severity level (Hamburg et al., 2019). This means that measures developed to assess AD-related cognitive decline in neurotypical populations (i.e., adults from the general population of similar age) are typically too difficult for adults with DS. As a result, the DS field often uses cognitive measures designed for younger populations (e.g., children), who are of matched mental age to adults with DS, and/or modified versions of measures originally created for the neurotypical adult population.

While the majority of adults with DS score in the mild to moderate range of intellectual functioning (based on cognitive measures and adaptive skill measures) prior to AD-related decline, a subset of adults with DS have cognitive and functional ability levels that are more severely affected and require extensive to pervasive support in everyday life (Karmiloff-Smith et al., 2016). The large heterogeneity in intellectual functioning across the DS population, creates further challenges for cognitive assessment. Among research samples of adults with DS, IQ scores have been reported to range from 8 to 67, with mental age equivalents ranging from $\leq$2 years to 12 years across IQ tests and samples (e.g., Carr, 1988; Dykens, Hodapp, & Evans, 2006; Godfrey & Lee, 2018). Expressive vocabulary on standardized tests has also ranged from $\leq$2 years to 12 years in adults with DS (e.g., Finestack & Abbeduto, 2010; Kristensen et al., 2022; Pennington, Moon, Edgin, Stedron, & Nadel, 2003). Most traditionally used cognitive measures are not designed for such a wide range of functioning.

Many of the existing cognitive measures relevant to the early progression of AD in DS have poor sensitivity and specificity in adults with DS with a mental age equivalent of $\leq$4 years or IQ <30 to 40 (Pezzuti et al., 2018). Heterogeneity in intellectual functioning level and expressive language ability across the DS population also means that single indicators (i.e., cutoff score) on measures of cognition are not relevant for tracking AD. Focusing on within-person change in scores on a measure overtime can help address this problem. However, to date, little is known about how much decline on a specific test is clinically relevant and indicative of AD-related change. This issue is complicated by the possibility that the amount of change on a specific test that signals clinically meaningful decline could vary as a function of premorbid level of intellectual disability.

3.1 Floor effects

One frequently encountered problem with cognitive measures for the DS population is floor effects (i.e., scores clustered at or near the lowest possible score). Floor effects occur when tests or parts of tests are too difficult for all or for a marked portion of the individuals assessed. Floor effects lead to skewing in the mean and in the distribution of scores, making it impossible to detect a reduction in the score over time. In order to minimize floor effects, many studies examining AD in DS have study inclusion criteria that involve an IQ cut off score that excludes adults with DS who have more severe intellectual impairments (e.g., IQ <50 and requiring extensive to pervasive support in everyday life) (e.g., Breia et al., 2014; Hamburg et al., 2019).

In recent years, z-scores, or approaches that derive true deviations from population norms, have been used in populations with intellectual disability including DS. These alternative approaches attempt to capture performance near the floor of the test by increasing the range of scores (e.g., Hessl et al., 2009; Pezzuti et al., 2018). Other researchers have recommended the use of raw scores, rather than standard scores (Hamburg et al., 2019). Creating measurement standards and understanding which scoring methods are most sensitive to AD-related changes for adults with DS, given their widely varying premorbid level of intellectual disability, is an important step for the field in the coming years. Indeed, these efforts are particularly important for establishing tests that have few floor effects in lower functioning adults with DS (i.e., those with severe/profound premorbid levels of intellectual disability based on cognitive and adaptive living skill support needs). Until the field has identified cognitive measures that are reliable and valid for capturing AD-related decline in adults with DS with severe or profound premorbid levels of intellectual disability, this subgroup will not be able to be included in clinical AD trials.

3.2 Co-occurring conditions

Another challenge to capturing AD-related cognitive decline in adults with DS is the high rate of co-occurring mental and physical health conditions. Many of these conditions can impair cognitive performance in ways that mirror what is seen early on in the progression to AD in adults with DS, leading to over- or under-diagnosis of clinical AD. In terms of physical health, adults with DS are at a higher risk for hypothyroidism than the general population (e.g., Guaraldi et al., 2017), which has been shown to impact learning and memory (Lai et al., 2021). Adults with DS are also at risk for vision (e.g., cataracts, strabismus, and keratoconus) (Hashemi, Mehravaran, Asgari, & Dehghanian Nasrabadi, 2021; Krinsky-McHale et al., 2014) and hearing problems (Bent, McShea, & Brennan, 2015) that may affect visual processing, comprehension of instructions, and performance on visual or verbal memory tests in ways that mimic AD-related cognitive decline. Adults with DS are also at risk for disrupted sleep (Giménez et al., 2018) and sleep disordered breathing problems (e.g., Trois et al., 2009), which are linked to memory and executive functioning difficulties in DS (Cody et al., 2020; Gandy et al., 2020) which can also mimic AD-related cognitive declines. Vitamin B2 and folate deficiency are also elevated in the DS populations and their effects on cognition can overlap with those seen in AD dementia (Prasher, 2005). Finally, adults with DS are at risk for late-onset epilepsy (De Simone, Puig, Gélisse, Crespel, & Genton, 2010;

Sharma et al., 2018), and this condition can cause diagnostic uncertainty, as it also contributes to cognitive decline and disrupts the performance of activities of daily living (Lott et al., 2012). More recently, late-onset epilepsy has been seen as an indicator of AD dementia (Altuna, Giménez, & Fortea, 2021).

Mental health problems also complicate the assessment of AD-related cognitive declines in DS, particularly if information about prior cognitive functioning is not available. Relative to their neurotypical peers, individuals with DS have a heightened prevalence of autism spectrum disorder (Moss, Richards, Nelson, & Oliver, 2013) and attention-deficit/hyperactivity disorder (Del Hoyo Soriano et al., 2020), which are both associated with their own profiles of cognitive strengths and weaknesses and variability in testing performance. As a result, these conditions can make it difficult to determine if AD-related cognitive declines are occurring. In a study by Tassé et al. (2016), depression and anxiety were found to be common mental health problems in adults with DS, and the rate of these problems increased across adulthood. Obsessive compulsive disorder, and ordering and tidiness in particular, also have an elevated prevalence in adults with DS relative to the neurotypical population (Prasher & Day, 1995; Vicari, Pontillo, & Armando, 2013). These mental health conditions can affect attention, motivation, working memory, processing speed, perseveration, and task completion and performance of everyday living skills (e.g., Culpepper, Lam, & McIntyre, 2017)—all of which may result in declines in testing performance that mirror what would be seen in the early stages of AD-dementia in DS.

3.3 Regression

The phenomenon of behavioral regression can also complicate the assessment of AD-related cognitive decline in DS. Regression involves the sudden onset or progressive "regression" (known by other names, including "DS disintegrative disorder" or "idiopathic regression in DS") that occurs in a subset of individuals with DS in late adolescence to early adulthood. Regression has been reported to involve a wide range of symptoms including the loss of daily living skills, language skills, and motor functions, changes in personality such as disinterest/withdrawal, and sleep disorders (see Rosso et al., 2020; Walpert, Zaman, & Holland, 2021).

It is now widely agreed that regression is not part of the early unfolding of AD pathology in DS. Indeed, treatment of regression, which most often involves anti-depressants or anti-psychotics, normally leads to at least partial recovery of cognitive and functional abilities with time. However, only a minority of adults with DS (about one-third; Walpert et al., 2021) who experience regression return to their baseline level of cognitive and functional abilities. Regression can thus complicate efforts to capture baseline levels of cognitive functioning prior to AD pathology. It can also be mistaken for early AD-related symptomology. While regression is not considered to be part of AD pathology, it remains unclear if it shares etiological mechanisms with AD and/or if regression at earlier life stages accelerates AD pathology or cognitive decline. In a recent small study (Handen et al., 2021), there was evidence that there may be subtle differences in AD-related proteomic biomarkers (i.e., tau and NfL) between adults with DS in their 20s through 40s that were reported to have experienced regression compared those who did not.

4. Cognitive measures and AT(N) biomarkers

Despite the challenges to assessing cognitive decline and in differentiating AD dementia from other co-occurring conditions in DS, a body of research has emerged on cognitive measures that appear to be promising for tracking AD-related progression in DS. A subset of this research has been aimed at identifying cognitive measures that are sensitive to early AD biomarkers of pathology, as has been done in the autosominal dominant AD population. In particular, a growing body of research has identified cognitive measures that are sensitive to AD biomarkers, drawing on the AT(N) framework. The AT(N) framework is an AD biomarker descriptive classification scheme used in non-DS populations to map the progression of AD pathology (Jack et al., 2016). The 'A' refers to biomarkers of Aβ (e.g., PET Aβ or CSF $A\beta_{42}$). The 'T' refers to biomarkers of tau (e.g., tau PET or CSF phospho tau). The '(N)' refers to biomarkers of neurodegeneration or neuronal injury (e.g., [^{18}F] fluorodeoxyglucose-positron emission tomography [FDG–PET], structural MRI, or CSF total tau).

Table 1 identifies some of the cognitive measures that have been associated with AT(N) biomarkers in the DS population. Much of the research around cognitive measures and the AT(N) model has been cross-sectional and focused on PET Aβ (i.e., 'A' in the AT(N) model (e.g., Annus et al., 2016; Hartley et al., 2014; Nelson et al., 2011). Among the handful of longitudinal studies (e.g., Hartley et al., 2017, 2020), there is evidence of an association between PET Aβ and early AD cognitive decline (e.g., transition to the prodromal stage). Using the PET imaging agent [^{11}C]PiB, Hartley et al. (2020) reported that non-demented adults with DS with marked Aβ

Table 1 Summary of cognitive measures highlighted in the current chapter and the Alzheimer's disease (AD) stage or variable domain that they have been associated with in Down syndrome.

				AD stage/variable domain		
Domain	**Measure**	**Measure citation**	**Type of measure**	**AT(N) biomarkers**	**Prodromal**	**AD dementia**
Adaptive behavior	American association for mental deficiency, adaptive behavior scale (AAMD-ABS)/Part I	Nihira et al. (1975), Nihira, Leland, and Lambert (1993); Hatton et al. (2001)	Informant		X	X
	Vineland adaptive behavior scale	Sparrow and Cicchetti (1989); Sparrow, Cicchetti, and Balla (2005); Sparrow, Cicchetti, and Saulnier (2016)	Informant	X	X	X
	Cambridge neuropsychological test automated battery (CANTAB)	CANTAB® (2016)	Direct		X	X
Overall cognitive functioning	Cambridge examination for mental disorders of older people with Down syndrome and others with disabilities (CAMDEX)	Ball et al. (2004) Beresford-Webb et al. (2021)	Informant		X	X
	Rapid assessment of developmental disabilities (RADD)	Walsh et al. (2007)	Direct			X
	Repeatable battery for the assessment of neuropsychological status total score (RBANS)	Randolph et al. (1998)	Direct	X		
	Down syndrome mental status examination (DSMSE)	Haxby (1989)	Direct	X	X	X

Continued

Table 1 Summary of cognitive measures highlighted in the current chapter and the Alzheimer's disease (AD) stage or variable domain that they have been associated with in Down syndrome.—cont'd

Domain	Measure	Measure citation	Type of measure	AD stage/variable domain: AT(N) biomarkers	Prodromal	AD dementia
Dementia symptoms	Dementia questionnaire for mentally retarded persons	Evenhuis (1992, 1996)	Informant	X		
	Dementia questionnaire for people with learning disabilities (DLD)	Evenhuis, Kengen, and Eurlings (1998, 2006)	Informant			X
	Dementia scale for Down syndrome (DSDS)	Gedye (1995)	Informant			X
	Dementia screening questionnaire for individuals with intellectual disabilities (DSQIDD)	Deb et al. (2007)	Informant			X
	National task group-early detection screen for dementia (NTG-EDSD)	Esralew et al. (2013)	Informant		X	X
	McCarthy category fluency test	McCarthy (1972)	Direct			X
Executive Functioning	Neuropsychological (NEPSY) word generation	Korkman et al. (2007)	Direct	X		
	NEPSY cancelation	Korkman et al. (2007)	Direct	X	X	X
	Stroop cats and dogs task	Ball et al. (2008)	Direct	X		
	Cued recall test	Zimmerli and Devenny (1995)	Direct	X	X	X

Memory	Observer memory questionnaire (OMQ)	O'Shea (1996)	Informant	X		
	Cambridge cognition examination (CAMCOG)	Roth et al. (1986)	Direct	X	X	X
	Selective reminding test	Buschke (1973)	Direct		X	
	WISC-IV digit span forward	Wechsler (2004)	Direct	X		
Mental Status	Modified Mini Mental Status Evaluation - DS	Wisniewski and Hill (1985)	Direct		X	
	Severe Impairment Battery (SIB)	Saxton et al. (2005)	Direct	X	X	X
	Test for Severe Impairment (TSI)	Albert and Cohen (1992)	Direct		X	X
Visuomotor Control and Planning	Developmental Test of Visuomotor Integration (VMI)	Beery et al. (2004)	Direct	X	X	X
	Purdue pegboard	Vega (1969)	Direct	X	X	X
	NEPSY-II car and motorbike score	Hatton et al. (2001)	Direct		X	
Visuospatial ability	Weschler intelligence scale for children-IV (WISC-IV) block design and haxby extension	Wechsler (2004); Haxby (1989)	Direct	X	X	X

accumulation (Aβ + group) performed worse on measures of memory, visual attention, executive function, and visuospatial ability than those without marked accumulation (Aβ-group). These cognitive domains were assessed using the Cued Recall Test (Zimmerli & Devenny, 1995), cancelation subtest of the Developmental Neuropsychological Assessment (NEPSY; Korkman, Kirk, & Kemp, 2007), Stroop Cats and Dogs Task (Ball, Holland, Treppner, Watson, & Huppert, 2008), and Block Design items from the Weschler Intelligence Scales for Children (WISC-IV; Wechsler, 2004) and Haxby extension (Haxby, 1989). Moreover, across time, the Aβ+ group had greater decline in memory, visual attention, and visuospatial ability than the Aβ− group. However, only the Cued Recall Test differentiated the Aβ+ group from the subset of adults with DS who converted from Aβ− to Aβ+ during the study (spanning 2–8 years). Thus, episodic memory was the cognitive domain affected earliest in the transition from preclinical to prodromal AD in DS (i.e., it was the only measure to differentiate those who recently converted from Aβ− to Aβ+ from those who were Aβ−). These early episodic memory declines appeared to be followed by declines in visual attention, executive functioning, and visuospatial abilities, with these non-memory domains differentiating the Aβ− group from the Aβ+ group. Episodic memory is similarly the earliest cognitive domain impacted by AD pathology (e.g., PET Aβ and PET tau) in the autosomal dominant and late-onset AD populations (Gagliardi et al., 2019; Tromp, Dufour, Lithfous, Pebayle, & Després, 2015). Recent DS research (Hom, Taylor, et al., 2021; Hom, Walsh, et al., 2021) suggests that PET Aβ accumulation in the frontal lobe specifically, may lead to early impairments in memory and other cognitive domains as assessed by the Rapid Assessment of Developmental Disabilities (RADD; Walsh et al., 2007), WISC-IV Digit Span Forward, and Stroop Cats and Dogs Task.

There is also evidence of an association between CSF biomarkers of the "A" in AT(N) and clinical ratings of AD based on a battery of cognitive measures (e.g., Fortea et al., 2018), including the Cambridge Examination for Mental Disorders of Older People with Down Syndrome and others with Intellectual Disabilities (CAMDEX-DS; Ball et al., 2004) and the Cambridge Cognition Examination (CAMCOG; Roth et al., 1986). Mixed evidence has been reported for an association between biomarkers of plasma Aβ (e.g., Aβ 1–40 and Aβ 1–42 and their ratio) and AD-related cognitive decline (Fortea et al., 2018; Iulita et al., 2016) and AD clinical status (Petersen et al., 2021).

Cognitive measures have also been found to correlate with biomarkers of PET tau (i.e., 'T' in the AT(N) model) prior to AD dementia in DS. In a small sample ($n = 12$), Rafii et al. (2017) found that PET tau measured via 18F-AV-1451 was negatively associated with performance on the Observer Memory Questionnaire (OMQ; O'Shea, 1996), Vineland-II (Sparrow & Cicchetti, 1989), recent memory items of the CAMCOG, and the Repeatable Battery for the Assessment of Neuropsychological Status Total score (RBANS; Randolph, Tierney, Mohr, & Chase, 1998). In a sample of 92 non-demented adults with DS, Tudorascu et al. (2021) found that higher tau PET 18F-AV-1451 was associated with lower episodic memory scores (on the Cued Recall Test), motor control and planning (on the Purdue Pegboard (Vega, 1969), and dementia symptoms on the Down Syndrome Mental Status Examination (DSMSE; Haxby, 1989).

In a follow-up study on the same sample of non-demented adults with DS analyzed by Tudorascu et al. (2021), elevated PET tau predicted lower episodic memory performance in models that controlled for Aβ. Thus, early declines in episodic memory on the Cued Recall Test were most closely associated with the presence of PET tau than Aβ accumulation alone (Hartley et al., 2022). Research by Fortea et al. (2018) also found that biomarkers of CSF (e.g., 181-phosphorylated tau and total tau) differentiated adults with DS deemed to be symptomatic for AD dementia (i.e., in prodromal stage) versus those deemed to be asymptomatic based on the CAMOG and CAMDEX-DS. Plasma biomarkers of total tau have also been found to be sensitive to AD-related cognitive decline in DS, both in terms of differentiating those in the cognitively stable stage from the prodromal stage of AD and from AD dementia (e.g., Fortea et al., 2018; Petersen et al., 2021).

Less has been published on cognitive measures sensitive to biomarkers of (N) in the AT(N) model in the DS population, and there appears to be little consensus on what the optimal biomarkers of (N) are for DS within or across various domains of biomarkers (e.g., imaging, plasma, and CSF). PET FDG studies of adults with DS have shown an association with AD dementia status (Haier, Head, Head, & Lott, 2008; Neale, Padilla, Fonseca, Holland, & Zaman, 2017; Rafii et al., 2015), as well as cognitive impairments on the DSMSE (Dani et al., 1996) and Dementia Questionnaire for Mentally Retarded Persons (Evenhuis, 1992, 1996; Haier et al., 2008). Structural MRI changes (e.g., T1-weighted indices) have been associated with a status of AD dementia in DS (Matthews et al., 2016; Rafii et al., 2015). Diffusion tensor imaging biomarkers of white matter degeneration have also been associated with cognitive declines (including specifically in memory) prior to AD dementia in DS (Bazydlo et al., 2021; Rosas et al., 2020), and have been associated with AD dementia status (Lin et al., 2016; Powell et al., 2014). Finally, plasma and CSF biomarkers of neuroinflammation, and specifically NfL, have been reported to be an indicator of both prodromal and AD dementia status in DS (Fortea et al., 2018; Petersen et al., 2021) and associated with scores on the CAMOG, Cambridge Neuropsychological Test Automated Battery (CANTAB®, 2016) Paired Associates Learning subtest, and OMQ (Rafii et al., 2019).

In summary, a growing body of research has identified cognitive correlates of biomarkers (imaging, CSF, and plasma) of AD pathology in DS drawing on the AT(N) framework. These studies have found associations between biomarkers of Aβ and tau and early and subtle memory declines, with the presence of elevated Aβ and tau being most sensitive to memory impairments in PET imaging studies. These early cognitive declines were closely followed by associations between biomarkers and declines in attention and executive functioning and then declines in other cognitive domains, as show in Fig. 2. Biomarkers of (N) have also been linked to AD-related cognitive decline. Going forward, it will be important for the

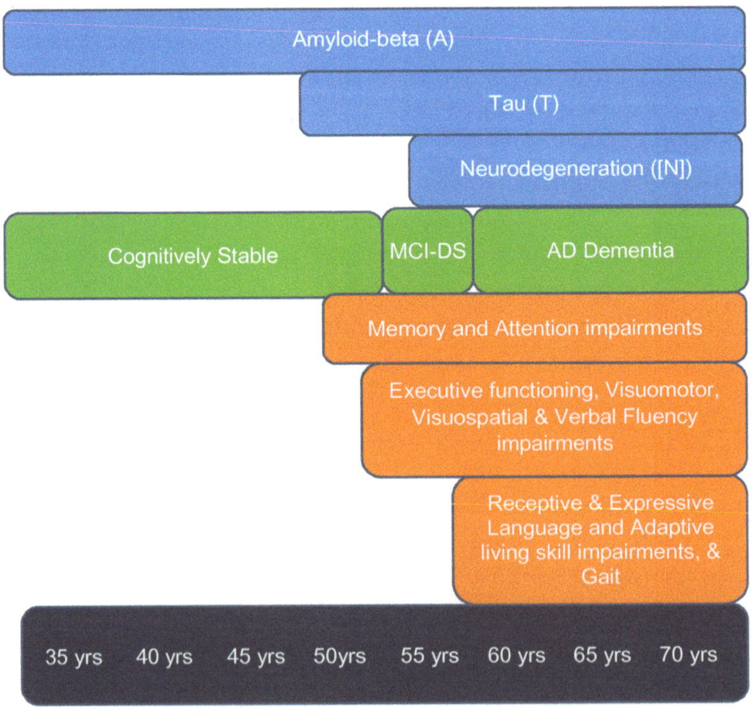

Fig. 2 Mapping of Alzheimer's biomarkers (blue), clinical Alzheimer's disease status (green), cognitive and functional declines (orange) and chronological age in the progression of Alzheimer's disease in Down syndrome.

field to examine profiles (A+/T+/(N)− vs A+/T+/(N)+) of biomarkers of A, T, and (N) in adults with DS in order to better understand the time-ordered sequence of AD pathology in relation to changes in cognition.

5. Measures sensitive to AD-related decline and dementia symptoms

5.1 Prodromal stage

Another line of DS research has been aimed at identifying measures sensitive to cognitive decline indicative of the prodromal stage, which is often when an MCI clinical status is given. Much of this research has focused on identifying cognitive measures that can capture subtle cognitive declines that occur prior to the onset of AD dementia and understanding which cognitive domains decline first (i.e., their sequence of decline). This work has leveraged data-driven methods and pooled data across studies to estimate long-term trends from cross-sectional and short-term longitudinal studies of adults with DS (e.g., Aschenbrenner et al., 2021; Firth et al., 2018; Silverman et al., 2021). In general, research studies on cognitive measures of the prodromal stage of AD in DS have found that directly-administered measures of cognition are more sensitive to early decline than informant-based measures (Firth et al., 2018; Prasher, 2018).

Findings from two large-scale efforts have largely converged in terms of the cognitive domains affected in the transition to prodromal AD (Aschenbrenner et al., 2021; Firth et al., 2018; Krinsky-McHale, Zigman, Lee, et al., 2020). Firth et al. (2018) explored the sequence of cognitive decline prior to clinical dementia, drawing on a cross-sectional sample of 283 young (16–35 years) and middle-aged (36+ years) adults with DS. Using an event-based model, the earliest decline occurred in memory, attention, visuomotor ability, and verbal fluency; this decline was assessed based on the first trial memory score from the CANTAB paired associates learning task, NEPSY-II car and motorbike score (Hatton et al., 2001) and a semantic verbal fluency task.

Aschenbrenner et al. (2021) compiled data from five large longitudinal studies to identify measures sensitive to the early indicators of transition to the prodromal stage of AD in DS. A machine-learning approach was used to examine the items and measures, which differed across the five studies. Their sample included 312 adults with DS, all without a diagnosis of clinical AD dementia, with at least two cycles of data. After adjusting for age and baseline level of intellectual functioning, their models showed that declines in memory and attention occurred early on, and that these declines were followed by declines in measures of executive function. The authors concluded that that the Cued Recall Test and CANTAB paired associate learning test were promising directly-administered measures of memory for consideration in AD clinical trials in DS (see Aschenbrenner et al., 2021 for full list of recommended measures).

A third large-scale recent study has also focused on cognitive measures of the prodromal stage in adults with DS. In this study, researchers examined cognitive measures that could differentiate adults with DS with a clinical status of MCI from those deemed to be cognitively stable (Silverman et al., 2021). It is important to note that the MCI stage continues to be debated within other AD populations (Dubois & Albert, 2004; Petersen, 2009), and is difficult to diagnose within the DS population. In the Silverman et al. (2021) study, a clinical status of MCI was based on within-person change (to the extent possible) and the individual's overall profile of performance on directly-administered cognitive measures as well as informant-report measures. Drawing on a large ($n = 269$) longitudinal study, Silverman et al. (2021) examined cognitive measures that differentiated the 67 adults with DS who developed MCI from those who remained cognitively stable. They found that adults with DS who developed MCI had greater declines in memory, mental status, visuospatial ability, and adaptive behavior relative to those who remained cognitively stable. These cognitive domains were measured using the Selective Reminding Test (Buschke, 1973), Modified Mini Mental Status Evaluation–Down syndrome (Wisniewski & Hill, 1985), DSMSE; Test for Severe Impairment (Albert & Cohen, 1992), Block Design subtests of WISC-Revised (Wechsler, 1974), and adaptive behavior on the American Association on Mental Deficient Adaptive Behavior Scale, Part I (ABSI; Nihira, 1976). In this study, performances on a measure of verbal fluency (McCarthy Category Fluency Test: McCarthy, 1972) and on the Beery-Buktenica Test of Visuomotor Integration (Beery, Buktenica, & Beery, 2004) did not differentiate those who developed MCI-DS from those who remained cognitively stable, but these measures were associated with transition to AD dementia.

Overall, recent data-driven and large sample efforts are remarkably consistent in identifying memory and attention as the domains impacted early on in the transition to prodromal AD in DS, with subsequent changes in visuospatial ability, executive functioning, verbal fluency, motor control and planning, and mental status, all prior to AD dementia (Fig. 2). This sequence is well-aligned with studies examining the cognitive correlates of AD biomarkers of Aβ and tau reviewed earlier (e.g., Hartley et al., 2017; Tudorascu et al., 2020) which also suggest that declines in memory, followed by declines in attention and executive functioning, are associated with biomarkers of early AD pathology in DS. These findings also align with other recent studies that have reported that measures that assess a range of cognitive domains, including memory, attention, and executive functioning, differentiate adults with DS clinically deemed to be in the prodromal stage (or have MCI) from those who were cognitively stable (e.g., Benejam et al., 2020; Fortea et al., 2018; Hom, Taylor, et al., 2021; Hom, Walsh, et al., 2021; Krinsky-McHale et al., 2020). Table 1 displays cognitive measures that have been found to be associated with cognitive changes associated with the prodromal stage of AD, including a clinical status of MCI, in DS.

5.2 AD dementia

Identifying feasible, valid, and sensitive cognitive measures of the AD dementia stage is also critical for the longitudinal evaluation of the effectiveness of AD clinical trials in DS. Insight into how to track change during the dementia stage can also yield information to help caregivers and health providers anticipate care needs and the course of progression following clinical dementia diagnosis (Jozsvai, Hewitt, & Gedye, 2018). Direct measures of cognition can become increasingly difficult for individuals with AD dementia, due to their reduced level of cognitive functioning (which exacerbates floor effects), and because lengthy testing batteries can be taxing. The late onset of seizures, which is linked to AD dementia in DS (e.g., De Simone et al., 2010; Möller, Hamer, Oertel, & Rosenow, 2001), can also make direct testing difficult (Lott et al., 2012).

In DS, AD dementia is characterized by cognitive, physical, and behavioral deterioration, including memory loss, communication problems, loss of mobility, change in eating, weight loss, and problems with continence (McCarron et al., 2018). It has also been associated with nighttime confusion, agitation, wandering, and visual hallucinations (Urv, Zigman, & Silverman, 2010). There is also evidence that the rate of cognitive decline in adults with DS accelerates after the transition to AD dementia (Keator et al., 2020) and that men and women with DS may decline at different rates; specifically, women decline faster than men following AD dementia (e.g., Keator et al., 2020), which is also true in non-DS populations (see Ferreira, Ferreira Santos-Galduróz, Ferri, & Fernandes Galduróz, 2014).

5.3 Direct measures

Table 1 highlights some of the direct measures that have shown promise for detecting AD dementia in DS. The RADD measures overall cognition using selected items from tests that were designed for neurotypical populations. On the RADD, a total score of <20 had a sensitivity of 0.89 and a specificity of 0.75 for detecting AD dementia in adults with DS with severe ID, and a total score of <60 had a sensitivity of 0.95 and specificity of 0.79 for classifying AD dementia in those with mild ID (Hom, Walsh, Doran, & Lott, 2018). The CAMCOG-DS has also been shown to differentiate individuals with DS who are cognitively stable from those with AD dementia (Fonseca, Ball, & Holland, 2018), with a sensitivity of 0.75 and specificity of 0.88 for people with mild ID and a sensitivity of 0.84 and specificity of 0.84 for people with moderate ID (Benejam et al., 2020). The CAMCOG-DS also has limited floor effects in adults with DS with mild and moderate premorbid ID levels (Hon, Huppert, Holland, & Watson, 1998). The Severe Impairment Battery (SIB; Saxton et al., 2005), which measures nine domains of cognitive functioning has also been shown to be effective in differentiating between early-stage and late-stage AD dementia in adults with DS (Koehl, Harp, Van Pelt, Head, & Schmitt, 2020), with a sensitivity of 0.63 and specificity of 0.59 (Wallace et al., 2021). The Test for Severe Impairment (TSI) covers a range of cognitive functions and was found to have few floor effects in adults with DS with premorbid ID in the moderate to severe range (Tyrrell et al., 2001). The TSI has been found to differentiate adults with DS with versus without AD dementia (Tyrrell et al., 2001), but there are no published rates of sensitivity or specificity for the DS population. The DSMSE has also been found to differentiate adults with DS with versus without AD dementia, although some researchers have noted that this measure was better suited for adults with DS with mild to moderate premorbid ID (McCarron, McCallion, Reilly, & Mulryan, 2014). Using a Total score (Free + Cued), the Cued Recall Test was recently found to have a sensitivity of 0.84 and specificity of 0.81 for distinguishing cognitively stable adults with DS from those with AD dementia (Krinsky-McHale, Silverman, Lee, et al., 2022, and a sensitivity of 0.91 and specificity of 0.75 in a previous study (Devenny, Krinsky-McHale, & Kittler, 2006).

5.4 Informant measures

Informant reports aimed at capturing cognitive and functional decline have also been found to be sensitive to clinical AD in DS. The Dementia

Questionnaire for People with Learning Disabilities (DLD; Evenhuis, 2018) is an informant-report of cognitive and behavioral changes. The criterion for clinical AD is an increase in the Sum of Cognitive Scores of ≥7 points and/or an increase of the Sum of Social Scores of ≥5 points in comparison to baseline (premorbid) functioning. The standardization study using these criteria found the DLD to have a sensitivity of 1.00 and a specificity of 0.75 for classifying AD dementia in DS (Deb & Braganza, 1999; Evenhuis, 2018), whereas Shultz et al. (2004) found the DLD to have a sensitivity of 0.65 and specificity of 0.93 among their sample of DS participants with and without AD dementia. Additionally, McCarron et al. (2014) found the DLD to be sensitive to change across time and Harp et al. (2021) demonstrated that the DLD Sum of Cognitive Scores combined with the Vineland-II Community subdomain score had a sensitivity of 1.00 and a specificity of 0.81 for detecting clinical AD in a sample of adults with DS, in which 31% had profound ID. In other studies, however, the DLD was reported to be plagued by floor effects in adults with profound ID (McKenzie, Metcalfe, & Murray, 2018). Regardless of premorbid ID level, a single assessment cut-off score was found to be less sensitive and specific to AD dementia compared to longitudinal changes in scores (Evenhuis, 1996, 2018).

The Dementia Scale for Down Syndrome scale (DSDS; Gedye, 1995) was designed to measure cognitive decline in adults with DS, especially those with severe or profound ID. In the standardization study 76% had severe or profound ID, and the DSDS had a sensitivity of 0.85 and specificity of 0.89 for AD dementia. By comparison, the DLD had a sensitivity and specificity of 0.92 for the same sample. In a subsequent study by Shultz et al. (2004), the DSDS had a sensitivity of 0.65 and specificity of 1.00, whereas the DLD's corresponding values were 0.65 and 0.93, respectively. For adults with DS with mild to moderate ID, the DSDS was found to be better at detecting individuals with middle or late stages of dementia relative to those in the early stage of dementia (Prasher, 2018).

The CAMDEX-DS includes an informant interview and is available in English, Portuguese, Spanish, and German. Using cohorts from the United Kingdom, the CAMDEX-DS had a sensitivity of 0.88 to1.00 and specificity of 0.94 for classifying the clinical AD in DS samples (Ball et al., 2004; Beresford-Webb et al., 2021). The CAMDEX-DS also successfully differentiated between adults with AD dementia from those with co-occurring mental conditions and without dementia (Beresford-Webb et al., 2021). In Brazil, the Portuguese version was reported to have a sensitivity of 1.00 and specificity of 0.98 (Fonseca et al., 2019). The CAMDEX-DS has recently been updated and is now the CAMDEX-II (Beresford-Webb et al., 2021). The Dementia Screening Questionnaire for Individuals with Intellectual Disabilities (DSQIID; Deb, Hare, Prior, & Bhaumik, 2007) is also effective for classifying AD dementia in DS, with a published sensitivity of 0.92 and specificity of 0.97. However, it has been noted that the DSQIID may not be as useful for adults with severe or premorbid ID or advanced dementia if using the fixed cut-off score of 20 (O'Caoimh, Clune, & Molloy, 2013).

The National Task Group-Early Detection Screen for Dementia (NTG-EDSD) is a freely available measure (Esralew, Janicki, DiSipio, Jokinen, & Keller, 2013; Esralew, Janicki, & Keller, 2018) that has been translated into at least 18 languages and was designed for use in adults with DS with varying premorbid ID levels. A recent study by Silverman and colleges (2021), however, highlighted limitations of the measure in terms of screening for MCI-DS. Using a criterion of one or more total concerns on the NTG-EDSD, in a sample of 185 adults with DS, sensitivity was 0.89 and specificity was 0.52. When using a more severely affected criterion of two or more total concerns, sensitivity dropped to 0.83 but specificity increased to 0.64. Among the domains, sensitivity was highest within the Memory and Language domain and specificity was highest in the Language and Communication domain.

In terms of informant-report of adaptive behavior, the *Adaptive Behavior Assessment System* (ABAS; Harrison & Oakland, 2000) has been used in AD research in DS (e.g., Strydom, Dickinson, Shende, Pratico, & Walker, 2009), but little has been published about its ability to detect AD dementia. The *Adaptive Behavior Scale* (ABS; Nihira, Foster, Shellhaas, & Leland, 1975) and its abbreviated version (short ABS; Hatton et al., 2001) has been found to be a valid and reliable measure with few ceiling or floor effects in the DS population (Kay et al., 2003; Startin et al., 2016). Margallo-Lana et al. (2007) followed a cohort of 92 institutionalized adults with DS over a period of 15 years and <10% of their participants had ABS total scores that deteriorated by more than one standard deviation. However, a limitation of that study was that none of the participants resided in a home, where there would likely be more opportunities and variability in daily responsibilities and community experiences. In contrast, Zigman, Krinsky-McHale, Schupf, Urv, and Silverman (2018) followed 133 adults with DS at 18-month intervals for at least five cycles. The ABS Part I scores changed more for those converting to AD dementia compared to those who were cognitively stable at each time point, both before and after the onset of AD dementia.

The *Vineland Adaptive Behavior Scales* is the most commonly used adaptive living skills instrument in AD research in DS (e.g., Hamburg et al., 2019; Keeling et al., 2017). When considered in combination with other measures, the Vineland shows promise in detecting AD dementia in DS. In a study of 141 adults with DS (51% with AD dementia and 38% had severe to profound ID), the Vineland-II Community subdomain score was particularly effective at classifying those with versus without AD dementia (Harp et al., 2021). Meanwhile, in a study of 168 adults with DS (20% with AD dementia, all with mild or moderate ID), the Vineland-III Communication domain score was the only composite score that differentiated those with and without AD dementia (Pulsifer et al., 2020). Hence, the Vineland Communication score appears to be the best indicator of clinical AD in higher functioning individuals with DS, whereas the Vineland Community score may be the best indicator for lower functioning individuals at baseline.

6. Conclusions and next steps

DS is now recognized as a genetic type of AD, given the near universal presence of AD pathology by age 40 years (Lott & Head, 2019) and 90% lifetime risk of clinical AD dementia in DS (McCarron et al., 2014). Over the past decade, a growing body of DS research has been aimed at identifying measures of cognition that correspond to AD biomarkers and are sensitive to early declines and progressive stages of AD. The driving goal of this research is to prepare the field for AD-DS clinical trials. The research that explores the progression of AD is complicated by the challenges of assessing cognition in the DS population. Research in DS has begun to identify associations between AD biomarkers and transition to the prodromal stage and the AD clinical status including a variety of PET imaging, CSF, and plasma biomarkers that map onto the AT(N) model. Overall, research to-date has generally been consistent in revealing a pattern of AD-related cognitive decline in DS that is similar to that of autosomal dominant and late-onset AD. Specifically, research suggests a sequence of decline that starts with changes in memory and attention, and has found that measures of these domains correlate with PET biomarkers of A and T in the AT(N) model. These early cognitive changes are then followed by changes in executive functioning, visuospatial and visuomotor ability, and verbal fluency.

In this chapter, we highlighted several direct and caregiver-reported measures (Table 1) that have shown promise for detecting adults with DS in the prodromal stage (including a clinical rating of MCI-DS) and/or who have AD dementia. Many are also good candidates for inclusion in AD intervention trials that are focused on the transition from the preclinical to prodromal stage of AD in DS. Some of these measures, however, work better for those with mild to moderate premorbid intellectual disability and when used longitudinally to track change in performance over time. It should be noted that in some studies, there was circularity in that the measure evaluated for sensitivity or specificity in detecting MCI or AD dementia was also used in making the clinical rating of MCI or AD dementia. Thus, there remains a strong need for more work aimed at understanding the reliability and validity of these cognitive measures in isolation and when used across samples and clinicians.

Looking forward, there are several important next steps for DS research on cognitive measures in order to prepare for clinical AD intervention trials. While varying levels of premorbid intellectual disability may preclude reliance on a single cut-point on many cognitive measures, guidelines should be developed that are focused on within-person change when possible and that reference premorbid level of functioning. It is also important for the field to establish best practices on specific measures in terms of using raw (vs standard scores) and true deviation approaches to maximize variability in measures at both the between-person and within-person across time level. It is possible that the amount of decline on specific measures that are clinically relevant will differ as a function of premorbid intellectual and functional ability level. Guidelines for differentiating AD-related decline from the effect of co-occurring physical and mental health would also be valuable in clinical and research settings. Finally, there is a critical need for more research to identify more reliable and valid measures for individuals with DS with severe and profound levels of premorbid intellectual disability, as many of the promising cognitive measures are prone to floor effects.

To-date, research on cognitive measures of AD-related decline in DS have predominantly involved individuals who identify as white, non-Hispanic. Moreover, most studies have limited participation to adults with DS who are fluent in the dominant language of that country (e.g., English for studies in the U.S.). There is a critical need for DS researchers to focus on recruiting more racially/ethnically diverse samples and to work to ensure that research opportunities are available for individuals who speak multiple languages, as important subgroups of adults with DS are being left out of science.

Finally, in the coming years there is also a need to understand how genetic factors such as mosaicism, translocation, and APOE status impact the trajectory of AD-related cognitive decline in DS. For example, it is possible that the cognitive domains and/or timeline for cognitive decline differs as a function of these genetic factors. If so, screening recommendations and clinical trial planning may need to differ based on these genetic considerations. Indeed, there is evidence that cognitive declines may occur 2 years earlier in adults with DS who have the APOE e4 gene (Fortea et al., 2020). Genetic factors may have an important role in the progression of AD within the DS population. Similarly, it is possible that lifestyle factors such as physical activity and leisure activities (Fleming et al., 2021; Mihaila et al., 2019) and co-occurring conditions such as sleep disruptions and sleep disordered breathing (Chen, Spanò, & Edgin, 2013; Cody et al., 2020) also alter the rate of cognitive decline associated with AD in DS; the potential role of these environmental and health factors on profiles of cognitive decline need to be explored in the coming years.

As the DS field nears its first large-scale AD prevention trials, there is critical need for research that continues to focus on identifying feasible, reliable, valid, and sensitive measures of cognitive decline and dementia symptoms in full array of adults with DS. It is important that this research consider measures that are suitable for the wide array of premorbid intellectual levels and support needs. It is also critical that this research focus on identifying cognitive measures that are sensitive to the transition from preclinical to prodromal AD in DS, including measures that correlate with AD biomarkers during these stages. These measures will play a key role in participant screening/recruitment for selection into AD clinical trials, tracking intervention efficacy, and characterizing the progression of AD in DS.

Funding

NIH funding: U19 AG070043; R01 AG070028, U01 AG15001, U01 AG051412, and P50HD105353.

References

Abbeduto, L., Warren, S. F., & Conners, F. A. (2007). Language development in down syndrome: From the prelinguistic period to the acquisition of literacy. *Mental Retardation and Developmental Disabilities Research Reviews*, *13*(3), 247–261. https://doi.org/10.1002/MRDD.20158.

Albert, M., & Cohen, C. (1992). The test for severe impairment: An instrument for the assessment of patients with severe cognitive dysfunction. *Journal of the American Geriatrics Society*, *40*(5), 449–453. https://doi.org/10.1111/j.1532-5415.1992.tb02009.x.

Altuna, M., Giménez, S., & Fortea, J. (2021). Epilepsy in down syndrome: A highly prevalent comorbidity. *Journal of Clinical Medicine*, *10*(13), 2776. https://doi.org/10.3390/jcm10132776.

Annus, T., Wilson, L. R., Hong, Y. T., Acosta-Cabronero, J., Fryer, T. D., Cardenas-Blanco, A., et al. (2016). The pattern of amyloid accumulation in the brains of adults with Down syndrome. *Alzheimer's & Dementia, 12*(5), 538–545. https://doi.org/10.1016/J.JALZ.2015.07.490.

Aschenbrenner, A. J., Baksh, R. A., Benejam, B., Beresford-Webb, J. A., Coppus, A., Fortea, J., et al. (2021). Markers of early changes in cognition across cohorts of adults with down syndrome at risk of Alzheimer's disease. *Alzheimer's & Dementia: Diagnosis, Assessment & Disease Monitoring, 13*(1), e12184. https://doi.org/10.1002/dad2.12184.

Ball, S. L., Holland, A. J., Huppert, F. A., Treppner, P., Watson, P., & Hon, J. (2004). The modified CAMDEX informant interview is a valid and reliable tool for use in the diagnosis of dementia in adults with Down's syndrome. *Journal of Intellectual Disability Research, 48*(Pt 6), 611–620. https://doi.org/10.1111/j.1365-2788.2004.00630.x.

Ball, S. L., Holland, A. J., Treppner, P., Watson, P. C., & Huppert, F. A. (2008). Executive dysfunction and its association with personality and behaviour changes in the development of Alzheimer's disease in adults with down syndrome and mild to moderate learning disabilities. *The British Journal of Clinical Psychology, 47*(Pt. 1), 1–29. https://doi.org/10.1348/014466507X230967.

Bazydlo, A., Zammit, M., Wu, M., Dean, D., Johnson, S., Tudorascu, D., et al. (2021). White matter microstructure associations with episodic memory in adults with down syndrome: A tract-based spatial statistics study. *Journal of Neurodevelopmental Disorders, 13*(1), 17. https://doi.org/10.1186/s11689-021-09366-1.

Beery, K. E., Buktenica, N. A., & Beery, N. A. (2004). *The Beery-Buktencia developmental test of visual motor integration* (5th ed.). Bloomington, MN: Pearson.

Benejam, B., Videla, L., Vilaplana, E., Barroeta, I., Carmona-Iragui, M., Altuna, M., et al. (2020). Diagnosis of prodromal and Alzheimer's disease dementia in adults with Down syndrome using neuropsychological tests. *Alzheimer's & Dementia (Amsterdam), 12*(1), e12047. https://doi.org/10.1002/dad2.12047.

Bent, S., McShea, L., & Brennan, S. (2015). The importance of hearing: A review of the literature on hearing loss for older people with learning disabilities. *British Journal of Learning Disability, 43*, 277–284. https://doi.org/10.1111/bld.12148.

Beresford-Webb, J. A., Mak, E., Grigorova, M., Daffern, S. J., Holland, A. J., & Zaman, S. H. (2021). Establishing diagnostic thresholds for Alzheimer's disease in adults with Down syndrome: The Cambridge Examination for mental disorders of older people with Down's syndrome and others with intellectual disabilities (CAMDEX-DS). *British Journal of Psychology*, 7(3), e79. https://doi.org/10.1192/bjo.2021.36.

Bhattacharyya, R., Sanyal, D., & Bhattacharyya, S. (2018). Diagnostic algorithm of Down syndrome by minor physical anomaly. *Indian Journal of Psychiatry, 60*(4), 398–403. https://doi.org/10.4103/psychiatry.IndianJPsychiatry_401_17.

Breia, P., Mendes, R., Silvestre, A., Gonçalves, M. J., Figueira, M. J., & Bispo, R. (2014). Adults with Down syndrome: Characterization of a Portuguese Sample. *Acta Médica Portuguesa, 27*(3), 357–363. https://doi.org/10.20344/AMP.4898.

Buschke, H. (1973). Selective reminding for analysis of memory and learning. *Journal of Verbal Learning and Verbal Behavior, 12*(5), 543–550.

CANTAB®. (2016). *Cambridge neuropsychological test automated battery (CANTAB®)*. Cambridge, UK: Cambridge Cognition Ltd.

Carr, J. (1988). Six weeks to twenty-one years old: A longitudinal study of children wit Down's syndrome and their families. *Journal of Child Psychology and Psychiatry, 29*(4), 407–431. https://doi.org/10.1111/J.1469-7610.1988.TB00734.X.

Chen, C. C., Spanò, G., & Edgin, J. O. (2013). The impact of sleep disruption on executive function in Down syndrome. *Research in Developmental Disabilities, 34*(6), 2033–2039. https://doi.org/10.1016/j.ridd.2013.03.009.

Cody, K. A., Piro-Gambetti, B., Zammit, M. D., Christian, B. T., Handen, B. L., Klunk, W. E., et al. (2020). Association of sleep with cognition and beta amyloid accumulation in adults with Down syndrome. *Neurobiology of Aging*, *93*, 44–51. https://doi.org/10.1016/j.neurobiolaging.2020.04.018.

Culpepper, L., Lam, R. W., & McIntyre, R. S. (2017). Cognitive impairment in patients with depression: Awareness, assessment, and management. *The Journal of Clinical Psychiatry*, *78*(9), 1383–1394. https://doi.org/10.4088/JCP.tk16043ah5c.

Dani, A., Pietrini, P., Furey, M. L., McIntosh, A. R., Grady, C. L., Horwitz, B., et al. (1996). Brain cognition and metabolism in Down syndrome adults in association with development of dementia. *Neuroreport*, 7(18), 2933–2936. https://doi.org/10.1097/00001756-199611250-00026.

De Simone, R., Puig, X. S., Gélisse, P., Crespel, A., & Genton, P. (2010). Senile myoclonic epilepsy: Delineation of a common condition associated with Alzheimer's disease in Down syndrome. *Seizure*, *19*(7), 383–389. https://doi.org/10.1016/j.seizure.2010.04.008.

Deb, S., & Braganza, J. (1999). Comparison of rating scales for the diagnosis of dementia in adults with Down's syndrome. *Journal of Intellectual Disability Research*, *43*(Pt 5), 400–407. https://doi.org/10.1046/j.1365-2788.1999.043005400.x.

Deb, S., Hare, M., Prior, L., & Bhaumik, S. (2007). Dementia screening questionnaire for individuals with intellectual disabilities. *British Journal of Psychiatry*, *190*, 440–444. https://doi.org/10.1192/bjp.bp.106.024984.

Dekker, A. D., Fortea, J., Blesa, R., & De Deyn, P. P. (2017). Cerebrospinal fluid biomarkers for Alzheimer's disease in Down syndrome. *Alzheimer's & Dementia: Diagnosis, Assessment & Disease Monitoring*, *8*, 1–10. https://doi.org/10.1016/J.DADM.2017.02.006.

Del Hoyo Soriano, L., Rosser, T., Hamilton, D., Wood, T., Abbeduto, L., & Sherman, S. (2020). Gestational age is related to symptoms of attention-deficit/hyperactivity disorder in late-preterm to full-term children and adolescents with down syndrome. *Scientific Reports*, *10*(1), 20,345. https://doi.org/10.1038/s41598-020-77392-5.

Devenny, D., Krinsky-McHale, S., & Kittler, P. (2006). *Cognitive processes in early-stage dementia in adults with Down syndrome; [Paper presentation]. (9th World Down Syndrome Congress).*

Doran, E., Keator, D., Head, E., Phelan, M. J., Kim, R., Totoiu, M., et al. (2017). Down syndrome, partial trisomy 21, and absence of Alzheimer's disease: The role of APP. *Journal of Alzheimer's Disease*, *56*(2), 459–470. https://doi.org/10.3233/JAD-160836.

Dubois, B., & Albert, M. L. (2004). Amnestic MCI or prodromal Alzheimer's disease? *The Lancet. Neurology*, *3*(4), 246–248. https://doi.org/10.1016/S1474-4422(04)00710-0.

Dykens, E., Hodapp, R., & Evans, D. (2006). Profiles and development of adaptive behavior in children with Down syndrome. *Down Syndrome Research and Practice*, *9*(3), 45–50. https://doi.org/10.3104/reprints.293.

Esralew, L., Janicki, M. P., DiSipio, M., Jokinen, J., & Keller, S. M. (2013). Members of the National Task Group Section on Early Detection and Screening. *National Task Group Early Detection Screen for Dementia (NTGEDSD) manual*, *16*, 47–54.

Esralew, L., Janicki, M. P., & Keller, S. M. (2018). National task group early detection screen for dementia (NTG-EDSD). *Neuropsychological assessments of dementia in down syndrome and intellectual disabilities* (pp. 197–213). Cham: Springer.

Evenhuis, H. M. (1992). Evaluation of a screening instrument for dementia in aging mentally retarded persons. *Journal of Intellectual Disability Research*, *36*(Pt. 4), 337–347. https://doi.org/10.1111/j.1365-2788.1992.tb00532.x.

Evenhuis, H. M. (1996). Further evaluation of the Dementia Questionnaire for persons with mental retardation (DMR). *Journal of Intellectual Disability Research*, *40*(Pt. 4), 369–373. https://doi.org/10.1046/j.1365-2788.1996.786786.x.

Evenhuis, H. M. (2018). The dementia questionnaire for people with learning disabilities. In V. P. Prasher (Ed.), *Neuropsychological assessments of dementia in Down syndrome and intellectual disabilities* (pp. 43–56). UK: Springer.

Evenhuis, H. M., Kengen, M. M. F., & Eurlings, H. A. (1998). *Dementie Vragenlijst voor Verstandelijk Gehandicapten (DVZ)* (2nd). Amsterdam: Harcourt Test Publishers.
Evenhuis, H. M., Kengen, M. M. F., & Eurlings, H. A. (2006). *Dementia Questionaire for Persons with Intellectual Disabilities (DMR)*. Amsterdam: Harcourt Test Publishers.
Ferreira, L., Ferreira Santos-Galduróz, R., Ferri, C. P., & Fernandes Galduróz, J. C. (2014). Rate of cognitive decline in relation to sex after 60 years-of-age: A systematic review. *Geriatrics & Gerontology International*, *14*(1), 23–31. https://doi.org/10.1111/ggi.12093.
Finestack, L. H., & Abbeduto, L. (2010). Expressive language profiles of verbally expressive adolescents and young adults with Down syndrome or fragile X syndrome. *Journal of Speech, Language, and Hearing Research*, *53*(5), 1334–1348. https://doi.org/10.1044/1092-4388(2010/09-0125).
Firth, N. C., Startin, C. M., Hithersay, R., Hamburg, S., Wijeratne, P. A., Mok, K. Y., et al. (2018). Aging related cognitive changes associated with Alzheimer's disease in Down syndrome. *Annals of Clinical and Translational Neurology*, *5*(6), 741–751. https://doi.org/10.1002/acn3.571.
Fleming, V., Piro-Gambetti, B., Patrick, A., Zammit, M., Alexander, A., Christian, B. T., et al. (2021). Physical activity and cognitive and imaging biomarkers of Alzheimer's disease in down syndrome. *Neurobiology of Aging*, *107*, 118–127. https://doi.org/10.1016/j.neurobiolaging.2021.07.016.
Flores-Aguilar, L., Iulita, M. F., Kovecses, O., Torres, M. D., Levi, S. M., Zhang, Y., et al. (2020). Evolution of neuroinflammation across the lifespan of individuals with Down syndrome. *Brain*, *143*(12), 3653–3671. https://doi.org/10.1093/brain/awaa326.
Fonseca, L. M., Ball, S. L., & Holland, A. J. (2018). The Cambridge examination for mental disorders of older people with Down's syndrome and others with intellectual disabilities (CAMDEX-DS). In V. P. Prasher (Ed.), *Neuropsychological assessments of dementia in Down syndrome and intellectual disabilities* (pp. 123–144). UK: Springer International.
Fonseca, L. M., Haddad, G. G., Mattar, G. P., Oliveira, M. C., Simon, S. S., Guilhoto, L. M., et al. (2019). The validity and reliability of the CAMDEX-DS for assessing dementia in adults with Down syndrome in Brazil. *Brazil Journal of Psychiatry*, *41*(3), 225–233. https://doi.org/10.1590/1516-4446-2018-0033.
Fortea, J., Carmona-Iragui, M., Benejam, B., Fernández, S., Videla, L., Barroeta, I., et al. (2018). Plasma and CSF biomarkers for the diagnosis of Alzheimer's disease in adults with Down syndrome: A cross-sectional study. *The Lancet Neurology*, *17*(10), 860–869. https://doi.org/10.1016/S1474-4422(18)30285-0.
Fortea, J., Vilaplana, E., Carmona-Iragui, M., Benejam, B., Videla, L., Barroeta, I., et al. (2020). Clinical and biomarker changes of Alzheimer's disease in adults with Down syndrome: A cross-sectional study. *The Lancet*, *395*(10242), 1988–1997. https://doi.org/10.1016/S0140-6736(20)30689-9.
Fortea, J., Zaman, S. H., Hartley, S., Rafii, M. S., Head, E., & Carmona-Iragui, M. (2021). Alzheimer's disease associated with Down syndrome: A genetic form of dementia. *The Lancet. Neurology*, *20*(11), 930–942. https://doi.org/10.1016/S1474-4422(21)00245-3.
Gagliardi, G., Epelbaum, S., Houot, M., Bakardjian, H., Boukadida, L., Revillon, M., et al. (2019). Which episodic memory performance is associated with Alzheimer's disease biomarkers in elderly cognitive complainers? evidence from a longitudinal observational study with four episodic memory tests (insight-PreAD). *Journal of Alzheimer's Disease*, *70*(3), 811–824. https://doi.org/10.3233/JAD-180966.
Gandy, K. C., Castillo, H. A., Ouellette, L., Castillo, J., Lupo, P. J., Jacola, L. M., et al. (2020). The relationship between chronic health conditions and cognitive deficits in children, adolescents, and young adults with down syndrome: A systematic review. *PLoS One*, *15*(9), e0239040. https://doi.org/10.1371/journal.pone.0239040.
Gedye, A. (1995). *Manual for the dementia scale for Down syndrome*. Vancouver: Gedye Research and Consulting.

Giménez, S., Videla, L., Romero, S., Benejam, B., Clos, S., Fernández, S., et al. (2018). Prevalence of sleep disorders in adults with down syndrome: A comparative study of self-reported, actigraphic, and polysomnographic findings. *Journal of Clinical Sleep Medicine, 14*(10), 1725–1733. https://doi.org/10.5664/jcsm.7382.

Giri, M., Zhang, M., & Lü, Y. (2016). Genes associated with Alzheimer's disease: An overview and current status. *Clinical Interventions in Aging, 11*, 665–681. https://doi.org/10.2147/CIA.S105769.

Godfrey, M., & Lee, N. R. (2018). Memory profiles in Down syndrome across development: A review of memory abilities through the lifespan. *Journal of Neurodevelopmental Disorders, 10*(1), 5. https://doi.org/10.1186/s11689-017-9220-y.

Guaraldi, F., Rossetto Giaccherino, R., Lanfranco, F., Motta, G., Gori, D., Arvat, E., et al. (2017). Endocrine autoimmunity in Down's syndrome. *Frontiers of Hormone Research, 48*, 133–146. https://doi.org/10.1159/000452912.

Haier, R. J., Head, K., Head, E., & Lott, I. T. (2008). Neuroimaging of individuals with Down's syndrome at-risk for dementia: Evidence for possible compensatory events. *NeuroImage, 39*(3), 1324–1332. https://doi.org/10.1016/j.neuroimage.2007.09.064.

Hamburg, S., Lowe, B., Startin, C. M., Padilla, C., Coppus, A., Silverman, W., et al. (2019). Assessing general cognitive and adaptive abilities in adults with Down syndrome: A systematic review. *Journal of Neurodevelopmental Disorders, 11*, 16. https://doi.org/10.1186/s11689-019-9279-8.

Handen, B., Clare, I., Laymon, C., Petersen, M., Zaman, S., O'Bryant, S., et al. (2021). Acute regression in Down syndrome. *Brain Sciences, 11*(8), 1109. https://doi.org/10.3390/brainsci11081109.

Harp, J. P., Koehl, L. M., Pelt, K., Hom, C. L., Doran, E., Head, E., et al. (2021). Cognitive and behavioral domains that reliably differentiate normal aging and dementia in Down syndrome. *Brain Sciences, 11*(9), 1128. https://doi.org/10.3390/brainsci11091128.

Harrison, P. L., & Oakland, T. (2000). *Adaptive behavior assessment system*. San Antonio, TX: Psychological Corporation.

Hartley, S. L., Handen, B. L., Devenny, D. A., Hardison, R., Mihaila, I., Price, J. C., et al. (2014). Cognitive functioning in relation to brain amyloid-β in healthy adults with Down syndrome. *Brain, 137*(9), 2556–2563. https://doi.org/10.1093/brain/awu173.

Hartley, S. L., Handen, B. L., Devenny, D., Mihaila, I., Hardison, R., Lao, P. J., et al. (2017). Cognitive decline and brain amyloid-β accumulation across 3 years in adults with Down syndrome. *Neurobiology of Aging, 58*, 68–76. https://doi.org/10.1016/j.neurobiolaging.2017.05.019.

Hartley, S. L., Handen, B. L., Devenny, D., Tudorascu, D., Piro-Gambetti, B., Zammit, M. D., et al. (2020). Cognitive indicators of transition to preclinical and prodromal stages of Alzheimer's disease in Down syndrome. *Alzheimer's & Dementia: Diagnosis, Assessment & Disease Monitoring, 12*(1), e12096. https://doi.org/10.1002/dad2.12096.

Hartley, S. L., Handen, B. L., Tudorascu, D., Lee, L., Cohen, A., Piro-Gambetti, B., et al. (2022). Role of tau deposition in early cognitive decline in Down syndrome. *Alzheimer's and Dementia: Diagnosis, Assessment and Disease Monitoring, 14*(1), e12256. Epub ahead of print https://doi.org/10.1002/dad2.12256.

Hashemi, H., Mehravaran, S., Asgari, S., & Dehghanian Nasrabadi, F. (2021). Refractive and vision status in Down syndrome: A comparative study. *Turkish Journal of Ophthalmology, 51*(4), 199–205. https://doi.org/10.4274/tjo.galenos.2020.52959.

Hatton, C., Emerson, E., Robertson, J., Gregory, N., Kessissoglou, S., Perry, J., et al. (2001). The adaptive behavior scale-residential and community (part I): Towards the development of a short form. *Research in Developmental Disabilities, 22*(4), 273–288. https://doi.org/10.1016/s0891-4222(01)00072-5.

Haxby, J. V. (1989). Neuropsychological evaluation of adults with Down's syndrome: Patterns of selective impairment in non-demented old adults. *Journal of Mental Deficiency Research, 33*(Pt. 3), 193–210. https://doi.org/10.1111/j.1365-2788.1989.tb01467.x.
Head, E., & Ances, B. (2020). Biomarkers in Down syndrome can help us understand Alzheimer's disease. *The Lancet, 395*(10242), 1951–1953. https://doi.org/10.1016/S0140-6736(20)30916-8.
Head, E., Powell, D., Gold, B. T., & Schmitt, F. A. (2012). Alzheimer's disease in Down syndrome. *European Journal of Neurodegenerative Disease, 1*(3), 353–364.
Hessl, D., Nguyen, D. V., Green, C., Chavez, A., Tassone, F., Hagerman, R. J., et al. (2009). A solution to limitations of cognitive testing in children with intellectual disabilities: The case of fragile X syndrome. *Journal of Neurodevelopmental Disorders, 1*(1), 33–45. https://doi.org/10.1007/s11689-008-9001-8.
Hithersay, R., Startin, C. M., Hamburg, S., Mok, K. Y., Hardy, J., Fisher, E., et al. (2019). Association of dementia with mortality among adults with Down syndrome older than 35 years. *JAMA Neurology, 76*(2), 152–160. https://doi.org/10.1001/jamaneurol.2018.3616.
Hodapp, R. M., & Fidler, D. J. (2021). Down syndrome. In L. M. Glidden, L. Abbeduto, L. L. McIntyre, & M. J. Tassé (Eds.), *APA handbook of intellectual and developmental disabilities: Foundations* American Psychological Association. https://doi.org/10.1037/0000194-006. pp. 123–150.
Holland, A. J., Hon, J., Huppert, F. A., & Stevens, F. (2000). Incidence and course of dementia in people with Down's syndrome: Findings from a population-based study. *Journal of Intellectual Disability Research, 44*(Pt. 2), 138–146. https://doi.org/10.1046/j.1365-2788.2000.00263.x.
Hom, C., Taylor, L., Mapstone, M., Rosas, H. D., Silverman, W., Krinsky-McHale, S. J., et al. (2021). The relationship between regional amyloid deposition and executive function decline in adults with Down syndrome. *Alzheimer's & Dementia, 17*, e053302. https://doi.org/10.1002/alz.053302.
Hom, C. L., Walsh, D. M., Doran, E., & Lott, I. T. (2018). The rapid assessment for developmental disabilities. In *Neuropsychological assessments of dementia in Down Syndrome and intellectual disabilities* (pp. 215–233). Cham: Springer.
Hom, C. L., Walsh, D., Fernandez, G., Tournay, A., Touchette, P., & Lott, I. T. (2021). Cognitive assessment using the rapid assessment for developmental disabilities, second edition (RADD-2). *Journal of Intellectual Disability Research, 65*(9), 831–848. https://doi.org/10.1111/jir.12863.
Hon, J., Huppert, F. A., Holland, A. J., & Watson, P. (1998). The value of the Rivermead Behavioral Memory Test (Children's Version) in an epidemiological study of older adults with Down syndrome. *The British Journal of Clinical Psychology, 37*(1), 15–29. https://doi.org/10.1111/j.2044-8260.1998.tb01276.x.
Irum, S., Robert, H. M., Mahmood, A., Mahmood, R., Khurshid, A., & Khan, S. A. (2021). Frequency of clinical features and cytogenetic defects in down syndrome diagnosed at afip. *PAFMJ, 71*(Suppl. 1), S28–S31. https://doi.org/10.51253/pafmj.V71isuppl-1.6196.
Iulita, M. F., Ower, A., Barone, C., Pentz, R., Gubert, P., Romano, C., et al. (2016). An inflammatory and trophic disconnect biomarker profile revealed in Down syndrome plasma: Relation to cognitive decline and longitudinal evaluation. *Alzheimer's & Dementia, 12*(11), 1132–1148. https://doi.org/10.1016/j.jalz.2016.05.001.
Jack, C. R., Jr., Bennett, D. A., Blennow, K., Carrillo, M. C., Feldman, H. H., Frisoni, G. B., et al. (2016). A/T/N: An unbiased descriptive classification scheme for Alzheimer's disease biomarkers. *Neurology, 87*(5), 539. https://doi.org/10.1212/WNL.0000000000002923.

Jack, C. R., Knopman, D. S., Jagust, W. J., Petersen, R. C., Weiner, M. W., Aisen, P. S., et al. (2013). Update on hypothetical model of Alzheimer's disease biomarkers. *The Lancet Neurology, 12*(2). https://doi.org/10.1016/S1474-4422(12)70291-0.

Jennings, D., Seibyl, J., Sabbagh, M., Lai, F., Hopkins, W., Bullich, S., et al. (2015). Age dependence of brain β-amyloid deposition in Down syndrome: An [18F]florbetaben PET study. *Neurology, 84*(5), 500–507. https://doi.org/10.1212/WNL.0000000000001212.

Jozsvai, E., Hewitt, S., & Gedye, A. (2018). Gedye dementia scale for Down syndrome. In V. P. Prasher (Ed.), *Neuropsychological assessments of dementia in Down syndrome and intellectual disabilities* (2nd ed., pp. 57–71). London: Springer International Publishing.

Karmiloff-Smith, A., Al-Janabi, T., D'Souza, H., Groet, J., Massand, E., Mok, K., et al. (2016). The importance of understanding individual differences in Down syndrome. *F1000Research, 5*. F1000 Faculty Rev-389 https://doi.org/10.12688/f1000research.7506.1.

Karran, E., Mercken, M., & De Strooper, B. (2011). The amyloid cascade hypothesis for Alzheimer's disease: An appraisal for the development of therapeutics. *Nature Reviews. Drug Discovery, 10*(9), 698–712. https://doi.org/10.1038/nrd3505.

Kay, D. W., Tyrer, S. P., Margallo-Lana, M. L., Moore, P. B., Fletcher, R., Berney, T. P., et al. (2003). Preliminary evaluation of a scale to assess cognitive function in adults with Down's syndrome: The Prudhoe cognitive function test. *Journal of Intellectual Disability Research, 47*(Pt. 3), 155–168. https://doi.org/10.1046/j.1365-2788.2003.00451.x.

Keator, D. B., Doran, E., Taylor, L., Phelan, M. J., Hom, C., Tseung, K., et al. (2020). Brain amyloid and the transition to dementia in Down syndrome. *Alzheimer's & Dementia, 12*(1), e12126. https://doi.org/10.1002/dad2.12126.

Keeling, L. A., Spiridigliozzi, G. A., Hart, S. J., Baker, J. A., Jones, H. N., & Kishnani, P. S. (2017). Challenges in measuring the effects of pharmacological interventions on cognitive and adaptive functioning in individuals with Down syndrome: A systematic review. *American Journal of Medical Genetics Part A, 173*(11), 3058–3066. https://doi.org/10.1002/ajmg.a.38416.

Kim, J., Basak, J. M., & Holtzman, D. M. (2009). The role of apolipoprotein E in Alzheimer's disease. *Neuron, 63*(3), 287–303. https://doi.org/10.1016/j.neuron.2009.06.026.

Knox, K., Stanley, J., Hendrix, J. A., Hillerstrom, H., Dunn, T., Achenbach, J., et al. (2021). Development of a symptom menu to facilitate goal attainment scaling in adults with Down syndrome-associated Alzheimer's disease: A qualitative study to identify meaningful symptoms. *Journal of Patient-Reported Outcomes, 5*(1), 1–10. https://doi.org/10.1186/S41687-020-00278-7/FIGURES/1.

Koehl, L., Harp, J., Van Pelt, K. L., Head, E., & Schmitt, F. A. (2020). Longitudinal assessment of dementia measures in Down syndrome. *Alzheimer's & Dementia (Amsterdam), 12*(1), e12075. https://doi.org/10.1002/dad2.12075.

Korenberg, J. R., Chen, X. N., Schipper, R., Sun, Z., Gonsky, R., Gerwehr, S., et al. (1994). Down syndrome phenotypes: The consequences of chromosomal imbalance. *Proceedings of the National Academy of Sciences of the United States of America, 91*(11), 4997–5001. https://doi.org/10.1073/PNAS.91.11.4997.

Korkman, M., Kirk, U., & Kemp, S. (2007). *NEPSY-II* (2nd ed.). San Antonio: Harcourt Assessment.

Krinsky-McHale, S. J., Silverman, W., Gordon, J., Devenny, D. A., Oley, N., & Abramov, I. (2014). Vision deficits in adults with Down syndrome. *Journal of Applied Research in Intellectual Disabilities, 27*(3), 247–263.

Krinsky-McHale, S. J., Silverman, W., Lee, J. H., et al. (2022). *Sensitivity and specificity of the modified cued recall test for Alzheimer's disease in Down syndrome. [Meeting Presentation]. Alzheimer's Biomarker Consortium – Down Syndrome Annual Meeting, Long Beach, CA.*

Krinsky-McHale, S. J., Zigman, W. B., Lee, J. H., et al. (2020). Promising outcome measures of early Alzheimer's dementia in adults with Down syndrome. *Alzheimer's & Dementia, 2020*(12), e12044. https://doi.org/10.1002/dad2.

Kristensen, K., Lorenz, K. M., Zhou, X., Piro-Gambetti, B., Hartley, S. L., Godar, S. P., et al. (2022). Language and executive functioning in young adults with Down syndrome. *Journal of Intellectual Disability Research, 66*(1–2), 151–161. https://doi.org/10.1111/jir.12868.

Lai, F., Mercaldo, N. D., Wang, C. M., Hersch, M. S., Hersch, G. G., & Rosas, H. D. (2021). Association between hypothyroidism onset and Alzheimer's disease onset in adults with Down syndrome. *Brain Sciences, 11*(9), 1223. https://doi.org/10.3390/brainsci11091223.

Lai, F., & Williams, R. S. (1989). A prospective study of Alzheimer's disease in Down syndrome. *Archives of Neurology, 46*(8), 849–853. https://doi.org/10.1001/archneur.1989.00520440031017.

Lao, P. J., Gutierrez, J., Keator, D., Rizvi, B., Banerjee, A., Igwe, K. C., et al. (2020). Alzheimer-related cerebrovascular disease in Down syndrome. *Annals of Neurology, 88*(6), 1165–1177. https://doi.org/10.1002/ana.25905.

Lao, P. J., Handen, B. L., Betthauser, T. J., Mihaila, I., Hartley, S. L., Cohen, A. D., et al. (2017). Longitudinal changes in amyloid positron emission tomography and volumetric magnetic resonance imaging in the nondemented Down syndrome population. *Alzheimer's & Dementia (Amsterdam), 9*, 1–9. https://doi.org/10.1016/j.dadm.2017.05.001.

Lin, A. L., Powell, D., Caban-Holt, A., Jicha, G., Robertson, W., Gold, B. T., et al. (2016). (1)H-MRS metabolites in adults with Down syndrome: Effects of dementia. *Neuroimage: Clinical, 11*, 728–735. https://doi.org/10.1016/j.nicl.2016.06.001.

Lott, I. T., Doran, E., Nguyen, V. Q., Tournay, A., Movsesyan, N., & Gillen, D. L. (2012). Down syndrome and dementia: Seizures and cognitive decline. *Journal of Alzheimer's Disease, 29*(1), 177–185. https://doi.org/10.3233/JAD-2012-111,613.

Lott, I. T., & Head, E. (2019). Dementia in Down syndrome: Unique insights for Alzheimer's disease research. *Nature Reviews. Neurology, 15*(3), 135. https://doi.org/10.1038/S41582-018-0132-6.

Mai, C. T., Isenburg, J. L., Canfield, M. A., Meyer, R. E., Correa, A., Alverson, C. J., et al. (2019). National population-based estimates for major birth defects, 2010–2014. *Birth Defects Research, 111*(18), 1420–1435. https://doi.org/10.1002/bdr2.1589.

Mann, D. M. A., & Esiri, M. M. (1989). The pattern of acquisition of plaques and tangles in the brains of patients under 50 years of age with Down's syndrome. *Journal of the Neurological Sciences, 89*(2–3). https://doi.org/10.1016/0022-510X(89)90019-1.

Margallo-Lana, M. L., Moore, P. B., Kay, D. W., Perry, R. H., Reid, B. E., Berney, T. P., et al. (2007). Fifteen-year follow-up of 92 hospitalized adults with Down's syndrome: Incidence of cognitive decline, its relationship to age and neuropathology. *Journal of Intellectual Disability Research, 51*(Pt. 6), 463–477. https://doi.org/10.1111/j.1365-2788.2006.00902.x.

Martini, A. C., Helman, A. M., McCarty, K. L., Lott, I. T., Doran, E., Schmitt, F. A., et al. (2020). Distribution of microglial phenotypes as a function of age and Alzheimer's disease neuropathology in the brains of people with Down syndrome. *Alzheimer's & dementia (Amsterdam, Netherlands), 12*(1), e12113. https://doi.org/10.1002/dad2.12113.

Matthews, D. C., Lukic, A. S., Andrews, R. D., Marendic, B., Brewer, J., Rissman, R. A., et al. (2016). Dissociation of Down syndrome and Alzheimer's disease effects with imaging. *Alzheimer's & Dementia, 2*(2), 69–81. https://doi.org/10.1016/j.trci.2016.02.004.

McCarron, M., McCallion, P., Coppus, A., Fortea, J., Stemp, S., Janicki, M., et al. (2018). Supporting advanced dementia in people with Down syndrome and other intellectual disability: Consensus statement of the International Summit on Intellectual Disability and Dementia. *Journal of Intellectual Disability Research, 62*(7), 617–624. https://doi.org/10.1111/jir.12500.

McCarron, M., McCallion, P., Reilly, E., Dunne, P., Carroll, R., & Mulryan, N. (2017). A prospective 20-year longitudinal follow-up of dementia in persons with Down syndrome. *Journal of Intellectual Disability Research, 61*(9), 843–852. https://doi.org/10.1111/jir.12390.

McCarron, M., McCallion, P., Reilly, E., & Mulryan, N. (2014). A prospective 14-year longitudinal follow-up of dementia in persons with Down syndrome. *Journal of Intellectual Disability Research, 58*(1), 61–70. https://doi.org/10.1111/jir.12074.

McCarthy, D. (1972). McCarthy scales of children's abilities (MSCA). *Psychological Corporation.*

McKenzie, K., Metcalfe, D., & Murray, G. (2018). A review of measures used in the screening, assessment and diagnosis of dementia in people with an intellectual disability. *Journal of Applied Research in Intellectual Disabilities, 31*(5), 725–742. https://doi.org/10.1111/jar.12441.

Mihaila, I., Handen, B. L., Christian, B. T., Lao, P. J., Cody, K. A., Klunk, W. E., et al. (2019). Leisure activity, brain β-amyloid, and episodic memory in adults with Down syndrome. *Developmental Neurobiology, 79*(7), 738–749. https://doi.org/10.1002/dneu.22677.

Möller, J. C., Hamer, H. M., Oertel, W. H., & Rosenow, F. (2001). Late-onset myoclonic epilepsy in Down's syndrome (LOMEDS). *Seizure, 10*(4), 303–306. https://doi.org/10.1053/seiz.2000.0500.

Montoliu-Gaya, L., Strydom, A., Blennow, K., Zetterberg, H., & Ashton, N. J. (2021). Blood biomarkers for Alzheimer's disease in Down syndrome. *Journal of Clinical Medicine, 10*(16), 3639. https://doi.org/10.3390/JCM10163639.

Moss, J., Richards, C., Nelson, L., & Oliver, C. (2013). Prevalence of autism spectrum disorder symptomatology and related behavioral characteristics in individuals with Down syndrome. *Autism, 17*(4), 390–404. https://doi.org/10.1177/1362361312442790.

Neale, N., Padilla, C., Fonseca, L. M., Holland, T., & Zaman, S. (2017). Neuroimaging and other modalities to assess Alzheimer's disease in Down syndrome. *NeuroImage: Clinical, 17*, 263–271. https://doi.org/10.1016/j.nicl.2017.10.022.

Nelson, D. L. D., Siddarth, D. P., Kepe, D. V., Scheibel, M. K. E., Huang, D. S. C., Barrio, D. J. R., et al. (2011). Positron emission tomography of brain β-amyloid and tau levels in adults with Down syndrome. *Archives of Neurology, 68*(6), 768. https://doi.org/10.1001/ARCHNEUROL.2011.104.

Nihira, K. (1976). Dimensions of adaptive behavior in institutionalized mentally retarded children and adults: Developmental perspective. *American Journal of Mental Deficiency, 81*(3), 215–226.

Nihira, K., Foster, R., Shellhaas, M., & Leland, H. (1975). *AAMD adaptive behavior scale (Rev).* Washington, DC: American Association on Mental Deficiency.

Nihira, K., Leland, H., & Lambert, N. (1993). *Adaptive Behaviour Scale—Residential and community: Examination booklet.* Austin, TX: Pro-Ed.

O'Caoimh, R., Clune, Y., & Molloy, D. W. (2013). Screening for Alzheimer's disease in Down's syndrome. *Journal of Alzheimer's Disease and Parkinsonism*, S7(001). https://doi.org/10.4172/2161-0460.S7-001.

O'Shea, M. F. (1996). *The cognitive and affective correlates of the memory complaint in temporal lobe epilepsy (Doctoral dissertation).* University of Melbourne.

Pennington, B. F., Moon, J., Edgin, J., Stedron, J., & Nadel, L. (2003). The neuropsychology of Down syndrome: Evidence for hippocampal dysfunction. *Child Development, 74*(1), 75–93. https://doi.org/10.1111/1467-8624.00522.

Petersen, R. C. (2009). Early diagnosis of Alzheimer's disease: Is MCI too late? *Current Alzheimer Research, 6*(4), 324–330. https://doi.org/10.2174/156720509788929237.

Petersen, M. E., Rafii, M. S., Zhang, F., Hall, J., Julovich, D., Ances, B. M., et al. (2021). Plasma total-tau and neurofilament light chain as diagnostic biomarkers of Alzheimer's disease dementia and mild cognitive impairment in adults with Down syndrome. *Journal of Alzheimer's Disease: JAD, 79*(2), 671–681. https://doi.org/10.3233/JAD-201167.

Pezzuti, L., Nacinovich, R., Oggiano, S., Bomba, M., Ferri, R., La Stella, A., et al. (2018). Beyond the floor effect on the WISC-IV in individuals with Down syndrome: Are there cognitive strengths and weaknesses? *Journal of Intellectual Disability Research, 62*(7), 593–603. https://doi.org/10.1111/jir.12499.

Powell, D., Caban-Holt, A., Jicha, G., Robertson, W., Davis, R., Gold, B. T., et al. (2014). Frontal white matter integrity in adults with Down syndrome with and without dementia. *Neurobiology of Aging, 35*(7), 1562–1569. https://doi.org/10.1016/j.neurobiolaging.2014.01.137.

Prasher, V. P. (2005). *Alzheimer's disease and dementia in Down syndrome and intellectual disabilities*. Oxford: Milton Keynes: Radcliffe Publishing.

Prasher, V. P. (2018). *Neuropsychological assessments of dementia in Down syndrome and intellectual disabilities* (2nd ed.). UK: Springer.

Prasher, V. P., & Day, S. (1995). Brief report: Obsessive-compulsive disorder in adults with Down's syndrome. *Journal of Autism and Developmental Disorders, 25*(4), 453–458. https://doi.org/10.1007/BF02179379.

Prasher, V. P., Farrer, M. J., Kessling, A. M., Fisher, E. M., West, R. J., Barber, P. C., et al. (1998). Molecular mapping of Alzheimer-type dementia in Down's syndrome. *Annals of Neurology, 43*(3), 380–383. https://doi.org/10.1002/ana.410430316.

Prasher, V. P., Sajith, S. G., Rees, S. D., Patel, A., Tewari, S., Schupf, N., et al. (2008). Significant effect of APOE epsilon 4 genotype on the risk of dementia in Alzheimer's disease and mortality in persons with Down Syndrome. *International Journal of Geriatric Psychiatry, 23*(11), 1134–1140. https://doi.org/10.1002/GPS.2039.

Pulsifer, M. B., Evans, C. L., Hom, C., Krinsky-McHale, S. J., Silverman, W., Lai, F., et al. (2020). Language skills as a predictor of cognitive decline in adults with Down syndrome. *Alzheimer's & Dementia (Amsterdam), 12*(1), e12080. https://doi.org/10.1002/dad2.12080.

Rafii, M. S. (2020). Alzheimer's disease in Down syndrome: Progress in the design and conduct of drug prevention trials. *CNS Drugs, 34*(8), 785–794. https://doi.org/10.1007/s40263-020-00740-6.

Rafii, M. S., Donohue, M. C., Matthews, D. C., Muranevici, G., Ness, S., O'Bryant, S. E., et al. (2019). Plasma neurofilament light and Alzheimer's disease biomarkers in Down syndrome: Results from the Down syndrome biomarker initiative (DSBI). *Journal of Alzheimer's Disease, 70*(1), 131–138. https://doi.org/10.3233/JAD-190322.

Rafii, M. S., Lukic, A. S., Andrews, R. D., Brewer, J., Rissman, R. A., Strother, S. C., et al. (2017). PET imaging of tau pathology and relationship to amyloid, longitudinal MRI, and cognitive change in Down syndrome: Results from the Down syndrome biomarker initiative (DSBI). *Journal of Alzheimer's Disease, 60*(2), 439–450. https://doi.org/10.3233/JAD-170390.

Rafii, M. S., Wishnek, H., Brewer, J. B., Donohue, M. C., Ness, S., Mobley, W. C., et al. (2015). The down syndrome biomarker initiative (DSBI) pilot: Proof of concept for deep phenotyping of Alzheimer's disease biomarkers in down syndrome. *Frontiers in Behavioral Neuroscience, 9*, 239. https://doi.org/10.3389/fnbeh.2015.00239.

Randolph, C., Tierney, M. C., Mohr, E., & Chase, T. N. (1998). The repeatable battery for the assessment of neuropsychological status (RBANS): Preliminary clinical validity. *Journal of Clinical and Experimental Neuropsychology, 20*(3), 310–319. https://doi.org/10.1076/jcen.20.3.310.823.

Rosas, H. D., Hsu, E., Mercaldo, N. D., Lai, F., Pulsifer, M., Keator, D., et al. (2020). Alzheimer-related altered white matter microstructural integrity in Down syndrome: A model for sporadic AD? *Alzheimer's & Dementia (Amsterdam), 12*(1), e12040. https://doi.org/10.1002/dad2.12040.

Rossini, P. M., Di Iorio, R., Vecchio, F., Anfossi, M., Babiloni, C., Bozzali, M., et al. (2020). Early diagnosis of Alzheimer's disease: The role of biomarkers including advanced EEG signal analysis. Report from the IFCN-sponsored panel of experts. *Clinical Neurophysiology, 131*(6), 1287–1310. https://doi.org/10.1016/j.clinph.2020.03.003.

Rosso, M., Fremion, E., Santoro, S. L., Santoro, S. L., Oreskovic, N. M., Chitnis, T., et al. (2020). Down syndrome disintegrative disorder: A clinical regression syndrome of increasing importance. *Pediatrics, 145*(6). https://doi.org/10.1542/PEDS.2019-2939/76920.

Roth, M., Tym, E., Mountjoy, C. Q., Huppert, F. A., Hendrie, H., Verma, S., et al. (1986). CAMDEX. A standardized instrument for the diagnosis of mental disorder in the elderly with special reference to the early detection of dementia. *The British Journal of Psychiatry, 149*, 698–709. https://doi.org/10.1192/bjp.149.6.698.

Rubenstein, E., Hartley, S., & Bishop, L. (2020). Epidemiology of dementia and Alzheimer's disease in individuals With Down syndrome. *JAMA Neurology*, 77(2), 262–264. https://doi.org/10.1001/jamaneurol.2019.3666.

Saxton, J., Kastango, K. B., Hugonot-Diener, L., Boller, F., Verny, M., Sarles, C. E., et al. (2005). Development of a short form of the severe impairment battery. *The American Journal of Geriatric Psychiatry, 13*(11), 999–1005. https://doi.org/10.1176/appi.ajgp.13.11.999.

Schöll, M., Maass, A., Mattsson, N., Ashton, N. J., Blennow, K., Zetterberg, H., et al. (2019). Biomarkers for tau pathology. *Molecular and Cellular Neurosciences, 97*, 18. https://doi.org/10.1016/J.MCN.2018.12.001.

Sharma, R. A., Varga, A. W., Bubu, O. M., Pirraglia, E., Kam, K., Parekh, A., et al. (2018). Obstructive sleep apnea severity affects amyloid burden in cognitively normal elderly. A longitudinal study. *American Journal of Respiratory and Critical Care Medicine, 197*(7). https://doi.org/10.1164/rccm.201704-0704OC.

Shultz, J., Aman, M., Kelbley, T., LeClear Wallace, C., Burt, D. B., Primeaux-Hart, S., et al. (2004). Evaluation of screening tools for dementia in older adults with mental retardation. *American Journal of Mental Retardation, 109*(2), 98–110. https://doi.org/10.1352/0895-8017(2004)109<98:eostfd>2.0.co;2.

Silverman, W., Krinsky-McHale, S. J., Lai, F., Diana Rosas, H., Hom, C., Doran, E., et al. (2021). Evaluation of the National Task Group-Early Detection Screen for Dementia: Sensitivity to 'mild cognitive impairment' in adults with Down syndrome. *Journal of Applied Research in Intellectual Disabilities, 34*(3), 905–915. https://doi.org/10.1111/jar.12849.

Sinai, A., Mokrysz, C., Bernal, J., Bohnen, I., Bonell, S., Courtenay, K., et al. (2018). Predictors of age of diagnosis and survival of Alzheimer's disease in Down syndrome. *Journal of Alzheimer's Disease, 61*(2). https://doi.org/10.3233/JAD-170624.

Sparrow, S., Cicchetti, D., & Saulnier, C. (2016). *Vineland Adaptive Behavior Scales—Third edition (Vineland-3)*. Circle Pines, MN: American Guidance Service.

Sparrow, S. S., & Cicchetti, D. V. (1989). *The Vineland adaptive behavior scales*. Allyn & Bacon.

Sparrow, S. S., Cicchetti, D. V., & Balla, D. A. (2005). *Vineland Adaptive Behavior Scales—Second edition (Vineland–II)*. Circle Pines, MN: American Guidance Service.

Startin, C. M., Hamburg, S., Hithersay, R., Al-Janabi, T., Mok, K. Y., Hardy, J., et al. (2019). Cognitive markers of preclinical and prodromal Alzheimer's disease in Down syndrome. *Alzheimer's & Dementia, 15*(2), 245–257. https://doi.org/10.1016/j.jalz.2018.08.009.

Startin, C. M., Hamburg, S., Hithersay, R., Davies, A., Rodger, E., Aggarwal, N., et al. (2016). The LonDownS adult cognitive assessment to study cognitive abilities and decline in Down syndrome. *Wellcome Open Research, 1*, 11. https://doi.org/10.12688/wellcomeopenres.9961.1.

Strydom, A., Dickinson, M. J., Shende, S., Pratico, D., & Walker, Z. (2009). Oxidative stress and cognitive ability in adults with Down syndrome. *Progress in Neuro-psychopharmacology & Biological Psychiatry, 33*(1), 76–80. https://doi.org/10.1016/j.pnpbp.2008.10.006.

Tassé, M. J., Navas Macho, P., Havercamp, S. M., Benson, B. A., Allain, D. C., Manickam, K., et al. (2016). Psychiatric conditions prevalent among adults with Down syndrome. *Journal of Policy and Practice in Intellectual Disabilities*, *13*, 173–180. https://doi.org/10.1111/jppi.12156.

Teipel, S. J., & Hampel, H. (2006). Neuroanatomy of Down syndrome in vivo: A model of preclinical Alzheimer's disease. *Behavior Genetics*, *36*(3), 405–415. https://doi.org/10.1007/s10519-006-9047-x.

Trois, M. S., Capone, G. T., Lutz, J. A., Melendres, M. C., Schwartz, A. R., Collop, N. A., et al. (2009). Obstructive sleep apnea in adults with Down syndrome. *Journal of Clinical Sleep Medicine*, *5*(4), 317–323. https://doi.org/10.5664/jcsm.27541.

Tromp, D., Dufour, A., Lithfous, S., Pebayle, T., & Després, O. (2015). Episodic memory in normal aging and Alzheimer's disease: Insights from imaging and behavioral studies. *Aging Research Reviews*, *24*, 232–262. https://doi.org/10.1016/J.ARR.2015.08.006.

Tudorascu, D. L., Hartley, S. L., Zammit, M. D., Cody, K. A., Laymon, C. M., Minhas, D. S., et al. (2021). Associations between cognition, Aβ, and tau in adults with Down syndrome. *ALZ*. https://alz.confex.com/alz/2021/meetingapp.cgi/Paper/52887.

Tudorascu, D. L., Laymon, C. M., Zammit, M., Minhas, D. S., Anderson, S. J., Ellison, P. A., et al. (2020). Relationship of amyloid beta and neurofibrillary tau deposition in neurodegeneration in aging Down syndrome (NiAD) study at baseline. *Alzheimer's & Dementia (New York)*, *6*(1), e12096. https://doi.org/10.1002/trc2.12096.

Tyrrell, J., Cosgrave, M., McCarron, M., McPherson, J., Calvert, J., Kelly, A., et al. (2001). Dementia in people with Down's syndrome. *International Journal of Geriatric Psychiatry*, *16*(12), 1168–1174. https://doi.org/10.1002/gps.502.

Urv, T. K., Zigman, W. B., & Silverman, W. (2010). Psychiatric symptoms in adults with Down syndrome and Alzheimer's disease. *American Journal of Intellectual & Developmental Disabilities*, *115*(4), 265–276. https://doi.org/10.1352/1944-7558-115.4.265.

Vega, A. (1969). Use of purdue pegboard and finger tapping performance as a rapid screening test for brain damage. *Journal of Clinical Psychology*, *25*(3), 255–258. https://doi.org/10.1002/1097-4679(196907)25:3<255::aid-jclp2270250306>3.0.co;2-v.

Vicari, S., Pontillo, M., & Armando, M. (2013). Neurodevelopmental and psychiatric issues in Down's syndrome: Assessment and intervention. *Psychiatric Genetics*, *23*(3), 95–107. https://doi.org/10.1097/YPG.0b013e32835fe426.

Vilaplana, E., Videla, L., Carmona-Iragui, M., Benejam, B., Barroeta, I., Fernandez, S., et al. (2020). The effect of APOE ε4 in Alzheimer's disease biomarkers in Down syndrome. *ALZ*. https://alz.confex.com/alz/20amsterdam/meetingapp.cgi/Paper/48122.

Wallace, E. R., Harp, J. P., Van Pelt, K. L., Koehl, L. M., Caban-Holt, A. M., Anderson-Mooney, A. J., et al. (2021). Identifying dementia in Down syndrome with the severe impairment battery, brief praxis test and Dementia scale for people with learning disabilities. *Journal of Intellectual Disability Research*, *65*, 1085–1096. https://doi.org/10.1111/jir.12901.

Walpert, M., Zaman, S., & Holland, A. (2021). A systematic review of unexplained early regression in adolescents and adults with Down syndrome. *Brain Sciences*, *11*(9), 1197. https://doi.org/10.3390/BRAINSCI11091197.

Walsh, D. M., Finwall, J., Touchette, P. E., McGregor, M. R., Fernandez, G. E., Lott, I. T., et al. (2007). Rapid assessment of severe cognitive impairment in individuals with developmental disabilities. *Journal of Intellectual Disability Research*, *51*(2), 91–100. https://doi.org/10.1111/j.1365-2788.2006.00853.x.

Wechsler, D. (1974). *Wechsler intelligence scale for children—Revised edition*. San Antonio, TX: The Psychological Corporation.

Wechsler, D. (2004). *Wechsler memory scale-fourth edition: Administration and scoring manual*. San Antonio: The Psychological Corporation.

WHO | Life expectancy. (2018). *World Health Organization*. http://www.who.int/gho/mortality_burden_disease/life_tables/situation_trends_text/en/.

Wiseman, F. K., Al-Janabi, T., Hardy, J., Karmiloff-Smith, A., Nizetic, D., Tybulewicz, V. L. J. J., et al. (2015). A genetic cause of Alzheimer's disease: Mechanistic insights from Down syndrome. *Nature Reviews Neuroscience, 16*(9), 564–574. https://doi.org/10.1038/nrn3983.

Wisniewski, K., & Hill, A. L. (1985). Clinical aspects of dementia in mental retardation and developmental disabilities. *Aging and Developmental Disabilities, 195–207*.

Wisniewski, K., Wisniewski, H., & Wen, G. (1985). Occurrence of neuropathological changes and dementia of Alzheimer's disease in Down's syndrome. *Annals of Neurology, 17*(3), 278–282. https://doi.org/10.1002/ANA.410170310.

Yamazaki, Y., Zhao, N., Caulfield, T. R., Liu, C. C., & Bu, G. (2019). Apolipoprotein E and Alzheimer's disease: Pathobiology and targeting strategies. *Nature Reviews. Neurology, 15*(9), 501–518. https://doi.org/10.1038/s41582-019-0228-7.

Zigman, W. B., Krinsky-McHale, S. J., Schupf, N., Urv, T. K., & Silverman, W. (2018). Adaptive behavior change, mild cognitive impairment and dementia in Down Syndrome: Case classification using the adaptive behavior scale. In V. P. Prasher (Ed.), *Neuropsychological assessments of dementia in Down syndrome and intellectual disabilities* (pp. 99–122). London: Springer International Publishing.

Zigman, W. B., & Lott, I. T. (2007). Alzheimer's disease in Down syndrome: Neurobiology and risk. *Mental Retardation and Developmental Disabilities Research Reviews, 13*(3), 237–246. https://doi.org/10.1002/mrdd.20163.

Zimmerli, E., & Devenny, D. (1995). *Cued recall as a screen for dementia in the MR population, Gatlinburg Conference for Intellectual and Developmental Disabilities, Gatlinburg, TN.*

CHAPTER SEVEN

Measurement of social skills treatment outcome in autism: Moving beyond informant report and considering diversity

Christine T. Moody[a], Hillary K. Schiltz[a], Allison B. Ratto[b], Amanda C. Gulsrud[a], and Elizabeth A. Laugeson[a]
[a]Department of Psychiatry and Biobehavioral Sciences, Semel Institute for Neuroscience and Human Behavior, University of California, Los Angeles, Los Angeles, CA, United States
[b]Children's National Hospital, Washington, DC, United States

Contents

International Review of Research in Developmental Disabilities, Volume 62
ISSN 2211-6095
https://doi.org/10.1016/bs.irrdd.2022.05.007

Abstract

Social skills interventions (SSIs) are one of the most commonly utilized treatment approaches for autistic individuals across the lifespan, with the goal of mitigating negative impacts of the social communication differences associated with autism, including peer rejection, social isolation, and poor mental health. Thorough and accurate assessment of the efficacy of SSIs is critical in this population, given its widespread use in the autism community. The current paper serves as a scoping review of outcome measurement in SSI research in autistic populations. The strengths and limitations of measurement methodologies (e.g., questionnaires, observational measures) are considered, with commonly used outcome measures discussed in detail, including psychometric properties when available. The role of diversity factors, including race/ethnicity and gender, in relation to outcome measurement is reviewed. Overall, results of this review indicate a need for continued research in measurement to refine the field's ability to assess treatment response following SSIs. In particular, a greater understanding of how existing measures operate in autistic samples is needed. Further, given the historical heavy reliance on and limitations of questionnaire measures in SSI research, multi-method, multi-informant assessment approaches to outcome measurement are indicated for future SSI research.

Autism spectrum disorder (ASD) is a neurodevelopmental disorder characterized primarily by differences in social communication and restricted, repetitive behaviors. Common social communication differences in autism include difficulties utilizing and comprehending nonverbal and nonliteral language elements (e.g., gestures, eye contact, facial expressions, tone of voice), challenges with reciprocity and contingency in back-and-forth communication or play, and struggles understanding others' perspectives and emotions (American Psychiatric Association, 2013). Notably, restricted, repetitive behaviors and sensory differences, the other diagnostic component of autism (American Psychiatric Association, 2013), can also significantly impact social interactions and functioning (Tsai et al., 2020).

Following from these differences, autistic individuals often benefit from support in their pursuit of healthy social relationships, such as friendships and romantic relationships. Despite a common misconception that autistic people lack social motivation and prefer to be alone, there is growing research evidence that many people on the spectrum desire social connection and relationships—but may have difficulty achieving this goal (Locke, Ishijima, Kasari, & London, 2010; O'Hagan & Hebron, 2017). Recent research reviews and theoretical articles, incorporating qualitative accounts from autistic people themselves, have challenged the underlying assumption that autistic people are not motivated by belonging and connection (Jaswal & Akhtar, 2019; Mitchell, Sheppard, & Cassidy, 2021). Indeed, most autistic adolescents describe making and having friends as a top priority (Cresswell, Hinch, & Cage, 2019). Autistic adults frequently report "masking" and "camouflaging" their autistic traits to avoid rejection and develop social relationships (Cook, Hull, Crane, & Mandy, 2021). Further, evidence suggests that social factors strongly impact the well-being of autistic people; peer rejection and loneliness correlate with poor mental health and increased suicidality in this population (Hedley, Uljarević, Foley, Richdale, & Trollor, 2018; Rodriguez, Drastal, & Hartley, 2021), while social support emerges as a prominent predictor of quality of life in autistic adults, over and above disability characteristics (Renty & Roeyers, 2006).

Autistic traits have been directly linked to lower peer acceptance and greater loneliness (Sari, Luijk, Prinzie, van IJzendoorn, & Jansen, 2021; Schiltz, McVey, et al., 2021; Schiltz, Magnus, et al., 2021). In a large meta-analysis of school-aged boys on the autism spectrum, results revealed that although autistic youth were able to make friends, they had significantly fewer friends than neurotypical youth and their friendships were reported be of significantly lower quality (Mendelson, Gates, & Lerner, 2016). Unfortunately, evidence suggest that after exiting high school and in the absence of the structured social opportunities it provides, adults on the autism spectrum experience increased social isolation, with 28% of autistic adults being completely socially isolated (i.e., never see friends, friends never call, and never invited to social activities; Orsmond, Shattuck, Cooper, Sterzing, & Anderson, 2013). Social communication differences also significantly predict other important outcomes, including post-secondary educational attainment and obtaining employment (Nasamran, Witmer, & Los, 2017).

To help prevent and disrupt these negative outcomes associated with the social communication differences in autism, interventions are necessary. In this review, we will be focusing on outcome measurement in the predominant intervention method to date: social skills interventions (SSIs). The review will include a brief overview of social skills intervention methods and considerations, followed by a more comprehensive summary of outcome measurement methodologies. The strengths and limitations of various measures will be discussed, as well as what is known about how measures operate within diverse populations in the autism community.

1. Social skills intervention

SSIs typically aim to support autistic individuals in learning and navigating social norms, such as conversation skills (e.g., starting conversations), perspective taking, nonverbal communication skills, use of humor, and play skills (e.g., taking turns, good sportsmanship; Moody & Laugeson, 2020). The most common and well-studied SSI methods use didactic instruction of ecologically valid social skills, modeling, behavioral practice with coaching (by therapists, parents, and/or peers), and generalization homework assignments, within a small group treatment modality (Moody & Laugeson, 2020). However, there are also SSIs that utilize implicit instruction methods, through certain social group activities or peer-mediated supports (e.g., Corbett et al., 2019; Kasari, Rotheram-Fuller, Locke, & Gulsrud, 2012). Meta-analytic results have demonstrated that SSIs are effective at improving social communication outcomes in youth and young adults on the autism spectrum (Gates, Kang, & Lerner, 2017; Wolstencroft et al., 2018). However, these meta-analyses note limited generalization across contexts, as evidenced by no significant improvement in teacher-reported outcomes and attenuated effects in parent-reported outcomes. Additionally, improvements observed in self-report measures are often limited to changes in social knowledge, and not changes in applied social behavior (Gates et al., 2017).

Although established as an evidence-based practice in the treatment of autism, it is also important to note that SSIs are relatively new, with the vast majority of studies published in the last twenty years (Hume et al., 2021). Though there is more to learn and an ongoing need to refine SSIs, they are a potentially powerful tool to assist autistic people in reaching their social goals. With an increased call for autistic voices to be involved in intervention design and measurement, some have voiced concerns that SSIs contribute to the burden of having to camouflage autistic traits by teaching social norms of a neurotypical world (Monahan, Freedman, Pini, & Lloyd, 2021). We believe that alternative approaches to improve acceptance of neurodiversity within society are essential, as will be discussed later in this review; however, given that such cultural change takes time, it is also essential that supports are provided *now* to empower autistic people to form the relational connections that they desire and that contribute to their well-being as a marginalized population. That being said, SSIs should only be delivered to autistic individuals who *want* to participate in such programs; researchers might consider motivation to participate in SSI as an inclusion criterion when determining eligibility for treatment, as is the case with some evidence-based curricula (E.A. Laugeson, 2013; E. Laugeson, 2017; Laugeson & Frankel, 2011).

Beyond assessing motivation for participation, SSI programs must also continually adapt in a number of ways. Social skills are highly culturally laden and social norms can shift over time and across generations. This fact requires social skills curricula to be rigorously cross-culturally validated when being used in different cultural contexts and to conduct ongoing research into socially normative behavior to update curricula (e.g., changes in dating behavior following increased utilization of online dating applications, need for video-conferencing social skills following rapid uptick in use due to COVID-19 pandemic). There is also a need for adaptations across the lifespan and across social contexts. For example, ecologically valid social behavior among friends may not be considered ecologically valid within the workplace. Similarly, different sets of social skills are needed as children transition into adolescence as the primary social milieu moves from play to conversation and electronic communication. Such adaptations are not only necessary in social skills curricula, but also in measurement of success in SSIs for autistic individuals. With developmental and cultural shifts, social skills outcome measurement must shift too.

2. Outcome measurement

Valid and reliable measurement is at the heart of good science and intervention research. Empirically-based interventions rely upon psychometrically robust instruments that can capture the intended construct and are sensitive to change. In autism research, evidence suggests that measurement is particularly complex, such that tools developed for neurotypical people may not function in the same way for this population (Cassidy et al., 2020; Schiltz, Magnus, et al., 2021) and may be impacted by autism-specific factors (Schiltz & Magnus, 2021). Considering this, particular care needs to be taken when selecting outcome measures and, in turn, interpreting intervention effects among autistic youth and adults. Various measurement modalities have been used to assess treatment response in SSIs, each of which will be covered in detail in this chapter: (1) questionnaires tapping into the perspectives of caregivers and autistic individuals, (2) observational measures assessing in-vivo social skills, (3) in-depth qualitative interviews, and (4) neurobiological indices measuring brain-based and physiological changes. Given the measurement complexities in autism research and inherent limitations and strengths of each modality, as described in Table 1, a multi-method and multi-informant approach may be

Table 1 Strengths and limitations of measurement modalities used in SSI research.

Modality	Strengths	Limitations
Questionnaires	• Parallel versions (self, caregiver, other informant report) capture multiple perspectives • Easy to administer, low time and effort investment of researchers • Able to measure a variety of constructs including primary (e.g., social skills knowledge) and secondary outcomes (e.g., mental health) • Often include presence of standardization samples, norms, and/or empirically derived cut-off scores	• Caregiver and other informants are often limited to reporting upon observable behavior • Concerns about accessibility of self-reported instruments (e.g., confusing vocabulary and wording) • Many measures have not been validated in autism samples • Often unblinded to treatment condition, potential bias in reporters involved in treatment • Often discrepancies emerge between reporters
Neurobiological indices	• Provides objective quantitative information • Assesses potential mechanisms of change (e.g., neural plasticity)	• Lack of clear biomarkers for autism and related conditions in autism • Can be difficult to interpret due to confounding sample characteristics
Social cognitive assessments	• Often administered by computer or clinician • Offers objective evaluation of correct or incorrect responses • Assesses specific abilities that may be targeted by SSI	• Changes in specific social cognitive abilities do not always generalize to broader social functioning outcomes
Qualitative	• Captures more nuanced social information and/or subtle changes • At times, produces unexpected insights due to flexibility in interview structure • Creates space for stakeholders to share experiences	• Less well-controlled: susceptible to bias (e.g., during interview, theme extraction) and individual differences (e.g., response style of participants) • Time-intensive to administer, transcribe, and extract themes • Can be difficult to analyze statistically
Observational	• Blind to treatment condition • Assesses generalization of skills • Assesses change in specific behaviors	• Captures snapshot of behavior which may be context specific (i.e., time and setting) • Time and labor intensive to administer, train researchers, and code interactions

particularly useful for SSI intervention research. However, very few SSI research studies have employed such methods. Considering this gap, it is important to have a comprehensive understanding of various limitations and strengths of different types of outcome measures used in SSI research, which is the impetus for the current review.

3. Questionnaires

Many SSI studies rely solely upon questionnaire-based measures that capture the perspectives of caregivers, other informants (e.g., teachers), or the participants themselves. Within SSI research, questionnaires have been utilized to capture a variety of constructs ranging from aspects of social competence, to feelings of loneliness, to secondary outcomes such as mental health. While questionnaires are cost-effective, relatively easy to administer, and provide important information about participant's perspectives, the shortcomings of such instruments are equally important to consider with respect to both caregiver/other informant and self-reported outcomes. For example, caregivers and other informants are limited to reporting upon externally observed behaviors (e.g., has difficulty engaging in back-and-forth conversation) and experiences (e.g., hosting a get-together with another child) and may have limited knowledge about their child's internal experiences (e.g., desire for friendships) unless these have been vocalized. Further complicating use of caregiver-report questionnaires in autism research is the overlap between core features of autism (e.g., social communication differences) and symptoms associated with co-occurring mental health concerns (e.g., social anxiety, depression), which may impact accurate measurement of each construct (McVey et al., 2018; Schiltz & Magnus, 2021). Additionally, multiple studies point to significant discrepancies between caregiver and self-reported questionnaires in autism on various domains, including social skills (Lerner, Calhoun, Mikami, & De Los Reyes, 2012), quality of life (Sheldrick, Neger, Shipman, & Perrin, 2012), internalizing symptoms (Burrows et al., 2018), and empathy (Johnson, Filliter, & Murphy, 2009), with some evidence for better agreement on externalizing constructs (Stratis & Lecavalier, 2015). As such, these studies highlight potential differences in the perceptions of parents and autistic people when reporting on these constructs.

On the other hand, self-reported questionnaires have historically been underutilized (Kim & Lecavalier, 2021) due to concerns regarding difficulties identifying and conveying internal experiences (Kinnaird, Stewart, & Tchanturia, 2019). More recently, however, evidence suggests that self-report measures can be valid and useful in autistic samples (Kim & Lecavalier, 2021; Ozsivadjian, Hibberd, & Hollocks, 2014; Schiltz, McIntyre, Swain-Lerro, Zajic, & Mundy, 2017), which is accompanied by a heightened recognition of the need to elevate autistic perspectives and voices in autism research (Fletcher-Watson et al., 2019). While use of self-report in autism research is increasing, unfortunately, many self-reported questionnaires remain inaccessible by autistic individuals across the spectrum due to confusing vocabulary, complex sentence structure, lack of clarity in response options, ableist language, and failure to assess autism-specific dimensions of constructs (Nicolaidis et al., 2020). Although there are recent discussions regarding advancing measurement in autism research (Benevides & Cassidy, 2020) and empirical studies evaluating (Williams, Everaert, & Gotham, 2021), adapting (Nicolaidis et al., 2020), and developing (Cassidy et al., 2020) self-reported questionnaires that are valid for use with autistic youth and adults, much work remains to continue to improve measurement using self-reported questionnaires in autism (Kim & Lecavalier, 2021). In particular, studies involving rigorous psychometric analyses (e.g., differential item functioning analyses, validity analyses, test-retest reliability) in large samples across a range of constructs (e.g., friendship quality, loneliness, etc.), among adults, and focused on those with lower cognitive abilities are greatly needed (Kim & Lecavalier, 2021).

As one of the most used outcome measurement methodologies, this review will organize various questionnaires based on the construct being measured. Constructs captured by questionnaires range widely, including social skills and responsiveness, social knowledge, social engagement, friendship characteristics, loneliness, empathy, and mental health. The psychometric evidence for questionnaires vary, with some questionnaires being developed and psychometrically evaluated specifically within autistic samples while others were developed for the general population and have subsequently been used in autism research.

3.1 Social competence

Primary outcome measures of SSIs center upon aspects of social competence. Social competence is multi-dimensional and includes social skills, social responsiveness, social knowledge, and social contact, among other domains. We will discuss questionnaires used to assess each of these components, highlighting relevant strengths and limitations. Of note, common limitations across all these instruments include the unmasked nature of caregiver-report and self-report. Thus, independent teacher report questionnaires from those unaffiliated with SSI and masked to the conditions under investigation are uniquely positioned to obtain less-biased information. However, the availability and access to caregivers or teachers to provide informant reports may be more limited in adulthood.

Social Skills. The *Social Skills Rating System* (*SSRS*; Gresham & Elliott, 1990) and its revised version, the *Social Skills Improvement System (SSIS) Rating Scales* (Gresham & Elliot, 2008), are questionnaires that have been commonly used in SSI research (see Soares et al., 2021, for a review). Given that this measure is normed up to age 18, most studies have utilized this measure with children (e.g., Chester, Richdale, & McGillivray, 2019; Dekker et al., 2019; Frankel et al., 2010; Tripathi, Estabillo, Moody, & Laugeson, 2021) and adolescents (e.g., Laugeson, Frankel, Gantman, Dillon, & Mogil, 2012; Laugeson, Frankel, Mogil, & Dillon, 2009; Matthews et al., 2018; Schohl et al., 2014); however, some studies have also utilized SSIS raw scores with young adults (e.g., Gantman, Kapp, Orenski, & Laugeson, 2012; Laugeson, Gantman, Kapp, Orenski, & Ellingsen, 2015; McVey et al., 2016). A strength of these questionnaires is offering parallel versions for parent, teacher, and self-report, which allows researchers to capture multiple perspectives, as well as different norms based on the child's age to adjust for developmental appropriateness. The revised version (i.e., *SSIS*) covers a range of constructs including communication, cooperation, assertion, engagement, responsibility, empathy, and self-control, as well as areas of problem behavior (i.e., externalizing, internalizing, hyperactivity). Each item is rated on both frequency and importance using Likert-type response options. Across informant versions, high internal consistency and test-retest reliability of the *SSRS* (α's ranging from .73 to .94; *r*'s ranging from .65 to .87) and *SSIS* (α's ranging from .94 to .97; *r*'s ranging from .71 to .81) have been found (Gresham, Elliott, Vance, & Cook, 2011). Positively, differential item functioning analyses (DIF) of the *SSIS* revealed little evidence for DIF across gender, race, and ethnicity (Gresham & Elliot, 2008).

Social Responsiveness. The *Social Responsiveness Scale* (*SRS*; Constantino & Gruber, 2005) and its second edition, the *SRS-2* (Constantino & Gruber, 2012), are 65-item questionnaires that have been widely used to assess social communication and repetitive behaviors associated with autism in clinical trials of SSI among children (e.g., Freitag et al., 2016; Koning, Magill-Evans, Volden, & Dick, 2013; Tripathi et al., 2021), adolescents (e.g., Laugeson et al., 2012; Matthews et al., 2018; Schohl et al., 2014; Vernon, Miller, Ko, Barrett, & McGarry, 2018), and adults (e.g., Ashman, Banks, Philip,

Walley, & Stanfield, 2017; Baker-Ericzén et al., 2018; Cunningham, Sperry, Brady, Peluso, & Pauletti, 2016; Gantman et al., 2012; Hillier, Fish, Cloppert, & Beversdorf, 2007; Laugeson et al., 2015; McVey et al., 2016; Sung et al., 2019) on the autism spectrum. Similar to the *SSRS/SSIS*, the *SRS* and *SRS-2* offer parallel versions for parents/caregivers and teachers as well as a self-report version that can be completed by adults. The *SRS-2* yields T-scores based on age, reporter, and gender. Psychometric evaluation, especially in terms of structural validity, of the *SRS* and *SRS-2* have revealed somewhat mixed evidence. Early psychometric exploration indicated a one-factor solution (Constantino et al., 2004), while subsequent research demonstrated good fit of a two-factor structure consisting of social communication/interaction and restricted/repetitive behavior index scores (Frazier et al., 2014). Although there are five subscales including social awareness, social cognition, social communication, social motivation, and autistic mannerisms, they are "treatment subscales" (i.e., for treatment planning or intervention outcome) and do not have psychometric support (Constantino & Gruber, 2005; Wigham et al., 2012). Evidence for strict measurement invariance was found across sex and reporter (self vs. other and child vs. adult) and for partial scalar invariance across age (Frazier et al., 2014). Notably, metric measurement invariance was not found for ASD diagnosis (i.e., non-ASD siblings and ASD-affected siblings), indicating that the factor loadings (i.e., associations between the item packets and factor) are not equivalent across ASD and non-ASD groups (Frazier et al., 2014). The lack of invariance across ASD diagnosis has implications for the use of the SRS-2 in studies that utilize both neurotypical and autistic participants; this concern is fortunately less applicable to SSI research, which usually includes autistic participants only.

Regarding reliability, the current *SRS-2* demonstrates excellent internal consistency in autism and other clinical samples (parent $\alpha = .95$), temporal stability (parent $r = .88$–$.90$), and strong diagnostic performance (AUC = .97; sensitivity = .84–.93; specificity = .91–.94; Constantino & Gruber, 2012). The *SRS-2* has support for validity via correlations with other measures of autism-related features, such as the Social Communication Questionnaire ($r = .68$), although associations with observation and interview tend to not be as strong (e.g., *ADI-R* $r = .59$; *ADOS* $r = .48$; Charman et al., 2007). Notably, research has highlighted concerns regarding the influence of individual factors and characteristics such as behavior problems, language, anxiety, and cognitive abilities on *SRS* scores (Havdahl et al., 2016; Hus, Bishop, Gotham, Huerta, & Lord, 2013a; South, Carr, Stephenson, Maisel, & Cox, 2017; Zou et al., 2018), although there is debate about the interpretation and meaning of these associations (Constantino & Frazier, 2013; Hus, Bishop, Gotham, Huerta, & Lord, 2013b).

Social Knowledge. The *Test of Adolescent Social Skills Knowledge* (*TASSK*; Laugeson & Frankel, 2011) and modified version for young adults, the *Test of Young Adult Social Skills Knowledge* (*TYASSK*; Laugeson, 2017) were developed to evaluate social skills knowledge gained from PEERS for Adolescents and PEERS for Young Adults, respectively, which are evidence-based and well-established SSIs (Gantman et al., 2012; Laugeson & Frankel, 2011; McVey et al., 2016; Zheng, Kim, Salzman, Ankenman, & Bent, 2021). These assessments are criterion-based, assessing retention of knowledge and concepts that are taught within the curriculum. While a strength of these measures is the range of topics covered (i.e., two items derived from each key component of the intervention), the resulting multidimensionality may contribute to the low internal consistencies identified for the *TASSK* ($\alpha = .56$; Laugeson et al., 2009) and the *TYASSK* ($\alpha = .22$; McVey et al., 2016). Studies of other interventions have developed or adapted similar questionnaires to evaluate social skills knowledge gained from the intervention (e.g., Koning et al., 2013; Thomeer et al., 2012); however, these types of measures are also limited by their assessment of knowledge, which may differ from actual social behavior in context (i.e., generalized use of skills).

Social Engagement. The frequency and quality of social engagement has been assessed via the *Quality of Play Questionnaire* (*QPQ*; Frankel & Myatt, 2003; Laugeson & Frankel, 2011) which was subsequently adapted for older children as the *Quality of Socialization Questionnaire* (*QSQ*; Laugeson, 2017). The *QPQ and QSQ* assess the number of hosted and invited playdates or get-togethers, respectively, and the level of conflict during these interactions. These measures have both parent and self-report versions. Measuring social engagement is both concrete and observable, which is likely to improve validity and inter-rater reliability (i.e., agreement between parent and self-report). Further, such a measure may arguably be more representative of true social connection and friendships, often the ultimate goal of SSIs, than questionnaires focused on social behavior (e.g., frequency in which an individual greets others) or social skills knowledge.

3.2 Friendship

Some SSIs specifically teach social skills with an eye toward developing and maintaining friendships (e.g., PEERS; Laugeson, 2017; Laugeson & Frankel, 2011). As such, the *Friendship Qualities Scale* (*FQS*; Bukowski, Hoza, &

Boivin, 1994) has been used in SSI research to explore effects on the quality (e.g., closeness, security, conflict) of a close friendship (Laugeson et al., 2009; Schohl et al., 2014). The *FQS* has often been used in autism research to better understand the nature of friendship in autistic youth (Petrina, Carter, & Stephenson, 2014). Although it has robust psychometric properties in neurotypical samples (Bukowski et al., 1994), the FQS has yet to be validated in autism, although it has been used frequently to measure friendship quality in this population (Bottema-Beutel, Malloy, Cuda, Kim, & MacEvoy, 2019; Calder, Hill, & Pellicano, 2013; Locke et al., 2010). The *FQS* has shown sensitivity to treatment effects (Laugeson et al., 2009), although another study did not show significant change in the *FQS* across SSI (Schohl et al., 2014).

3.3 Loneliness

Loneliness refers to a negative emotional experience or discomfort due to a discrepancy between someone's desired social connections and actual experiences (Perlman, Peplau, & Goldston, 1984). As such, feeling lonely and being alone are not one in the same (Cacioppo, Grippo, London, Goossens, & Cacioppo, 2015). Higher levels of loneliness are reported by autistic youth and adults compared to neurotypical people (Bauminger, Shulman, & Agam, 2003; Ee et al., 2019) and are thought to partly underlie mental health challenges in this population (Schiltz, McVey, et al., 2021). Among children and adolescents, the *Children's Loneliness and Social Dissatisfaction Scale* (*CLS*; Asher, Hymel, & Renshaw, 1984) and *Revised UCLA Loneliness Scale* (Russell, Peplau, & Cutrona, 1980) have been used as outcome measures of SSI and have demonstrated significant change across intervention (Frankel et al., 2010; Matthews et al., 2018; Rabin, Israel-Yaacov, Laugeson, Mor-Snir, & Golan, 2018). The *Social Emotional Loneliness Scale for Adults* (*SELSA*; DiTommaso & Spinner, 1993) has been used in SSI studies of autistic adults and shown sensitivity to intervention in one study (Gantman et al., 2012), although no change in another (McVey et al., 2016). While these instruments have demonstrated adequate psychometric properties in neurotypical samples, none are designed to capture dimensions of loneliness that may be unique to autistic youth or adults or have been psychometrically evaluated in this population, possibly calling into question the validity of these measures of loneliness in autism research.

3.4 Empathy

There is common "mis-characterization of autistic people as lacking empathy" (Fletcher-Watson & Bird, 2020). Given the many steps involved in expressing empathy (i.e., noticing another's feelings, correctly interpreting their feelings, feeling empathy, and responding empathetically), one might argue that empathy among autistic people may be underestimated due to the neurotypical societal norms associated with empathetic responding (Fletcher-Watson & Bird, 2020). The *Empathy Quotient* (*EQ*; Baron-Cohen & Wheelwright, 2004) has been commonly used to measure empathy in SSI studies with autistic adults and shows some evidence for sensitivity to change (Cunningham et al., 2016; Gantman et al., 2012; Hillier et al., 2007; Laugeson et al., 2015; McVey et al., 2016). The *EQ* has been found to have excellent reliability including high internal consistency ($\alpha = .92$) and test-retest reliability ($r = .97$; Baron-Cohen & Wheelwright, 2004). Regarding validity, the *EQ* has shown to have good concurrent validity via correlations with the *FQ* (*Friendship Questionnaire*; Baron-Cohen & Wheelwright, 2004) ($r = .59$, $P < .001$) and an inverse association with the *AQ* (*Autism Spectrum Quotient*; Baron-Cohen, Wheelwright, Hill, Raste, & Plumb, 2001; Baron-Cohen, Wheelwright, Skinner, Martin, & Clubley, 2001) ($r = -.56$). The *EQ* has been found to have a three-factor solution—cognitive empathy (intellectual understanding or appreciation of another's affective state), emotional reactivity (tendency to have an emotional reaction to other's mental states), and social skills (Lawrence, Shaw, Baker, Baron-Cohen, & David, 2004; Muncer & Ling, 2006).

3.5 Mental health

Mental health concerns including anxiety and depression are highly prevalent among autistic youth and adults (Hollocks, Lerh, Magiati, Meiser-Stedman, & Brugha, 2019; Lai et al., 2019). Evidence indicates robust links between social functioning and mental health (McVey et al., 2018), and as such, studies have explored secondary effects of SSIs on anxiety (e.g., McVey et al., 2016; Schohl et al., 2014), depression (Schiltz, McVey, Barrington, et al., 2018; Schiltz, McVey, Dolan, et al., 2018; Yoo et al., 2014), and suicidality (Schiltz, McVey, Barrington, et al., 2018; Schiltz, McVey, Dolan, et al., 2018). Given the interplay between autism features and mental health symptoms, disentangling these constructs and ensuring precise and accurate measurement of mental health in autism samples is imperative.

Depression and Suicidality. Multiple instruments have been used to measure depression as an outcome of SSI for autistic individuals. Two self-report instruments, the Children's Depression Inventory (*CDI*; Kovacs, 1985) and Depression Self-Rating Scale for Children (*DSRS-C*; Birleson, Hudson, Buchanan, & Wolff, 1987), have been used among adolescents; the *CDI* demonstrated improvements in depression and suicidality (based on one item) across SSI (Schiltz, McVey, Barrington, et al., 2018; Schiltz, McVey, Dolan, et al., 2018; Yoo et al., 2014), but the *DSRS-C* did not (Yamada et al., 2020). In autistic adults, self-report on the *Beck Depression Inventory* (*BDI-II*; Beck, Steer, & Brown, 1996) and *Patient Health Questionnaire-9* (*PHQ-9*; Spitzer et al., 1999) have been used in SSI studies. However, only the *BDI-II* (Hillier, Fish, Siegel, & Beversdorf, 2011), and not the *PHQ-9* (Connor, Sung, Strain, Zeng, & Fabrizi, 2020; Morgan, Leatzow, Clark, & Siller, 2014), has shown significant improvement after SSI. No questionnaires specifically assessing suicidality have been used as outcome measures of SSI in autism.

Of these four instruments, the *BDI-II* and the *PHQ-9* have been psychometrically evaluated in autistic samples and demonstrate promising psychometric properties (Arnold et al., 2020; Williams et al., 2021). In particular, using item response theory (IRT) in a large sample of autistic adults, the *BDI-II* has been found to have evidence for unidimensionality, with strong model-based reliability (omega total = .95; omega hierarchical = .88; Williams et al., 2021). Criterion validity was supported by associations with measures of anxiety ($r = .74$) and quality of life ($r = .72$), with discriminant validity supported by a weaker correlation with a measure of autism features (*SRS-2*; $r = .50$) and a nonsignificant association with age ($r = .06$). The *BDI-II* produced fair-to- good discrimination ability between depressed vs non-depressed autistic adults using both latent trait scores (AUC = .80) and total scores (AUC = .79), and adequate sensitivity (.82; .74) and specificity (.65; .69). DIF analyses revealed few items with practically significant DIF between autistic and non-autistic adults, supporting valid comparisons of scores between these groups. In the study of the *PHQ-9* in autistic adults, this measure was found to fit a two-factor structure with cognitive-affective and somatic factors, as well as a bifactor analysis supporting utility of a total score (i.e., unidimensionality; Arnold et al., 2020). Excellent internal consistency was found for the total score ($\alpha = 0.91$) and subscales (cognitive affective $\alpha = .89$, somatic $\alpha = .79$). The PHQ-9 was also found to have good convergent validity via correlations with measures of quality of life ($r = -.76$) and well-being ($r = -.67$).

Anxiety. A variety of anxiety questionnaires have been used in SSI research with varying levels of psychometric evidence for their reliability and validity. The parent-report version of the *Spence Child Anxiety Scale* (*SCAS-P*; Spence, 1998) has been used as an SSI outcome, showing significant change in some (Beaumont, Rotolone, & Sofronoff, 2015), but not all studies (Andrews, Attwood, & Sofronoff, 2013). Multiple studies have explored the psychometric performance of the *SCAS-P* in autistic samples revealing that although there is evidence for acceptable sensitivity (.75) and specificity (.71), internal consistency (total $\alpha = .93$–.94; subscales $\alpha = .55$–.84; total $\alpha = .93$), convergent validity, diagnostic predictive validity (AUC = .84; sensitivity = .90; specificity = .66) and interrater agreement (intraclass correlation coefficient [ICC] = .59; Carruthers, Kent, Hollocks, & Simonoff, 2020; Jitlina et al., 2017; Magiati et al., 2017; Zainal et al., 2014), the factor structure in autism does not appear to be equivalent to the literature standard (Glod et al., 2017; Jitlina et al., 2017; Magiati et al., 2017; Toscano et al., 2020).

Among adolescents, the *Social Interaction Anxiety Scale* (*SIAS*; Mattick & Clarke, 1998), *Social Anxiety Scale for Adolescents* (*SAS-A;* La Greca & Lopez, 1998) and *State and Trait Anxiety Inventory for Children* (*STAIC-T* and STAIC-S; Spielberger, Edwards, Lushene, Montuori, & Platzek, 1973) have been used as outcomes of SSI programs (Matthews et al., 2018; Schohl et al., 2014; Yoo et al., 2014). Of these, the *SIAS* and *SAS-A* have some evidence of sensitivity to change (Factor, Moody, Sung, & Laugeson, 2022; Laugeson, Ellingsen, Sanderson, Tucci, & Bates, 2014; Schohl et al., 2014) and have received some psychometric examination in autistic samples (Boulton & Guastella, 2021; Schiltz, Magnus, et al., 2021). In a sample of autistic adolescents, the *SAS-A* has been found to have a two-factor structure (fear of negative evaluation and social avoidance/distress), as opposed to the literature standard three-factor structure, with modest evidence for convergent and discriminant validity via correlations with another measure of social anxiety ($r = .19$–.76), adolescent-reported depression ($r = .03$–.43), caregiver-reported depression ($r = .17$–.53), and caregiver-reported social responsiveness ($r = -.06$ to .30), though these correlations varied by informant (e.g., self, parent; Schiltz, Magnus, et al., 2021). Importantly, this study found poor agreement between caregiver and adolescent report (Cohen's weighted kappas: .09–.35: polychoric correlations: .10–.39) and a lack of measurement invariance beyond the configural level across reporters. As such, although the same underlying factor structure is present for adolescent and caregiver report, lack of higher levels of measurement invariance precludes comparisons of scores across reporters and suggests that caregiver report should not be used as a proxy for adolescent report (and vice-versa). Although psychometrically evaluated in autistic adults, not adolescents, the *SIAS* shows evidence for strong internal consistency ($\alpha = .91$; item-total correlations .22–.80), as well as concurrent validity via correlations with other measures of social anxiety ($r = .67$–.81), anxiety ($r = .59$), and depression ($r = .53$; Boulton & Guastella, 2021). Discriminant validity was also supported via nonsignificant correlation with age ($r = .04$).

Various questionnaires including the *General Anxiety Disorder Questionnaire-7* (*GAD-7*; Spitzer, Kroenke, Williams, & Löwe, 2006), *Liebowitz Social Anxiety Scale* (*LSAS*; Fresco et al., 2001), *Social Phobia Inventory (SPIN*; Connor et al., 2000), and *State-Trait Anxiety Inventory* (*STAI*; Spielberger, 1983) have been used in SSI studies with autistic adults (Connor et al., 2020; Hillier et al., 2011; McVey et al., 2016); all except the *SPIN* demonstrated significant improvement across SSI. To date, out of these measures used in adult SSI studies, only the *L-SAS* has preliminary and promising psychometric evidence in autism (Boulton & Guastella, 2021). The *L-SAS* shows excellent internal consistency (total score $\alpha = .96$), convergent validity with social anxiety ($r = .64$–.81) and depression ($r = .53$) measures. However, no studies to date have evaluated the factor structure or diagnostic performance of the *L-SAS* in autism.

4. Observational measures

Observational measures are powerful tools for assessing social skills and treatment outcome in autism (McConachie et al., 2015; Rotheram-Fuller et al., 2013). Unlike questionnaires, which can be influenced by reporter-bias and other limitations previously discussed, observational measures allow for direct assessment of the individual's skills. Observational measures may also have the advantage of targeting the known challenge of generalization in ASD (Church et al., 2015); namely, that skills learned in one context (e.g., a social skills group) may not be readily generalized to other settings (e.g., real-world social interactions) in autism. Through direct observation of social behaviors, observational measurement tools may allow for more ecologically valid assessment of SSI outcomes. Further, while questionnaires tend to provide ratings of change in global social skill and functioning, observational measures can more directly assess change in specific behaviors of interest (e.g., asking appropriate follow-up questions, identifying emotions in facial expressions; McConachie et al., 2015). This strength of observational measures, in turn, may bolster sensitivity to detecting the effects of treatment. Moreover, unlike for most questionnaire respondents, observational coders can be masked to treatment groups, potentially increasing their validity.

Yet, observational measures are not without limitations. By definition, they require direct observation of behavior and thus are necessarily limited by time and setting, in which behaviors observed under set conditions serve as a representation of behaviors and skills across settings. Observational measures are also more time and labor intensive than questionnaires or other approaches in their requirements for training, data collection, and often behavioral coding. Thus, they often require substantial investments in training research staff and ensuring coders remain reliable within the instrument and with one another over time. Observational measures also require significant adaptation across development to meaningfully represent appropriate social behavior. For example, SSIs developed for younger children (i.e., preschool and elementary school-aged youth) may utilize natural settings such as the playground, the cafeteria or lunchroom, or the classroom. In contrast, for autistic adolescents and adults, specific role play tasks (e.g., a mock job interview) are often the most feasible approach to observational assessment of social skills (Spence, 2003). Broadly, observational assessments are most useful when they can provide ecologically valid samples of social behaviors of interest, utilizing standardized rating systems to support objectivity.

4.1 ADOS and BOSCC

Some early intervention research targeting social communication in very young autistic children has utilized the *Autism Diagnostic Observation Schedule* (*ADOS*, and current edition, *ADOS-2*; Lord, Rutter, & DiLavore, 2012) algorithm scores or calibrated severity scores (e.g., Pickles et al., 2016; Rogers et al., 2019); however, this measure was originally designed as a diagnostic tool, and thus may be limited in its sensitivity to the smaller degrees of change that may be observed following SSI treatment. The developers of the *ADOS* recommend against its use as an outcome measure for this reason and have recently developed a novel coding system known as the *Brief Observation of Social Communication Change* (*BOSCC*; Grzadzinski et al., 2016) that can be applied to semi-structured social interactions, such as those that occur in the *ADOS* administration. Initial psychometric properties indicate excellent inter-rater reliability (ICC = .97), test-retest reliability (ICC = .90), responsiveness to treatment, and convergent validity with change in social communication behaviors on other measures (Grzadzinski et al., 2016). Though the psychometric properties and evidence base are still developing, the *BOSCC* shows promise as a potential outcome measure that is more appropriate and sensitive to change than *ADOS* algorithm and calibrated severity scores in early childhood interventions for autism features (e.g., Carruthers et al., 2021; Kim, Grzadzinski, Martinez, & Lord, 2019; Pijl et al., 2018). To our knowledge, the *BOSCC* has yet to be used as an outcome in traditional SSI clinical trials, which utilize didactic instruction to teach specific social skills, though research testing this is currently underway—including multiple randomized control trials being conducted by the authors testing various PEERS programs.

4.2 Playground interactions

Behavior in a naturalistic social setting, such as a playground for youth, may arguably be one of the most face valid measures of SSI outcome. Corbett and colleagues across several studies have developed and examined the *Peer Interaction Paradigm* (*PIP*; Corbett, Schupp, Simon, Ryan, & Mendoza, 2010) as an outcome in SSI intervention studies (Corbett et al., 2016; Corbett et al., 2019). The *PIP* involves a 20-min interaction between the target autistic youth and two same-aged peers, at least one of whom is given specific training and directions to solicit interaction in a series of semi-structured playground activities (e.g., free play, play on the equipment structures, cooperative play with toys). Though the specific behavioral codes applied vary slightly across studies, codes often capture interactive, group play as well as solitary play. The *PIP* shows good reliability ($k = .85$), ability to differentiate autistic youth from neurotypical youth, and responsiveness to SSI treatment.

While the *PIP* playground observation involves one or more confederates, other playground observation methods use a fully naturalistic observation in a typical social setting. In several studies of SSI approaches for school aged children on the autism spectrum (Kasari et al., 2012; Kasari et al., 2016; Locke, Rotheram-Fuller, Harker, Kasari, & Mandell, 2019) the *Playground Observation of Peer Engagement* (*POPE*; Kasari, Locke, Gulsrud, & Rotheram-Fuller, 2011) has been utilized. The *POPE* codes interaction and engagement between the target child and peers in repeated 1-min intervals (40-s observation, 20-second coding) in a playground recess setting at the target child's school. Engagement is rated as one of the following: solitary, proximity, onlooker, parallel, parallel aware, joint engagement, or games with rules.

The target child's initiations and responses are coded using a dichotomous structure (e.g., successful or failed, appropriate or missed). Inter-rater reliability on the *POPE* has been reported to be adequate (>0.80). Results suggest that SSI can lead to reduced time spent in solitary engagement, increased time spent in joint engagement, and more successful initiations—though specific significant effects varied based on the format of the SSI (e.g., peer-mediated vs didactic skills instruction; Kasari et al., 2012, Kasari et al., 2016; Locke et al., 2019). The *POPE* has also been shown to be responsive to alternative SSI methods in which school staff provide social coaching that promotes peer engagement and conversation more broadly, rather than teaching social skills to a specific target child (Kretzmann, Shih, & Kasari, 2015; Shih et al., 2019). A new, adapted version of the *POPE* for adolescents called the *Teen Observation of Peer Interaction* (*TOPI*) also showed adequate inter-rater reliability and responsiveness to SSI (Dean, Williams, Orlich, & Kasari, 2020).

4.3 Contextual assessment of social skills (CASS)

The *Contextual Assessment of Social Skills* (*CASS*) is a peer-enacted role play measure of social functioning designed for use with autistic adolescents and young adults (Ratto, Turner-Brown, Rupp, Mesibov, & Penn, 2011) that has been used as an outcome measure in SSI research. The *CASS* was designed to consist of two separate role plays, lasting 3 min each, in which the autistic participant interacts with trained confederates of similar age and opposite gender. Confederate selection was intended to capitalize upon the unique social demands of navigating peer interactions with individuals of the opposite gender that begin to take prominence in adolescence (Connolly, Craig, Goldberg, & Pepler, 2004). Different confederates are instructed to display social interest and boredom in the first and second role plays, respectively. Participants' behavior is coded in each role play, and the change in behavior across the two role plays is considered the "final score," as an indication of the participant's ability to change their social behavior in response to contextual social cues from their interaction partner. Whether in the interested or the bored condition, confederates are instructed to minimize the use of questions to maintain conversation and to try to speak for <50% of the time, to keep the burden of maintaining conversation primarily on the participant. The participants' behavior is coded using a nine-item behavioral coding system to assess the participant's social behavior including counts of Asking Questions and Topic Changes, as well as 7-point scales of Vocal Expressiveness, Gestures, Positive Affect, Kinesic Arousal, Social

Anxiety, Overall Involvement in the Conversation, and Overall Quality of Rapport. Coders receive training on the behavioral coding system and establish reliability with a set of training videos (White, Scarpa, Conner, Maddox, & Bonete, 2015). Variations on the original *CASS* include only utilizing a single role play (interested condition) when the social skills curriculum provides explicit instruction to end the conversation when conversational partners display boredom (White et al., 2015), use of same-gender, rather than cross-gender interactions, and application of the *CASS* coding system to other types of peer-based interactions (e.g., Dolan et al., 2016).

The *CASS* has strong psychometric support, with high internal consistency (standardized Cronbach's $\alpha = .83$) and intraclass correlation coefficients (ICCs) ranging from .50 to .97. In the development study, the *CASS* showed good concurrent validity via correlations with verbal IQ ($r = .32$, $p = .04$) and theory of mind ($r = .47$, $p = .002$) and discriminant validity, via lack of association with performance IQ ($r = .006$, *ns*). Predictive validity was also supported, as autistic participants scored significantly worse on the *CASS* than neurotypical participants. Subsequent studies using the *CASS* as an outcome measure have found that the *CASS* is sensitive to treatment outcome in SSIs (Bent et al., 2021; Dolan et al., 2016; Rabin et al., 2018; Simmons et al., 2021; White et al., 2015).

4.4 Mock job interview

For autistic adults, some SSIs have focused on promoting social skills relevant to the workplace (e.g., Sung et al., 2019). These "soft" skills are qualities that employers value and consider during the application and employment process (Robles, 2012), including nonverbal and verbal communication skills, ability to work in a team, networking, professionalism, and manners/courtesy. The vocational success of autistic adults has been linked to social communication skills by both quantitative data and qualitative stakeholder reports (Black et al., 2020; Chiang, Cheung, Li, & Tsai, 2013). The first barrier to employment for people on the autism spectrum is often the job interview, with autistic adults describing challenges with expressing oneself clearly, eye contact, coping with anxiety, and knowing how to present oneself (e.g., whether to be truthful when asked about weaknesses; Sarrett, 2017). As such, mock job interviews have been identified as potent observational outcome measure of employment-focused SSI. One such outcome measure is the *Mock Interview Rating Scale* (*MIRS*; Smith et al., 2014), which has been used in different populations, including autism (*A-MIRS*; Smith et al., 2021). The *A-MIRS* is coded via 5–7 point Likert scales, with a global rating of overall likeliness of being hired, as well as 11 codes of specific interview skills, including: confidence, being positive, professionalism, showing interest, honesty, being dependable/hardworking, working well with others, sharing strengths and skills, sharing past experiences, sharing past limitations, and overall rapport (Smith et al., 2021). The *A-MIRS* demonstrated strong reliability (ICC = 0.97) and responsiveness to SSI programs that target job interviewing skills (Genova et al., 2021; Smith et al., 2021). The *A-MIRS* has shown convergent and predictive validity through significant associations with *SRS-2* scores and employment outcomes, respectively (Smith et al., 2015; Smith et al., 2021).

4.5 Social cognition assessments

Clinicians have also utilized standardized assessments of social cognition, including tests of emotion recognition and theory of mind to assess improvements in these aspects of social skills following SSI. Though somewhat distinct from other observational assessments, which frequently attempt to reproduce a natural social context, social cognitive assessments elicit social decision-making in the moment when faced with social information (e.g., faces, situations). The "*Reading the Mind in the Eyes*" *Test* (*RMET*; Baron-Cohen, Wheelwright, Hill, et al., 2001; Baron-Cohen, Wheelwright, Skinner, et al., 2001) has been used as an SSI outcome measure (Ashman et al., 2017; Gorenstein et al., 2020; Soorya et al., 2015). The *RMET* was originally validated in autistic adolescents and adults and involves choosing the emotion best displayed by the male and female eyes. Test items are limited to complex emotions (e.g., none of the five basic emotions are listed: "happy," "sad," "angry," "afraid," "disgust"). A significant limitation of the *RMET* is the lack of racial and ethnic diversity in the displayed images, as stimuli in the original version utilize Caucasian faces. Of note, creation of versions of this test in other countries (e.g., Turkey, France, Japan) have utilized stimuli more representative of their citizens. Reviews of the psychometric properties of the *RMET* have highlighted inconsistent reliability, ranging from poor (e.g., $\alpha = .58$) to adequate internal consistency (e.g., $\alpha = .70$; Olderbak et al., 2015; Vellante et al., 2013). Further, mixed findings have been observed in factor analytic approaches on whether the test assesses a unidimensional construct (Olderbak et al., 2015; Vellante et al., 2013). In general, the *RMET* shows convergent validity with empathy, assessed by questionnaires, and differentiated autistic individuals from neurotypical individuals; however, some research showed significant relations between *RMET* scores and IQ, which may limit its validity across the full range of cognitive abilities present in autism (Olderbak et al., 2015; Vellante et al., 2013). Other similar emotion recognition measures exist and have been used to assess treatment response in SSIs (e.g., Ashman et al., 2017; McMahon, Lerner, & Britton, 2013; Stichter et al., 2010; Thomeer et al., 2012). These include the *Cambridge Mindreading Voice-Face Battery* (Golan, Baron-Cohen, & Hill, 2006), which presents stimuli (visual and auditory) of people enacting emotions, and the *Diagnostic Analysis of Nonverbal Accuracy-2 Child Facial Expressions* subtest (*DANVA-2-CF*; Nowicki & Carton, 1993).

Another social cognitive construct relevant to outcome measurement in SSI is theory of mind, or the ability to take another's perspective to understand and predict the other's emotions, beliefs, and desires, which has long been regarded as an area of challenge for autistic people (Baron-Cohen, 2000; Kimhi, 2014). False belief tasks (e.g., Sally-Anne task, Baron-Cohen, 2000; deceptive box task, Perner, Frith, Leslie, & Leekam, 1989) are often used to assess theory of mind in young children; however, they do not demonstrate responsiveness to SSI (Chin & Bernard-Opitz, 2000; Stichter et al., 2010), likely due to their limited range of scores (i.e., pass, fail). In contrast, other assessments with multiple items capturing theory of mind skills across a range of developmental complexity and situations are more sensitive to treatment response. For example, the *Strange Stories Test* (Happé, 1994; Revised versions: Brent, Rios, Happé, & Charman, 2004; O'Hare, Bremner, Nash, Happé, & Pettigrew, 2009) asks youth to interpret several more complex mentalizing situations, such as humor and sarcasm, persuading, and telling white lies. This assessment is appropriate for school aged children, 5–12 years old, differentiates autism and neurotypical samples, has high internal consistency ($\alpha = 0.95$), and shows developmental progression (O'Hare et al., 2009; Velloso, Duarte, & Schwartzman, 2013). As an outcome measure, autistic children and adolescents have shown significant improvements on the *Strange Stories Test* following SSIs (e.g., Cheung, Brown, Yu, & Siu, 2021; Soorya et al., 2015; Waugh & Peskin, 2015). Theory of mind has also been assessed via parent-report in youth ages 3–17 (Hutchins, Prelock, & Bonazinga, 2012), and more recently via self-report in adults (Hutchins, Lewis, Prelock, & Brien, 2021), using the *Theory of Mind Inventory* (*TOMI*). The *TOMI* parent-report demonstrated strong psychometric properties, including high internal consistency (neurotypical group $\alpha = .95$, autistic group $\alpha = .97$), test-rest reliability, convergent validity with other measures of theory of mind and social communication, sensitivity to expected developmental changes, and ability to differentiate autistic clinical samples from neurotypical samples (Greenslade & Coggins, 2016; Hutchins et al., 2012; Lerner, Hutchins, & Prelock, 2011).

Importantly, interventions that only teach emotion recognition or theory of mind skills may show benefits on these specific social cognitive skills, but these changes do not commonly generalize to change in real-world social behavior and outcomes more broadly (Begeer, Bouk, Boussaid, Terwogt, & Koot, 2009; Berggren et al., 2018; Tang, Chen, Falkmer, Bölte, & Girdler, 2019). However, when used to assess outcomes following a more comprehensive SSI, these measures have utility as a part of a larger battery to gather information on precise treatment effects.

5. Qualitative data

In the field of autism intervention research, quantitative data is much more commonly reported in scientific journals while qualitative data is consistently underutilized. However, qualitative and quantitative measures are best seen as complementary outcomes, both unique and necessary in evaluating SSI treatment (Bölte, 2014). Qualitative data from semi-structured interviews can be especially meaningful in capturing nuanced information about constructs, such as friendship, that may not be easily picked up in standardized assessments. Downstream and indirect effects of interventions, such as improved family functioning, may also be more readily elicited through semi-structured interviews and qualitative data. Such data can help inform future refinements to interventions, new hypotheses, or additions to assessment batteries. Qualitative interview data also tend to "bring to life" the impact and meaning of interventions for participants and families, and this type of data can be especially powerful in dissemination efforts to the public. Importantly, it is also essential for researchers to systematically gather these perspectives to honor and learn from the experiences of stakeholders receiving treatments. For example, despite positive effects on quantitative measures, some autistic self-advocates have spoken out against some forms applied behavioral analysis treatments as aversive and harmful experientially (McGill & Robinson, 2020).

In one of the very few applications of qualitative methods in SSI research, autistic youth and their parents were interviewed following participation in a manualized group SSI (KONTAKT; Choque Olsson, Rautio, Asztalos, Stoetzer, & Bölte, 2016). The researchers classified youth as either high responders or low responders based on their quantitative change on standardized outcome measures (e.g., *SRS*) to explore differences in experiences and perceived impact of SSI. Emergent themes from qualitative interviews revealed that, regardless of responder classification, youth and their families were satisfied with the SSI treatment and perceived positive changes in social skills and other areas (e.g., conflict resolution, emotion regulation, confidence) following treatment. A replication study with a larger sample using deductive content analysis of semi-structured interviews showed similar results (Afsharnejad et al., 2021). These data reinforce the possibility that qualitative data may capture more nuanced and subtle changes, which may still feel meaningful to the individual and family.

6. Neurobiological indices

Given the neurobiological underpinnings of autism (Neuhaus, Beauchaine, & Bernier, 2010; Parellada et al., 2014) and neural-plasticity that exists across the lifespan (Power & Schlaggar, 2017), there is a growing interest in exploring various neurological and physiological indices as outcome measures in autism intervention research (Stavropoulos, 2017). A growing number of SSI studies have leveraged use of neurobiological indices to better understand such plasticity processes. While these metrics offer objective quantitative data, the current state of the literature is characterized by inconsistencies across a limited number of studies, along with a lack of clear biomarkers for autism (Frye et al., 2019) and related conditions within autism (e.g., anxiety; McVey, 2019).

6.1 Electroencephalogram (EEG)

Studies have utilized EEG to evaluate changes in brain activity following SSI in autism. EEG is a direct measure of postsynaptic brain activity and has strong temporal resolution, but weaker spatial resolution. As EEG is relatively low-cost and non-invasive, this approach may be particularly well-suited for autism research. Other strengths of EEG include the tolerance of motion artifacts, especially compared to magnetic resonance imaging (MRI) research, and ability to record brain activity in naturalistic settings (Lau-Zhu, Lau, & McLoughlin, 2019). The sensory aspects of an EEG (i.e., pressure and wetness from the cap on the scalp), however, may be difficult to tolerate for some autistic individuals. Additionally, given the immense heterogeneity of autism, it has also been posited that researchers should consider EEG in relation to various domains of functioning including behavioral, linguistic, social, and cognitive factors (Jeste, Frohlich, & Loo, 2015). Other methodological considerations, and potential confounds, include age, gender, socio-economic status, paradigm condition, and electrode location and quantity (Heunis, Aldrich, & de Vries, 2016). Various EEG metrics, reviewed below, have been examined in SSI studies.

EEG Asymmetry. EEG asymmetry refers to the relative activation or dominance of one brain hemisphere compared to the other and has been found to relate to particular behavioral and emotional presentations (e.g., withdrawal, approach, anxiety), in neurotypical development (Blackhart, Minnix, & Kline, 2006; Harmon-Jones, Gable, & Peterson, 2010) and autism (Schiltz, McVey, Barrington, et al., 2018; Schiltz, McVey, Dolan, et al., 2018). Furthermore, research also indicates atypicalities in relative hemisphere dominance in autism (Wang et al., 2013) in addition to within group associations between asymmetry and autism features (Burnette et al., 2011). EEG asymmetry can be calculated in various brain regions (e.g., frontal, temporal, parietal) or across the entire hemisphere, and within various frequency bands (e.g., delta 0–4 Hz; theta 4–8 Hz, alpha 8–12 Hz, beta 12–30 Hz, and gamma 30–50 Hz). One study has explored hemispheric EEG asymmetry within all frequency bands across SSI for adolescents (Van Hecke et al., 2015). This study suggests that hemispheric gamma-band EEG asymmetry may be particularly sensitive to SSI in adolescents (Van Hecke et al., 2015).

EEG Coherence. The level of connectivity and integration between different brain regions is captured by EEG coherence and may be an important SSI outcome measure, given the differences in brain connectivity identified in autism (O'Reilly, Lewis, & Elsabbagh, 2017; Vissers, Cohen, & Geurts, 2012; Wang et al., 2013). Coherence can be calculated within hemispheres (intra-hemispheric) or between hemispheres (inter-hemispheric) and across various brain regions. A recent study of an SSI in autistic adolescents examined inter- and intra-hemispheric EEG coherence within the alpha band (Haendel et al., 2021). These findings revealed that connectivity between the left occipital to temporal region showed change following intervention, while other inter- and intra-hemispheric pairs did not.

Event-Related Potential (ERP). ERPs capture brain activity specific to a particular stimulus. In SSI research, ERPs have been used to tap into neural responses related to the reward system (Baker, Veytsman, Choy, Blacher, & Stavropoulos, 2021; Baker, Veytsman, Martin, Blacher, & Stavropoulos, 2020), habituation (Baker et al., 2020), face processing (Baker et al., 2021), and facial memory (Corbett et al., 2016). Building on evidence that autistic youth display slower rates of habituation to social stimuli (e.g., Kleinhans et al., 2009) and lower reward-related activation to faces

(Stavropoulos & Carver, 2014), Baker et al. (2020) examined a difference wave (reward positivity; RewP) between correct and incorrect feedback in social and nonsocial conditions, during the first and second halves of the task, and from pre- to post-SSI. Compared to the non-autistic group ($n=7$), who did not receive SSI, the autistic youth ($n=7$) demonstrated larger RewP post-intervention in the first half of the task, indicating enhanced reward processing (i.e., more responsive to reward) due to SSI. Although a second study did not find changes in RewP across SSI, a marginally significant decrease in stimulus-preceding negativity (SPN; anticipation of social reward) and increase in N170 (face processing) in the right hemisphere was detected (Baker et al., 2021). Notably, not only has RewP been found to predict treatment response (Baker et al., 2020), but level of social motivation prior to intervention was predictive of degree of change in ERPs (RewP and SPN) across SSI (Baker et al., 2021). Corbett et al. (2016, 2019) used the incidental face memory task to explore whether neutral processes involved in facial memory change due to SSI using a randomized trial design. Stimuli included social (faces) and non-social (houses) images; one image in each category was presented repeatedly (50 times), while the others were presented only once. These studies examined the ERP amplitude difference between repeated and single stimulus conditions at the partial electrodes 300-500ms after stimuli presentation, which was found to be sensitive to SSI (Corbett et al., 2016, 2019).

6.2 Cortisol

In addition to directly measuring brain activity via EEG, functioning of the hypothalamic-pituitary-adrenal (HPA) axis—a key part of the stress response system—has also been examined. Stressful or threatening situations can activate the HPA axis, yielding release of cortisol. Salivary cortisol is a non-invasive way to capture the physiological stress response to a particular stimulus, and studies have revealed altered response patterns to psychosocial stressors in autistic youth (Taylor & Corbett, 2014). Studies of SSI in autistic youth have collected salivary cortisol to explore diurnal cortisol, cortisol response to play with peers, and cortisol before and after intervention sessions. Although no significant changes in diurnal cortisol were detected across treatment (Corbett et al., 2011; Corbett et al., 2014; Corbett, Blain, Ioannou, & Balser, 2017), cortisol levels before and after intervention sessions and during interaction with peers have demonstrated some sensitivity to change (Corbett et al., 2011; Corbett et al., 2014).

7. Diversity considerations in SSI outcome measurement

Historically, autism research has paid relatively little attention to the potential impacts of race and ethnicity on the autistic experience and on commonly used assessment procedures (Wallis & Pinto-Martin, 2008). Although racial gaps in the identification of autism and diagnostic timing have been narrowing over time (Maenner et al., 2021; Shaw et al., 2021), individuals from historically marginalized ethnoracial groups continue to be significantly underrepresented in autism research (West et al., 2016), and especially in autism intervention research (Davenport, Mazurek, Brown, & McCollom, 2018; Safer-Lichtenstein, Hamilton, & McIntyre, 2019). This lack of representative samples, in part due to the significant barriers to participation in clinical treatment trials (e.g., mistrust of academic research, competing demands on time, concerns about legal status; George, Duran, & Norris, 2014; Ratto et al., 2017), precludes researchers' ability to adequately explore cultural influences on outcome measures and limits the generalizability of findings.

Although there is little empirical data on potential cultural effects on the measurement of SSI outcomes, it is clear from prior literature that these factors should be further explored. For example, informant report measures of psychopathology have been found to differ by ethnicity in terms of the rates of parent endorsement of behavioral and emotional concerns, parental response styles, and fit of existing factor analytic models of measure domains (Mano, Davies, Klein-Tasman, & Adesso, 2009; Miller, Nigg, & Miller, 2009; Tyson, Teasley, & Ryan, 2011). Relatedly, parent report of autism features have been found to vary on the basis of race/ethnicity (e.g., Blacher, Cohen, & Azad, 2014; Donohue, Childs, Richards, & Robins, 2019). Although the core symptoms of social-communication differences and associated impairment in autism are likely invariant, or at least highly similar, across cultural lines, there are known differences in what is considered socially appropriate behavior across cultures (Soto et al., 2015). Cultural differences in social behaviors that are most highly valued or concerning may also influence the measurement of SSI outcomes (Bernier, Mao, & Yen, 2010).

Yet, parents are not alone in being subject to the influences of societal and cultural norms. Clinician perceptions of autism and other symptoms have been found to vary by the race/ethnicity of the individual being assessed, even when all other information is held constant (Begeer et al., 2009; Sullivan, 2013). The potential influence of these biases is evident in differences in diagnostic rates by race/ethnicity based on geographic location (Maenner et al., 2021) and in continued (though improving) disparities in identification and diagnostic timing based on race/ethnicity (Jarquin, Wiggins, Schieve, & Naarden-Braun, 2011; Nowell, Brewton, Allain, & Mire, 2015). Most critically, the under-representation of racially and ethnically marginalized groups in autism SSI research limits knowledge about the potential impacts of culture on the assessment of social behaviors and treatment outcomes. Moving forward, clinical researchers must prioritize diversity, equity, inclusion, and accessibility in their samples to enhance our understanding of how SSIs operate across cultural lines and how to evaluate SSI outcome in autistic people from the broad range of cultural backgrounds (Davenport et al., 2018; Safer-Lichtenstein et al., 2019).

In comparison to the relative lack of attention given to cultural factors in autism research, measurement considerations around sex assigned at birth and gender have received relatively more attention (Kaat et al., 2021). However, sex/gender differences likely cannot be fully understood utilizing the strictly characterized samples commonly included in most autism research, which are prone to excluding individuals whose autism manifests later in life and/or in more subtle ways; Ratto, 2021). A recent meta-analysis of epidemiological studies suggests that autistic females are more likely to be missed, and that the true sex ratio in autism is likely closer to 3:1 than the oft-cited 4:1 (Loomes, Hull, & Mandy, 2017). There has also been increasing attention in recent years to the elevated co-occurrence of gender diversity and autism, which may affect phenotypic presentations (Dewinter, De Graaf, & Begeer, 2017; Warrier et al., 2020). The distinct effects of sex and gender are increasingly emerging as a critical focus of autism research aiming to understanding the manifestation, identification, and treatment of autism (Strang et al., 2020), and in turn, valid and reliable SSI outcome measurement.

In assessing SSI outcome, avenues by which sex and gender may influence social behaviors are of clear importance, as these factors may influence the baseline from which participants enter treatment and the measurement of relevant constructs. One avenue that has received much attention recently is "camouflaging" or "masking,"—compensatory behaviors (whether conscious or unconscious) an autistic individual uses to navigate (neurotypical) social expectations—and has been central to discussions about sex/gender differences in autism (Hull et al., 2017). Although camouflaging is a somewhat new and at times controversial concept, autistic cisgender girls and women, as well as gender diverse autistic people, have frequently described camouflaging as a part of their experience of autism (Hull, Petrides, & Mandy, 2020; Wiskerke, Stern, & Igelström, 2018). Moreover, newer evidence seems to indicate that autistic females assigned at birth may show better social-communication skills than their male assigned at birth peers. For example, autistic females have been found to have better language skills, more intact play abilities, higher social motivation, and subtle advantages in social-communication skills (Conlon et al., 2019; Head, McGillivray, & Stokes, 2014; Kirkovski, Enticott, & Fitzgerald, 2013). At this time, however, it is unclear how camouflaging may or may not impact measurement of SSI outcomes.

Further, expectations for appropriate social behavior are inherently influenced by sex and gender, as there is evidence that parents and other adults perceive and respond differently to children based on sex/gender, beginning in infancy (Zahn-Waxler, Shirtcliff, & Marceau, 2008). Given these gender-differences, many commonly used questionnaire measures of general psychopathology (e.g., the *ASEBA* scales) and more specific domains of child and adult psychopathology (e.g., the *CDI-2*) are separately normed by gender. In contrast, autism diagnostic instruments and SSI outcome measures are usually not separately normed by gender, with the notable exception of the *SRS-2*. This is an important consideration, in light of the sex/gender differences described above. One study, for example, found that autistic girls were rated similarly to neurotypical boys in their social competence (Dean et al., 2014). Other studies have also found that parents may rate autistic children differently by gender on standardized measures (Halladay et al., 2015; Ratto et al., 2017). Additionally, clinicians may also be impacted by issues of sex and gender in their perceptions of autistic individuals (Dworzynski, Ronald, Bolton, & Happé, 2012; Kreiser & White, 2014). Utilizing outcome measurement tools that do not differentiate by gender may therefore impact our conclusions regarding treatment response in SSIs, for autistic girls in particular.

8. Discussion

In sum, there is a wealth of measurement tools and modalities (e.g., questionnaires, observation, interview) used to assess SSI outcomes of interest (e.g., social skills, social behavior, mental health). Given the inherent strengths and limitations of each modality (see Table 1), varied psychometric support specific to autism samples, and scant consideration of diversity, a carefully curated, multi-method, multi-informant assessment battery in SSI autism research is critically important to leverage the strengths of available instruments. We also noted a marked diversity in assessments across studies—with very few measures, with the exception of the *SRS* and *SSIS* (see Soares et al., 2021, for a review), being used widely across many studies. As the literature base grows, it will be of utmost importance for SSI researchers to stay attuned to the most rigorously tested outcome measures, harmonizing toward gold standard outcomes—which will better enable meta-analytic and collaborative research to investigate moderators of response, treatment mechanisms, and diversity factors relevant to SSI.

One particularly critical flaw in current SSI outcome measurement is the over-reliance on parent-report questionnaires, which is especially problematic as autistic people age. In the authors' experiences conducting research and clinical work in the autism community, many autistic young adults have taken steps toward independence with reduced parental involvement. We have observed a diverse level of parental involvement in our participants' lives, with several adult participants who did not consent to parents completing questionnaires at all for various reasons. As such, in adulthood, use of parent-report measurement may be biased or limited by levels of parental knowledge and interaction. The validity of parent-report questionnaires for autistic adults needs to be further specified, with exploration of the influence of factors such as age of autistic adult, amount of contact with parent, and living situation on psychometric properties (e.g., testing for DIF) to assist with interpretation and selection of measures. These challenges in parent-report have led us to increasingly pursue observational measures (e.g., *BOSCC*, *CASS*, mock job interviews) and qualitative interviews to supplement self-report questionnaires in our own SSI research in the UCLA PEERS Clinic (affiliated with authors CM, HS, AG, and EL). Such methods more closely mirror best practices in assessments of adults in other clinical populations (e.g., depression, anxiety, attention-deficit/hyperactivity disorder). Colleagues of ours have also led efforts to incorporate neurobiological indicators into measurement batteries assessing the PEERS interventions (Baker et al., 2020; Baker et al., 2021; Van Hecke et al., 2015). These studies have also begun to increase our understanding of how brain changes correspond to behavioral changes, another important area of study. Baker et al. (2020), for example, identified significant correlations between changes in social knowledge and increased reward positivity amplitude in social conditions after SSI treatment.

Further, with the rapid shift toward virtual interactions and telehealth services brought about by the COVID-19 pandemic, the field needs to be thoughtful in considering how to adapt current practices. It is likely that telehealth services will remain, given the expanded reach and ease of access they afford. At the UCLA PEERS Clinic, we have pivoted our outcome measurement battery to adapt to this new reality, collecting questionnaire measures online and adapting both the CASS and mock job interview observational assessments to a video-conferencing format. To our knowledge, the CASS has not yet been rigorously studied through a virtual modality, and we plan to explore the psychometric properties from our data in the future. For example, specific codes, such as Gestures, may be more or less valid and informative in the video-conferencing format, where hands are often not visible in the frame (typically focused on the shoulders and head). In addition to looking at the CASS data from autistic people, it is also essential to collect comparable neurotypical control data using the same video-conferencing format to determine its utility as an outcome and its comparability to the original measure. Perhaps most importantly, though some of the field's current outcome measures can be readily transferred to online administration (e.g., questionnaires), it is unclear how our current measures capture successful social functioning in an increasingly online world. Standardized and commonly utilized questionnaire measures of social skills and social responsiveness have few to no questions examining online social behavior and etiquette (e.g., texting, social media, emails, video-conferencing). There has been a recent call into investigating the electronic communication of autistic individuals (Livingston, Ashwin, & Shah, 2020), and development of measures in this domain could be another important, ecologically relevant outcome for SSIs.

Given the need to continue to improve outcome measurement for SSI studies in autism research, we encourage researchers to utilize advanced psychometric approaches and participatory research designs. In particular, use of IRT offers many advantages over traditional classical test theory (CTT) approaches including evaluating item bias (i.e., DIF), estimating latent variable scores based on person and item parameters, and allowing measurement error to vary across the latent variable, among others (Reise & Henson, 2003; Thomas, 2011). Furthermore, recent dialogue in the autism research community highlights the need for researchers, clinicians, and funders to work alongside community partners (e.g., autistic adults) to ensure that researchers are "measuring what matters in autism research and practice" (Benevides & Cassidy, 2020). We believe this collaborative approach is of the utmost importance in SSI outcome measure adaptation and development to not only identify relevant constructs but also to enhance accessibility of instruments (Nicolaidis et al., 2020).

Although SSIs are the most commonly used approach to support successful social interactions of autistic individuals in a neurotypical-majority society, it is also important to examine other possible avenues as well. In the spirit of the neurodiversity movement, an alternative method would be to intervene in the context of peers, social and vocational settings, and society as a whole to increase awareness and acceptance of the social communication and behavioral differences associated with neurodiverse individuals. Recently, there have been some interventions focused on changing the environment, rather than the autistic person. Examples include a workshop for college residential life advisors about autism and how to support autistic students in the dorm settings (Bolourian, Veytsman, Galligan, & Blacher, 2021) and an online training for college students about autism (Gillespie-Lynch et al., 2015). Both sought to increase knowledge of autism with the ultimate goal of enabling greater supports, understanding, and acceptance of autistic individuals in college settings. These two studies indeed found that participants had significantly more accurate knowledge of autism and reduced stigma (Bolourian et al., 2021; Gillespie-Lynch et al., 2015). Another critical outcome measure for such an approach would be the downstream effects of such trainings on the lived experience of autistic people. Outcome measures such as comparisons of academic success, social inclusion, and mental health at these colleges, compared to colleges that did not implement such training, would demonstrate true ecological validity. Significant changes observed on those outcomes would be indicative of far more than a change in an individual, but instead a change in the culture of a school or other setting. Such cultural shifts may also more naturally proliferate and transfer than would traditional social skills training, which teaches a more limited number of participants at a time. As such, encouraging societal embrace of neurodiversity may also ultimately be a more cost-effective approach than SSIs for people on the spectrum. One recent study incorporating such elements designed an "ecosystem" intervention approach with layers of supports for autistic individuals preparing for employment—from the individual level, to the family, to co-workers and supervisors (Nicholas, Mitchell, Dudley, Clarke, & Zulla, 2018). Ultimately, broadening our lens beyond the individual is essential for the field of autism SSI in the future and will require a refined and expanded scope of outcome measures.

References

Afsharnejad, B., Falkmer, M., Picen, T., Black, M. H., Alach, T., Fridell, A., et al. (2021). "I Met Someone Like Me!": Autistic Adolescents and Their Parents' Experience of the KONTAKT® Social Skills Group Training. *Journal of Autism and Developmental Disorders*, 1–20.

American Psychiatric Association. (2013). *Diagnostic and statistical manual of mental disorders* (5th ed.).

Andrews, L., Attwood, T., & Sofronoff, K. (2013). Increasing the appropriate demonstration of affectionate behavior, in children with Asperger syndrome, high functioning autism, and PDD-NOS: A randomized controlled trial. *Research in Autism Spectrum Disorders*, 7(12), 1568–1578.

Arnold, S. R., Uljarević, M., Hwang, Y. I., Richdale, A. L., Trollor, J. N., & Lawson, L. P. (2020). Brief report: Psychometric properties of the Patient Health Questionaire-9 (PHQ-9) in autistic adults. *Journal of Autism and Developmental Disorders, 50*(6).

Asher, S. R., Hymel, S., & Renshaw, P. D. (1984). Loneliness in children. *Child Development*, 1456–1464.

Ashman, R., Banks, K., Philip, R. C., Walley, R., & Stanfield, A. C. (2017). A pilot randomised controlled trial of a group based social skills intervention for adults with autism spectrum disorder. *Research in Autism Spectrum Disorders, 43*, 67–75.

Baker, E., Veytsman, E., Choy, T., Blacher, J., & Stavropoulos, K. K. M. (2021). Investigating changes in reward-related neural correlates after PEERS intervention in adolescents with ASD: Preliminary evidence of a 'precision medicine' approach. *Frontiers in Psychiatry, 12*, 742280.

Baker, E., Veytsman, E., Martin, A. M., Blacher, J., & Stavropoulos, K. K. (2020). Increased neural reward responsivity in adolescents with ASD after social skills intervention. *Brain Sciences, 10*(6), 402.

Baker-Ericzén, M. J., Fitch, M. A., Kinnear, M., Jenkins, M. M., Twamley, E. W., Smith, L., et al. (2018). Development of the Supported Employment, Comprehensive Cognitive Enhancement, and Social Skills program for adults on the autism spectrum: Results of initial study. *Autism, 22*(1), 6–19.

Baron-Cohen, S. (2000). Theory of mind and autism: A fifteen year review. *Understanding Other Minds: Perspectives from Developmental Cognitive Neuroscience, 2*(3-20), 102.

Baron-Cohen, S., & Wheelwright, S. (2004). The empathy quotient: An investigation of adults with Asperger syndrome or high functioning autism, and normal sex differences. *Journal of Autism and Developmental Disorders, 34*(2), 163–175.

Baron-Cohen, S., Wheelwright, S., Hill, J., Raste, Y., & Plumb, I. (2001). The "Reading the Mind in the Eyes" Test revised version: A study with normal adults, and adults with Asperger syndrome or high-functioning autism. *The Journal of Child Psychology and Psychiatry and Allied Disciplines, 42*(2), 241–251.

Baron-Cohen, S., Wheelwright, S., Skinner, R., Martin, J., & Clubley, E. (2001). The autism-spectrum quotient (AQ): Evidence from Asperger syndrome/high-functioning autism, males and females, scientists and mathematicians. *Journal of Autism and Developmental Disorders, 31*(1), 5–17.

Bauminger, N., Shulman, C., & Agam, G. (2003). Peer interaction and loneliness in high-functioning children with autism. *Journal of Autism and Developmental Disorders, 33*(5), 489–507.

Beaumont, R., Rotolone, C., & Sofronoff, K. (2015). The secret agent society social skills program for children with high-functioning autism spectrum disorders: A comparison of two school variants. *Psychology in the Schools, 52*(4), 390–402.

Beck, A. T., Steer, R. A., & Brown, G. K. (1996). *Beck depression inventory (BDI-II)*. Pearson.

Begeer, S., Bouk, S. E., Boussaid, W., Terwogt, M. M., & Koot, H. M. (2009). Underdiagnosis and referral bias of autism in ethnic minorities. *Journal of Autism and Developmental Disorders*, *39*(1), 142–148.

Benevides, T. W., & Cassidy, S. A. (2020). Measuring what matters in autism research and practice. *Autism in Adulthood*, *2*(1), 1–3.

Bent, S., McDonald, M. G., Chen, Y., Widjaja, F., Wahlberg, J., Hossain, B., et al. (2021). Brief report: Game day: A Novel method of assessing change in social competence in students with autism spectrum disorder (ASD). *Research in Autism Spectrum Disorders*, *84*, 101766.

Berggren, S., Fletcher-Watson, S., Milenkovic, N., Marschik, P. B., Bölte, S., & Jonsson, U. (2018). Emotion recognition training in autism spectrum disorder: A systematic review of challenges related to generalizability. *Developmental Neurorehabilitation*, *21*(3), 141–154.

Bernier, R., Mao, A., & Yen, J. (2010). Psychopathology, families, and culture: Autism. *Child and Adolescent Psychiatric Clinics*, *19*(4), 855–867.

Birleson, P., Hudson, I., Buchanan, D. G., & Wolff, S. (1987). Clinical evaluation of a self-rating scale for depressive disorder in childhood (Depression Self-Rating Scale). *Journal of Child Psychology and Psychiatry*, *28*(1), 43–60.

Blacher, J., Cohen, S. R., & Azad, G. (2014). In the eye of the beholder: Reports of autism symptoms by Anglo and Latino mothers. *Research in Autism Spectrum Disorders*, *8*(12), 1648–1656.

Black, M. H., Mahdi, S., Milbourn, B., Scott, M., Gerber, A., Esposito, C., et al. (2020). Multi-informant international perspectives on the facilitators and barriers to employment for autistic adults. *Autism Research*, *13*(7), 1195–1214.

Blackhart, G. C., Minnix, J. A., & Kline, J. P. (2006). Can EEG asymmetry patterns predict future development of anxiety and depression? A preliminary study. *Biological Psychology*, *72*(1), 46–50.

Bolourian, Y., Veytsman, E., Galligan, M. L., & Blacher, J. (2021). Autism goes to college: A workshop for residential life advisors (practice brief). *Journal of Postsecondary Education & Disability*, *34*(2).

Bölte, S. (2014). The power of words: Is qualitative research as important as quantitative research in the study of autism? *Autism*, *18*(2), 67–68.

Bottema-Beutel, K., Malloy, C., Cuda, J., Kim, S. Y., & MacEvoy, J. P. (2019). Friendship expectations may be similar for mental age-matched children with autism spectrum disorder and typically developing children. *Journal of Autism and Developmental Disorders*, *49*(10), 4346–4354.

Boulton, K. A., & Guastella, A. J. (2021). Social anxiety symptoms in autism spectrum disorder and social anxiety disorder: Considering the reliability of self-report instruments in adult cohorts. *Autism Research*, *14*(11), 2383–2392.

Brent, E., Rios, P., Happé, F., & Charman, T. (2004). Performance of children with autism spectrum disorder on advanced theory of mind tasks. *Autism*, *8*(3), 283–299.

Bukowski, W. M., Hoza, B., & Boivin, M. (1994). Measuring friendship quality during pre-and early adolescence: The development and psychometric properties of the Friendship Qualities Scale. *Journal of Social and Personal Relationships*, *11*(3), 471–484.

Burnette, C. P., Henderson, H. A., Inge, A. P., Zahka, N. E., Schwartz, C. B., & Mundy, P. C. (2011). Anterior EEG asymmetry and the modifier model of autism. *Journal of Autism and Developmental Disorders*, *41*(8), 1113–1124.

Burrows, C. A., Usher, L. V., Becker-Haimes, E. M., McMahon, C. M., Mundy, P. C., Jensen-Doss, A., et al. (2018). Profiles and correlates of parent–child agreement on social anxiety symptoms in youth with autism spectrum disorder. *Journal of Autism and Developmental Disorders*, *48*(6), 2023–2037.

Cacioppo, S., Grippo, A. J., London, S., Goossens, L., & Cacioppo, J. T. (2015). Loneliness: Clinical import and interventions. *Perspectives on Psychological Science, 10*(2), 238–249.

Calder, L., Hill, V., & Pellicano, E. (2013). 'Sometimes I want to play by myself': Understanding what friendship means to children with autism in mainstream primary schools. *Autism, 17*(3), 296–316.

Carruthers, S., Kent, R., Hollocks, M. J., & Simonoff, E. (2020). Brief report: Testing the psychometric properties of the spence children's anxiety scale (scas) and the screen for child anxiety related emotional disorders (scared) in autism spectrum disorder. *Journal of Autism and Developmental Disorders, 50*(7), 2625–2632.

Carruthers, S., Charman, T., El Hawi, N., Kim, Y. A., Randle, R., Lord, C., et al. (2021). Utility of the autism diagnostic observation schedule and the brief observation of social and communication change for measuring outcomes for a parent-mediated early autism intervention. *Autism Research, 14*(2), 411–425.

Cassidy, S. A., Bradley, L., Cogger-Ward, H., Shaw, R., Bowen, E., Glod, M., et al. (2020). Measurement properties of the suicidal behaviour questionnaire-revised in autistic adults. *Journal of Autism and Developmental Disorders, 50*(10), 3477–3488.

Charman, T., Baird, G., Simonoff, E., Loucas, T., Chandler, S., Meldrum, D., et al. (2007). Efficacy of three screening instruments in the identification of autistic-spectrum disorders. *The British Journal of Psychiatry, 191*(6), 554–559.

Chester, M., Richdale, A. L., & McGillivray, J. (2019). Group-based social skills training with play for children on the autism spectrum. *Journal of Autism and Developmental Disorders, 49*(6), 2231–2242.

Cheung, P. P., Brown, T., Yu, M. L., & Siu, A. M. (2021). The effectiveness of a school-based social cognitive intervention on the social participation of Chinese children with autism. *Journal of Autism and Developmental Disorders, 51*(6), 1894–1908.

Chiang, H. M., Cheung, Y. K., Li, H., & Tsai, L. Y. (2013). Factors associated with participation in employment for high school leavers with autism. *Journal of Autism and Developmental Disorders, 43*(8), 1832–1842.

Chin, H. Y., & Bernard-Opitz, V. (2000). Teaching conversational skills to children with autism: Effect on the development of a theory of mind. *Journal of Autism and Developmental Disorders, 30*(6), 569–583.

Choque Olsson, N., Rautio, D., Asztalos, J., Stoetzer, U., & Bölte, S. (2016). Social skills group training in high-functioning autism: A qualitative responder study. *Autism, 20*(8), 995–1010.

Church, B. A., Rice, C. L., Dovgopoly, A., Lopata, C. J., Thomeer, M. L., Nelson, A., et al. (2015). Learning, plasticity, and atypical generalization in children with autism. *Psychonomic Bulletin & Review, 22*(5), 1342–1348.

Conlon, O., Volden, J., Smith, I. M., Duku, E., Zwaigenbaum, L., Waddell, C., et al. (2019). Gender differences in pragmatic communication in school-aged children with autism spectrum disorder (ASD). *Journal of Autism and Developmental Disorders, 49*(5), 1937–1948.

Connolly, J., Craig, W., Goldberg, A., & Pepler, D. (2004). Mixed-gender groups, dating, and romantic relationships in early adolescence. *Journal of Research on Adolescence, 14*(2), 185–207.

Connor, K. M., Davidson, J. R., Churchill, L. E., Sherwood, A., Weisler, R. H., & Foa, E. (2000). Psychometric properties of the Social Phobia Inventory (SPIN): New self-rating scale. *The British Journal of Psychiatry, 176*(4), 379–386.

Connor, A., Sung, C., Strain, A., Zeng, S., & Fabrizi, S. (2020). Building skills, confidence, and wellness: Psychosocial effects of soft skills training for young adults with autism. *Journal of Autism and Developmental Disorders, 50*(6), 2064–2076.

Constantino, J. N., & Frazier, T. W. (2013). Commentary: The observed association between autistic severity measured by the Social Responsiveness Scale (SRS) and general psychopathology–a response to. *Journal of Child Psychology and Psychiatry, and Allied Disciplines*, *54*(6), 695.

Constantino, J. N., & Gruber, C. P. (2005). *Social Responsiveness Scale (SRS)*. Los Angeles, CA: Western Psychological Services.

Constantino, J. N., & Gruber, C. P. (2012). *Social responsiveness scale: SRS-2*. Torrance, CA: Western Psychological Services.

Constantino, J. N., Gruber, C. P., Davis, S., Hayes, S., Passanante, N., & Przybeck, T. (2004). The factor structure of autistic traits. *Journal of Child Psychology and Psychiatry*, *45*(4), 719–726.

Cook, J., Hull, L., Crane, L., & Mandy, W. (2021). Camouflaging in autism: A systematic review. *Clinical Psychology Review*, *89*, 102080.

Corbett, B. A., Blain, S. D., Ioannou, S., & Balser, M. (2017). Changes in anxiety following a randomized control trial of a theatre-based intervention for youth with autism spectrum disorder. *Autism*, *21*(3), 333–343.

Corbett, B. A., Gunther, J. R., Comins, D., Price, J., Ryan, N., Simon, D., et al. (2011). Brief report: Theatre as therapy for children with autism spectrum disorder. *Journal of Autism and Developmental Disorders*, *41*(4), 505–511.

Corbett, B. A., Ioannou, S., Key, A. P., Coke, C., Muscatello, R., Vandekar, S., et al. (2019). Treatment effects in social cognition and behavior following a theater-based intervention for youth with autism. *Developmental Neuropsychology*, *44*(7), 481–494.

Corbett, B. A., Key, A. P., Qualls, L., Fecteau, S., Newsom, C., Coke, C., et al. (2016). Improvement in social competence using a randomized trial of a theatre intervention for children with autism spectrum disorder. *Journal of Autism and Developmental Disorders*, *46*(2), 658–672.

Corbett, B. A., Schupp, C. W., Simon, D., Ryan, N., & Mendoza, S. (2010). Elevated cortisol during play is associated with age and social engagement in children with autism. *Molecular Autism*, *1*(1), 1–12.

Corbett, B. A., Swain, D. M., Coke, C., Simon, D., Newsom, C., Houchins-Juarez, N., et al. (2014). Improvement in social deficits in autism spectrum disorders using a theatre-based, peer-mediated intervention. *Autism Research*, 7(1), 4–16.

Cresswell, L., Hinch, R., & Cage, E. (2019). The experiences of peer relationships amongst autistic adolescents: A systematic review of the qualitative evidence. *Research in Autism Spectrum Disorders*, *61*, 45–60.

Cunningham, A., Sperry, L., Brady, M. P., Peluso, P. R., & Pauletti, R. E. (2016). The effects of a romantic relationship treatment option for adults with autism spectrum disorder. *Counseling Outcome Research and Evaluation*, 7(2), 99–110.

Davenport, M., Mazurek, M., Brown, A., & McCollom, E. (2018). A systematic review of cultural considerations and adaptation of social skills interventions for individuals with autism spectrum disorder. *Research in Autism Spectrum Disorders*, *52*, 23–33.

Dean, M., Kasari, C., Shih, W., Frankel, F., Whitney, R., Landa, R., et al. (2014). The peer relationships of girls with ASD at school: Comparison to boys and girls with and without ASD. *Journal of Child Psychology and Psychiatry*, *55*(11), 1218–1225.

Dean, M., Williams, J., Orlich, F., & Kasari, C. (2020). Adolescents with autism spectrum disorder and social skills groups at school: A randomized trial comparing intervention environment and peer composition. *School Psychology Review*, *49*(1), 60–73.

Dekker, V., Nauta, M. H., Timmerman, M. E., Mulder, E. J., van der Veen-Mulders, L., van den Hoofdakker, B. J., et al. (2019). Social skills group training in children with autism spectrum disorder: A randomized controlled trial. *European Child & Adolescent Psychiatry*, *28*(3), 415–424.

Dewinter, J., De Graaf, H., & Begeer, S. (2017). Sexual orientation, gender identity, and romantic relationships in adolescents and adults with autism spectrum disorder. *Journal of Autism and Developmental Disorders*, *47*(9), 2927–2934.

DiTommaso, E., & Spinner, B. (1993). The development and initial validation of the Social and Emotional Loneliness Scale for Adults (SELSA). *Personality and Individual Differences*, *14*(1), 127–134.

Dolan, B. K., Van Hecke, A. V., Carson, A. M., Karst, J. S., Stevens, S., Schohl, K. A., et al. (2016). Brief report: Assessment of intervention effects on in vivo peer interactions in adolescents with autism spectrum disorder (ASD). *Journal of Autism and Developmental Disorders*, *46*(6), 2251–2259.

Donohue, M. R., Childs, A. W., Richards, M., & Robins, D. L. (2019). Race influences parent report of concerns about symptoms of autism spectrum disorder. *Autism*, *23*(1), 100–111.

Dworzynski, K., Ronald, A., Bolton, P., & Happé, F. (2012). How different are girls and boys above and below the diagnostic threshold for autism spectrum disorders? *Journal of the American Academy of Child & Adolescent Psychiatry*, *51*(8), 788–797.

Ee, D., Hwang, Y. I., Reppermund, S., Srasuebkul, P., Trollor, J. N., Foley, K. R., et al. (2019). Loneliness in adults on the autism spectrum. *Autism in Adulthood*, *1*(3), 182–193.

Factor, R. S., Moody, C. T., Sung, K. Y., & Laugeson, E. A. (2022). Improving social anxiety and social responsiveness in autism spectrum disorder through PEERS®. *Evidence-Based Practice in Child and Adolescent Mental Health*, 7(1), 142–159.

Fletcher-Watson, S., Adams, J., Brook, K., Charman, T., Crane, L., Cusack, J., et al. (2019). Making the future together: Shaping autism research through meaningful participation. *Autism*, *23*(4), 943–953.

Fletcher-Watson, S., & Bird, G. (2020). Autism and empathy: What are the real links? *Autism*, *24*(1), 3–6.

Frankel, F., & Myatt, R. (2003). *Children's friendship training*. New York: Brunner-Routledge.

Frankel, F., Myatt, R., Sugar, C., Whitham, C., Gorospe, C. M., & Laugeson, E. (2010). A randomized controlled study of parent-assisted children's friendship training with children having autism spectrum disorders. *Journal of Autism and Developmental Disorders*, *40*(7), 827–842.

Frazier, T. W., Ratliff, K. R., Gruber, C., Zhang, Y., Law, P. A., & Constantino, J. N. (2014). Confirmatory factor analytic structure and measurement invariance of quantitative autistic traits measured by the Social Responsiveness Scale-2. *Autism*, *18*(1), 31–44.

Freitag, C. M., Jensen, K., Elsuni, L., Sachse, M., Herpertz-Dahlmann, B., Schulte-Rüther, M., et al. (2016). Group-based cognitive behavioural psychotherapy for children and adolescents with ASD: The randomized, multicentre, controlled SOSTA–net trial. *Journal of Child Psychology and Psychiatry*, *57*(5), 596–605.

Fresco, D. M., Coles, M. E., Heimberg, R. G., Liebowitz, M. R., Hami, S., Stein, M. B., et al. (2001). The Liebowitz Social Anxiety Scale: A comparison of the psychometric properties of self-report and clinician-administered formats. *Psychological Medicine*, *31*(6), 1025–1035.

Frye, R. E., Vassall, S., Kaur, G., Lewis, C., Karim, M., & Rossignol, D. (2019). Emerging biomarkers in autism spectrum disorder: A systematic review. *Annals of Translational Medicine*, 7(23), 792.

Gantman, A., Kapp, S. K., Orenski, K., & Laugeson, E. A. (2012). Social skills training for young adults with high-functioning autism spectrum disorders: A randomized controlled pilot study. *Journal of Autism and Developmental Disorders*, *42*(6), 1094–1103.

Gates, J. A., Kang, E., & Lerner, M. D. (2017). Efficacy of group social skills interventions for youth with autism spectrum disorder: A systematic review and meta-analysis. *Clinical Psychology Review*, *52*, 164–181.

Genova, H. M., Lancaster, K., Morecraft, J., Haas, M., Edwards, A., DiBenedetto, M., et al. (2021). A pilot RCT of virtual reality job interview training in transition-age youth on the autism spectrum. *Research in Autism Spectrum Disorders, 89*, 101878.

George, S., Duran, N., & Norris, K. (2014). A systematic review of barriers and facilitators to minority research participation among African Americans, Latinos, Asian Americans, and Pacific Islanders. *American Journal of Public Health, 104*(2), e16–e31.

Gillespie-Lynch, K., Brooks, P. J., Someki, F., Obeid, R., Shane-Simpson, C., Kapp, S. K., et al. (2015). Changing college students' conceptions of autism: An online training to increase knowledge and decrease stigma. *Journal of Autism and Developmental Disorders, 45*(8), 2553–2566.

Glod, M., Creswell, C., Waite, P., Jamieson, R., McConachie, H., South, M. D., et al. (2017). Comparisons of the factor structure and measurement invariance of the spence children's anxiety scale—parent version in children with autism spectrum disorder and typically developing anxious children. *Journal of Autism and Developmental Disorders, 47*(12), 3834–3846.

Golan, O., Baron-Cohen, S., & Hill, J. (2006). The Cambridge mindreading (CAM) face-voice battery: Testing complex emotion recognition in adults with and without Asperger syndrome. *Journal of Autism and Developmental Disorders, 36*(2), 169–183.

Gorenstein, M., Giserman-Kiss, I., Feldman, E., Isenstein, E. L., Donnelly, L., Wang, A. T., et al. (2020). Brief report: A Job-Based Social Skills Program (JOBSS) for adults with autism spectrum disorder: A pilot randomized controlled trial. *Journal of Autism and Developmental Disorders, 50*(12), 4527–4534.

Greenslade, K. J., & Coggins, T. E. (2016). Brief report: An independent replication and extension of psychometric evidence supporting the theory of mind inventory. *Journal of Autism and Developmental Disorders, 46*(8), 2785–2790.

Gresham, F. M., & Elliot, S. N. (2008). *Social skills improvement system: Rating scales*. Bloomington: Pearson Assessments.

Gresham, F. M., & Elliott, S. (1990). *The social skills rating system: Manual*. Circle Pines: American Guidance Service.

Gresham, F. M., Elliott, S. N., Vance, M. J., & Cook, C. R. (2011). Comparability of the social skills rating system to the social skills improvement system: Content and psychometric comparisons across elementary and secondary age levels. *School Psychology Quarterly, 26*(1), 27.

Grzadzinski, R., Carr, T., Colombi, C., McGuire, K., Dufek, S., Pickles, A., et al. (2016). Measuring changes in social communication behaviors: Preliminary development of the Brief Observation of Social Communication Change (BOSCC). *Journal of Autism and Developmental Disorders, 46*(7), 2464–2479.

Haendel, A. D., Barrington, A., Magnus, B., Arias, A. A., McVey, A., Pleiss, S., et al. (2021). Changes in Electroencephalogram Coherence in Adolescents With Autism Spectrum Disorder After a Social Skills Intervention. *Autism Research, 14*(4), 787–803.

Halladay, A. K., Bishop, S., Constantino, J. N., Daniels, A. M., Koenig, K., Palmer, K., et al. (2015). Sex and gender differences in autism spectrum disorder: Summarizing evidence gaps and identifying emerging areas of priority. *Molecular. Autism, 6*(1).

Happé, F. G. (1994). An advanced test of theory of mind: Understanding of story characters' thoughts and feelings by able autistic, mentally handicapped, and normal children and adults. *Journal of Autism and Developmental Disorders, 24*(2), 129–154.

Harmon-Jones, E., Gable, P. A., & Peterson, C. K. (2010). The role of asymmetric frontal cortical activity in emotion-related phenomena: A review and update. *Biological Psychology, 84*(3), 451–462.

Havdahl, K. A., Bal, V. H., Huerta, M., Pickles, A., Øyen, A. S., Stoltenberg, C., et al. (2016). Multidimensional influences on autism symptom measures: Implications for use in etiological research. *Journal of the American Academy of Child & Adolescent Psychiatry, 55*(12), 1054–1063.

Head, A. M., McGillivray, J. A., & Stokes, M. A. (2014). Gender differences in emotionality and sociability in children with autism spectrum disorders. *Molecular Autism*, *5*(1), 1–9.
Hedley, D., Uljarević, M., Foley, K. R., Richdale, A., & Trollor, J. (2018). Risk and protective factors underlying depression and suicidal ideation in autism spectrum disorder. *Depression and Anxiety*, *35*(7), 648–657.
Heunis, T. M., Aldrich, C., & de Vries, P. J. (2016). Recent advances in resting-state electroencephalography biomarkers for autism spectrum disorder—a review of methodological and clinical challenges. *Pediatric Neurology*, *61*, 28–37.
Hillier, A., Fish, T., Cloppert, P., & Beversdorf, D. Q. (2007). Outcomes of a social and vocational skills support group for adolescents and young adults on the autism spectrum. *Focus on Autism and Other Developmental Disabilities*, *22*(2), 107–115.
Hillier, A. J., Fish, T., Siegel, J. H., & Beversdorf, D. Q. (2011). Social and vocational skills training reduces self-reported anxiety and depression among young adults on the autism spectrum. *Journal of Developmental and Physical Disabilities*, *23*(3), 267–276.
Hollocks, M. J., Lerh, J. W., Magiati, I., Meiser-Stedman, R., & Brugha, T. S. (2019). Anxiety and depression in adults with autism spectrum disorder: A systematic review and meta-analysis. *Psychological Medicine*, *49*(4), 559–572.
Hull, L., Petrides, K. V., Allison, C., Smith, P., Baron-Cohen, S., Lai, M. C., et al. (2017). "Putting on my best normal": Social camouflaging in adults with autism spectrum conditions. *Journal of Autism and Developmental Disorders*, *47*(8), 2519–2534.
Hull, L., Petrides, K. V., & Mandy, W. (2020). The female autism phenotype and camouflaging: A narrative review. *Review Journal of Autism and Developmental Disorders*, 1–12.
Hume, K., Steinbrenner, J. R., Odom, S. L., Morin, K. L., Nowell, S. W., Tomaszewski, B., et al. (2021). Evidence-based practices for children, youth, and young adults with autism: Third generation review. *Journal of Autism and Developmental Disorders*, 1–20.
Hus, V., Bishop, S., Gotham, K., Huerta, M., & Lord, C. (2013a). Factors influencing scores on the social responsiveness scale. *Journal of Child Psychology and Psychiatry*, *54*(2), 216–224.
Hus, V., Bishop, S., Gotham, K., Huerta, M., & Lord, C. (2013b). *Commentary: Advancing measurement of ASD severity and social competence: A reply to Constantino and Frazier (2013).*
Hutchins, T. L., Lewis, L., Prelock, P. A., & Brien, A. (2021). The Development and Preliminary Psychometric Evaluation of the Theory of Mind Inventory: Self report—Adult (ToMI: SR-Adult). *Journal of Autism and Developmental Disorders*, *51*(6), 1839–1851.
Hutchins, T. L., Prelock, P. A., & Bonazinga, L. (2012). Psychometric evaluation of the Theory of Mind Inventory (ToMI): A study of typically developing children and children with autism spectrum disorder. *Journal of Autism and Developmental Disorders*, *42*(3), 327–341.
Jarquin, V. G., Wiggins, L. D., Schieve, L. A., & Naarden-Braun, K. V. (2011). Racial disparities in community identification of autism spectrum disorders over time; Metropolitan Atlanta, Georgia, 2000-2006. *Journal of Developmental & Behavioral Pediatrics*, *32*(3), 179–187.
Jaswal, V. K., & Akhtar, N. (2019). Being versus appearing socially uninterested: Challenging assumptions about social motivation in autism. *Behavioral and Brain Sciences*, *42*, 1–73, e82.
Jeste, S. S., Frohlich, J., & Loo, S. K. (2015). Electrophysiological biomarkers of diagnosis and outcome in neurodevelopmental disorders. *Current Opinion in Neurology*, *28*(2), 110.
Jitlina, K., Zumbo, B., Mirenda, P., Ford, L., Bennett, T., Georgiades, S., et al. (2017). Psychometric properties of the spence children's anxiety scale: Parent report in children with autism spectrum disorder. *Journal of Autism and Developmental Disorders*, *47*(12), 3847–3856.

Johnson, S. A., Filliter, J. H., & Murphy, R. R. (2009). Discrepancies between self-and parent-perceptions of autistic traits and empathy in high functioning children and adolescents on the autism spectrum. *Journal of Autism and Developmental Disorders, 39*(12), 1706–1714.
Kaat, A. J., Shui, A. M., Ghods, S. S., Farmer, C. A., Esler, A. N., Thurm, A., et al. (2021). Sex differences in scores on standardized measures of autism symptoms: A multisite integrative data analysis. *Journal of Child Psychology and Psychiatry, 62*(1), 97–106.
Kasari, C., Dean, M., Kretzmann, M., Shih, W., Orlich, F., Whitney, R., et al. (2016). Children with autism spectrum disorder and social skills groups at school: A randomized trial comparing intervention approach and peer composition. *Journal of Child Psychology and Psychiatry, 57*(2), 171–179.
Kasari, C., Locke, J., Gulsrud, A., & Rotheram-Fuller, E. (2011). Social networks and friendships at school: Comparing children with and without ASD. *Journal of Autism and Developmental Disorders, 41*(5), 533–544.
Kasari, C., Rotheram-Fuller, E., Locke, J., & Gulsrud, A. (2012). Making the connection: Randomized controlled trial of social skills at school for children with autism spectrum disorders. *Journal of Child Psychology and Psychiatry, 53*(4), 431–439.
Kim, S. H., Grzadzinski, R., Martinez, K., & Lord, C. (2019). Measuring treatment response in children with autism spectrum disorder: Applications of the Brief Observation of Social Communication Change to the Autism Diagnostic Observation Schedule. *Autism, 23*(5), 1176–1185.
Kim, S. Y., & Lecavalier, L. (2021). Evaluating the use of self-reported measures in autistic individuals in the context of psychiatric assessment: A systematic review. *Journal of Autism and Developmental Disorders*, 1–20.
Kimhi, Y. (2014). Theory of mind abilities and deficits in autism spectrum disorders. *Topics in Language Disorders, 34*(4), 329–343.
Kinnaird, E., Stewart, C., & Tchanturia, K. (2019). Investigating alexithymia in autism: A systematic review and meta-analysis. *European Psychiatry, 55*, 80–89.
Kirkovski, M., Enticott, P. G., & Fitzgerald, P. B. (2013). A Review of the Role of Female Gender in Autism Spectrum Disorders. *Journal of Autism and Developmental Disorders, 43*(11), 2584–2603. https://doi.org/10.1007/s10803-013-1811-1.
Kleinhans, N. M., Johnson, L. C., Richards, T., Mahurin, R., Greenson, J., Dawson, G., et al. (2009). Reduced neural habituation in the amygdala and social impairments in autism spectrum disorders. *American Journal of Psychiatry, 166*(4), 467–475.
Koning, C., Magill-Evans, J., Volden, J., & Dick, B. (2013). Efficacy of cognitive behavior therapy-based social skills intervention for school-aged boys with autism spectrum disorders. *Research in Autism Spectrum Disorders*, 7(10), 1282–1290.
Kovacs, M. (1985). The Children's Depression, Inventory (CDI). *Psychopharmacology Bulletin, 21*(4), 995–998.
Kreiser, N. L., & White, S. W. (2014). ASD in females: Are we overstating the gender difference in diagnosis? *Clinical Child and Family Psychology Review, 17*(1), 67–84.
Kretzmann, M., Shih, W., & Kasari, C. (2015). Improving peer engagement of children with autism on the school playground: A randomized controlled trial. *Behavior Therapy, 46*(1), 20–28.
La Greca, A. M., & Lopez, N. (1998). Social anxiety among adolescents: Linkages with peer relations and friendships. *Journal of Abnormal Child Psychology, 26*, 83–94.
Lai, M. C., Kassee, C., Besney, R., Bonato, S., Hull, L., Mandy, W., et al. (2019). Prevalence of co-occurring mental health diagnoses in the autism population: A systematic review and meta-analysis. *The Lancet Psychiatry, 6*(10), 819–829.
Laugeson, E. A. (2013). *The PEERS® curriculum for school based professionals: Social skills training for adolescents with autism spectrum disorder*. Routledge.
Laugeson, E. (2017). *PEERS® for young adults: Social skills training for adults with autism spectrum disorder and other social challenges*. Routledge.

Laugeson, E. A., Ellingsen, R., Sanderson, J., Tucci, L., & Bates, S. (2014). The ABC's of teaching social skills to adolescents with autism spectrum disorder in the classroom: The UCLA PEERS® program. *Journal of Autism and Developmental Disorders*, *44*(9), 2244–2256.

Laugeson, E. A., & Frankel, F. (2011). *Social skills for teenagers with developmental and autism spectrum disorders: The PEERS treatment manual*. Routledge.

Laugeson, E. A., Frankel, F., Gantman, A., Dillon, A. R., & Mogil, C. (2012). Evidence-based social skills training for adolescents with autism spectrum disorders: The UCLA PEERS program. *Journal of Autism and Developmental Disorders*, *42*(6), 1025–1036.

Laugeson, E. A., Frankel, F., Mogil, C., & Dillon, A. R. (2009). Parent-assisted social skills training to improve friendships in teens with autism spectrum disorders. *Journal of Autism and Developmental Disorders*, *39*(4), 596–606.

Laugeson, E. A., Gantman, A., Kapp, S. K., Orenski, K., & Ellingsen, R. (2015). A randomized controlled trial to improve social skills in young adults with autism spectrum disorder: The UCLA PEERS® program. *Journal of Autism and Developmental Disorders*, *45*(12), 3978–3989.

Lau-Zhu, A., Lau, M. P., & McLoughlin, G. (2019). Mobile EEG in research on neurodevelopmental disorders: Opportunities and challenges. *Developmental Cognitive Neuroscience*, *36*, 100635.

Lawrence, E. J., Shaw, P., Baker, D., Baron-Cohen, S., & David, A. S. (2004). Measuring empathy: Reliability and validity of the Empathy Quotient. *Psychological Medicine*, *34*(5), 911–920.

Lerner, M. D., Calhoun, C. D., Mikami, A. Y., & De Los Reyes, A. (2012). Understanding parent–child social informant discrepancy in youth with high functioning autism spectrum disorders. *Journal of Autism and Developmental Disorders*, *42*(12), 2680–2692.

Lerner, M. D., Hutchins, T. L., & Prelock, P. A. (2011). Brief report: Preliminary evaluation of the theory of mind inventory and its relationship to measures of social skills. *Journal of Autism and Developmental Disorders*, *41*(4), 512–517.

Livingston, L. A., Ashwin, C., & Shah, P. (2020). Electronic communication in autism spectrum conditions. *Molecular Autism*, *11*, 1–3.

Locke, J., Ishijima, E. H., Kasari, C., & London, N. (2010). Loneliness, friendship quality and the social networks of adolescents with high-functioning autism in an inclusive school setting. *Journal of Research in Special Educational Needs*, *10*, 74–81.

Locke, J., Rotheram-Fuller, E., Harker, C., Kasari, C., & Mandell, D. S. (2019). Comparing a practice-based model with a research-based model of social skills interventions for children with autism in schools. *Research in Autism Spectrum Disorders*, *62*, 10–17.

Loomes, R., Hull, L., & Mandy, W. P. L. (2017). What is the male-to-female ratio in autism spectrum disorder? A systematic review and meta-analysis. *Journal of the American Academy of Child & Adolescent Psychiatry*, *56*(6), 466–474.

Lord, C., Rutter, M., & DiLavore, P. C. (2012). *Autism Diagnostic Observation Schedule (ADOS-2) (Modules 1–4)* (2nd ed.). Los Angeles, CA: Western Psychological Services.

Maenner, M. J., Shaw, K. A., Bakian, A. V., Bilder, D. A., Durkin, M. S., Esler, A., et al. (2021). Prevalence and characteristics of autism spectrum disorder among children aged 8 years—Autism and Developmental Disabilities Monitoring Network, 11 sites, United States, 2018. *MMWR Surveillance Summaries*, *70*(11), 1.

Magiati, I., Lerh, J. W., Hollocks, M. J., Uljarevic, M., Rodgers, J., McConachie, H., et al. (2017). The measurement properties of the spence children's anxiety scale-parent version in a large international pooled sample of young people with autism spectrum disorder. *Autism Research*, *10*(10), 1629–1652.

Mano, K. E. J., Davies, W. H., Klein-Tasman, B. P., & Adesso, V. J. (2009). Measurement equivalence of the Child Behavior Checklist among parents of African American adolescents. *Journal of Child and Family Studies*, *18*(5), 606–620.

Matthews, N. L., Orr, B. C., Warriner, K., DeCarlo, M., Sorensen, M., Laflin, J., et al. (2018). Exploring the effectiveness of a peer-mediated model of the PEERS curriculum: A pilot randomized control trial. *Journal of Autism and Developmental Disorders, 48*(7), 2458–2475.
Mattick, R. P., & Clarke, J. C. (1998). Development and validation of measures of social phobia scrutiny fear and social interaction anxiety. *Behaviour Research and Therapy, 36*(4), 455–470.
McConachie, H., Parr, J. R., Glod, M., Hanratty, J., Livingstone, N., Oono, I. P., et al. (2015). Systematic review of tools to measure outcomes for young children with autism spectrum disorder. *Health Technology Assessment, 19*(41).
McGill, O., & Robinson, A. (2020). "Recalling hidden harms": Autistic experiences of childhood applied behavioural analysis (ABA). *Advances in Autism,* 7(4), 269–282.
McMahon, C. M., Lerner, M. D., & Britton, N. (2013). Group-based social skills interventions for adolescents with higher-functioning autism spectrum disorder: A review and looking to the future. *Adolescent Health, Medicine and Therapeutics, 4,* 23.
McVey, A. J. (2019). The neurobiological presentation of anxiety in autism spectrum disorder: A systematic review. *Autism Research, 12*(3), 346–369.
McVey, A. J., Dolan, B. K., Willar, K. S., Pleiss, S., Karst, J. S., Casnar, C. L., et al. (2016). A replication and extension of the PEERS® for young adults social skills intervention: Examining effects on social skills and social anxiety in young adults with autism spectrum disorder. *Journal of Autism and Developmental Disorders, 46*(12), 3739–3754.
McVey, A. J., Schiltz, H. K., Haendel, A. D., Dolan, B. K., Willar, K. S., Pleiss, S. S., et al. (2018). Social difficulties in youth with autism with and without anxiety and ADHD symptoms. *Autism Research, 11*(12), 1679–1689.
Mendelson, J. L., Gates, J. A., & Lerner, M. D. (2016). Friendship in school-age boys with autism spectrum disorders: A meta-analytic summary and developmental, process-based model. *Psychological Bulletin, 142*(6), 601.
Miller, T. W., Nigg, J. T., & Miller, R. L. (2009). Attention deficit hyperactivity disorder in African American children: What can be concluded from the past ten years? *Clinical Psychology Review, 29*(1), 77–86.
Mitchell, P., Sheppard, E., & Cassidy, S. (2021). Autism and the double empathy problem: Implications for development and mental health. *British Journal of Developmental Psychology, 39*(1), 1–18.
Monahan, J., Freedman, B., Pini, K., & Lloyd, R. (2021). Autistic input in social skills interventions for young adults: A systematic review of the literature. *Review Journal of Autism and Developmental Disorders,* 1–21.
Moody, C. T., & Laugeson, E. A. (2020). Social skills training in autism spectrum disorder across the lifespan. *Child and Adolescent Psychiatric Clinics, 29*(2), 359–371.
Morgan, L., Leatzow, A., Clark, S., & Siller, M. (2014). Interview skills for adults with autism spectrum disorder: A pilot randomized controlled trial. *Journal of Autism and Developmental Disorders, 44*(9), 2290–2300.
Muncer, S. J., & Ling, J. (2006). Psychometric analysis of the empathy quotient (EQ) scale. *Personality and Individual Differences, 40*(6), 1111–1119.
Nasamran, A., Witmer, S. E., & Los, J. E. (2017). Exploring predictors of postsecondary outcomes for students with autism spectrum disorder. *Education and Training in Autism and Developmental Disabilities, 52*(4), 343–356.
Neuhaus, E., Beauchaine, T. P., & Bernier, R. (2010). Neurobiological correlates of social functioning in autism. *Clinical Psychology Review, 30*(6), 733–748.
Nicholas, D. B., Mitchell, W., Dudley, C., Clarke, M., & Zulla, R. (2018). An ecosystem approach to employment and autism spectrum disorder. *Journal of Autism and Developmental Disorders, 48*(1), 264–275.

Nicolaidis, C., Raymaker, D. M., McDonald, K. E., Lund, E. M., Leotti, S., Kapp, S. K., et al. (2020). Creating accessible survey instruments for use with autistic adults and people with intellectual disability: Lessons learned and recommendations. *Autism in Adulthood*, *2*(1), 61–76.

Nowell, K. P., Brewton, C. M., Allain, E., & Mire, S. S. (2015). The influence of demographic factors on the identification of autism spectrum disorder: A review and call for research. *Review Journal of Autism and Developmental Disorders*, *2*(3), 300–309.

Nowicki, S., & Carton, J. (1993). The measurement of emotional intensity from facial expressions. *Journal of Social Psychology*, *133*(5), 749–750.

O'Hagan, S., & Hebron, J. (2017). Perceptions of friendship among adolescents with autism spectrum conditions in a mainstream high school resource provision. *European Journal of Special Needs Education*, *32*(3), 314–328.

O'Hare, A., Bremner, L., Nash, M., Happé, F., & Pettigrew, L. (2009). A clinical assessment tool for advanced theory of mind performance in 5–12 year olds. *Journal of Autism and Developmental Disorders*, *39*(6), 916–928.

O'Reilly, C., Lewis, J. D., & Elsabbagh, M. (2017). Is functional brain connectivity atypical in autism? A systematic review of EEG and MEG studies. *PLoS One*, *12*(5), e0175870.

Olderbak, S., Wilhelm, O., Olaru, G., Geiger, M., Brenneman, M. W., & Roberts, R. D. (2015). A psychometric analysis of the reading the mind in the eyes test: Toward a brief form for research and applied settings. *Frontiers in Psychology*, *6*, 1503.

Orsmond, G. I., Shattuck, P. T., Cooper, B. P., Sterzing, P. R., & Anderson, K. A. (2013). Social participation among young adults with an autism spectrum disorder. *Journal of Autism and Developmental Disorders*, *43*(11), 2710–2719.

Ozsivadjian, A., Hibberd, C., & Hollocks, M. J. (2014). Brief report: The use of self-report measures in young people with autism spectrum disorder to access symptoms of anxiety, depression and negative thoughts. *Journal of Autism and Developmental Disorders*, *44*(4), 969–974.

Parellada, M., Penzol, M. J., Pina, L., Moreno, C., González-Vioque, E., Zalsman, G., et al. (2014). The neurobiology of autism spectrum disorders. *European Psychiatry*, *29*(1), 11–19.

Perlman, D., Peplau, L. A., & Goldston, S. E. (1984). Loneliness research: A survey of empirical findings. *Preventing the harmful consequences of severe and persistent loneliness*, 13–46.

Perner, J., Frith, U., Leslie, A. M., & Leekam, S. R. (1989). Exploration of the autistic child's theory of mind: Knowledge, belief, and communication. *Child Development*, 689–700.

Petrina, N., Carter, M., & Stephenson, J. (2014). The nature of friendship in children with autism spectrum disorders: A systematic review. *Research in Autism Spectrum Disorders*, *8*(2), 111–126.

Pickles, A., Le Couteur, A., Leadbitter, K., Salomone, E., Cole-Fletcher, R., Tobin, H., et al. (2016). Parent-mediated social communication therapy for young children with autism (PACT): Long-term follow-up of a randomised controlled trial. *The Lancet*, *388*(10059), 2501–2509.

Pijl, M. K., Rommelse, N. N., Hendriks, M., De Korte, M. W., Buitelaar, J. K., & Oosterling, I. J. (2018). Does the Brief Observation of Social Communication Change help moving forward in measuring change in early autism intervention studies? *Autism*, *22*(2), 216–226.

Power, J. D., & Schlaggar, B. L. (2017). Neural plasticity across the lifespan. *Wiley Interdisciplinary Reviews: Developmental Biology*, *6*(1), e216.

Rabin, S. J., Israel-Yaacov, S., Laugeson, E. A., Mor-Snir, I., & Golan, O. (2018). A randomized controlled trial evaluating the Hebrew adaptation of the PEERS® intervention: Behavioral and questionnaire-based outcomes. *Autism Research*, *11*(8), 1187–1200.

Ratto, A. B. (2021). Commentary: What's so special about girls on the autism spectrum?— A commentary on Kaat et al. (2020). *Journal of Child Psychology and Psychiatry, 62*(1), 107–109.

Ratto, A. B., Anthony, B. J., Pugliese, C., Mendez, R., Safer-Lichtenstein, J., Dudley, K. M., et al. (2017). Lessons learned: Engaging culturally diverse families in neurodevelopmental disorders intervention research. *Autism, 21*(5), 622–634.

Ratto, A. B., Turner-Brown, L., Rupp, B. M., Mesibov, G. B., & Penn, D. L. (2011). Development of the Contextual Assessment of Social Skills (CASS): A role play measure of social skill for individuals with high-functioning autism. *Journal of Autism and Developmental Disorders, 41*(9), 1277–1286.

Reise, S. P., & Henson, J. M. (2003). A discussion of modern versus traditional psychometrics as applied to personality assessment scales. *Journal of Personality Assessment, 81*(2), 93–103.

Renty, J. O., & Roeyers, H. (2006). Quality of life in high-functioning adults with autism spectrum disorder: The predictive value of disability and support characteristics. *Autism, 10*(5), 511–524.

Robles, M. M. (2012). Executive perceptions of the top 10 soft skills needed in today's workplace. *Business Communication Quarterly, 75*(4), 453–465.

Rodriguez, G., Drastal, K., & Hartley, S. L. (2021). Cross-lagged model of bullying victimization and mental health problems in children with autism in middle to older childhood. *Autism, 25*(1), 90–101.

Rogers, S. J., Estes, A., Lord, C., Munson, J., Rocha, M., Winter, J., et al. (2019). A multisite randomized controlled two-phase trial of the Early Start Denver Model compared to treatment as usual. *Journal of the American Academy of Child & Adolescent Psychiatry, 58*(9), 853–865.

Rotheram-Fuller, E., Kim, M., Seiple, D., Locke, J., Greenwell, R., & Levin, D. (2013). Social skills assessments for children with autism spectrum disorders. *Autism, 3*(3), 122.

Russell, D., Peplau, L. A., & Cutrona, C. E. (1980). The revised UCLA Loneliness Scale: Concurrent and discriminant validity evidence. *Journal of Personality and Social Psychology, 39*(3), 472.

Safer-Lichtenstein, J., Hamilton, J. C., & McIntyre, L. L. (2019). Examining demographics in randomized controlled trials of group-based social skills interventions for individuals with autism spectrum disorder. *Journal of Autism and Developmental Disorders, 49*(8), 3453–3461.

Sari, N. P., Luijk, M. P., Prinzie, P., van IJzendoorn, M. H., & Jansen, P. W. (2021). Children's autistic traits and peer relationships: Do non-verbal IQ and externalizing problems play a role? *Child and Adolescent Psychiatry and Mental Health, 15*(1), 1–12.

Sarrett, J. (2017). Interviews, disclosures, and misperceptions: Autistic adults' perspectives on employment related challenges. *Disability Studies Quarterly, 37*(2).

Schiltz, H. K., & Magnus, B. E. (2021). Differential item functioning based on autism features, IQ, and age on the Screen for Child Anxiety Related Disorders (SCARED) among youth on the autism spectrum. *Autism Research, 14*(6), 1220–1226.

Schiltz, H. K., Magnus, B. E., McVey, A. J., Haendel, A. D., Dolan, B. K., Stanley, R. E., et al. (2021). A psychometric analysis of the social anxiety scale for adolescents among youth with autism spectrum disorder: Caregiver–adolescent agreement, factor structure, and validity. *Assessment, 28*(1), 100–115.

Schiltz, H., McIntyre, N., Swain-Lerro, L., Zajic, M., & Mundy, P. (2017). The stability of self-reported anxiety in youth with autism versus ADHD or typical development. *Journal of Autism and Developmental Disorders, 47*(12), 3756–3764.

Schiltz, H. K., McVey, A. J., Barrington, A., Haendel, A. D., Dolan, B. K., Willar, K. S., et al. (2018). Behavioral inhibition and activation as a modifier process in autism spectrum disorder: Examination of self-reported BIS/BAS and alpha EEG asymmetry. *Autism Research, 11*(12), 1653–1666.

Schiltz, H. K., McVey, A. J., Dolan, B. K., Willar, K. S., Pleiss, S., Karst, J. S., et al. (2018). Changes in depressive symptoms among adolescents with ASD completing the PEERS® social skills intervention. *Journal of Autism and Developmental Disorders, 48*(3), 834–843.
Schiltz, H. K., McVey, A. J., Dolan Wozniak, B., Haendel, A. D., Stanley, R., Arias, A., et al. (2021). The role of loneliness as a mediator between autism features and mental health among autistic young adults. *Autism, 25*(2), 545–555.
Schohl, K. A., Van Hecke, A. V., Carson, A. M., Dolan, B., Karst, J., & Stevens, S. (2014). A replication and extension of the PEERS intervention: Examining effects on social skills and social anxiety in adolescents with autism spectrum disorders. *Journal of Autism and Developmental Disorders, 44*(3), 532–545.
Shaw, K. A., Maenner, M. J., Bakian, A. V., Bilder, D. A., Durkin, M. S., Furnier, S. M., et al. (2021). Early identification of autism spectrum disorder among children aged 4 years—Autism and Developmental Disabilities Monitoring Network, 11 sites, United States, 2018. *MMWR Surveillance Summaries, 70*(10), 1.
Sheldrick, R. C., Neger, E. N., Shipman, D., & Perrin, E. C. (2012). Quality of life of adolescents with autism spectrum disorders: Concordance among adolescents' self-reports, parents' reports, and parents' proxy reports. *Quality of Life Research, 21*(1), 53–57.
Shih, W., Dean, M., Kretzmann, M., Locke, J., Senturk, D., Mandell, D. S., et al. (2019). Remaking recess intervention for improving peer interactions at school for children with autism spectrum disorder: Multisite randomized trial. *School Psychology Review, 48*(2), 133–144.
Simmons, G. L., Ioannou, S., Smith, J. V., Corbett, B. A., Lerner, M. D., & White, S. W. (2021). Utility of an observational social skill assessment as a measure of social cognition in autism. *Autism Research, 14*(4), 709–719.
Smith, M. J., Fleming, M. F., Wright, M. A., Losh, M., Humm, L. B., Olsen, D., et al. (2015). Brief report: Vocational outcomes for young adults with autism spectrum disorders at six months after virtual reality job interview training. *Journal of Autism and Developmental Disorders, 45*(10), 3364–3369.
Smith, M. J., Ginger, E. J., Wright, K., Wright, M. A., Taylor, J. L., Humm, L. B., et al. (2014). Virtual reality job interview training in adults with autism spectrum disorder. *Journal of Autism and Developmental Disorders, 44*(10), 2450–2463.
Smith, M. J., Sherwood, K., Ross, B., Smith, J. D., DaWalt, L., Bishop, L., et al. (2021). Virtual interview training for autistic transition age youth: A randomized controlled feasibility and effectiveness trial. *Autism, 25*(6), 1536–1552.
Soares, E. E., Bausback, K., Beard, C. L., Higinbotham, M., Bunge, E. L., & Gengoux, G. W. (2021). Social skills training for autism spectrum disorder: A meta-analysis of in-person and technological interventions. *Journal of Technology in Behavioral Science, 6*(1), 166–180.
Soorya, L. V., Siper, P. M., Beck, T., Soffes, S., Halpern, D., Gorenstein, M., et al. (2015). Randomized comparative trial of a social cognitive skills group for children with autism spectrum disorder. *Journal of the American Academy of Child & Adolescent Psychiatry, 54*(3), 208–216.
Soto, S., Linas, K., Jacobstein, D., Biel, M., Migdal, T., & Anthony, B. J. (2015). A review of cultural adaptations of screening tools for autism spectrum disorders. *Autism, 19*(6), 646–661.
South, M., Carr, A. W., Stephenson, K. G., Maisel, M. E., & Cox, J. C. (2017). Symptom overlap on the SRS-2 adult self-report between adults with ASD and adults with high anxiety. *Autism Research, 10*(7), 1215–1220.
Spence, S. H. (1998). A measure of anxiety symptoms among children. *Behaviour Research and Therapy, 36*(5), 545–566.
Spence, S. H. (2003). Social skills training with children and young people: Theory, evidence and practice. *Child and Adolescent Mental Health, 8*(2), 84–96.

Spielberger, C. D. (1983). *State-trait anxiety inventory for adults*. Mind Garden.
Spielberger, C. D., Edwards, C. D., Lushene, R. E., Montuori, J., & Platzek, D. (1973). *State-trait anxiety inventory for children*. Palo Alto, CA: Consulting Psychologists Press.
Spitzer, R. L., Kroenke, K., Williams, J. B., & Löwe, B. (2006). A brief measure for assessing generalized anxiety disorder: The GAD-7. *Archives of Internal Medicine, 166*(10), 1092–1097.
Spitzer, R. L., Kroenke, K., Williams, J. B., & Patient Health Questionnaire Primary Care Study Group, & Patient Health Questionnaire Primary Care Study Group. (1999). Validation and utility of a self-report version of PRIME-MD: The PHQ primary care study. *JAMA, 282*(18), 1737–1744.
Stavropoulos, K. K. M. (2017). Using neuroscience as an outcome measure for behavioral interventions in Autism spectrum disorders (ASD): A review. *Research in Autism Spectrum Disorders, 35*, 62–73.
Stavropoulos, K. K., & Carver, L. J. (2014). Reward anticipation and processing of social versus nonsocial stimuli in children with and without autism spectrum disorders. *Journal of Child Psychology and Psychiatry, 55*(12), 1398–1408.
Stichter, J. P., Herzog, M. J., Visovsky, K., Schmidt, C., Randolph, J., Schultz, T., et al. (2010). Social competence intervention for youth with Asperger syndrome and high-functioning autism: An initial investigation. *Journal of Autism and Developmental Disorders, 40*(9), 1067–1079.
Strang, J. F., van der Miesen, A., Caplan, R., Hughes, C., daVanport, S., & Lai, M. (2020). Both sex-and gender-related factors should be considered in autism research and clinical practice. *Autism, 24*(3), 539–543.
Stratis, E. A., & Lecavalier, L. (2015). Informant agreement for youth with autism spectrum disorder or intellectual disability: A meta-analysis. *Journal of Autism and Developmental Disorders, 45*(4), 1026–1041.
Sullivan, A. L. (2013). School-based autism identification: Prevalence, racial disparities, and systemic correlates. *School Psychology Review, 42*(3), 298–316.
Sung, C., Connor, A., Chen, J., Lin, C. C., Kuo, H. J., & Chun, J. (2019). Development, feasibility, and preliminary efficacy of an employment-related social skills intervention for young adults with high-functioning autism. *Autism, 23*(6), 1542–1553.
Tang, J. S., Chen, N. T., Falkmer, M., Bölte, S., & Girdler, S. (2019). A systematic review and meta-analysis of social emotional computer based interventions for autistic individuals using the serious game framework. *Research in Autism Spectrum Disorders, 66*, 101412.
Taylor, J. L., & Corbett, B. A. (2014). A review of rhythm and responsiveness of cortisol in individuals with autism spectrum disorders. *Psychoneuroendocrinology, 49*, 207–228.
Thomas, M. L. (2011). The value of item response theory in clinical assessment: A review. *Assessment, 18*(3), 291–307.
Thomeer, M. L., Lopata, C., Volker, M. A., Toomey, J. A., Lee, G. K., Smerbeck, A. M., et al. (2012). Randomized clinical trial replication of a psychosocial treatment for children with high-functioning autism spectrum disorders. *Psychology in the Schools, 49*(10), 942–954.
Toscano, R., Baillie, A. J., Lyneham, H. J., Kelly, A., Kidd, T., & Hudson, J. L. (2020). Assessment of anxiety in children and adolescents: A comparative study on the validity and reliability of the Spence Children's Anxiety Scale in children and adolescents with anxiety and autism spectrum disorder. *Journal of Affective Disorders, 260*, 569–576.
Tripathi, I., Estabillo, J. A., Moody, C. T., & Laugeson, E. A. (2021). Long-term treatment outcomes of PEERS® for preschoolers: A parent-mediated social skills training program for children with autism spectrum disorder. *Journal of Autism and Developmental Disorders*, 1–17.

Tsai, C. H., Chen, K. L., Li, H. J., Chen, K. H., Hsu, C. W., Lu, C. H., et al. (2020). The symptoms of autism including social communication deficits and repetitive and restricted behaviors are associated with different emotional and behavioral problems. *Scientific Reports*, *10*(1), 1–8.

Tyson, E. H., Teasley, M., & Ryan, S. (2011). Using the child behavior checklist with African American and Caucasian American adopted youth. *Journal of Emotional and Behavioral Disorders*, *19*(1), 17–26.

Van Hecke, A. V., Stevens, S., Carson, A. M., Karst, J. S., Dolan, B., Schohl, K., et al. (2015). Measuring the plasticity of social approach: A randomized controlled trial of the effects of the PEERS intervention on EEG asymmetry in adolescents with autism spectrum disorders. *Journal of Autism and Developmental Disorders*, *45*(2), 316–335.

Vellante, M., Baron-Cohen, S., Melis, M., Marrone, M., Petretto, D. R., Masala, C., et al. (2013). The "Reading the Mind in the Eyes" test: Systematic review of psychometric properties and a validation study in Italy. *Cognitive Neuropsychiatry*, *18*(4), 326–354.

Velloso, R. D. L., Duarte, C. P., & Schwartzman, J. S. (2013). Evaluation of the theory of mind in autism spectrum disorders with the Strange Stories test. *Arquivos de Neuro-Psiquiatria*, *71*, 871–876.

Vernon, T., Miller, R. A., Ko, J. A., Barrett, C. A., & McGarry, S. E. (2018). A randomized controlled trial of the Social Tools And Rules for Teens (START) program: An immersive socialization intervention for adolescents with autism spectrum disorder. *Journal of Autism and Developmental Disorders*, *48*(3), 892–904.

Vissers, M. E., Cohen, M. X., & Geurts, H. M. (2012). Brain connectivity and high functioning autism: A promising path of research that needs refined models, methodological convergence, and stronger behavioral links. *Neuroscience & Biobehavioral Reviews*, *36*(1), 604–625.

Wallis, K., & Pinto-Martin, J. (2008). The challenge of screening for autism spectrum disorder in a culturally diverse society. *Acta Paediatrica*, *97*(5), 539–540.

Wang, J., Barstein, J., Ethridge, L. E., Mosconi, M. W., Takarae, Y., & Sweeney, J. A. (2013). Resting state EEG abnormalities in autism spectrum disorders. *Journal of Neurodevelopmental Disorders*, *5*(1), 1–14.

Warrier, V., Greenberg, D. M., Weir, E., Buckingham, C., Smith, P., Lai, M. C., et al. (2020). Elevated rates of autism, other neurodevelopmental and psychiatric diagnoses, and autistic traits in transgender and gender-diverse individuals. *Nature Communications*, *11*(1), 1–12.

Waugh, C., & Peskin, J. (2015). Improving the social skills of children with HFASD: An intervention study. *Journal of Autism and Developmental Disorders*, *45*(9), 2961–2980.

West, E. A., Travers, J. C., Kemper, T. D., Liberty, L. M., Cote, D. L., McCollow, M. M., et al. (2016). Racial and ethnic diversity of participants in research supporting evidence-based practices for learners with autism spectrum disorder. *The Journal of Special Education*, *50*(3), 151–163.

White, S. W., Scarpa, A., Conner, C. M., Maddox, B. B., & Bonete, S. (2015). Evaluating change in social skills in high-functioning adults with autism spectrum disorder using a laboratory-based observational measure. *Focus on Autism and Other Developmental Disabilities*, *30*(1), 3–12.

Wigham, S., McConachie, H., Tandos, J., Le Couteur, A. S., & Gateshead Millennium Study Core Team. (2012). The reliability and validity of the Social Responsiveness Scale in a UK general child population. *Research in Developmental Disabilities*, *33*(3), 944–950.

Williams, Z. J., Everaert, J., & Gotham, K. O. (2021). Measuring depression in autistic adults: Psychometric validation of the Beck Depression Inventory–II. *Assessment*, *28*(3), 858–876.

Wiskerke, J., Stern, H., & Igelström, K. (2018). Camouflaging of repetitive movements in autistic female and transgender adults. *BioRxiv*, 412619.

Wolstencroft, J., Robinson, L., Srinivasan, R., Kerry, E., Mandy, W., & Skuse, D. (2018). A systematic review of group social skills interventions, and meta-analysis of outcomes, for children with high functioning ASD. *Journal of Autism and Developmental Disorders*, *48*(7), 2293–2307.

Yamada, T., Miura, Y., Oi, M., Akatsuka, N., Tanaka, K., Tsukidate, N., et al. (2020). Examining the treatment efficacy of PEERS in Japan: Improving social skills among adolescents with Autism Spectrum Disorder. *Journal of Autism and Developmental Disorders*, *50*(3), 976–997.

Yoo, H., Bahn, G., Cho, I., Kim, E., Kim, J., Min, J., & Laugeson, E. A. (2014). A randomized controlled trial of the Korean version of the PEERS® parent-assisted social skills training program for teens with ASD. *Autism Research*, 7(1), 145–161.

Zahn-Waxler, C., Shirtcliff, E. A., & Marceau, K. (2008). Disorders of childhood and adolescence: Gender and psychopathology. *Annual Review of Clinical Psychology*, *4*, 275–303.

Zainal, H., Magiati, I., Tan, J. W. L., Sung, M., Fung, D. S., & Howlin, P. (2014). A preliminary investigation of the Spence Children's Anxiety Parent Scale as a screening tool for anxiety in young people with autism spectrum disorders. *Journal of Autism and Developmental Disorders*, *44*(8), 1982–1994.

Zheng, S., Kim, H., Salzman, E., Ankenman, K., & Bent, S. (2021). Improving social knowledge and skills among adolescents with autism: Systematic review and meta-analysis of UCLA PEERS® for adolescents. *Journal of Autism and Developmental Disorders*, *51*, 4488–4503.

Zou, M., Sun, C., Wang, J., Kang, J., Xu, Z., Ma, Y., et al. (2018). Factors influencing the severity of behavioral phenotype in autism spectrum disorders: Implications for research. *Psychiatry Research*, *261*, 290–297.

FSC
www.fsc.org
MIX
Papier | Fördert
gute Waldnutzung
FSC® C083411

Kolibri 360 GmbH
Ferdinand-Jühlke-Straße 7
99095 Erfurt, Deutschland
produktsicherheit@kolibri360.de